P9-DHE-534

PLUNKITT OF TAMMANY HALL

Ex-Senator George Washington Plunkitt, on his rostrum, the New York County Court House Bootblack Stand
(Copy of the original frontispiece in the first edition of 1905)

PLUNKITT
of
Tammany Hall

A SERIES OF VERY PLAIN TALKS ON VERY PRACTICAL POLITICS, DELIVERED BY EX-SENATOR GEORGE WASHINGTON PLUNKITT, THE TAMMANY PHILOSOPHER, FROM HIS ROSTRUM—THE NEW YORK COUNTY COURT HOUSE BOOTBLACK STAND

Recorded by
WILLIAM L. RIORDON

Introduction by Arthur Mann

Amereon House

Library of Congress Catalog Card Number 82-72477
International Standard Book Number 0-88411-977-7

Republished 1982
AMEREON HOUSE, the publishing division of
Amereon Ltd.
Box 1200
Mattituck, New York 11952

Printed in the United States of America by
The Mad Printers of Mattituck

CONTENTS

Introduction by Arthur Mann vii

Preface by William L. Riordon xxiii

A Tribute by Charles F. Murphy xxvi

Honest Graft and Dishonest Graft 3

How To Become a Statesman 7

The Curse of Civil Service Reform 11

Reformers Only Mornin' Glories 17

New York City Is Pie for the Hayseeds 21

To Hold Your District: Study Human Nature and Act Accordin' 25

On *The Shame of the Cities* 29

Ingratitude in Politics 33

Reciprocity in Patronage 37

Brooklynites Natural-Born Hayseeds 41

Tammany Leaders Not Bookworms 45

Dangers of the Dress Suit in Politics 50

On Municipal Ownership 54

Tammany the Only Lastin' Democracy 57

Concerning Gas in Politics 61

Plunkitt's Fondest Dream 65

Tammany's Patriotism 69

On the Use of Money in Politics 73

The Successful Politician Does Not Drink 77

Bosses Preserve the Nation 81

Concerning Excise 84

A Parting Word on the Future of the Democratic Party in America 88

Strenuous Life of the Tammany District Leader 90

When Tammany Was Supreme

IT WAS just a hundred and twenty years ago that George Washington Plunkitt was born in a shantytown called Nanny Goat Hill on Manhattan's upper west side. He died wealthy and renowned in 1924 at the age of eighty-two near the site of his birth. Obituary writers mourned his passing and celebrated him as a political sage. His claim to fame derived from a series of very plain talks on very practical politics that he gave at the turn of the century and were published first in the newspapers and then as a book by McClure, Phillips & Co. in 1905. Reissued in 1948, the little volume is a minor classic and required reading in the more sophisticated college courses in American government.

But Plunkitt wasn't a writer, nor was he a political philosopher by trade. He was a Tammany district leader, which is to say that he was a ward boss. Politics was his profession; more—his faith, his hobby, his club, his inspiration and reason for being; politics was a way of life for him. In books he had no interest, and it is doubtful if he ever read one in his long life. "Of course, we ain't . . . bookworms," he said of himself and his fellow Tammany leaders. That his name appears on the title page of the book in your hands is due to a chance meeting with William L. Riordon of the *New York*

Evening Post, who interviewed him and preserved his philosophy for posterity.

Their talks took place at what Plunkitt called his office: Graziano's bootblack stand in the old New York County Court House off Foley Square. Riordon, like so many newspapermen of the day, was fascinated by New York City's endless variety of characters. Plunkitt was one of them. His views on politics—and the rhythm, inflection, and idiom of his speech, not to mention his handlebar mustache and top hat—intrigued Riordon. He is Plunkitt's Boswell, and like Plunkitt, he is remembered today for the *Series of Very Plain Talks on Very Practical Politics.*

It is hard to say who deserves to be called the author of the book. The substance is Plunkitt's, but the conception, the organization, the artistry, and the actual writing are Riordon's. In the end it doesn't matter who has first claim to the copyright. *A Series of Very Plain Talks* is a collaborative work, that rare example in American journalism where the writer enters fully into the mind and world of the man whose profile he is sketching. Riordon had the good sense, moreover, to know when Plunkitt was talking claptrap or blarney instead of wisdom. But he didn't feel superior to his subject, as Lincoln Steffens, his more celebrated contemporary, so often did to the bosses he interviewed. Riordon wanted to understand, not to score points; to record, not to prove a theory.

Plunkitt, for his own part, revealed himself with gusto and talked and talked to the point of being garrulous. There can be no doubt that he enjoyed talking immensely. How typical, one is inclined to say; that's how the old-fashioned bosses were. Most of them weren't, and no stereotype dies harder than the one of the ward politician as a gabby, jovial extrover

The tin box brigade that Judge Samuel Seabury investigated in the early 1930's, for example, was as dour a crew as ever appeared in court. They had good reason not to be frank and merry; many of them stood just an answer away from the penitentiary. Yet few of their kind had ever voluntarily given away the secrets of their trade. John Kelly, Richard Croker, and Charles F. Murphy, the greatest of the Tammany leaders, were anything but affable; they were cold, distant, reticent men. Once, at a Fourth-of-July celebration, a reporter wondered and later asked why Mr. Murphy (he was always Mister even to his closest associates) did not join in the singing of the National Anthem. "Perhaps he didn't want to commit himself," the boss's aide explained.

Plunkitt committed himself to Riordon, who, with a reporter's instinct for an unusual story, recognized in his informant an exceptional frankness that set him apart from his fellow bosses. The reception of the book confirmed Riordon's belief that readers would be grateful to him for admitting them to an area of life that mystified middle-class Americans. "One who masters the philosophy of these charming discourses," wrote the *Review of Reviews* in 1905, "will have mastered the whole secret of New York metropolitan politics—Tammany's secret."

II

Tammany's secret was that it knew how to get power, hold on to it, and exploit it for personal gain. "I seen my opportunities and I took 'em," Plunkitt boasted. Of that there can be no doubt. It is a matter of opinion, though, if in serving itself Tammany Hall served the public good. But before turning to that question, we must first establish the fact of Tammany's remarkable durability. Let's look at the record, as the Hall's most famous Sachem used to say.

Between the founding of modern Tammany in 1854 and Mayor Fiorello H. La Guardia's inauguration in 1934, the Democratic machine governed New York City for a total of seventy years. Those seven decades were Tammany's golden age. In spite of recurrent scandals beginning with the exposé of the thieving Tweed Ring of the 1860's, anti-machine reformers held office for only ten years until the three-term La Guardia administration. Tammany's Eden was the mugwump's nadir. Small wonder that Plunkitt dismissed reformers as "Only Mornin' Glories" and exclaimed: "Look at the bosses of Tammany Hall. . . . What magnificent men!" They were the ruling class of New York City.

As leader of the Fifteenth Assembly District, Plunkitt knew through nearly fifty years of practice the techniques that kept his kind in power. His book is an insider's manual of how the machine worked. Do you want to break into politics? Plunkitt tells you how: don't go to college and stuff your head with rubbish, but get out among your neighbors and relatives and round up a few votes that you can call your own. Is there a formula for staying continually on top? Study human nature, Plunkitt advises, and make government warm and personal. But what happens when the Party loses an election? Be patient, Plunkitt says; Tammany is the ocean, reform the waves, and there's lots of unofficial patronage to ride out the storm if you know the ropes. Why don't reformers last in politics? Because they're amateurs, Plunkitt points out, and there's nothing like a pro. Must politicians steal to make a living? Of course not, Plunkitt answers; he became a millionaire through "honest graft." A man who steals is not only a crook, he's a fool. And so on and on. With only slight editing of the format, this little volume by the sage of Graziano's bootblack stand could be offered to the public under the title of *Plunkitt's Compleat Catechism* of machine politics.

But it lacks an important dimension, the historical dimension, and the reader must look elsewhere to learn why and when the machine originated. And what—in the first place—is a machine? Plunkitt assumed a knowledge on the part of the public that he shouldn't have. The American creed, deriving from classical democratic political theory, has no room for machines. Citizens are supposed to vote without benefit of intermediaries for the men who will represent them in government. Bosses and machines are dirty words and the dirtiest of them all is Tammany Hall; they are to be shunned and censured. But we must examine them if we are to understand how our political system has worked in so many parts of this country.

What the citizen calls a machine the professional politician calls the organization (note carefully Murphy's choice of words in his tribute to Plunkitt). And the organization, if we can be neutral for the moment, is simply *the party structure and the men who run it.* The structure of both the Democratic and Republican parties has been substantially the same for more than a hundred years. Put in another way, the two major parties took shape before the Civil War and have changed in form only in detail.

In New York City the smallest unit is the election district committee, headed by a captain. Many election districts make up an assembly district, headed by a leader in charge of still another committee. The assembly district leaders constitute the county executive committee, headed by a chairman. Assembly district leaders are elected in party primaries, and in turn, choose their own election district captains and elect the party chairman.

At its height in the twentieth century, the New York City Democratic organization numbered 32,000 committee men spread over five counties, and Madison Square Garden was the only place large enough in which to hold a meeting.

And the purpose of that vast bureaucracy? To nominate candidates for public office, get out the vote, and win elections. Once in power the organization enjoyed a patronage feast, as Plunkitt joyfully points out. In 1888, when New York City comprised only Manhattan (New York County) and a slice of the Bronx, the victorious party had some twelve thousand municipal jobs to distribute. Ten years later, when the Albany legislature created Greater New York out of Manhattan, the Bronx, Brooklyn, Queens, and Staten Island, patronage multiplied. But by then civil service reform was just beginning to menace the spoils system. Plunkitt's denunciation of that menace sounds comical today, but he was serious. Why should a man work for the organization without a guarantee that a job will be his reward?

Tammany was the popular term for New York's Democratic organization, but it had separate origins and a different structure. The Society of Saint Tammany, named after a legendary Delaware Indian chief, was founded in 1789 for patriotic, charitable, and fraternal purposes. Most of the members were artisans and tradesmen; one-third were bankers. In the Society they were ranked in ascending order as hunters, warriors, and Sachems (chiefs). A Grand Sachem presided. The clubhouse was known as The Wigwam, months were called moons, seasons bore pseudo-Indian names. On patriotic holidays the braves donned feathers and war paint to go whooping through the streets. Tammany began essentially as a non-political club—in short, with the aims, mumbo-jumbo ritual, and hoopla common to service organizations that dot the American landscape today.

But over the years it came to be the club to which the leading Democrats of the city belonged. By the 1840's and 1850's Tammany was to the Democratic party what the Union League Club would be to the Republican party during and after the Civil War. In 1854 Fernando Wood became the first Tammany Democrat Mayor of New York City. An even better symbol of the merger that had taken place was the election in 1860 of William Marcy Tweed as chairman of the Democratic party's central committee for New York County and in 1863 as Grand Sachem of Tammany. Thereafter, membership in Tammany and leadership in the Democratic organization were so parallel as to be interchangeable, although rival Democratic clubs continued to exist, as Plunkitt points out.

But why—to return to the original question—the organization? The men who wrote the Constitution did not expect political parties to develop and they would have turned over in their graves had they known that Tweed and his sort were the masters of a great city. Plunkitt's explanation, that the Irish were born to rule, is less an explanation than a tribal boast. The Irish in Ireland of his day were governed, after all, by Englishmen. Tweed and Fernando Wood, the founders of the modern New York Democracy, were Anglo-Saxon Protestants. Not until the last quarter of the nineteenth century did the Irish claim Tammany as their own; by then they were the largest, also the most self-conscious, ethnic group in town.

Historians have not yet fully looked into the origins of modern party organizations, but available evidence for New York City points to the convergence of four changes during the quarter-century or so before the Civil War.

First, the franchise was extended and the ballot lengthened as a result of the egalitarianism of the Age of Jackson. To get out the larger vote and designate candidates for office, party managers perfected the rudimentary machinery that had previously existed. Second, mass immigration, particularly from Ireland and Germany, created a huge new electorate, which the Democrats exploited more artfully than the nativist-tinged Whigs and the Republicans who later succeeded the Whigs. Third, the city expanded physically, opening opportunities for graft—both honest and dishonest in Plunkitt's vocabulary—through the letting of franchises and the construction of such public improvements as schools and sewers and streets (Plunkitt made his fortune partly as a contractor and built a number of Hudson River docks). Fourth, the gentry, which traditionally had managed municipal affairs, were outnumbered, overrun, and displaced by men of obscure origins who had fought their way up from the bottom of the social pyramid.

This new breed, typified by Tweed and Fernando Wood, was the first generation of professional politicians in New York City. Their rise was so sudden that Chancellor Kent, a New York patrician, could write as late as 1835 that "the office of assistant alderman could be pleasant and desirable to persons of leisure, of intelligence, and of disinterested zeal for the wise and just regulation of the public concerns of the city." Thirty years later Boss Tweed called the aldermen "The Forty Thieves," remarking that "there never was a time when you couldn't buy" them. Tweed should have known.

By the time Plunkitt met Riordon the process that had begun before the Civil War was complete. The old families had been routed except for an occasional maverick like Theodore Roosevelt; "I intend(ed) to be one of the governing class," he said to blueblood friends astonished by his decision to join a Republican district club with headquarters above a saloon. Tammany, supported by continuing immigration, sustained by patronage, fattened by loot deriving from the still expanding city, organized down to the block level (there were even tenement-house captains), and led by men who were on the job day in and day out, seemed invincible.

III

But institutions, as a New England philosopher once observed, are merely the lengthened shadows of men. Plunkitt would have put it in a different way, but he would have agreed with the idea. Tammany was as successful as the leaders were resourceful, and a word is necessary about their more important characteristics.

The Sachems of the Hall were with few exceptions native Americans born of immigrant parents. They were what sociologists call marginal men, products of both the immigrant and American cultures. That they were of Irish parentage by Plunkitt's day is less important. Tweed's father came from Scotland. Other big-city machines, whether headed by Germans in Saint Louis, Yankees and Scandinavians in Minneapolis, Jews in San Francisco—or in our own day by Poles in Buffalo and Italians in Rhode Island—differ only in detail from Tammany when the Plunkitts and Murphys ran New York City.

Being a hyphenate had obvious advantages when three out of four New Yorkers were either immigrants or the children of immigrants. Most people vote for their own kind. Equally important, the Tammany leaders knew their own kind through direct experience. This knowledge was denied to the old-stock Americans whom they displaced in local politics. Tammany, because of the background of the Sachems, served as a bridge between the Old and the New worlds.

The immigrants brought from their peasant villages the conception that politics was a personal affair; government was vested in the powerful local ruler who could help or hurt you. In the district Tammany chieftain the newcomers found a replica of the kind of authority they had respected in Europe. Neither there nor in America did they think of politics in terms of issues. This was also true of Tammany. Plunkitt broke into politics in the 1850's, yet he has not a word to say about the most explosive issue of that decade: slavery. Richard Croker, one of the county chairmen under whom Plunkitt served, when asked for his opinion of free silver, the most controversial political question of the 1890's, merely said: "I'm in favor of all kinds of money—the more the better."

If one grasps the point that to most New Yorkers government meant what the leader could do for you, not his party's stand on some "fool issue" like free silver or the annexation of the Philippines, then one must admit that men like Plunkitt gave the people the kind of government they wanted. You went to the district leader with your *personal* problems, and all he asked in exchange for his help was your vote. He was the man to see for a job, a liquor or a pushcart licence, a bucket of coal when there was no money to buy one, help in making out citizenship papers, or in bailing a husband or son out of jail. There's no need to go on; Plunkitt supplies the details and his concluding chapter in particular is a classic of its kind.

Equally important as the hyphenate backgrounds of the Tammany leaders was the poverty that surrounded them during their early years. It explains their drive, their tenacity, their willingness to work around the clock, and their fierce desire for a fair share of riches and respect. Politics was a way out of the slums. In this way Tammany was equal to the Catholic Church's hierarchy as an engine of social mobility for gifted, ambitious Irish-Americans who lacked the capital, the educational advantages, and the connections of the sons of established families. In both institutions careers were open to talent.

Plunkitt's career was typical. The Irish neighborhood in which his immigrant parents settled and he was born had previously been known as Nigger Hill. Quitting school at the age of eleven after "three winters of it," he went to work in a butcher shop and eventually opened his own store in Washington Market. He sold out in 1876 to go into business as a contractor specializing in harbor construction. By then he had worked his way up, through means he describes, from election district captain to assembly district leader. The fact that he held public office was unimportant apart from the titles it conferred on him. At one time he wore four hats simultaneously, those of Magistrate, Alderman, Supervisor, and State Senator. But elected public officials come and go; only the leader enjoys long tenure.

The techniques that carried Plunkitt to the top and made him a millionaire were available, however, to other men with the vision to see and the ambition to rise. Plunkitt complains in one chapter of his book about the treachery of a younger and aggressive rival, The (Thomas J.) McManus, who ultimately defeated the aging politician (then in his sixties) in a party primary for leader of the Fifteenth Assembly District. The McManus seen *his* opportunities and took 'em.

The county chairmen during Plunkitt's life also came from working-class, immigrant neighborhoods and climbed the party hierarchy through methods similar to

Plunkitt's until they got to be Grand Sachem. Tweed was originally a chairmaker's apprentice, John Kelly a soapstone cutter, Richard Croker an unskilled laborer (and chief brawler of the Fourth Avenue Tunnel Gang), Charles F. Murphy a horse-car driver. All of them died rich and except for Tweed—who passed away in Ludlow Street Jail—in office. By common consent Murphy, who grew up in the Gashouse district, was the ablest of the big bosses, but his three predecessors had to prove that they were the most resourceful of their fellow assembly district leaders before becoming Number One.

Plunkitt tells us how he became a "statesman," but not why. Perhaps he would have thought the answer obvious. One can't read him without sensing that politics was to him what buying and selling railroads was to Jim Fisk. It was the thing he liked to do best and did best. It also made him rich, famous, and powerful, satisfying appetites that governed successful Americans in the business world. And make no mistake about it; Tammany Hall was big business. With twelve thousand municipal jobs to give and a payroll of twelve million dollars in the 1880's, the leaders of the Hall were in charge of an even bigger corporation than the Scottish-born Andrew Carnegie's iron and steel works.

IV

New York City was obviously good for the Plunkitts of Tammany Hall, but were they good for New York City? To the legions of mugwumps who are fighting the machine, and whose predecessors fought it from the beginning, there can be only one answer to that question. Tammany was a blight, a curse, an abominable excresence on the body politic. It debased standards of public conduct, the leaders looking out only for their own good, not the community's, and debauching the city while taking their opportunities. The proof? Once a generation the Hall was investigated, and once a generation it was thrown out of office for its record of boodle, corruption, and incompetence.

But Tammany also has its partisans, not just among the Plunkitts, but among historians, political scientists, and journalists. Their point is that the Hall acted as a social welfare agency when the poor and the immigrants had nowhere else to turn. What is more, the machine familiarized millions of newcomers to this country with representative government. This last is no mean achievement when one considers that the underdeveloped nations today have yet to discover a formula that can acquaint their people with the processes of self-government.

Richard Croker, though ordinarily a harsh, hard man, could nevertheless speak emotionally about Tammany's formula: "Think," he said, "what New York is and what the people of New York are. One half, more than one half, are of foreign birth. . . . They do not speak our language, they do not know our laws, they are the raw material with which we have to build up the state. . . . There is no denying the service which Tammany has rendered to the Republic. There is no such organization for taking hold of the untrained, friendless man and converting him into a citizen. Who else would do it if we did not? . . . There is not a mugwump in the city who would shake hands with him."

Tammany, Croker continued, "looks after them for the sake of their vote, grafts them upon the Republic, makes citizens of them, in short; and although you may not like our motives or our methods, what other agency is there by which so long a row could have been hoed so quickly or so well?"

When George Washington Plunkitt died in 1924, *The Nation,* one of the outstanding journals of advanced opinion, commemorated the Senator as "one of the wisest men in American politics. . . ." He understood that in politics "honesty doesn't matter; efficiency doesn't matter; progressive vision doesn't matter. What matters is the chance of a better job, a better price for wheat, better business conditions." Plunkitt's legacy is his practicality.

Yet the men who make a profession of being practical are not necessarily the men who get the right things done. This point is developed in a brilliant article by Daniel P. Moynihan,* a political scientist who spent his boyhood in Hell's Kitchen when The McManus, Plunkitt's successful rival, was still . legendary name. Moynihan concedes that Tammany built a formidable bureaucracy that succeeded in controlling New York City for nearly three-quarters of a century. But what is there to show for that régime? Very little, Moynihan proves; "the Irish didn't know what to do with power once they got it. . . . They never thought of politics as an instrument of social change. . . ."

But neither did the German, Scandinavian, or old-stock American bosses whom Lincoln Steffens described some sixty years ago in *The Shame of the Cities.* What is involved here is the entire breed of organization leader, irrespective of ethnic origins. No matter who ran them, the big-city machines were designed and fueled to win elections and divide the spoils. That takes cunning, industry, sobriety, and organizational know-how, but it requires no social vision. Tammany failed to use, and also misused and abused, the immense power it won because its leaders could not envision a more just and more

* "When the Irish Ran New York," *The Reporter* (June 8, 1961), pp. 32-34.

beautiful city than the mean and ugly neighborhoods in which they grew to manhood.

V

New York is still a Democratic town, but it is no longer run by the Irish. The racially balanced ticket, which dates from the political coming-of-age of other ethnic groups since the 1920's, is here to stay. Plunkitt would have been amused had anyone predicted sixty years ago that a Tammany leader would arise with the name of Carmine De Sapio. The time is not too distant when a Negro will direct the affairs of the Hall.

The machine today tries to carry on in the old ways in sections of the city where the middle class seldom penetrates. But it has never been the same since the rise of the welfare state and trade unionism during the Roosevelt-La Guardia era. Unemployment insurance, social security, collective bargaining, and the guaranteed minimum wage have undermined the role of the district leader as the benefactor of the poor. The bucket of coal and turkey at Christmas are as archaic as the gas-lit, horse-car age from which they came.

Since La Guardia's régime (1934-1945), moreover, there has been less patronage to go around. Plunkitt was right to fear civil service reform as a mortal threat to the life of the machine. But La Guardia was no mugwump. He knew how to get power and to hold on to it, just as Tammany did, but in addition he was motivated by a generous conception of what a great city should be like. The Little Flower combined the cunning of the ward politician with the aspirations of the reformer and demonstrated that the government of big cities need not be, as Lord Bryce observed, the most conspicuous failure in American life.

Tammany was as unprepared for its downfall in the 1930's as Chancellor Kent had been for the obsolescence of his class a century before. In 1929, the year that the Hall's golden boy, Jimmy (Beau James) Walker, was elected for a second term as mayor, the Sachems built the most imposing Wigwam in their history. Then came the New Deal and Mayor La Guardia. In 1943 Tammany was unable to meet the mortgage payments on its gorgeous new building, and the bank sold it to Local 91 of David Dubinsky's International Ladies' Garment Workers Union. Present headquarters for the Hall is a rented office on Madison Avenue.

But back to Plunkitt, when Tammany was supreme. All the world loves a sinner, and Plunkitt has endeared himself to innumerable readers already familiar with his book as a lovable rogue. The fairest way to evaluate him is by his own standards. To Riordon he said that if "my worst enemy was given the job of writin' my epitaph when I'm gone, he couldn't do more than write: 'George W. Plunkitt. He Seen His Opportunities and He Took 'Em.' " Is that a fitting epitaph for what Plunkitt called himself: a statesman?

ARTHUR MANN

Smith College
1962

Preface

This volume discloses the mental operations of perhaps the most thoroughly practical politician of the day—George Washington Plunkitt, Tammany leader of the Fifteenth Assembly District, Sachem of the Tammany Society and Chairman of the Elections Committee of Tammany Hall, who has held the offices of State Senator, Assemblyman, Police Magistrate, County Supervisor and Alderman, and who boasts of his record in filling four public offices in one year and drawing salaries from three of them at the same time.

The discourses that follow were delivered by him from his rostrum, the bootblack stand in the County Courthouse, at various times in the last half-dozen years. Their absolute frankness and vigorous unconventionality of thought and expression charmed me. Plunkitt said right out what all practical politicians think but are afraid to say. Some of the discourses I published as interviews in the *New York Evening Post,* the *New York Sun,* the *New York World,* and the *Boston Transcript.* They were reproduced in newspapers throughout the country and several of them, notably the talks on "The Curse of Civil Service Reform" and "Honest Graft and Dishonest Graft," became subjects of discussion in the United States Senate and in college lectures. There seemed to be a general recognition of Plunkitt as a striking type of the practical politician, a politician, moreover, who dared to say publicly what others in his class whisper among themselves in the City Hall corridors and the hotel lobbies.

I thought it a pity to let Plunkitt's revelations of himself—as frank in their way as Rousseau's *Confessions*—perish in the files of the newspapers; so I collected the talks I had published, added several new ones, and now give to the world in this volume a system of political philosophy which is as unique as it is refreshing.

No New Yorker needs to be informed who George Washington Plunkitt is. For the information of others, the following sketch of his career is given. He was born, as he proudly tells, in Central Park—that is, in the territory now included in the park. He began life as a driver of a cart, then became a butcher's boy, and later went into the butcher business for himself. How he entered politics he explains in one of his discourses. His advancement was rapid. He was in the Assembly soon after he cast his first vote and has held office most of the time for forty years.

In 1870, through a strange combination of circumstances, he held the places of Assemblyman, Alderman, Police Magistrate and County Supervisor and drew three salaries at once—a record unexampled in New York politics.

Plunkitt is now a millionaire. He owes his fortune mainly to his political pull, as he confesses in "Honest Graft and Dishonest Graft." He is in the contracting, transportation, real estate, and every other business out of which he can make money. He has no office. His headquarters is the County Courthouse bootblack stand. There he receives his constituents, transacts his general business and pours forth his philosophy.

Plunkitt has been one of the great powers in Tammany Hall for a quarter of a century. While he was in the

Assembly and the State Senate he was one of the most influential members and introduced the bills that provided for the outlying parks of New York City, the Harlem River Speedway, the Washington Bridge, the 155th Street Viaduct, the grading of Eighth Avenue north of Fifty-seventh Street, additions to the Museum of Natural History, the West Side Court, and many other important public improvements. He is one of the closest friends and most valued advisers of Charles F. Murphy, leader of Tammany Hall.

William L. Riordon

A Tribute to Plunkitt by the Leader of Tammany Hall

SENATOR PLUNKITT is a straight organization man. He believes in party government; he does not indulge in cant and hypocrisy and he is never afraid to say exactly what he thinks. He is a believer in thorough political organization and all-the-year-around work, and he holds to the doctrine that, in making appointments to office, party workers should be preferred if they are fitted to perform the duties of the office. Plunkitt is one of the veteran leaders of the organization; he has always been faithful and reliable, and he has performed valuable services for Tammany Hall.

CHARLES F. MURPHY

PLUNKITT OF TAMMANY HALL

Honest Graft and Dishonest Graft

EVERYBODY is talkin' these days about Tammany men growin' rich on graft, but nobody thinks of drawin' the distinction between honest graft and dishonest graft. There's all the difference in the world between the two. Yes, many of our men have grown rich in politics. I have myself. I've made a big fortune out of the game, and I'm gettin' richer every day, but I've not gone in for dishonest graft—blackmailin' gamblers, saloonkeepers, disorderly people, etc.—and neither has any of the men who have made big fortunes in politics.

There's an honest graft, and I'm an example of how it works. I might sum up the whole thing by sayin': "I seen my opportunities and I took 'em."

Just let me explain by examples. My party's in power in the city, and it's goin' to undertake a lot of public improvements. Well, I'm tipped off, say, that they're going to lay out a new park at a certain place.

I see my opportunity and I take it. I go to that place and I buy up all the land I can in the neighborhood. Then the board of this or that makes its plan public, and there is a rush to get my land, which nobody cared particular for before.

Ain't it perfectly honest to charge a good price and make a profit on my investment and foresight? Of course, it is. Well, that's honest graft.

Or supposin' it's a new bridge they're goin' to build. I get tipped off and I buy as much property as I can that has to be taken for approaches. I sell at my own price later on and drop some more money in the bank.

Wouldn't you? It's just like lookin' ahead in Wall Street or in the coffee or cotton market. It's honest graft, and I'm lookin' for it every day in the year. I will tell you frankly that I've got a good lot of it, too.

I'll tell you of one case. They were goin' to fix up a big park, no matter where. I got on to it, and went lookin' about for land in that neighborhood.

I could get nothin' at a bargain but a big piece of swamp, but I took it fast enough and held on to it. What turned out was just what I counted on. They couldn't make the park complete without Plunkitt's swamp, and they had to pay a good price for it. Anything dishonest in that?

Up in the watershed I made some money, too. I bought up several bits of land there some years ago and made a pretty good guess that they would be bought up for water purposes later by the city.

Somehow, I always guessed about right, and shouldn't I enjoy the profit of my foresight? It was rather amusin' when the condemnation commissioners came along and found piece after piece of the land in the name of George Plunkitt of the Fifteenth Assembly District, New York City. They wondered how I knew just what to buy. The answer is—I seen my opportunity and I took it. I haven't confined myself to land; anything that pays is in my line.

For instance, the city is repavin' a street and has several hundred thousand old granite blocks to sell. I am on hand to buy, and I know just what they are worth.

How? Never mind that. I had a sort of monopoly of this business for a while, but once a newspaper tried to do me. It got some outside men to come over from Brooklyn and New Jersey to bid against me.

Was I done? Not much. I went to each of the men and said: "How many of these 250,000 stones do you want?" One said 20,000, and another wanted 15,000, and other wanted 10,000. I said: "All right, let me bid for the lot, and I'll give each of you all you want for nothin'."

They agreed, of course. Then the auctioneer yelled: "How much am I bid for these 250,000 fine pavin' stones?"

"Two dollars and fifty cents," says I.

"Two dollars and fifty cents!" screamed the auctioneer. "Oh, that's a joke! Give me a real bid."

He found the bid was real enough. My rivals stood silent. I got the lot for $2.50 and gave them their share. That's how the attempt to do Plunkitt ended, and that's how all such attempts end.

I've told you how I got rich by honest graft. Now, let me tell you that most politicians who are accused of robbin' the city get rich the same way.

They didn't steal a dollar from the city treasury. They just seen their opportunities and took them. That is why, when a reform administration comes in and spends a half million dollars in tryin' to find the public robberies they talked about in the campaign, they don't find them.

The books are always all right. The money in the city treasury is all right. Everything is all right. All they can show is that the Tammany heads of departments looked after their friends, within the law, and gave them what opportunities they could to make honest graft. Now, let me tell you that's never goin' to hurt Tammany with the people. Every good man looks after his friends, and any man who doesn't isn't likely to be popular. If I have a good thing to hand out in private life, I give it to a friend. Why shouldn't I do the same in public life?

Another kind of honest graft. Tammany has raised a good many salaries. There was an awful howl by the reformers, but don't you know that Tammany gains ten votes for every one it lost by salary raisin'?

The Wall Street banker thinks it shameful to raise a department clerk's salary from $1500 to $1800 a year, but every man who draws a salary himself says: "That's all right. I wish it was me." And he feels very much like votin' the Tammany ticket on election day, just out of sympathy.

Tammany was beat in 1901 because the people were deceived into believin' that it worked dishonest graft. They didn't draw a distinction between dishonest and honest graft, but they saw that some Tammany men grew rich, and supposed they had been robbin' the city treasury or levyin' blackmail on disorderly houses, or workin' in with the gamblers and lawbreakers.

As a matter of policy, if nothing else, why should the Tammany leaders go into such dirty business, when there is so much honest graft lyin' around when they are in power? Did you ever consider that?

Now, in conclusion, I want to say that I don't own a dishonest dollar. If my worst enemy was given the job of writin' my epitaph when I'm gone, he couldn't do more than write:

"George W. Plunkitt. He Seen His Opportunities, and He Took 'Em."

How to Become a Statesman

THERE'S thousands of young men in this city who will go to the polls for the first time next November. Among them will be many who have watched the careers of successful men in politics, and who are longin' to make names and fortunes for themselves at the same game. It is to these youths that I want to give advice. First, let me say that I am in a position to give what the courts call expert testimony on the subject. I don't think you can easily find a better example than I am of success in politics. After forty years' experience at the game I am—well, I'm George Washington Plunkitt. Everybody knows what figure I cut in the greatest organization on earth, and if you hear people say that I've laid away a million or so since I was a butcher's boy in Washington Market, don't come to me for an indignant denial. I'm pretty comfortable, thank you.

Now, havin' qualified as an expert, as the lawyers say, I am goin' to give advice free to the young men who are goin' to cast their first votes, and who are lookin' forward to political glory and lots of cash. Some young men think they can learn how to be successful in politics from books, and they cram their heads with all sorts of college rot. They couldn't make a bigger mistake. Now, understand me, I ain't sayin' nothin' against colleges. I guess they'll have to exist as long as there's bookworms, and I suppose they do some good in a certain way, but they don't count in politics. In fact, a young man who has gone through the college course is handicapped at the outset. He may succeed in politics, but the chances are 100 to 1 against him.

Another mistake: some young men think that the best way to prepare for the political game is to practice speakin' and becomin' orators. That's all wrong. We've got some orators in Tammany Hall, but they're chiefly ornamental. You never heard of Charlie Murphy delivering a speech, did you? Or Richard Croker, or John Kelly, or any other man who has been a real power in the organization? Look at the thirty-six district leaders of Tammany Hall today. How many of them travel on their tongues? Maybe one or two, and they don't count when business is doin' at Tammany Hall. The men who rule have practiced keepin' their tongues still, not exercisin' them. So you want to drop the orator idea unless you mean to go into politics just to perform the skyrocket act.

Now, I've told you what not to do; I guess I can explain best what to do to succeed in politics by tellin' you what I did. After goin' through the apprenticeship of the business while I was a boy by workin' around the district headquarters and hustlin' about the polls on election day, I set out when I cast my first vote to win fame and money in New York City politics. Did I offer my services to the district leader as a stump-speaker? Not much. The woods are always full of speakers. Did I get up a book on municipal government and show it to the leader? I wasn't such a fool. What I did was to get some marketable goods before goin' to the leaders. What do I mean by marketable goods? Let me tell you: I had a cousin, a young man who didn't take any particular interest in politics. I went to him and said: "Tommy,

I'm goin' to be a politician, and I want to get a followin'; can I count on you?" He said: "Sure, George." That's how I started in business. I got a marketable commodity —one vote. Then I went to the district leader and told him I could command two votes on election day, Tommy's and my own. He smiled on me and told me to go ahead. If I had offered him a speech or a bookful of learnin', he would have said, "Oh, forget it!"

That was beginnin' business in a small way, wasn't it? But that is the only way to become a real lastin' statesman. I soon branched out. Two young men in the flat next to mine were school friends. I went to them, just as I went to Tommy, and they agreed to stand by me. Then I had a followin' of three voters and I began to get a bit chesty. Whenever I dropped into district headquarters, everybody shook hands with me, and the leader one day honored me by lightin' a match for my cigar. And so it went on like a snowball rollin' down a hill. I worked the flat-house that I lived in from the basement to the top floor, and I got about a dozen young men to follow me. Then I tackled the next house and so on down the block and around the corner. Before long I had sixty men back of me, and formed the George Washington Plunkitt Association.

What did the district leader say then when I called at headquarters? I didn't have to call at headquarters. He came after me and said: "George, what do you want? If you don't see what you want, ask for it. Wouldn't you like to have a job or two in the departments for your friends?" I said: "I'll think it over; I haven't yet decided what the George Washington Plunkitt Association will do in the next campaign." You ought to have seen how I was courted and petted then by the leaders of the rival organizations. I had marketable goods and there was bids for them from all sides, and I was a risin' man in politics. As time went on, and my association grew, I thought I would like to go to the Assembly. I just had to hint at what I wanted, and three different organizations offered me the nomination. Afterwards, I went to the Board of Aldermen, then to the State Senate, then became leader of the district, and so on up and up till I became a statesman.

That is the way and the only way to make a lastin' success in politics. If you are goin' to cast your first vote next November and want to go into politics, do as I did. Get a followin', if it's only one man, and then go to the district leader and say: "I want to join the organization. I've got one man who'll follow me through thick and thin." The leader won't laugh at your one-man followin'. He'll shake your hand warmly, offer to propose you for membership in his club, take you down to the corner for a drink and ask you to call again. But go to him and say: "I took first prize at college in Aristotle; I can recite all Shakespeare forwards and backwards; there ain't nothin' in science that ain't as familiar to me as blockades on the elevated roads and I'm the real thing in the way of silver-tongued orators." What will he answer? He'll probably say: "I guess you are not to blame for your misfortunes, but we have no use for you here."

The Curse of Civil Service Reform

THIS civil service law is the biggest fraud of the age. It is the curse of the nation. There can't be no real patriotism while it lasts. How are you goin' to interest our young men in their country if you have no offices to give them when they work for their party? Just look at things in this city today. There are ten thousand good offices, but we can't get at more than a few hundred of them. How are we goin' to provide for the thousands of men who worked for the Tammany ticket? It can't be done. These men were full of patriotism a short time ago. They expected to be servin' their city, but when we tell them that we can't place them, do you think their patriotism is goin' to last? Not much. They say: "What's the use of workin' for your country anyhow? There's nothin' in the game." And what can they do? I don't know, but I'll tell you what I do know. I know more than one young man in past years who worked for the ticket and was just overflowin' with patriotism, but when he was knocked out by the civil service humbug he got to hate his country and became an Anarchist.

This ain't no exaggeration. I have good reason for sayin' that most of the Anarchists in this city today are men who ran up against civil service examinations. Isn't it enough to make a man sour on his country when he wants to serve it and won't be allowed unless he answers a lot of fool questions about the number of cubic inches of water in the Atlantic and the quality of sand in the Sahara desert? There was once a bright young man in my district who tackled one of these examinations. The next I heard of him he had settled down in Herr Most's saloon smokin' and drinkin' beer and talkin' socialism all day. Before that time he had never drank anything but whisky. I knew what was comin' when a young Irishman drops whisky and takes to beer and long pipes in a German saloon. That young man is today one of the wildest Anarchists in town. And just to think! He might be a patriot but for that cussed civil service.

Say, did you hear about that Civil Service Reform Association kickin' because the tax commissioners want to put their fifty-five deputies on the exempt list, and fire the outfit left to them by Low? That's civil service for you. Just think! Fifty-five Republicans and mugwumps holdin' $3000 and $4000 and $5000 jobs in the tax department when 1555 good Tammany men are ready and willin' to take their places! It's an outrage! What did the people mean when they voted for Tammany? What is representative government, anyhow? Is it all a fake that this is a government of the people, by the people and for the people? If it isn't a fake, then why isn't the people's voice obeyed and Tammany men put in all the offices?

When the people elected Tammany, they knew just what they were doin'. We didn't put up any false pretenses. We didn't go in for humbug civil service and all that rot. We stood as we have always stood, for rewardin' the men that won the victory. They call that the spoils system. All right; Tammany is for the spoils system, and when we go in we fire every anti-Tammany man from office that can be fired under the law. It's an elastic sort of law and you can bet it will be stretched to the limit. Of course the Republican State Civil Service Board will stand in the way of our local Civil Service Commission all it can; but say!—suppose we carry the State sometime, won't we fire the upstate Board all right? Or we'll make it work in harmony with the local board, and that means that Tammany will get everything in sight. I know that the civil service humbug is stuck into the constitution, too, but, as Tim Campbell said: "What's the constitution among friends?"

Say, the people's voice is smothered by the cursed civil service law; it is the root of all evil in our government. You hear of this thing or that thing goin' wrong in the nation, the State or the city. Look down beneath the surface and you can trace everything wrong to civil service. I have studied the subject and I know. The civil service humbug is underminin' our institutions and if a halt ain't called soon this great republic will tumble down like a Park Avenue house when they were buildin' the subway, and on its ruins will rise another Russian government.

This is an awful serious proposition. Free silver and the tariff and imperialism and the Panama Canal are triflin' issues when compared to it. We could worry along without any of these things, but civil service is sappin' the foundation of the whole shootin' match. Let me argue it out for you. I ain't up on sillygisms, but I can give you some arguments that nobody can answer.

First, this great and glorious country was built up by political parties; second, parties can't hold together if their workers don't get the offices when they win; third, if the parties go to pieces, the government they built up must go to pieces, too; fourth, then there'll be h—— to pay.

Could anything be clearer than that? Say, honest now;

can you answer that argument? Of course you won't deny that the government was built up by the great parties. That's history, and you can't go back of the returns. As to my second proposition, you can't deny that either. When parties can't get offices, they'll bust. They ain't far from the bustin' point now, with all this civil service business keepin' most of the good things from them. How are you goin' to keep up patriotism if this thing goes on? You can't do it. Let me tell you that patriotism has been dying out fast for the last twenty years. Before then when a party won, its workers got everything in sight. That was somethin' to make a man patriotic. Now, when a party wins and its men come forward and ask for their rewards, the reply is, "Nothin' doin', unless you can answer a list of questions about Egyptian mummies and how many years it will take for a bird to wear out a mass of iron as big as the earth by steppin' on it once in a century?"

I have studied politics and men for forty-five years, and I see how things are driftin'. Sad indeed is the change that has come over the young men, even in my district, where I try to keep up the fire of patriotism by gettin' a lot of jobs for my constituents, whether Tammany is in or out. The boys and men don't get excited any more when they see a United States flag or hear "The Star-Spangled Banner." They don't care no more for firecrackers on the Fourth of July. And why should they? What is there in it for them? They know that no matter how hard they work for their country in a campaign, the jobs will go to fellows who can tell about the mummies and the bird steppin' on the iron. Are you surprised then that the young men of the country are beginnin' to look coldly on the flag and don't care to put up a nickel for firecrackers?

Say, let me tell of one case. After the battle of San Juan Hill, the Americans found a dead man with a light complexion, red hair and blue eyes. They could see he wasn't a Spaniard, although he had on a Spanish uniform. Several officers looked him over, and then a private of the Seventy-first Regiment saw him and yelled, "Good Lord, that's Flaherty." That man grew up in my district, and he was once the most patriotic American boy on the West Side. He couldn't see a flag without yellin' himself hoarse.

Now, how did he come to be lying dead with a Spanish uniform on? I found out all about it, and I'll vouch for the story. Well, in the municipal campaign of 1897, that young man, chockful of patriotism, worked day and night for the Tammany ticket. Tammany won, and the young man determined to devote his life to the service of the city. He picked out a place that would suit him, and sent in his application to the head of department. He got a reply that he must take a civil service examination to get the place. He didn't know what these examinations were, so he went, all lighthearted, to the Civil Service Board. He read the questions about the mummies, the bird on the iron, and all the other fool questions—and he left that office an enemy of the country that he had loved so well. The mummies and the bird blasted his patriotism. He went to Cuba, enlisted in the Spanish army at the breakin' out of the war, and died fightin' his country.

That is but one victim of the infamous civil service. If that young man had not run up against the civil examination, but had been allowed to serve his country as he wished, he would be in a good office today, drawin' a good salary. Ah, how many young men have had their patriotism blasted in the same way!

Now, what is goin' to happen when civil service crushes out patriotism? Only one thing can happen: the republic will go to pieces. Then a czar or a sultan will turn up, which brings me to the fourthly of my argument—that is, there will be h—— to pay. And that ain't no lie.

Reformers Only Mornin' Glories

College professors and philosophers who go up in a balloon to think are always discussin' the question: "Why Reform Administrations Never Succeed Themselves!" The reason is plain to anybody who has learned the a, b, c of politics.

I can't tell just how many of these movements I've seen started in New York during my forty years in politics, but I can tell you how many have lasted more than a few years—none. There have been reform committees of fifty, of sixty, of seventy, of one hundred and all sorts of numbers that started out to do up the regular political organizations. They were mornin' glories—looked lovely in the mornin' and withered up in a short time, while the regular machines went on flourishin' forever, like fine old oaks. Say, that's the first poetry I ever worked off. Ain't it great?

Just look back a few years. You remember the People's Municipal League that nominated Frank Scott for mayor in 1890? Do you remember the reformers that got up that league? Have you ever heard of them since? I haven't. Scott himself survived because he had always been a first-rate politician, but you'd have to look in the newspaper almanacs of 1891 to find out who made up the People's Municipal League. Oh, yes! I remember one name: Ollie Teall; dear, pretty Ollie and his big dog. They're about all that's left of the League.

Now take the reform movement of 1894. A lot of good politicians joined in that—the Republicans, the State Democrats, the Stecklerites and the O'Brienites, and they gave us a lickin', but the real reform part of the affair, the Committee of Seventy that started the thing goin', what's become of those reformers? What's become of Charles Stewart Smith? Where's Bangs? Do you ever hear of Cornell, the iron man, in politics now? Could a search party find R. W. G. Welling? Have you seen the name of Fulton McMahon or McMahon Fulton —I ain't sure which—in the papers lately? Or Preble Tucker? Or—but it's no use to go through the list of the reformers who said they sounded in the death knell of Tammany in 1894. They're gone for good, and Tammany's pretty well, thank you. They did the talkin' and posin', and the politicians in the movement got all the plums. It's always the case.

The Citizens' Union has lasted a little bit longer than the reform crowd that went before them, but that's because they learned a thing or two from us. They learned how to put up a pretty good bluff—and bluff counts a lot in politics. With only a few thousand members, they had the nerve to run the whole Fusion movement, make the Republicans and other organizations come to their headquarters to select a ticket and dictate what every candidate must do or not do. I love nerve, and I've had a sort of respect for the Citizens' Union lately, but the Union can't last. Its people haven't been trained to politics, and whenever Tammany calls their bluff they lay right down. You'll never hear of the Union again after a year or two.

And, by the way, what's become of the good government clubs, the political nurseries of a few years ago?

Do you ever hear of Good Government Club D and P and Q and Z any more? What's become of the infants who were to grow up and show us how to govern the city? I know what's become of the nursery that was started in my district. You can find pretty much the whole outfit over in my headquarters, Washington Hall.

The fact is that a reformer can't last in politics. He can make a show for a while, but he always comes down like a rocket. Politics is as much a regular business as the grocery or the dry-goods or the drug business. You've got to be trained up to it or you're sure to fail. Suppose a man who knew nothing about the grocery trade suddenly went into the business and tried to conduct it according to his own ideas. Wouldn't he make a mess of it? He might make a splurge for a while, as long as his money lasted, but his store would soon be empty. It's just the same with a reformer. He hasn't been brought up in the difficult business of politics and he makes a mess of it every time.

I've been studyin' the political game for forty-five years, and I don't know it all yet. I'm learnin' somethin' all the time. How, then, can you expect what they call "business men" to turn into politics all at once and make a success of it? It is just as if I went up to Columbia University and started to teach Greek. They usually last about as long in politics as I would last at Columbia.

You can't begin too early in politics if you want to succeed at the game. I began several years before I could vote, and so did every successful leader in Tammany Hall. When I was twelve years old I made myself useful around the district headquarters and did work at all the polls on election day. Later on, I hustled about gettin' out voters who had jags on or who were too lazy to come to the polls. There's a hundred ways that boys can help, and they get an experience that's the first real step in statesmanship. Show me a boy that hustles for the organization on election day, and I'll show you a comin' statesman.

That's the a, b, c of politics. It ain't easy work to get up to y and z. You have to give nearly all your time and attention to it. Of course, you may have some business or occupation on the side, but the great business of your life must be politics if you want to succeed in it. A few years ago Tammany tried to mix politics and business in equal quantities, by havin' two leaders for each district, a politician and a business man. They wouldn't mix. They were like oil and water. The politician looked after the politics of his district; the business man looked after his grocery store or his milk route, and whenever he appeared at an executive meeting, it was only to make trouble. The whole scheme turned out to be a farce and was abandoned mighty quick.

Do you understand now, why it is that a reformer goes down and out in the first or second round, while a politician answers to the gong every time? It is because the one has gone into the fight without trainin', while the other trains all the time and knows every fine point of the game.

New York City Is Pie for the Hayseeds

THIS city is ruled entirely by the hayseed legislators at Albany. I've never known an upstate Republican who didn't want to run things here, and I've met many thousands of them in my long service in the Legislature. The hayseeds think we are like the Indians to the National Government—that is, sort of wards of the State, who don't know how to look after ourselves and have to be taken care of by the Republicans of St. Lawrence, Ontario, and other backwoods counties. Why should anybody be surprised because ex-Governor Odell comes down here to direct the Republican machine? Newburg ain't big enough for him. He, like all the other upstate Republicans, wants to get hold of New York City. New York is their pie.

Say, you hear a lot about the downtrodden people of Ireland and the Russian peasants and the sufferin' Boers. Now, let me tell you that they have more real freedom and home rule than the people of this grand and imperial city. In England, for example, they make a pretense of givin' the Irish some self-government. In this State the Republican government makes no pretense at all. It says right out in the open: "New York City is a nice big fat Goose. Come along with your carvin' knives and have a slice." They don't pretend to ask the Goose's consent.

We don't own our streets or our docks or our waterfront or anything else. The Republican Legislature and Governor run the whole shootin' match. We've got to eat and drink what they tell us to eat and drink, and have got to choose our time for eatin' and drinkin' to suit them. If they don't feel like takin' a glass of beer on Sunday, we must abstain. If they have not got any amusements up in their backwoods, we mustn't have none. We've got to regulate our whole lives to suit them. And then we have to pay their taxes to boot.

Did you ever go up to Albany from this city with a delegation that wanted anything from the Legislature? No? Well, don't. The hayseeds who run all the committees will look at you as if you were a child that didn't know what it wanted, and will tell you in so many words to go home and be good and the Legislature will give you whatever it thinks is good for you. They put on a sort of patronizing air, as much as to say, "These children are an awful lot of trouble. They're wantin' candy all the time, and they know that it will make them sick. They ought to thank goodness that they have us to take care of them." And if you try to argue with them, they'll smile in a pityin' sort of way as if they were humorin' a spoiled child.

But just let a Republican farmer from Chemung or Wayne or Tioga turn up at the Capital. The Republican Legislature will make a rush for him and ask him what he wants and tell him if he doesn't see what he wants to ask for it. If he says his taxes are too high, they reply to him: "All right, old man, don't let that worry you. How much do you want us to take off?"

"I guess about fifty per cent will about do for the present," says the man. "Can you fix me up?"

"Sure," the Legislature agrees. "Give us somethin'

harder, don't be bashful. We'll take off sixty per cent if you wish. That's what we're here for."

Then the Legislature goes and passes a law increasin' the liquor tax or some other tax in New York City, takes a half of the proceeds for the State Treasury and cuts down the farmers' taxes to suit. It's as easy as rollin' off a log—when you've got a good workin' majority and no conscience to speak of.

Let me give you another example. It makes me hot under the collar to tell about this. Last year some hayseeds along the Hudson River, mostly in Odell's neighborhood, got dissatisfied with the docks where they landed their vegetables, brickbats, and other things they produce in the river counties. They got together and said: "Let's take a trip down to New York and pick out the finest dock we can find. Odell and the Legislature will do the rest." They did come down here, and what do you think they hit on? The finest dock in my district. Invaded George W. Plunkitt's district without sayin' as much as "by your leave." Then they called on Odell to put through a bill givin' them this dock, and he did.

When the bill came before Mayor Low I made the greatest speech of my life. I pointed out how the Legislature could give the whole waterfront to the hayseeds over the head of the Dock Commissioner in the same way, and warned the Mayor that nations had rebelled against their governments for less. But it was no go. Odell and Low were pards and—well, my dock was stolen.

You heard a lot in the State campaign about Odell's great work in reducin' the State tax to almost nothin', and you'll hear a lot more about it in the campaign next year. How did he do it? By cuttin' down the expenses of the State Government? Oh, no! The expenses went up. He simply performed the old Republican act of milkin' New York City. The only difference was that he nearly milked the city dry. He not only ran up the liquor tax, but put all sorts of taxes on corporations, banks, insurance companies, and everything in sight that could be made to give up. Of course, nearly the whole tax fell on the city. Then Odell went through the country districts and said: "See what I have done for you. You ain't got any more taxes to pay the State. Ain't I a fine feller?"

Once a farmer in Orange County asked him: "How did you do it, Ben?"

"Dead easy," he answered. "Whenever I want any money for the State Treasury, I know where to get it," and he pointed toward New York City.

And then all the Republican tinkerin' with New York City's charter. Nobody can keep up with it. When a Republican mayor is in, they give him all sorts of power. If a Tammany mayor is elected next fall I wouldn't be surprised if they changed the whole business and arranged it so that every city department should have four heads, two of them Republicans. If we make a kick, they would say: "You don't know what's good for you. Leave it to us. It's our business."

To Hold Your District: Study Human Nature and Act Accordin'

THERE's only one way to hold a district: you must study human nature and act accordin'. You can't study human nature in books. Books is a hindrance more than anything else. If you have been to college, so much the worse for you. You'll have to unlearn all you learned before you can get right down to human nature, and unlearnin' takes a lot of time. Some men can never forget what they learned at college. Such men may get to be district leaders by a fluke, but they never last.

To learn real human nature you have to go among the people, see them and be seen. I know every man, woman, and child in the Fifteenth District, except them that's been born this summer—and I know some of them, too. I know what they like and what they don't like, what they are strong at and what they are weak in, and I reach them by approachin' at the right side.

For instance, here's how I gather in the young men. I hear of a young feller that's proud of his voice, thinks that he can sing fine. I ask him to come around to Washington Hall and join our Glee Club. He comes and sings, and he's a follower of Plunkitt for life. Another young feller gains a reputation as a baseball player in a vacant lot. I bring him into our baseball club. That fixes him. You'll find him workin' for my ticket at the polls next election day. Then there's the feller that likes rowin' on the river, the young feller that makes a name as a waltzer on his block, the young feller that's handy with his dukes—I rope them all in by givin' them opportunities to show themselves off. I don't trouble them with political arguments. I just study human nature and act accordin'.

But you may say this game won't work with the high-toned fellers, the fellers that go through college and then join the Citizens' Union. Of course it wouldn't work. I have a special treatment for them. I ain't like the patent medicine man that gives the same medicine for all diseases. The Citizens' Union kind of a young man! I love him! He's the daintiest morsel of the lot, and he don't often escape me.

Before telling you how I catch him, let me mention that before the election last year, the Citizens' Union said they had four hundred or five hundred enrolled voters in my district. They had a lovely headquarters, too, beautiful roll-top desks and the cutest rugs in the world. If I was accused of havin' contributed to fix up the nest for them, I wouldn't deny it under oath. What do I mean by that? Never mind. You can guess from the sequel, if you're sharp.

Well, election day came. The Citizens' Union's candidate for Senator, who ran against me, just polled five votes in the district, while I polled something more than 14,000 votes. What became of the 400 or 500 Citizens' Union enrolled voters in my district? Some people guessed that many of them were good Plunkitt men all along and worked with the Cits just to bring them into the Plunkitt camp by election day. You can guess that way, too, if you want to. I never contradict stories about me, especially in hot weather. I just call your attention to the fact that on last election day 395 Citizens' Union enrolled voters in my district were missin' and unaccounted for.

I tell you frankly, though, how I have captured some of the Citizens' Union's young men. I have a plan that never fails. I watch the City Record to see when there's civil service examinations for good things. Then I take my young Cit in hand, tell him all about the good thing and get him worked up till he goes and takes an examination. I don't bother about him any more. It's a cinch that he comes back to me in a few days and asks to join Tammany Hall. Come over to Washington Hall some night and I'll show you a list of names on our rolls marked "C.S." which means, "bucked up against civil service."

As to the older voters, I reach them, too. No, I don't send them campaign literature. That's rot. People can get all the political stuff they want to read—and a good deal more, too—in the papers. Who reads speeches, nowadays, anyhow? It's bad enough to listen to them. You ain't goin' to gain any votes by stuffin' the letter boxes with campaign documents. Like as not you'll lose votes, for there's nothin' a man hates more than to hear the letter carrier ring his bell and go to the letter box expectin' to find a letter he was lookin' for, and find only a lot of printed politics. I met a man this very mornin' who told me he voted the Democratic State ticket last year just because the Republicans kept crammin' his letter box with campaign documents.

What tells in holdin' your grip on your district is to go right down among the poor families and help them in the different ways they need help. I've got a regular system for this. If there's a fire in Ninth, Tenth, or Eleventh Avenue, for example, any hour of the day or night, I'm usually there with some of my election district captains as soon as the fire engines. If a family is burned out I don't ask whether they are Republicans or Democrats, and I don't refer them to the Charity Organization Society, which would investigate their case in a month or two and decide they were worthy of help about the time they are dead from starvation. I just get quarters for them, buy clothes for them if their clothes were burned up, and fix them up till they get things runnin' again. It's philanthropy, but it's politics, too—mighty good politics. Who can tell how many votes one of these fires bring me? The poor are the most grateful people in the world, and, let me tell you, they have more friends in their neighborhoods than the rich have in theirs.

If there's a family in my district in want I know it before the charitable societies do, and me and my men are first on the ground. I have a special corps to look up such cases. The consequence is that the poor look up to George W. Plunkitt as a father, come to him in trouble—and don't forget him on election day.

Another thing, I can always get a job for a deservin' man. I make it a point to keep on the track of jobs, and it seldom happens that I don't have a few up my sleeve ready for use. I know every big employer in the district and in the whole city, for that matter, and they ain't in the habit of sayin' no to me when I ask them for a job.

And the children—the little roses of the district! Do I forget them? Oh, no! They know me, every one of them, and they know that a sight of Uncle George and candy means the same thing. Some of them are the best kind of vote-getters. I'll tell you a case. Last year a little Eleventh Avenue rosebud, whose father is a Republican, caught hold of his whiskers on election day and said she wouldn't let go till he'd promise to vote for me. And she didn't.

On *The Shame of the Cities*

I'VE been readin' a book by Lincoln Steffens on *The Shame of the Cities*. Steffens means well but, like all reformers, he don't know how to make distinctions. He can't see no difference between honest graft and dishonest graft and, consequent, he gets things all mixed up. There's the biggest kind of a difference between political looters and politicians who make a fortune out of politics by keepin' their eyes wide open. The looter goes in for himself alone without considerin' his organization or his city. The politician looks after his own interests, the organization's interests, and the city's interests all at the same time. See the distinction? For instance, I ain't no looter. The looter hogs it. I never hogged. I made my pile in politics, but, at the same time, I served the organization and got more big improvements for New York City than any other livin' man. And I never monkeyed with the penal code.

The difference between a looter and a practical politician is the difference between the Philadelphia Republican gang and Tammany Hall. Steffens seems to think they're both about the same; but he's all wrong. The Philadelphia crowd runs up against the penal code. Tammany don't. The Philadelphians ain't satisfied with robbin' the bank of all its gold and paper money. They stay to pick up the nickels and pennies and the cop comes and nabs them. Tammany ain't no such fool. Why, I remember, about fifteen or twenty years ago, a Republican superintendent of the Philadelphia almshouse stole the zinc roof off the buildin' and sold it for junk. That was carryin' things to excess. There's a limit to everything, and the Philadelphia Republicans go beyond the limit. It seems like they can't be cool and moderate like real politicians. It ain't fair, therefore, to class Tammany men with the Philadelphia gang. Any man who undertakes to write political books should never for a moment lose sight of the distinction between honest graft and dishonest graft, which I explained in full in another talk. If he puts all kinds of graft on the same level, he'll make the fatal mistake that Steffens made and spoil his book.

A big city like New York or Philadelphia or Chicago might be compared to a sort of Garden of Eden, from a political point of view. It's an orchard full of beautiful apple trees. One of them has got a big sign on it, marked: "Penal Code Tree—Poison." The other trees have lots of apples on them for all. Yet the fools go to the Penal Code Tree. Why? For the reason, I guess, that a cranky child refuses to eat good food and chews up a box of matches with relish. I never had any temptation to touch the Penal Code Tree. The other apples are good enough for me, and O Lord! how many of them there are in a big city!

Steffens made one good point in his book. He said he found that Philadelphia, ruled almost entirely by Americans, was more corrupt than New York, where the Irish do almost all the governin'. I could have told him that before he did any investigatin' if he had come to me. The Irish was born to rule, and they're the honestest people in the world. Show me the Irishman who would steal a roof off an almhouse! He don't exist. Of course, if an Irishman had the political pull and the roof was much worn, he might get the city authorities to put on a new one and get the contract for it himself, and buy the old roof at a bargain—but that's honest graft. It's goin' about the thing like a gentleman, and there's more money in it than in tearin' down an old roof and cartin' it to the junkman's—more money and no penal code.

One reason why the Irishman is more honest in politics than many Sons of the Revolution is that he is grateful to the country and the city that gave him protection and prosperity when he was driven by oppression from the Emerald Isle. Say, that sentence is fine, ain't it? I'm goin' to get some literary feller to work it over into poetry for next St. Patrick's Day dinner.

Yes, the Irishman is grateful. His one thought is to serve the city which gave him a home. He has this thought even before he lands in New York, for his friends here often have a good place in one of the city departments picked out for him while he is still in the old country. Is it any wonder that he has a tender spot in his heart for old New York when he is on its salary list the mornin' after he lands?

Now, a few words on the general subject of the so-called shame of cities. I don't believe that the government of our cities is any worse, in proportion to opportunities, than it was fifty years ago. I'll explain what I mean by "in proportion to opportunities." A half a century ago, our cities were small and poor. There wasn't many temptations lyin' around for politicians. There was hardly anything to steal, and hardly any opportunities for even honest graft. A city could count its money every night before goin' to bed, and if three cents was missin', all the fire bells would be rung. What credit was there in bein' honest under them circumstances? It makes me tired to hear of old codgers back in the thirties or forties boastin' that they retired from politics without a dollar except what they earned in their profession or business. If they lived today, with all the existin' opportunities, they would be just the same as twentieth-century politicians. There ain't any more honest people in the world just now than the convicts in Sing Sing. Not one of them steals anything. Why? Because they can't. See the application?

Understand, I ain't defendin' politicians of today who steal. The politician who steals is worse than a thief. He is a fool. With the grand opportunities all around for the man with a political pull, there's no excuse for stealin' a cent. The point I want to make is that if there is some stealin' in politics, it don't mean that the politicians of 1905 are, as a class, worse than them of 1835. It just means that the old-timers had nothin' to steal, while the politicians now are surrounded by all kinds of temptations and some of them naturally—the fool ones —buck up against the penal code.

Ingratitude in Politics

THERE'S no crime so mean as ingratitude in politics, but every great statesman from the beginnin' of the world has been up against it. Caesar had his Brutus; that king of Shakespeare's—Leary, I think you call him—had his own daughters go back on him; Platt had his Odell, and I've got my "The" McManus. It's a real proof that a man is great when he meets with political ingratitude. Great men have a tender, trustin' nature. So have I, outside of the contractin' and real estate business. In politics I have trusted men who have told me they were my friends, and if traitors have turned up in my camp—well, I only had the same experience as Caesar, Leary, and the others. About my Brutus. McManus, you know, has seven brothers and they call him "The" because he is the boss of the lot, and to distinguish him from all other McManuses. For several years he was a political bushwhacker. In campaigns he was sometimes on the fence, sometimes on both sides of the fence, and sometimes under the fence. Nobody knew where to find him at any particular time, and nobody trusted him—that is, nobody but me. I thought there was some good in him after all and that, if I took him in hand, I could make a man of him yet.

I did take him in hand, a few years ago. My friends

told me it would be the Brutus-Leary business all over again, but I didn't believe them. I put my trust in "The." I nominated him for the Assembly, and he was elected. A year afterwards, when I was runnin' for re-election as Senator, I nominated him for the Assembly again on the ticket with me. What do you think happened? We both carried the Fifteenth Assembly District, but he ran away ahead of me. Just think! Ahead of me in my own district! I was just dazed. When I began to recover, my election district captains came to me and said that McManus had sold me out with the idea of knockin' me out of the Senatorship, and then tryin' to capture the leadership of the district. I couldn't believe it. My trustin' nature couldn't imagine such treachery.

I sent for McManus and said, with my voice tremblin' with emotions: "They say you have done me dirt, 'The.' It can't be true. Tell me it ain't true."

"The" almost wept as he said he was innocent.

"Never have I done you dirt, George," he declared. "Wicked traitors have tried to do you. I don't know just who they are yet, but I'm on their trail, and I'll find them or abjure the name of 'The' McManus. I'm goin' out right now to find them."

Well, "The" kept his word as far as goin' out and findin' the traitors was concerned. He found them all right—and put himself at their head. Oh, no! He didn't have to go far to look for them. He's got them gathered in his clubrooms now, and he's doin' his best to take the leadership from the man that made him. So you see that Caesar and Leary and me's in the same boat, only I'll come out on top while Caesar and Leary went under.

Now let me tell you that the ingrate in politics never flourishes long. I can give you lots of examples. Look at the men who done up Roscoe Conkling when he resigned from the United States Senate and went to Albany to ask for re-election! What's become of them? Passed from view like a movin' picture. Who took Conkling's place in the Senate? Twenty dollars even that you can't remember his name without looking in the almanac. And poor old Platt! He's down and out now and Odell is in the saddle, but that don't mean that he'll always be in the saddle. His enemies are workin' hard all the time to do him, and I wouldn't be a bit surprised if he went out before the next State campaign.

The politicians who make a lastin' success in politics are the men who are always loyal to their friends, even up to the gate of State prison, if necessary; men who keep their promises and never lie. Richard Croker used to say that tellin' the truth and stickin' to his friends was the political leader's stock in trade. Nobody ever said anything truer, and nobody lived up to it better than Croker. That is why he remained leader of Tammany Hall as long as he wanted to. Every man in the organization trusted him. Sometimes he made mistakes that hurt in campaigns, but they were always on the side of servin' his friends.

It's the same with Charles F. Murphy. He has always stood by his friends even when it looked like he would be downed for doin' so. Remember how he stuck to McClellan in 1903 when all the Brooklyn leaders were against him, and it seemed as if Tammany was in for a grand smash-up! It's men like Croker and Murphy that stay leaders as long as they live; not men like Brutus and McManus.

Now I want to tell you why political traitors, in New York City especially, are punished quick. It's because the Irish are in a majority. The Irish, above all people in the world, hates a traitor. You can't hold them back when a traitor of any kind is in sight and, rememberin' old Ireland, they take particular delight in doin' up a political traitor. Most of the voters in my district are Irish or of Irish descent; they've spotted "The" McManus, and when they get a chance at him at the polls next time, they won't do a thing to him.

The question has been asked: Is a politician ever justified in goin' back on his district leader? I answer: "No; as long as the leader hustles around and gets all the jobs possible for his constituents." When the voters elect a man leader, they make a sort of a contract with him. They say, although it ain't written out: "We've put you here to look out for our interests. You want to see that this district gets all the jobs that's comin' to it. Be faithful to us, and we'll be faithful to you."

The district leader promises and that makes a solemn contract. If he lives up to it, spends most of his time chasin' after places in the departments, picks up jobs from railroads and contractors for his followers, and shows himself in all ways a true statesman, then his followers are bound in honor to uphold him, just as they're bound to uphold the Constitution of the United States. But if he only looks after his own interests or shows no talent for scenting out jobs or ain't got the nerve to demand and get his share of the good things that are goin', his followers may be absolved from their allegiance and they may up and swat him without bein' put down as political ingrates.

Reciprocity in Patronage

WHENEVER Tammany is whipped at the polls, the people set to predictin' that the organization is goin' to smash. They say we can't get along without the offices and that the district leaders are goin' to desert wholesale. That was what was said after the throwdowns in 1894 and 1901. But it didn't happen, did it? Not one big Tammany man deserted, and today the organization is stronger than ever.

How was that? It was because Tammany has more than one string to its bow.

I acknowledge that you can't keep an organization together without patronage. Men ain't in politics for nothin'. They want to get somethin' out of it.

But there is more than one kind of patronage. We lost the public kind, or a greater part of it, in 1901, but Tammany has an immense private patronage that keeps things goin' when it gets a setback at the polls.

Take me, for instance. When Low came in, some of my men lost public jobs, but I fixed them all right. I don't know how many jobs I got for them on the surface and elevated railroads—several hundred.

I placed a lot more on public works done by contractors, and no Tammany man goes hungry in my district. Plunkitt's O.K. on an application for a job is never turned down, for they all know that Plunkitt and Tammany don't stay out long. See!

Let me tell you, too, that I got jobs from Republicans in office—Federal and otherwise. When Tammany's on top I do good turns for the Republicans. When they're on top they don't forget me.

Me and the Republicans are enemies just one day in the year—election day. Then we fight tooth and nail. The rest of the time it's live and let live with us.

On election day I try to pile up as big a majority as I can against George Wanmaker, the Republican leader of the Fifteenth. Any other day George and I are the best of friends. I can go to him and say: "George, I want you to place this friend of mine." He says: "All right, Senator." Or vice versa.

You see, we differ on tariffs and currencies and all them things, but we agree on the main proposition that when a man works in politics, he should get something out of it.

The politicians have got to stand together this way or there wouldn't be any political parties in a short time. Civil service would gobble up everything, politicians would be on the bum, the republic would fall and soon there would be the cry of "Vevey le roi!"

The very thought of this civil service monster makes my blood boil. I have said a lot about it already, but another instance of its awful work just occurs to me.

Let me tell you a sad but true story. Last Wednesday a line of carriages wound into Cavalry Cemetery. I was in one of them. It was the funeral of a young man from my district—a bright boy that I had great hopes of.

When he went to school, he was the most patriotic boy in the district. Nobody could sing "The Star-Spangled Banner" like him, nobody was as fond of waving a flag, and nobody shot off as many firecrackers on the Fourth of July. And when he grew up he made up his mind to serve his country in one of the city departments. There was no way of gettin' there without passin' a civil service examination. Well, he went down to the civil service office and tackled the fool questions. I saw him next day—it was Memorial Day, and soldiers were marchin' and flags flyin' and people cheerin'.

Where was my young man? Standin' on the corner, scowlin' at the whole show. When I asked him why he was so quiet, he laughed in a wild sort of way and said: "What rot all this is!"

Just then a band came along playing "Liberty." He laughed wild again and said: "Liberty? Rats!"

I don't guess I need to make a long story of it.

From the time that young man left the civil service office he lost all patriotism. He didn't care no more for his country. He went to the dogs.

He ain't the only one. There's a gravestone over some bright young man's head for every one of them infernal civil service examinations. They are underminin' the manhood of the nation and makin' the Declaration of Independence a farce. We need a new Declaration of Independence—independence of the whole fool civil service business.

I mention all this now to show why it is that the politicians of two big parties help each other along, and why Tammany men are tolerably happy when not in power in the city. When we win I won't let any deservin' Republican in my neighborhood suffer from hunger or thirst, although, of course, I look out for my own people first.

Now, I've never gone in for nonpartisan business, but I do think that all the leaders of the two parties should get together and make an open, nonpartisan fight against civil service, their common enemy. They could keep up their quarrels about imperialism and free silver and high tariff. They don't count for much alongside of civil service, which strikes right at the root of the government.

The time is fast coming when civil service or the politicians will have to go. And it will be here sooner than they expect if the politicians don't unite, drop all them minor issues for a while and make a stand against the civil service flood that's sweepin' over the country like them floods out West.

Brooklynites Natural-Born Hayseeds

SOME people are wonderin' why it is that the Brooklyn Democrats have been sidin' with David B. Hill and the upstate crowd. There's no cause for wonder. I have made a careful study of the Brooklynite, and I can tell you why. It's because a Brooklynite is a natural-born hayseed, and can never become a real New Yorker. He can't be trained into it. Consolidation didn't make him a New Yorker, and nothin' on earth can. A man born in Germany can settle down and become a good New Yorker. So can an Irishman; in fact, the first word an Irish boy learns in the old country is "New York," and when he grows up and comes here, he is at home right away. Even a Jap or a Chinaman can become a New Yorker, but a Brooklynite never can.

And why? Because Brooklyn don't seem to be like any other place on earth. Once let a man grow up amidst Brooklyn's cobblestones, with the odor of Newton Creek and Gowanus Canal ever in his nostrils, and there's no place in the world for him except Brooklyn. And even if he don't grow up there; if he is born there and lives there only in his boyhood and then moves away, he is still beyond redemption. In one of my speeches in the Legislature, I gave an example of this, and it's worth repeatin' now. Soon after I became a leader on the West

Side, a quarter of a century ago, I came across a bright boy, about seven years old, who had just been brought over from Brooklyn by his parents. I took an interest in the boy, and when he grew up I brought him into politics. Finally, I sent him to the Assembly from my district. Now remember that the boy was only seven years old when he left Brooklyn, and was twenty-three when he went to the Assembly. You'd think he had forgotten all about Brooklyn, wouldn't you? I did, but I was dead wrong. When that young fellow got into the Assembly he paid no attention to bills or debates about New York City. He didn't even show any interest in his own district. But just let Brooklyn be mentioned, or a bill be introduced about Gowanus Canal, or the Long Island Railroad, and he was all attention. Nothin' else on earth interested him.

The end came when I caught him—what do you think I caught him at? One mornin' I went over from the Senate to the Assembly chamber, and there I found my young man readin'—actually readin' a Brooklyn newspaper! When he saw me comin' he tried to hide the paper, but it was too late. I caught him dead to rights, and I said to him: "Jimmy, I'm afraid New York ain't fascinatin' enough for you. You had better move back to Brooklyn after your present term." And he did. I met him the other day crossin' the Brooklyn Bridge, carryin' a hobbyhorse under one arm, and a doll's carriage under the other, and lookin' perfectly happy.

McCarren and his men are the same way. They can't get it into their heads that they are New Yorkers, and just tend naturally toward supportin' Hill and his hayseeds against Murphy. I had some hopes of McCarren till lately. He spends so much of his time over here and has seen so much of the world that I thought he might be an exception, and grow out of his Brooklyn surroundings, but his course at Albany shows that there is no exception to the rule. Say, I'd rather take a Hottentot in hand to bring up as a good New Yorker than undertake the job with a Brooklynite. Honest, I would.

And, by the way, come to think of it, is there really any upstate Democrats left? It has never been proved to my satisfaction that there is any. I know that some upstate members of the State committee call themselves Democrats. Besides these, I know at least six more men above the Bronx who make a livin' out of professin' to be Democrats, and I have just heard of some few more. But if there is any real Democrats up the State, what becomes of them on election day? They certainly don't go near the polls or they vote the Republican ticket. Look at the last three State elections! Roosevelt piled up more than 100,000 majority above the Bronx; Odell piled up about 160,000 majority the first time he ran and 131,000 the second time. About all the Democratic votes cast were polled in New York City. The Republicans can get all the votes they want up the State. Even when we piled up 123,000 majority for Coler in the city in 1902, the Republicans went it 8000 better above the Bronx.

That's why it makes me mad to hear about upstate Democrats controllin' our State convention, and sayin' who we shall choose for President. It's just like Staten Island undertakin' to dictate to a New York City convention. I remember once a Syracuse man came to Richard Croker at the Democratic Club, handed him a letter of introduction and said: "I'm lookin' for a job in the Street Cleanin' Department; I'm backed by a hundred upstate Democrats." Croker looked hard at the man a minute and then said: "Upstate Democrats! Upstate

Democrats! I didn't know there was any upstate Democrats. Just walk up and down a while till I see what an upstate Democrat looks like."

Another thing. When a campaign is on, did you ever hear of an upstate Democrat makin' a contribution? Not much. Tammany has had to foot the whole bill, and when any of Hill's men came down to New York to help him in the campaign, we had to pay their board. Whenever money is to be raised, there's nothin' doin' up the State. The Democrats there—always providin' that there is any Democrats there—take to the woods. Supposin' Tammany turned over the campaigns to the Hill men and then held off, what would happen? Why, they would have to hire a shed out in the suburbs of Albany for a headquarters, unless the Democratic National Committee put up for the campaign expenses. Tammany's got the votes and the cash. The Hill crowd's only got hot air.

Tammany Leaders Not Bookworms

You hear a lot of talk about the Tammany district leaders bein' illiterate men. If illiterate means havin' common sense, we plead guilty. But if they mean that the Tammany leaders ain't got no education and ain't gents they don't know what they're talkin' about. Of course, we ain't all bookworms and college professors. If we were, Tammany might win an election once in four thousand years. Most of the leaders are plain American citizens, of the people and near to the people, and they have all the education they need to whip the dudes who part their name in the middle and to run the City Government. We've got bookworms, too, in the organization. But we don't make them district leaders. We keep them for ornaments on parade days.

Tammany Hall is a great big machine, with every part adjusted delicate to do its own particular work. It runs so smooth that you wouldn't think it was a complicated affair, but it is. Every district leader is fitted to the district he runs and he wouldn't exactly fit any other district. That's the reason Tammany never makes the mistake the Fusion outfit always makes of sendin' men into the districts who don't know the people, and have no sympathy with their peculiarities. We don't put a silk stockin' on the Bowery, nor do we make a man who is handy with his fists leader of the Twenty-ninth. The Fusionists make about the same sort of a mistake that a repeater made at an election in Albany several years ago. He was hired to go to the polls early in a half-dozen election districts and vote on other men's names before these men reached the polls. At one place, when he was asked his name by the poll clerk, he had the nerve to answer "William Croswell Doane."

"Come off. You ain't Bishop Doane," said the poll clerk.

"The hell I ain't, you———!" yelled the repeater.

Now, that is the sort of bad judgment the Fusionists are guilty of. They don't pick men to suit the work they have to do.

Take me, for instance. My district, the Fifteenth, is made up of all sorts of people, and a cosmopolitan is needed to run it successful. I'm a cosmopolitan. When I get into the silk-stockin' part of the district, I can talk grammar and all that with the best of them. I went to school three winters when I was a boy, and I learned a lot of fancy stuff that I keep for occasions. There ain't a silk stockin' in the district who ain't proud to be seen talkin' with George Washington Plunkitt, and maybe they learn a thing or two from their talks with me. There's one man in the district, a big banker, who said to me one day: "George, you can sling the most vigorous English I ever heard. You remind me of Senator Hoar of Massachusetts." Of course, that was puttin' it on too thick; but say, honest, I like Senator Hoar's speeches. He once quoted in the United States Senate some of my remarks on the curse of civil service, and, though he didn't agree with me altogether, I noticed that our ideas are alike in some things, and we both have the knack of puttin' things strong, only he put on more frills to suit his audience.

As for the common people of the district, I am at home with them at all times. When I go among them, I don't try to show off my grammar, or talk about the Constitution, or how many volts there is in electricity or make it appear in any way that I am better educated than they are. They wouldn't stand for that sort of thing. No; I drop all monkeyshines. So you see, I've got to be several sorts of a man in a single day, a lightnin' change artist, so to speak. But I am one sort of man always in one respect: I stick to my friends high and low, do them a good turn whenever I get a chance, and hunt up all the jobs going for my constituents. There ain't a man in New York who's got such a scent for political jobs as I have. When I get up in the mornin' I can almost tell every time whether a job has become vacant over night, and what department it's in and I'm the first man on the ground to get it. Only last week I turned up at the office of Water Register Savage at 9 A.M. and told him I wanted a vacant place in his office for one of my constituents. "How did you know that O'Brien had got out?" he asked me. "I smelled it in the air when I got up this mornin'," I answered. Now, that was the fact. I didn't know there was a man in the department named O'Brien, much less that he had got out, but my scent led me to the Water Register's office, and it don't often lead me wrong.

A cosmopolitan ain't needed in all the other districts, but our men are just the kind to rule. There's Dan Finn, in the Battery district, bluff, jolly Dan, who is now on the bench. Maybe you'd think that a court justice is not the man to hold a district like that, but you're mistaken. Most of the voters of the district are the janitors of the big office buildings on lower Broadway and their helpers. These janitors are the most dignified and haughtiest of men. Even I would have trouble in holding them. Nothin' less than a judge on the bench is good enough for them. Dan does the dignity act with the janitors, and when he is with the boys he hangs up the ermine in the closet and becomes a jolly good fellow.

Big Tom Foley, leader of the Second District, fits in exactly, too. Tom sells whisky, and good whisky, and he is able to take care of himself against a half dozen thugs if he runs up against them on Cherry Hill or in Chatham Square. Pat Ryder and Johnnie Ahearn of the Third and Fourth Districts are just the men for the places. Ahearn's constituents are about half Irishmen and half Jews. He is as popular with one race as with the other. He eats corned beef and kosher meat with equal nonchalance, and it's all the same to him whether he takes off his hat in the church or pulls it down over his ears in the synagogue.

The other downtown leaders, Barney Martin of the Fifth, Tim Sullivan of the Sixth, Pat Keahon of the Seventh, Florrie Sullivan of the Eighth, Frank Goodwin of the Ninth, Julius Harburger of the Tenth, Pete Dooling of the Eleventh, Joe Scully of the Twelfth, Johnnie Oakley of the Fourteenth, and Pat Keenan of the Sixteenth are just built to suit the people they have to deal with. They don't go in for literary business much downtown, but these men are all real gents, and that's what the people want—even the poorest tenement dwellers. As you go farther uptown you find a rather different kind of district leader. There's Victor Dowling who was until lately the leader of the Twenty-fourth. He's a lulu. He knows the Latin grammar backward. What's strange, he's a sensible young fellow, too. About once in a century we come across a fellow like that in Tammany politics. James J. Martin, leader of the Twenty-seventh, is also something of a hightoner, and publishes a law paper, while Thomas E. Rush, of the Twenty-ninth, is a lawyer, and Isaac Hopper, of the Thirty-first, is a big contractor. The downtown leaders wouldn't do uptown, and vice versa. So, you see, these fool critics don't know what they're talkin' about when they criticize Tammany Hall, the most perfect political machine on earth.

Dangers of the Dress Suit in Politics

Puttin' on style don't pay in politics. The people won't stand for it. If you've got an achin' for style, sit down on it till you have made your pile and landed a Supreme Court Justiceship with a fourteen-year term at $17,500 a year, or some job of that kind. Then you've got about all you can get out of politics, and you can afford to wear a dress suit all day and sleep in it all night if you have a mind to. But, before you have caught onto your life meal ticket, be simple. Live like your neighbors even if you have the means to live better. Make the poorest man in your district feel that he is your equal, or even a bit superior to you.

Above all things, avoid a dress suit. You have no idea of the harm that dress suits have done in politics. They are not so fatal to young politicians as civil service reform and drink, but they have scores of victims. I will mention one sad case. After the big Tammany victory in 1897, Richard Croker went down to Lakewood to make up the slate of offices for Mayor Van Wyck to distribute. All the district leaders and many more Tammany men went down there, too, to pick up anything good that was goin.' There was nothin' but dress suits at dinner at Lakewood, and Croker wouldn't let any Tammany men go to dinner without them. Well, a bright young West

Side politician, who held a three-thousand-dollar job in one of the departments, went to Lakewood to ask Croker for something better. He wore a dress suit for the first time in his life. It was his undoin'. He got stuck on himself. He thought he looked too beautiful for anything, and when he came home he was a changed man. As soon as he got to his house every evenin' he put on that dress suit and set around in it until bedtime. That didn't satisfy him long. He wanted others to see how beautiful he was in a dress suit; so he joined dancin' clubs and began goin' to all the balls that was given in town. Soon he began to neglect his family. Then he took to drinkin', and didn't pay any attention to his political work in the district. The end came in less than a year. He was dismissed from the department and went to the dogs. The other day I met him rigged out almost like a hobo, but he still had a dress-suit vest on. When I asked him what he was doin', he said: "Nothin' at present, but I got a promise of a job enrollin' voters at Citizens' Union headquarters." Yes, a dress suit had brought him that low!

I'll tell you another case right in my own Assembly District. A few years ago I had as one of my lieutenants a man named Zeke Thompson. He did fine work for me and I thought he had a bright future. One day he came to me, said he intended to buy an option on a house, and asked me to help him out. I like to see a young man acquirin' property and I had so much confidence in Zeke that I put up for him on the house.

A month or so afterwards I heard strange rumors. People told me that Zeke was beginnin' to put on style. They said he had a billiard table in his house and had hired Jap servants. I couldn't believe it. The idea of a Democrat, a follower of George Washington Plunkitt in the Fifteenth Assembly District havin' a billiard table and Jap servants! One mornin' I called at the house to give Zeke a chance to clear himself. A Jap opened the door for me. I saw the billiard table. Zeke was guilty! When I got over the shock, I said to Zeke: "You are caught with the goods on. No excuses will go. The Democrats of this district ain't used to dukes and princes and we wouldn't feel comfortable in your company. You'd overpower us. You had better move up to the Nineteenth or Twenty-seventh District, and hang a silk stocking on your door." He went up to the Nineteenth, turned Republican, and was lookin' for an Albany job the last I heard of him.

Now, nobody ever saw me puttin' on any style. I'm the same Plunkitt I was when I entered politics forty years ago. That is why the people of the district have confidence in me. If I went into the stylish business, even I, Plunkitt, might be thrown down in the district. That was shown pretty clearly in the senatorial fight last year. A day before the election, my enemies circulated a report that I had ordered a $10,000 automobile and a $125 dress suit. I sent out contradictions as fast as I could, but I wasn't able to stamp out the infamous slander before the votin' was over, and I suffered some at the polls. The people wouldn't have minded much if I had been accused of robbin' the city treasury, for they're used to slanders of that kind in campaigns, but the automobile and the dress suit were too much for them.

Another thing that people won't stand for is showin' off your learnin'. That's just puttin' on style in another way. If you're makin' speeches in a campaign, talk the language the people talk. Don't try to show how the situation is by quotin' Shakespeare. Shakespeare was all right in his way, but he didn't know anything about Fifteenth District politics. If you know Latin and Greek and have a hankerin' to work them off on somebody, hire a stranger to come to your house and listen to you for a couple of hours; then go out and talk the language of the Fifteenth to the people. I know it's an awful temptation, the hankerin' to show off your learnin'. I've felt it myself, but I always resist it. I know the awful consequences.

On Municipal Ownership

I AM for municipal ownership on one condition: that the civil service law be repealed. It's a grand idea—the city ownin' the railroads, the gas works and all that. Just see how many thousands of new places there would be for the workers in Tammany! Why, there would be almost enough to go around, if no civil service law stood in the way. My plan is this: first get rid of that infamous law, and then go ahead and by degrees get municipal ownership.

Some of the reformers are sayin' that municipal ownership won't do because it would give a lot of patronage to the politicians. How those fellows mix things up when they argue! They're givin' the strongest argument in favor of municipal ownership when they say that. Who is better fitted to run the railroads and the gas plants and the ferries than the men who make a business of lookin' after the interests of the city? Who is more anxious to serve the city? Who needs the jobs more?

Look at the Dock Department! The city owns the docks, and how beautiful Tammany manages them! I can't tell you how many places they provide for our workers. I know there is a lot of talk about dock graft, but that talk comes from the outs. When the Republicans had the docks under Low and Strong, you didn't hear them sayin' anything about graft, did you? No; they just went in and made hay while the sun shone. That's always the case. When the reformers are out they raise the yell that Tammany men should be sent to jail. When they get in, they're so busy keepin' out of jail themselves that they don't have no time to attack Tammany.

All I want is that municipal ownership be postponed till I get my bill repealin' the civil service law before the next legislature. It would be all a mess if every man who wanted a job would have to run up against a civil service examination. For instance, if a man wanted a job as motorman on a surface car, it's ten to one that they would ask him: "Who wrote the Latin grammar, and, if so, why did he write it? How many years were you at college? Is there any part of the Greek language you don't know? State all you don't know, and why you don't know it. Give a list of all the sciences with full particulars about each one and how it came to be discovered. Write out word for word the last ten decisions of the United States Supreme Court and show if they conflict with the last ten decisions of the police courts of New York City."

Before the would-be motorman left the civil service room, the chances are he would be a raving lunatic. Anyhow I wouldn't like to ride on his car. Just here I want to say one last final word about civil service. In the last ten years I have made an investigation which I've kept quiet till this time. Now I have all the figures together, and I'm ready to announce the result. My investigation was to find out how many civil service reformers and how many politicians were in state prisons. I discovered that there was forty per cent more civil service reformers among the jailbirds. If any legislative committee wants the detailed figures, I'll prove what I say. I don't want to give the figures now, because I want to keep them to back me up when I go to Albany to get the civil service law repealed. Don't you think that when I've had my inning, the civil service law will go down, and the people will see that the politicians are all right, and that they ought to have the job of runnin' things when municipal ownership comes?

One thing more about municipal ownership. If the city owned the railroads, etc., salaries would be sure to go up. Higher salaries is the cryin' need of the day. Municipal ownership would increase them all along the line and would stir up such patriotism as New York City never knew before. You can't be patriotic on a salary that just keeps the wolf from the door. Any man who pretends he can will bear watchin'. Keep your hand on your watch and pocketbook when he's about. But, when a man has a good fat salary, he finds himself hummin' "Hail Columbia," all unconscious and he fancies, when he's ridin' in a trolley car, that the wheels are always sayin': "Yankee Doodle Came to Town." I know how it is myself. When I got my first good job from the city I bought up all the firecrackers in my district to salute this glorious country. I couldn't wait for the Fourth of July. I got the boys on the block to fire them off for me, and I felt proud of bein' an American. For a long time after that I use to wake up nights singin' "The Star-Spangled Banner."

Tammany the Only Lastin' Democracy

I'VE seen more than one hundred "Democracies" rise and fall in New York City in the last quarter of a century. At least a half-dozen new so-called Democratic organizations are formed every year. All of them go in to down Tammany and take its place, but they seldom last more than a year or two, while Tammany's like the everlastin' rocks, the eternal hills and the blockades on the "L" road—it goes on forever.

I recall offhand the County Democracy, which was the only real opponent Tammany has had in my time, the Irving Hall Democracy, the New York State Democracy, the German-American Democracy, the Protection Democracy, the Independent County Democracy, the Greater New York Democracy, the Jimmy O'Brien Democracy, the Delicatessen Dealers' Democracy, the Silver Democracy, and the Italian Democracy. Not one of them is livin' today, although I hear somethin' about the ghost of the Greater New York Democracy bein' seen on Broadway once or twice a year.

In the old days of the County Democracy, a new Democratic organization meant some trouble for Tammany—for a time anyhow. Nowadays a new Democracy means nothin' at all except that about a dozen bone-hunters have got together for one campaign only to try to induce Tammany to give them a job or two, or in order to get in with the reformers for the same purpose. You might think that it would cost a lot of money to get up one of these organizations and keep it goin' for even one campaign, but, Lord bless you! it costs next to nothin'. Jimmy O'Brien brought the manufacture of "Democracies" down to an exact science, and reduced the cost of production so as to bring it within the reach of all. Any man with $50 can now have a "Democracy" of his own.

I've looked into the industry, and can give rock-bottom figures. Here's the items of cost of a new "Democracy":

A dinner to twelve bone-hunters	$12.00
A speech on Jeffersonian Democracy	00.00
A proclamation of principles (typewriting)	2.00
Rent of a small room one month for headquarters	12.00
Stationery	2.00
Twelve secondhand chairs	6.00
One secondhand table	2.00
Twenty-nine cuspidors	9.00
Sign painting	5.00
Total	$50.00

Is there any reason for wonder, then, that "Democracies" spring up all over when a municipal campaign is comin' on? If you land even one small job, you get a big return on your investment. You don't have to pay for advertisin' in the papers. The New York papers tumble over one another to give columns to any new organization that comes out against Tammany. In describin' the formation of a "Democracy" on the $50 basis, accordin' to the items I give, the papers would say somethin' like this: "The organization of the Delicatessen Democracy last night threatens the existence of Tammany Hall. It is a grand move for a new and pure Democracy in this city. Well may the Tammany leaders be alarmed; panic has already broke loose in Fourteenth Street. The vast crowd that gathered at the launching of the new organization, the stirrin' speeches and the proclamation of principles mean that, at last, there is an uprisin' that will end Tammany's career of corruption. The Delicatessen Democracy will open in a few days spacious headquarters where all true Democrats may gather and prepare for the fight."

Say, ain't some of the papers awful gullible about politics? Talk about come-ons from Iowa or Texas—they ain't in it with the childlike simplicity of these papers.

It's a wonder to me that more men don't go into this kind of manufacturin' industry. It has bigger profits generally than the green-goods business and none of the risks. And you don't have to invest as much as the green-goods men. Just see what good things some of these "Democracies" got in the last few years! The New York State Democracy in 1897 landed a Supreme Court Justiceship for the man who manufactured the concern—a fourteen-year term at $17,500 a year, that is $245,000. You see, Tammany was rather scared that year and was bluffed into givin' this job to get the support of the State Democracy which, by the way, went out of business quick and prompt the day after it got this big plum. The next year the German Democracy landed a place of the same kind. And then see how the Greater New York Democracy worked the game on the reformers in 1901! The men who managed this concern were former Tammanyites who had lost their grip; yet they made the Citizens' Union innocents believe that they were the real thing in the way of reformers, and that they had 100,000 votes back of them. They got the Borough President of Manhattan, the President of the Board of Aldermen, the Register and a lot of lesser places. It was the greatest bunco game of modern times.

And then, in 1894, when Strong was elected mayor, what a harvest it was for all the little "Democracies" that was made to order that year! Every one of them got somethin' good. In one case, all the nine men in an organization got jobs payin' from $2000 to $5000. I happen to know exactly what it cost to manufacture that organization. It was $42.04. They left out the stationery, and had only twenty-three cuspidors. The extra four cents was for two postage stamps.

The only reason I can imagine why more men don't go into this industry is because they don't know about it. And just here it strikes me that it might not be wise to publish what I've said. Perhaps if it gets to be known what a snap this manufacture of "Democracies" is, all the green-goods men, the bunco-steerers, and the young Napoleons of finance will go into it and the public will be humbugged more than it has been. But, after all, what difference would it make? There's always a certain number of suckers and a certain number of men lookin' for a chance to take them in, and the suckers are sure to be took one way or another. It's the everlastin' law of demand and supply.

Concerning Gas in Politics

SINCE the eighty-cent gas bill was defeated in Albany, everybody's talkin' about senators bein' bribed. Now, I wasn't in the Senate last session, and I don't know the ins and outs of everything that was done, but I can tell you that the legislators are often hauled over the coals when they are all on the level. I've been there and I know. For instance, when I voted in the Senate in 1904, for the Remsen Bill that the newspapers called the "Astoria Gas Grab Bill," they didn't do a thing to me. The papers kept up a howl about all the supporters of the bill bein' bought up by the Consolidated Gas Company, and the Citizens' Union did me the honor to call me the commander-in-chief of the "Black Horse Cavalry."

The fact is that I was workin' for my district all this time, and I wasn't bribed by nobody. There's several of these gashouses in the district, and I wanted to get them over to Astoria for three reasons: first, because they're nuisances; second, because there's no votes in them for me any longer; third, because—well, I had a little private reason which I'll explain further on. I needn't explain how they're nuisances. They're worse than open sewers. Still, I might have stood that if they hadn't degenerated so much in the last few years.

Ah, gashouses ain't what they used to be! Not very

long ago, each gashouse was good for a couple of hundred votes. All the men employed in them were Irishmen and Germans who lived in the district. Now, it is all different. The men are dagoes who live across in Jersey and take no interest in the district. What's the use of havin' ill-smellin' gashouses if there's no votes in them?

Now, as to my private reason. Well, I'm a business man and go in for any business that's profitable and honest. Real estate is one of my specialties. I know the value of every foot of ground in my district, and I calculated long ago that if them gashouses was removed, surroundin' property would go up 100 per cent. When the Remsen Bill, providin' for the removal of the gashouses to Queens County came up, I said to myself: "George, hasn't your chance come?" I answered: "Sure." Then I sized up the chances of the bill. I found it was certain to pass the Senate and the Assembly, and I got assurances straight from headquarters that Governor Odell would sign it. Next I came down to the city to find out the mayor's position. I got it straight that he would approve the bill, too.

Can't you guess what I did then? Like any sane man who had my information, I went in and got options on a lot of the property around the gashouses. Well, the bill went through the Senate and the Assembly all right and the mayor signed it, but Odell backslided at the last minute and the whole game fell through. If it had succeeded, I guess I would have been accused of graftin'. What I want to know is, what do you call it when I got left and lost a pot of money?

I not only lost money, but I was abused for votin' for the bill. Wasn't that outrageous? They said I was in with the Consolidated Gas Company and all other kinds of rot, when I was really only workin' for my district and tryin' to turn an honest penny on the side. Anyhow I got a little fun out of the business. When the Remsen Bill was up, I was tryin' to put through a bill of my own, the Spuyten Duyvil Bill, which provided for fillin' in some land under water that the New York Central Railroad wanted. Well, the Remsen managers were afraid of bein' beaten and they went around offerin' to make trades with senators and assemblymen who had bills they were anxious to pass. They came to me and offered six votes for my Spuyten Duyvil Bill in exchange for my vote on the Remsen Bill. I took them up in a hurry, and they felt pretty sore afterwards when they heard I was goin' to vote for the Remsen Bill anyhow.

A word about that Spuyten Duyvil Bill—I was criticized a lot for introducin' it. They said I was workin' in the interest of the New York Central, and was goin' to get the contract for fillin' in. The fact is, that the fillin' in was a good thing for the city, and if it helped the New York Central, too, what of it? The railroad is a great public institution, and I was never an enemy of public institutions. As to the contract, it hasn't come along yet. If it does come, it will find me at home at all proper and reasonable hours, if there is a good profit in sight.

The papers and some people are always ready to find wrong motives in what us statesmen do. If we bring about some big improvement that benefits the city and it just happens, as a sort of coincidence, that we make a few dollars out of the improvement, they say we are grafters. But we are used to this kind of ingratitude. It falls to the lot of all statesmen, especially Tammany statesmen. All we can do is to bow our heads in silence and wait till time has cleared our memories.

Just think of mentionin' dishonest graft in connection with the name of George Washington Plunkitt, the man who gave the city its magnificent chain of parks, its Washington Bridge, its Speedway, its Museum of Natural

History, its One Hundred and Fifty-fifth Street Viaduct and its West Side Courthouse! I was the father of the bills that provided for all these; yet, because I supported the Remsen and Spuyten Duyvil bills, some people have questioned my honest motives. If that's the case, how can you expect legislators to fare who are not the fathers of the parks, the Washington Bridge, the Speedway and the Viaduct?

Now, understand; I ain't defendin' the senators who killed the eighty-cent gas bill. I don't know why they acted as they did; I only want to impress the idea to go slow before you make up your mind that a man, occupyin' the exalted position that I held for so many years, has done wrong. For all I know, these senators may have been as honest and high-minded about the gas bill as I was about the Remsen and Spuyten Duyvil bills.

Plunkitt's Fondest Dream

THE time is comin' and though I'm no youngster, I may see it, when New York City will break away from the State and become a state itself. It's got to come. The feelin' between this city and the hayseeds that make a livin' by plunderin' it is every bit as bitter as the feelin' between the North and South before the war. And, let me tell you, if there ain't a peaceful separation before long, we may have the horrors of civil war right here in New York State. Why, I know a lot of men in my district who would like nothin' better today than to go out gunnin' for hayseeds!

New York City has got a bigger population than most of the states in the Union. It's got more wealth than any dozen of them. Yet the people here, as I explained before, are nothin' but slaves of the Albany gang. We have stood the slavery a long, long time, but the uprisin' is near at hand. It will be a fight for liberty, just like the American Revolution. We'll get liberty peacefully if we can; by cruel war if we must.

Just think how lovely things would be here if we had a Tammany Governor and Legislature meetin', say in the neighborhood of Fifty-ninth Street, and a Tammany Mayor and Board of Aldermen doin' business in City Hall! How sweet and peaceful everything would go on!

The people wouldn't have to bother about nothin'. Tammany would take care of everything for them in its nice quiet way. You wouldn't hear of any conflicts between the state and city authorities. They would settle everything pleasant and comfortable at Tammany Hall, and every bill introduced in the Legislature by Tammany would be sure to go through. The Republicans wouldn't count.

Imagine how the city would be built up in a short time! At present we can't make a public improvement of any consequence without goin' to Albany for permission, and most of the time we get turned down when we go there. But, with a Tammany Governor and Legislature up at Fifty-ninth Street, how public works would hum here! The Mayor and Aldermen could decide on an improvement, telephone the Capitol, have a bill put through in a jiffy and—there you are. We could have a state constitution, too, which would extend the debt limit so that we could issue a whole lot more bonds. As things are now, all the money spent for docks, for instance, is charged against the city in calculatin' the debt limit, although the Dock Department provides immense revenues. It's the same with some other departments. This humbug would be dropped if Tammany ruled at the Capitol and the City Hall, and the city would have money to burn.

Another thing—the constitution of the new state wouldn't have a word about civil service, and if any man dared to introduce any kind of a civil service bill in the Legislature, he would be fired out the window. Then we would have government of the people by the people who were elected to govern them. That's the kind of government Lincoln meant. O what a glorious future for the city! Whenever I think of it I feel like goin' out and celebratin', and I'm really almost sorry that I don't drink.

You may ask what would become of the upstate people if New York City left them in the lurch and went into the State business on its own account. Well, we wouldn't be under no obligation to provide for them; still I would be in favor of helpin' them along for a while until they could learn to work and earn an honest livin', just like the United States Government looks after the Indians. These hayseeds have been so used to livin' off of New York City that they would be helpless after we left them. It wouldn't do to let them starve. We might make some sort of an appropriation for them for a few years, but it would be with the distinct understandin' that they must get busy right away and learn to support themselves. If, after say five years, they weren't self-supportin', we could withdraw the appropriation and let them shift for themselves. The plan might succeed and it might not. We'd be doin' our duty anyhow.

Some persons might say: "But how about it if the hayseed politicians moved down here and went in to get control of the government of the new state?" We could provide against that easy by passin' a law that these politicians couldn't come below the Bronx without a sort of passport limitin' the time of their stay here, and forbiddin' them to monkey with politics here. I don't know just what kind of a bill would be required to fix this, but with a Tammany Constitution, Governor, Legislature and Mayor, there would be no trouble in settlin' a little matter of that sort.

Say, I don't wish I was a poet, for if I was, I guess I'd be livin' in a garret on no dollars a week instead of runnin' a great contractin' and transportation business which is doin' pretty well, thank you; but, honest, now, the notion takes me sometimes to yell poetry of the red-hot-hail-glorious-land kind when I think of New York City as a state by itself.

Tammany's Patriotism

TAMMANY's the most patriotic organization on earth, notwithstandin' the fact that the civil service law is sappin' the foundations of patriotism all over the country. Nobody pays any attention to the Fourth of July any longer except Tammany and the small boy. When the Fourth comes, the reformers, with Revolutionary names parted in the middle, run off to Newport or the Adirondacks to get out of the way of the noise and everything that reminds them of the glorious day. How different it is with Tammany! The very constitution of the Tammany Society requires that we must assemble at the wigwam on the Fourth, regardless of the weather, and listen to the readin' of the Declaration of Independence and patriotic speeches.

You ought to attend one of these meetin's. They're a liberal education in patriotism. The great hall upstairs is filled with five thousand people, suffocatin' from heat and smoke. Every man Jack of these five thousand knows that down in the basement there's a hundred cases of champagne and two hundred kegs of beer ready to flow when the signal is given. Yet that crowd stick to their seats without turnin' a hair while, for four solid hours, the Declaration of Independence is read, long-winded orators speak, and the glee club sings itself hoarse.

Talk about heroism in the battlefield! That comes and passes away in a moment. You ain't got time to be anything but heroic. But just think of five thousand men sittin' in the hottest place on earth for four long hours, with parched lips and gnawin' stomachs, and knowin' all the time that the delights of the oasis in the desert were only two flights downstairs! Ah, that is the highest kind of patriotism, the patriotism of long sufferin' and endurance. What man wouldn't rather face a cannon for a minute or two than thirst for four hours, with champagne and beer almost under his nose?

And then see how they applaud and yell when patriotic things are said! As soon as the man on the platform starts off with "when, in the course of human events," word goes around that it's the Declaration of Independence, and a mighty roar goes up. The Declaration ain't a very short document and the crowd has heard it on every Fourth but they give it just as fine a send-off as if it was brand-new and awful excitin'. Then the "long talkers" get in their work, that is two or three orators who are good for an hour each. Heat never has any effect on these men. They use every minute of their time. Sometimes human nature gets the better of a man in the audience and he begins to nod, but he always wakes up with a hurrah for the Declaration of Independence.

The greatest hero of the occasion is the Grand Sachem of the Tammany Society who presides. He and the rest of us Sachems come on the stage wearin' stovepipe hats, accordin' to the constitution, but we can shed ours right off, while the Grand Sachem is required to wear his hat all through the celebration. Have you any idea what that means? Four hours under a big silk hat in a hall where the heat registers 110 and the smoke 250! And the Grand Sachem is expected to look pleasant all the time and say nice things when introducin' the speakers! Often his hand goes to his hat, unconscious-like, then he catches himself up in time and looks around like a man who is in the tenth story of a burnin' buildin' seekin' a way to escape. I believe that Fourth-of-July silk hat shortened the life of one of our Grand Sachems, the late Supreme Court Justice Smyth, and I know that one of our Sachems refused the office of Grand Sachem because he couldn't get up sufficient patriotism to perform this four-hour hat act. You see, there's degrees of patriotism just as there's degrees in everything else.

You don't hear of the Citizens' Union people holdin' Fourth-of-July celebrations under a five-pound silk hat, or any other way, do you? The Cits take the Fourth like a dog I had when I was a boy. That dog knew as much as some Cits and he acted just like them about the glorious day. Exactly forty-eight hours before each Fourth of July, the dog left our house on a run and hid himself in the Bronx woods. The day after the Fourth he turned up at home as regular as clockwork. He must have known what a dog is up against on the Fourth. Anyhow, he kept out of the way. The name-parted-in-the-middle aristocrats act in just the same way. They don't want to be annoyed with firecrackers and the Declaraction of Independence, and when they see the Fourth comin' they hustle off to the woods like my dog.

Tammany don't only show its patriotism at Fourth-of-July celebrations. It's always on deck when the country needs its services. After the Spanish-American War broke out, John J. Scannell, the Tammany leader of the Twenty-fifth District, wrote to Governor Black offerin' to raise a Tammany regiment to go to the front. If you want proof, go to Tammany Hall and see the beautiful set of engrossed resolutions about this regiment. It's true that the Governor didn't accept the offer, but it showed

Tammany's patriotism. Some enemies of the organization have said that the offer to raise the regiment was made after the Governor let it be known that no more volunteers were wanted, but that's the talk of envious slanderers.

Now, a word about Tammany's love for the American flag. Did you ever see Tammany Hall decorated for a celebration? It's just a mass of flags. They even take down the window shades and put flags in place of them. There's flags everywhere except on the floors. We don't care for expense where the American flag is concerned, especially after we have won an election. In 1904 we originated the custom of givin' a small flag to each man as he entered Tammany Hall for the Fourth-of-July celebration. It took like wildfire. The men waved their flags whenever they cheered and the sight made me feel so patriotic that I forgot all about civil service for a while. And the good work of the flags didn't stop there. The men carried them home and gave them to the children, and the kids got patriotic, too. Of course, it all cost a pretty penny, but what of that? We had won at the polls the precedin' November, had the offices and could afford to make an extra investment in patriotism.

On the Use of Money in Politics

THE civil service gang is always howlin' about candidates and officeholders puttin' up money for campaigns and about corporations chippin' in. They might as well howl about givin' contributions to churches. A political organization has to have money for its business as well as a church, and who has more right to put up than the men who get the good things that are goin'? Take, for instance, a great political concern like Tammany Hall. It does missionary work like a church, it's got big expenses and it's got to be supported by the faithful. If a corporation sends in a check to help the good work of the Tammany Society, why shouldn't we take it like other missionary societies? Of course, the day may come when we'll reject the money of the rich as tainted, but it hadn't come when I left Tammany Hall at 11:25 A.M. today.

Not long ago some newspapers had fits because the Assemblyman from my district said he had put up $500 when he was nominated for the Assembly last year. Every politician in town laughed at these papers. I don't think there was even a Citizens' Union man who didn't know that candidates of both parties have to chip in for campaign expenses. The sums they pay are accordin' to their salaries and the length of their terms of office, if elected.

Even candidates for the Supreme Court have to fall in line. A Supreme Court Judge in New York County gets $17,500 a year, and he's expected, when nominated, to help along the good cause with a year's salary. Why not? He has fourteen years on the bench ahead of him, and ten thousand other lawyers would be willin' to put up twice as much to be in his shoes. Now, I ain't sayin' that we sell nominations. That's a different thing altogether. There's no auction and no regular biddin'. The man is picked out and somehow he gets to understand what's expected of him in the way of a contribution, and he ponies up—all from gratitude to the organization that honored him, see?

Let me tell you an instance that shows the difference between sellin' nominations and arrangin' them in the way I described. A few years ago a Republican district leader controlled the nomination for Congress in his Congressional district. Four men wanted it. At first the leader asked for bids privately, but decided at last that the best thing to do was to get the four men together in the back room of a certain saloon and have an open auction. When he had his men lined up, he got on a chair, told about the value of the goods for sale, and asked for bids in regular auctioneer style. The highest bidder got the nomination for $5000. Now, that wasn't right at all. These things ought to be always fixed up nice and quiet.

As to officeholders, they would be ingrates if they didn't contribute to the organization that put them in office. They needn't be assessed. That would be against the law. But they know what's expected of them, and if they happen to forget they can be reminded polite and courteous. Dan Donegan, who used to be the Wiskinkie of the Tammany Society, and received contributions from grateful officeholders, had a pleasant way of remindin'.

If a man forgot his duty to the organization that made him, Dan would call on the man, smile as sweet as you please and say: "You haven't been round at the Hall lately, have you?" If the man tried to slide around the question, Dan would say: "It's gettin' awful cold." Then he would have a fit of shiverin' and walk away. What could be more polite and, at the same time, more to the point? No force, no threats—only a little shiverin' which any man is liable to even in summer.

Just here, I want to charge one more crime to the infamous civil service law. It has made men turn ungrateful. A dozen years ago, when there wasn't much civil service business in the city government, and when the administration could turn out almost any man holdin' office, Dan's shiver took effect every time and there was no ingratitude in the city departments. But when the civil service law came in and all the clerks got lead-pipe cinches on their jobs, ingratitude spread right away. Dan shivered and shook till his bones rattled, but many of the city employees only laughed at him. One day, I remember, he tackled a clerk in the Public Works Department, who used to give up pretty regular, and, after the usual question, began to shiver. The clerk smiled. Dan shook till his hat fell off. The clerk took ten cents out of his pocket, handed it to Dan and said: "Poor man! Go and get a drink to warm yourself up." Wasn't that shameful? And yet, if it hadn't been for the civil service law, that clerk would be contributin' right along to this day.

The civil service law don't cover everything, however. There's lots of good jobs outside its clutch, and the men that get them are grateful every time. I'm not speakin' of Tammany Hall alone, remember! It's the same with the Republican Federal and State officeholders, and every organization that has or has had jobs to give out—except, of course, the Citizens' Union. The Cits held office only a couple of years and, knowin' that they would never be in again, each Cit officeholder held on for dear life to every dollar that came his way.

Some people say they can't understand what becomes of all the money that's collected for campaigns. They would understand fast enough if they were district leaders. There's never been half enough money to go around. Besides the expenses for meetin's, bands and all that, there's the bigger bill for the district workers who get men to the polls. These workers are mostly men who want to serve their country but can't get jobs in the city departments on account of the civil service law. They do the next best thing by keepin' track of the voters and seein' that they come to the polls and vote the right way. Some of these deservin' citizens have to make enough on registration and election days to keep them the rest of the year. Isn't it right that they should get a share of the campaign money?

Just remember that there's thirty-five Assembly districts in New York County, and thirty-six district leaders reachin' out for the Tammany dough-bag for somethin' to keep up the patriotism of ten thousand workers, and you wouldn't wonder that the cry for more, more, is goin' up from every district organization now and forevermore. Amen.

The Successful Politician Does Not Drink

I HAVE explained how to succeed in politics. I want to add that no matter how well you learn to play the political game, you won't make a lastin' success of it if you're a drinkin' man. I never take a drop of any kind of intoxicatin' liquor. I ain't no fanatic. Some of the saloonkeepers are my best friends, and I don't mind goin' into a saloon any day with my friends. But as a matter of business I leave whisky and beer and the rest of that stuff alone. As a matter of business, too, I take for my lieutenants in my district men who don't drink. I tried the other kind for several years, but it didn't pay. They cost too much. For instance, I had a young man who was one of the best hustlers in town. He knew every man in the district, was popular everywhere and could induce a half-dead man to come to the polls on election day. But, regularly, two weeks before election, he started on a drunk, and I had to hire two men to guard him day and night and keep him sober enough to do his work. That cost a lot of money, and I dropped the young man after a while.

Maybe you think I'm unpopular with the saloonkeepers because I don't drink. You're wrong. The most successful saloonkeepers don't drink themselves and they understand that my temperance is a business proposition, just like their own. I have a saloon under my headquarters. If a saloonkeeper gets into trouble, he always knows that Senator Plunkitt is the man to help him out. If there is a bill in the Legislature makin' it easier for the liquor dealers, I am for it every time. I'm one of the best friends the saloon men have—but I don't drink their whisky. I won't go through the temperance lecture dodge and tell you how many bright young men I've seen fall victims to intemperance, but I'll tell you that I could name dozens—young men who had started on the road to statesmanship, who could carry their districts every time, and who could turn out any vote you wanted at the primaries. I honestly believe that drink is the greatest curse of the day, except, of course, civil service, and that it has driven more young men to ruin than anything except civil service examinations.

Look at the great leaders of Tammany Hall! No regular drinkers among them. Richard Croker's strongest drink was vichy. Charlie Murphy takes a glass of wine at dinner sometimes, but he don't go beyond that. A drinkin' man wouldn't last two weeks as leader of Tammany Hall. Nor can a man manage an assembly district long if he drinks. He's got to have a clear head all the time. I could name ten men who, in the last few years, lost their grip in their districts because they began drinkin'. There's now thirty-six district leaders in Tammany Hall, and I don't believe a half-dozen of them ever drink anything except at meals. People have got an idea that because the liquor men are with us in campaigns, our district leaders spend most of their time leanin' against bars. There couldn't be a wronger idea. The district leader makes a business of politics, gets his livin' out of it, and, in order to succeed, he's got to keep sober just like in any other business.

Just take as examples "Big Tim" and "Little Tim" Sullivan. They're known all over the country as the Bowery leaders and, as there's nothin' but saloons on the Bowery, people might think that they are hard drinkers. The fact is that neither of them has ever touched a drop of liquor in his life or even smoked a cigar. Still they don't make no pretenses of being better than anybody else, and don't go around deliverin' temperance lectures. Big Tim made money out of liquor—sellin' it to other people. That's the only way to get good out of liquor.

Look at all the Tammany heads of city departments! There's not a real drinkin' man in the lot. Oh, yes, there are some prominent men in the organization who drink sometimes, but they are not the men who have power. They're ornaments, fancy speakers and all that, who make a fine show behind the footlights, but ain't in it when it comes to directin' the city government and the Tammany organization. The men who sit in the executive committee room at Tammany Hall and direct things are men who celebrate on apollinaris or vichy. Let me tell you what I saw on election night in 1897, when the Tammany ticket swept the city: Up to 10 P.M. Croker, John F. Carroll, Tim Sullivan, Charlie Murphy, and myself sat in the committee room receivin' returns. When nearly all the city was heard from and we saw that Van Wyck was elected by a big majority, I invited the crowd to go across the street for a little celebration. A lot of small politicians followed us, expectin' to see magnums of champagne opened. The waiters in the restaurant expected it, too, and you never saw a more disgusted lot of waiters when they got our orders. Here's the orders: Croker, vichy and bicarbonate of soda; Carroll, seltzer lemonade; Sullivan, apollinaris; Murphy, vichy; Plunkitt, ditto. Before midnight we were all in bed, and next mornin' we were up bright and early attendin' to business, while other men were nursin' swelled heads. Is there anything the matter with temperance as a pure business proposition?

Bosses Preserve the Nation

When I retired from the Senate, I thought I would take a good, long rest, such a rest as a man needs who has held office for about forty years, and has held four different offices in one year and drawn salaries from three of them at the same time. Drawin' so many salaries is rather fatiguin', you know, and, as I said, I started out for a rest; but when I seen how things were goin' in New York State, and how a great big black shadow hung over us, I said to myself: "No rest for you, George. Your work ain't done. Your country still needs you and you mustn't lay down yet."

What was the great big black shadow? It was the primary election law, amended so as to knock out what are called the party bosses by lettin' in everybody at the primaries and givin' control over them to state officials. Oh, yes, that is a good way to do up the so-called bosses, but have you ever thought what would become of the country if the bosses were put out of business, and their places were taken by a lot of cart-tail orators and college graduates? It would mean chaos. It would be just like takin' a lot of dry-goods clerks and settin' them to run express trains on the New York Central Railroad. It makes my heart bleed to think of it. Ignorant people are always talkin' against party bosses, but just wait till the bosses are gone! Then, and not until then, will they get the right sort of epitaphs, as Patrick Henry or Robert Emmet said.

Look at the bosses of Tammany Hall in the last twenty years. What magnificent men! To them New York City owes pretty much all it is today. John Kelly, Richard Croker, and Charles F. Murphy—what names in American history compares with them, except Washington and Lincoln? They built up the grand Tammany organization, and the organization built up New York. Suppose the city had to depend for the last twenty years on irresponsible concerns like the Citizens' Union, where would it be now? You can make a pretty good guess if you recall the Strong and Low administrations when there was no boss, and the heads of departments were at odds all the time with each other, and the Mayor was at odds with the lot of them. They spent so much time in arguin' and makin' grandstand play, that the interests of the city were forgotten. Another administration of that kind would put New York back a quarter of a century.

Then see how beautiful a Tammany city government runs, with a so-called boss directin' the whole shootin' match! The machinery moves so noiseless that you wouldn't think there was any. If there's any differences of opinion, the Tammany leader settles them quietly, and his orders go every time. How nice it is for the people to feel that they can get up in the mornin' without bein' afraid of seein' in the papers that the Commissioner of Water Supply has sandbagged the Dock Commissioner, and that the Mayor and heads of the departments have been taken to the police court as witnesses! That's no joke. I remember that, under Strong, some commissioners came very near sandbaggin' one another.

Of course, the newspapers like the reform administration. Why? Because these administrations, with their daily rows, furnish as racy news as prizefights or divorce cases. Tammany don't care to get in the papers. It goes right along attendin' to business quietly and only wants to be let alone. That's one reason why the papers are against us.

Some papers complain that the bosses get rich while devotin' their lives to the interests of the city. What of it? If opportunities for turnin' an honest dollar comes their way, why shouldn't they take advantage of them, just as I have done? As I said, in another talk, there is honest graft and dishonest graft. The bosses go in for the former. There is so much of it in this big town that they would be fools to go in for dishonest graft.

Now, the primary election law threatens to do away with the boss and make the city government a menagerie. That's why I can't take the rest I counted on. I'm goin' to propose a bill for the next session of the legislature repealin' this dangerous law, and leavin' the primaries entirely to the organizations themselves, as they used to be. Then will return the good old times, when our district leaders could have nice comfortable primary elections at some place selected by themselves and let in only men that they approved of as good Democrats. Who is a better judge of the Democracy of a man who offers his vote than the leader of the district? Who is better equipped to keep out undesirable voters?

The men who put through the primary law are the same crowd that stand for the civil service blight and they have the same objects in view—the destruction of governments by party, the downfall of the constitution and hell generally.

Concerning Excise

ALTHOUGH I'm not a drinkin' man myself, I mourn with the poor liquor dealers of New York City, who are taxed and oppressed for the benefit of the farmers up the state. The Raines liquor law is infamous. It takes away nearly all the profits of the saloonkeepers, and then turns in a large part of the money to the State treasury to relieve the hayseeds from taxes. Ah, who knows how many honest, hard-workin' saloonkeepers have been driven to untimely graves by this law! I know personally of a half-dozen who committed suicide because they couldn't pay the enormous license fee, and I have heard of many others. Every time there is an increase of the fee, there is an increase in the suicide record of the city. Now, some of these Republican hayseeds are talkin' about makin' the liquor tax $1500, or even $2000 a year. That would mean the suicide of half of the liquor dealers in the city.

Just see how these poor fellows are oppressed all around! First, liquor is taxed in the hands of the manufacturer by the United States Government; second, the wholesale dealer pays a special tax to the government; third, the retail dealer is specially taxed by the United States Government; fourth, the retail dealer has to pay a big tax to the State government.

Now, liquor dealing is criminal or it ain't. If it's criminal, the men engaged in it ought to be sent to prison. If it ain't criminal, they ought to be protected and encouraged to make all the profit they honestly can. If it's right to tax a saloonkeeper $1000, it's right to put a heavy tax on dealers in other beverages—in milk, for instance—and make the dairymen pay up. But what a howl would be raised if a bill was introduced in Albany to compel the farmers to help support the State government! What would be said of a law that put a tax of, say $60 on a grocer, $150 on a dry-goods man, and $500 more if he includes the other goods that are kept in a country store?

If the Raines law gave the money extorted from the saloonkeepers to the city, there might be some excuse for the tax. We would get some benefit from it, but it gives a big part of the tax to local option localities where the people are always shoutin' that liquor dealin' is immoral. Ought these good people be subjected to the immoral influence of money taken from the saloons—tainted money? Out of respect for the tender consciences of these pious people, the Raines law ought to exempt them from all contamination from the plunder that comes from the saloon traffic. Say, mark that sarcastic. Some people who ain't used to fine sarcasm might think I meant it.

The Raines people make a pretense that the high license fee promotes temperance. It's just the other way around. It makes more intemperance and, what is as bad, it makes a monopoly in dram-shops. Soon the saloons will be in the hands of a vast trust, and any stuff can be sold for whisky or beer. It's gettin' that way already. Some of the poor liquor dealers in my district have been forced to sell wood alcohol for whisky, and many deaths have followed. A half-dozen men died in a

A Parting Word on the Future of the Democratic Party in America

THE Democratic party of the nation ain't dead, though it's been givin' a lifelike imitation of a corpse for several years. It can't die while it's got Tammany for its backbone. The trouble is that the party's been chasin' after theories and stayin' up nights readin' books instead of studyin' human nature and actin' accordin', as I've advised in tellin' how to hold your district. In two Presidential campaigns, the leaders talked themselves red in the face about silver bein' the best money and gold bein' no good, and they tried to prove it out of books. Do you think the people cared for all that guff? No. They heartily indorsed what Richard Croker said at the Hoffman House one day in 1900. "What's the use of discussin' what's the best kind of money?" said Croker. "I'm in favor of all kinds of money—the more the better." See how a real Tammany statesman can settle in twenty-five words a problem that monopolized two campaigns!

Then imperialism. The Democratic party spent all its breath on that in the last national campaign. Its position was all right, sure, but you can't get people excited about the Philippines. They've got too much at home to interest them; they're too busy makin' a livin' to bother about the niggers in the Pacific. The party's got to drop all them put-you-to-sleep issues and come out in 1908 for somethin' that will wake the people up; somethin' that will make it worth while to work for the party.

There's just one issue that would set this country on fire. The Democratic party should say in the first plank of its platform: "We hereby declare, in national convention assembled, that the paramount issue now, always and forever, is the abolition of the iniquitous and villainous civil service laws which are destroyin' all patriotism, ruinin' the country and takin' away good jobs from them that earn them. We pledge ourselves, if our ticket is elected, to repeal those laws at once and put every civil service reformer in jail."

Just imagine the wild enthusiasm of the party, if that plank was adopted, and the rush of Republicans to join us in restorin' our country to what it was before this college professor's nightmare, called civil service reform, got hold of it! Of course, it would be all right to work in the platform some stuff about the tariff and sound money and the Philippines, as no platform seems to be complete without them, but they wouldn't count. The people would read only the first plank and then hanker for election day to come to put the Democratic party in office.

I see a vision. I see the civil service monster lyin' flat on the ground. I see the Democratic party standin' over it with foot on its neck and wearin' the crown of victory. I see Thomas Jefferson lookin' out from a cloud and sayin': "Give him another sockdologer; finish him." And I see millions of men wavin' their hats and singin' "Glory Hallelujah!"

Strenuous Life of the Tammany District Leader

NOTE: *This chapter is based on extracts from Plunkitt's Diary and on my daily observation of the work of the district leader.*—W.L.R.

THE life of the Tammany district leader is strenuous. To his work is due the wonderful recuperative power of the organization.

One year it goes down in defeat and the prediction is made that it will never again raise its head. The district leader, undaunted by defeat, collects his scattered forces, organizes them as only Tammany knows how to organize, and in a little while the organization is as strong as ever.

No other politician in New York or elsewhere is exactly like the Tammany district leader or works as he does. As a rule, he has no business or occupation other than politics. He plays politics every day and night in the year, and his headquarters bears the inscription, "Never closed."

Everybody in the district knows him. Everybody knows where to find him, and nearly everybody goes to him for assistance of one sort or another, especially the poor of the tenements.

He is always obliging. He will go to the police courts

to put in a good word for the "drunks and disorderlies" or pay their fines, if a good word is not effective. He will attend christenings, weddings, and funerals. He will feed the hungry and help bury the dead.

A philanthropist? Not at all. He is playing politics all the time.

Brought up in Tammany Hall, he has learned how to reach the hearts of the great mass of voters. He does not bother about reaching their heads. It is his belief that arguments and campaign literature have never gained votes.

He seeks direct contact with the people, does them good turns when he can, and relies on their not forgetting him on election day. His heart is always in his work, too, for his subsistence depends on its results.

If he holds his district and Tammany is in power, he is amply rewarded by a good office and the opportunities that go with it. What these opportunities are has been shown by the quick rise to wealth of so many Tammany district leaders. With the examples before him of Richard Croker, once leader of the Twentieth District; John F. Carroll, formerly leader of the Twenty-ninth; Timothy ("Dry Dollar") Sullivan, late leader of the Sixth, and many others, he can always look forward to riches and ease while he is going through the drudgery of his daily routine.

This is a record of a day's work by Plunkitt:

2 A.M.: Aroused from sleep by the ringing of his doorbell; went to the door and found a bartender, who asked him to go to the police station and bail out a saloonkeeper who had been arrested for violating the excise law. Furnished bail and returned to bed at three o'clock.

6 A.M.: Awakened by fire engines passing his house. Hastened to the scene of the fire, according to the custom of the Tammany district leaders, to give assistance to

the fire sufferers, if needed. Met several of his election district captains who are always under orders to look out for fires, which are considered great vote-getters. Found several tenants who had been burned out, took them to a hotel, supplied them with clothes, fed them, and arranged temporary quarters for them until they could rent and furnish new apartments.

8:30 A.M.: Went to the police court to look after his constituents. Found six "drunks." Secured the discharge of four by a timely word with the judge, and paid the fines of two.

9 A.M.: Appeared in the Municipal District Court. Directed one of his district captains to act as counsel for a widow against whom dispossess proceedings had been instituted and obtained an extension of time. Paid the rent of a poor family about to be dispossessed and gave them a dollar for food.

11 A.M.: At home again. Found four men waiting for him. One had been discharged by the Metropolitan Railway Company for neglect of duty, and wanted the district leader to fix things. Another wanted a job on the road. The third sought a place on the Subway and the fourth, a plumber, was looking for work with the Consolidated Gas Company. The district leader spent nearly three hours fixing things for the four men, and succeeded in each case.

3 P.M.: Attended the funeral of an Italian as far as the ferry. Hurried back to make his appearance at the funeral of a Hebrew constituent. Went conspicuously to the front both in the Catholic church and the synagogue, and later attended the Hebrew confirmation ceremonies in the synagogue.

7 P.M.: Went to district headquarters and presided over a meeting of election district captains. Each captain

submitted a list of all the voters in his district, reported on their attitude toward Tammany, suggested who might be won over and how they could be won, told who were in need, and who were in trouble of any kind and the best way to reach them. District leader took notes and gave orders.

8 P.M.: Went to a church fair. Took chances on everything, bought ice cream for the young girls and the children. Kissed the little ones, flattered their mothers and took their fathers out for something down at the corner.

9 P.M.: At the clubhouse again. Spent $10 on tickets for a church excursion and promised a subscription for a new church bell. Bought tickets for a baseball game to be played by two nines from his district. Listened to the complaints of a dozen pushcart peddlers who said they were persecuted by the police and assured them he would go to Police Headquarters in the morning and see about it.

10:30 P.M.: Attended a Hebrew wedding reception and dance. Had previously sent a handsome wedding present to the bride.

12 P.M.: In bed.

That is the actual record of one day in the life of Plunkitt. He does some of the same things every day, but his life is not so monotonous as to be wearisome.

Sometimes the work of a district leader is exciting, especially if he happens to have a rival who intends to make a contest for the leadership at the primaries. In that case, he is even more alert, tries to reach the fires before his rival, sends out runners to look for "drunks and disorderlies" at the police stations, and keeps a very close watch on the obituary columns of the newspapers.

A few years ago there was a bitter contest for the Tammany leadership of the Ninth District between John

C. Sheehan and Frank J. Goodwin. Both had had long experience in Tammany politics and both understood every move of the game.

Every morning their agents went to their respective headquarters before seven o'clock and read through the death notices in all the morning papers. If they found that anybody in the district had died, they rushed to the homes of their principals with the information and then there was a race to the house of the deceased to offer condolences, and, if the family were poor, something more substantial.

On the day of the funeral there was another contest. Each faction tried to surpass the other in the number and appearance of the carriages it sent to the funeral, and more than once they almost came to blows at the church or in the cemetery.

On one occasion the Goodwinites played a trick on their adversaries which has since been imitated in other districts. A well-known liquor dealer who had a considerable following died, and both Sheehan and Goodwin were eager to become his political heir by making a big showing at the funeral.

Goodwin managed to catch the enemy napping. He went to all the livery stables in the district, hired all the carriages for the day, and gave orders to two hundred of his men to be on hand as mourners.

Sheehan had never had any trouble about getting all the carriages that he wanted, so he let the matter go until the night before the funeral. Then he found that he could not hire a carriage in the district.

He called his district committee together in a hurry and explained the situation to them. He could get all the vehicles he needed in the adjoining district, he said, but if he did that, Goodwin would rouse the voters of the Ninth by declaring that he (Sheehan) had patronized foreign industries.

Finally, it was decided that there was nothing to do but to go over to Sixth Avenue and Broadway for carriages. Sheehan made a fine turnout at the funeral, but the deceased was hardly in his grave before Goodwin raised the cry of "Protection to home industries," and denounced his rival for patronizing livery-stable keepers outside of his district. The cry had its effect in the primary campaign. At all events, Goodwin was elected leader.

A recent contest for the leadership of the Second District illustrated further the strenuous work of the Tammany district leaders. The contestants were Patrick Divver, who had managed the district for years, and Thomas F. Foley.

Both were particularly anxious to secure the large Italian vote. They not only attended all the Italian christenings and funerals, but also kept a close lookout for the marriages in order to be on hand with wedding presents.

At first, each had his own reporter in the Italian quarter to keep track of the marriages. Later, Foley conceived a better plan. He hired a man to stay all day at the City Hall marriage bureau, where most Italian couples go through the civil ceremony, and telephone to him at his saloon when anything was doing at the bureau.

Foley had a number of presents ready for use and, whenever he received a telephone message from his man, he hastened to the City Hall with a ring or a watch or a piece of silver and handed it to the bride with his congratulations. As a consequence, when Divver got the news and went to the home of the couple with his present, he always found that Foley had been ahead of him. Toward the end of the campaign, Divver also stationed a man at the marriage bureau and then there were daily foot races and fights between the two heelers.

Sometimes the rivals came into conflict at the deathbed. One night a poor Italian peddler died in Roosevelt Street. The news reached Divver and Foley about the same time, and as they knew the family of the man was destitute, each went to an undertaker and brought him to the Roosevelt Street tenement.

The rivals and the undertakers met at the house and an altercation ensued. After much discussion the Divver undertaker was selected. Foley had more carriages at the funeral, however, and he further impressed the Italian voters by paying the widow's rent for a month, and sending her half a ton of coal and a barrel of flour.

The rivals were put on their mettle toward the end of the campaign by the wedding of a daughter of one of the original Cohens of the Baxter Street region. The Hebrew vote in the district is nearly as large as the Italian vote, and Divver and Foley set out to capture the Cohens and their friends.

They stayed up nights thinking what they would give the bride. Neither knew how much the other was prepared to spend on a wedding present, or what form it would take; so spies were employed by both sides to keep watch on the jewelry stores, and the jewelers of the district were bribed by each side to impart the desired information.

At last Foley heard that Divver had purchased a set of silver knives, forks and spoons. He at once bought a duplicate set and added a silver tea service. When the presents were displayed at the home of the bride, Divver was not in a pleasant mood and he charged his jeweler with treachery. It may be added that Foley won at the primaries.

One of the fixed duties of a Tammany district leader is to give two outings every summer, one for the men of his district and the other for the women and children, and a beefsteak dinner and a ball every winter. The scene of the outings is, usually, one of the groves along the Sound.

The ambition of the district leader on these occasions is to demonstrate that his men have broken all records in the matter of eating and drinking. He gives out the exact number of pounds of beef, poultry, butter, etc., that they have consumed and professes to know how many potatoes and ears of corn have been served.

According to his figures, the average eating record of each man at the outing is about ten pounds of beef, two or three chickens, a pound of butter, a half peck of potatoes, and two dozen ears of corn. The drinking records, as given out, are still more phenomenal. For some reason, not yet explained, the district leader thinks that his popularity will be greatly increased if he can show that his followers can eat and drink more than the followers of any other district leader.

The same idea governs the beefsteak dinners in the winter. It matters not what sort of steak is served or how it is cooked; the district leader considers only the question of quantity, and when he excels all others in this particular, he feels, somehow, that he is a bigger man and deserves more patronage than his associates in the Tammany Executive Committee.

As to the balls, they are the events of the winter in the extreme East Side and West Side society. Mamie and Maggie and Jennie prepare for them months in advance, and their young men save up for the occasion just as they save for the summer trips to Coney Island.

The district leader is in his glory at the opening of the ball. He leads the cotillion with the prettiest woman present—his wife, if he has one, permitting—and spends almost the whole night shaking hands with his constituents. The ball costs him a pretty penny, but he has found that the investment pays.

By these means the Tammany district leader reaches out into the homes of his district, keeps watch not only on the men, but also on the women and children; knows their needs, their likes and dislikes, their troubles and their hopes, and places himself in a position to use his knowledge for the benefit of his organization and himself. Is it any wonder that scandals do not permanently disable Tammany and that it speedily recovers from what seems to be crushing defeat?

W9-ASK-177

Praise for Ellen Herrick's books:

The Forbidden Garden

"*The Forbidden Garden* is a romantic, bighearted novel that celebrates femininity in all its nurturing, resilient, and fearless power."
—Heather Young, author of *The Lost Girls*

"*The Forbidden Garden* is misnamed. It should be titled: *The Enchanted, Page-turning, Beautiful, Absorbing, Magical Garden.* You'll be swept up in this transformative tale that reinforces your belief that sometimes in life there's more than we can understand with logic and instead must give ourselves up to our hearts. Readers who loved Alice Hoffman's *Practical Magic* and Audrey Niffenegger's *The Time Traveler's Wife* are in for a wonderful treat with Ellen Herrick's lovely new novel."
—*New York Times* bestselling author M. J. Rose

The Sparrow Sisters

"If you're looking for a read à la Elin Hilderbrand with a touch of magic, look no further than *The Sparrow Sisters*, Ellen Herrick's wicked and romantic debut."
—*New York Times* and *USA Today* bestselling author Sarah Jio

"A haunting, magical, modern-day fairy tale. A feast for the senses."
—*New York Times* bestselling author Sarah Addison Allen

"A delightfully intriguing debut, gracefully paced and skillfully crafted. Ellen Herrick's attention to sensory detail is magical and moving. Evocative to the last page."
—Susan Meissner

Women's Fiction Best Bets for September, 2015
—Heroes and Heartbreakers

2015 BookExpo Books that Buzzed
—*Library Journal*

29 New Books You'll Want to Read this Fall (2015)
—PopSugar

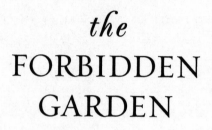

the FORBIDDEN GARDEN

Also by Ellen Herrick

The Sparrow Sisters

the FORBIDDEN GARDEN

ELLEN HERRICK

wm

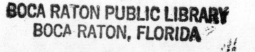

WILLIAM MORROW

An Imprint of HarperCollins*Publishers*

This is a work of fiction. Names, characters, places, and incidents are products of the author's imagination or are used fictitiously and are not to be construed as real. Any resemblance to actual events, locales, organizations, or persons, living or dead, is entirely coincidental.

HarperCollins books may be purchased for educational, business, or sales promotional use. For information, please email the Special Markets Department at SPsales@harpercollins.com.

FIRST EDITION

Designed by Diahann Sturge

Illustrated map copyright © by Laura Hartman Maestro

Library of Congress Cataloging-in-Publication Data has been applied for.

ISBN 978-0-06-249995-0 (paperback)
ISBN 978-0-06-265962-0 (library edition)

17 18 19 20 21 RRD 10 9 8 7 6 5 4 3 2 1

For my beloved family without whom I might have met my first deadline, or at least my second

Hiraeth

(n.) a homesickness for a home to which you cannot return, a home which maybe never was: the nostalgia, the yearning, the grief for the lost places of your past.

the FORBIDDEN GARDEN

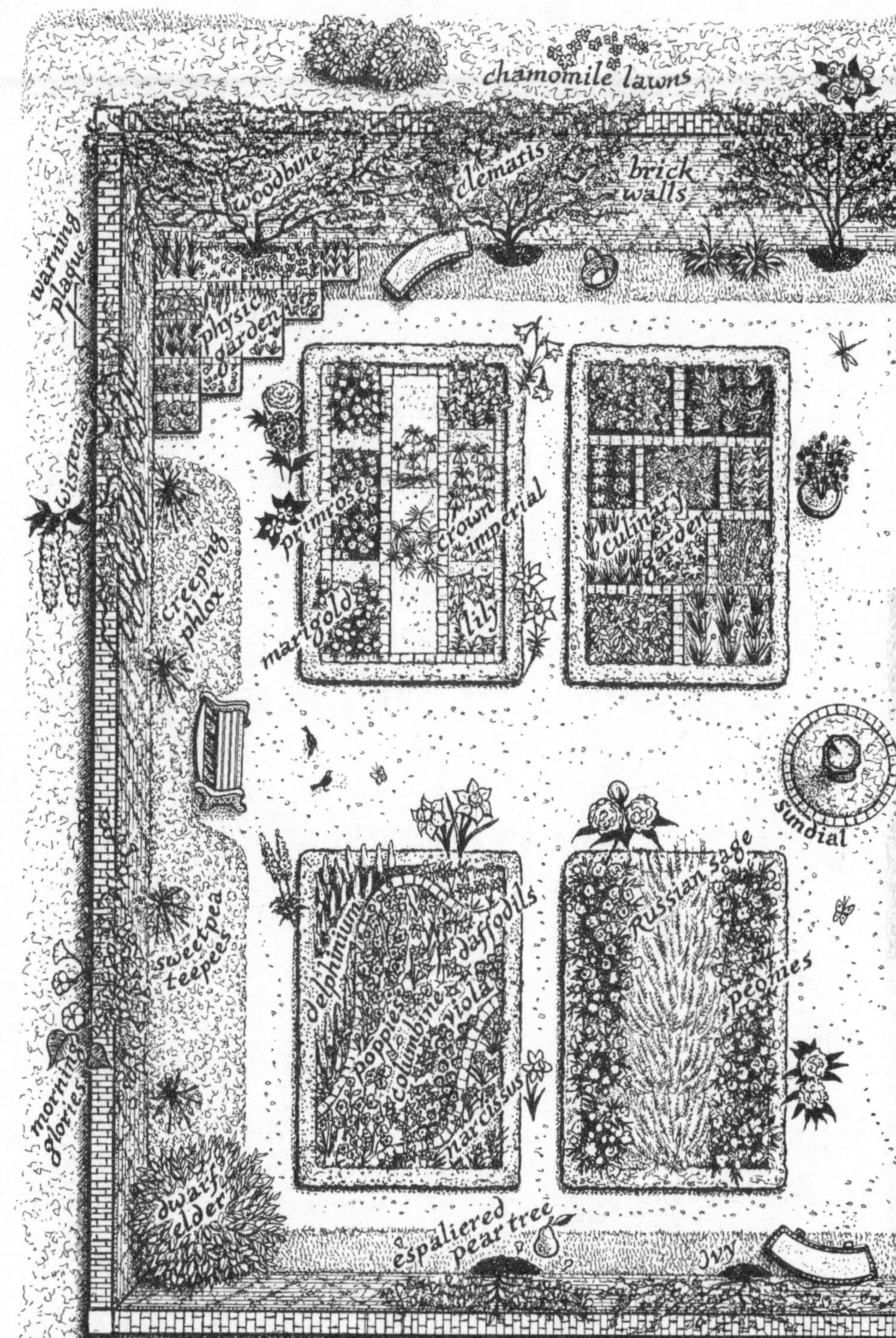
chamomile lawns
woodbine
clematis
brick walls
warning plaque
physic garden
wisteria
primrose
crown imperial
culinary garden
creeping phlox
marigold
lily
sundial
delphinium
daffodils
Russian sage
sweetpea teepees
poppies
columbine
viola
peonies
morning glories
narcissus
dwarf elder
espaliered pear tree
ivy
chamomile lawns

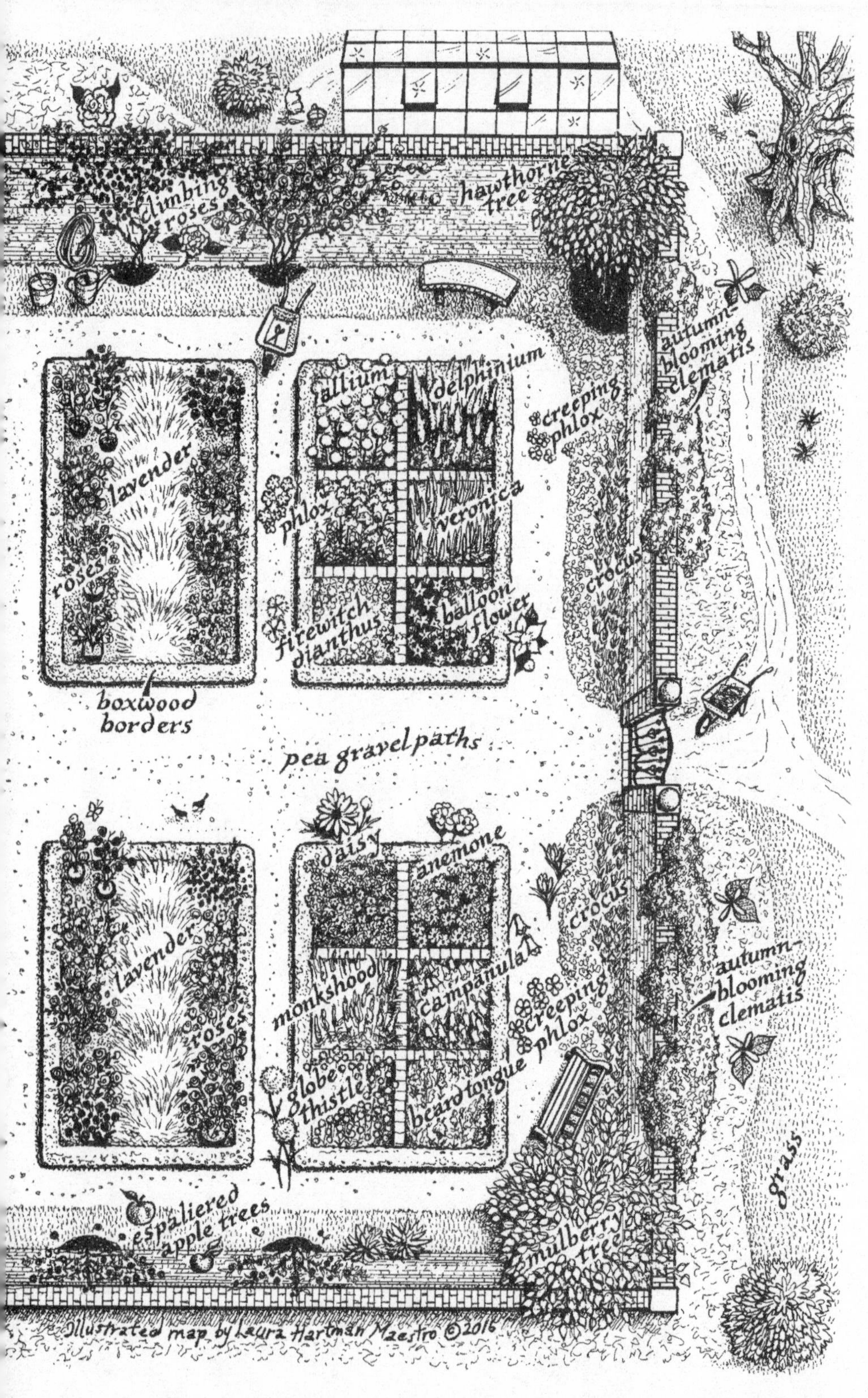
climbing roses
hawthorne tree
autumn-blooming clematis
allium
delphinium
creeping phlox
lavender
phlox
veronica
roses
crocus
firewitch dianthus
balloon flower
boxwood borders
pea gravel paths
daisy
anemone
crocus
lavender
monkshood
campanula
autumn-blooming clematis
creeping phlox
roses
globe thistle
beardtongue
grass
espaliered apple trees
mulberry tree
Illustrated map by Laura Hartman Maestro © 2016

PROLOGUE

The garden waited. Behind the yew hedges, beyond the crumbling brick wall, within sight of the ancient house, under skies both heavy and light, the garden waited for someone to save it. Beneath the soil, now emptied of any nourishment, seeds huddled, asleep or worse, and still the garden waited.

First there were the birds that flew over and settled to pick at the bones of the garden. Then the small creatures dug and scrabbled until bulbs were gnawed raw and white. Finally, the larger animals came, deer and dog, a lost soldier, shoes worn to paper, a farmer broken by blight. These animals were hungry too, their ribs pressed sharp against their fur, their fingers frost-tipped, their eyes as empty as the garden had become.

Years passed with nothing to show in a land once so enchanted that bees and butterflies slept safe in the blossoms after

their nectar was gathered. Here was a place that defined beauty in petals and leaves, scent and sight, hue and touch. Now, no matter the trowels pressed into the earth, the care taken with each tiny seedling, the garden would not wake. It was waiting for one pair of hands, one heart, one fine and tender soul to rouse it and release its magic.

CHAPTER 1

Thistledown

Graham, Lord Kirkwood put the phone down and turned to his wife, Stella.

"Fiona says she's found a gardener," he said.

"In America? What good does that do us here?" Stella asked, looking up from her book.

"Fiona thinks this person may be willing to travel—something about a bad summer in her village, a child's death, townspeople on edge, not a good thing. It's been nearly a year, but apparently everyone's still a bit shell-shocked." Graham tapped away at his laptop for a moment in silence.

"Yes, here it is in the papers over there: modern-day witch hunt involving three sisters and their own gardens, all very peasants-with-pitchforks-and-torches. I'll send you over the

story. Perfect for us, right, my love? A professional to sort things out at last and time for you to regain your strength."

Stella's head came up. "I am hardly an invalid," she said. "Whatever made me ill is gone now, and I am none the worse for it. Besides, is that the kind of thing we need right now, Gray?" she asked. "Isn't the garden enough of an uncanny mystery without dropping some poor innocent into the middle of our rather 'interesting' lives?"

"But that's just it, Stella," Graham said. "That's why this Sorrel Sparrow must come to England. With all she has suffered in that town—the ruination of her own gardens—and all she has recovered in this year with her sisters, I am hoping that she can find the key to our ruined garden, and perhaps more. I know you think I'm silly to feel that the place needs more than just time and compost. There is something to the old stories and to this young woman. Fiona agrees and she knows Sorrel. I believe they are meant for each other, the garden and the girl."

"I don't know why you won't let me continue with this project. I am perfectly capable of working with someone here to put the place right again. Others may have failed, but I am determined," Stella said.

"Yes, my love, this is true but I have no wish to lose you to this garden when a capable young woman has presented herself to us."

"She hasn't, Gray," Stella said. "You and your sister are going to press-gang her into coming to England."

Graham laughed. "We can be very persuasive."

Stella looked at her husband with all the love she felt in her heart and the indulgence she had come to need when Graham got hold of a project, even if it had been her project from the start.

"My darling," she said and held out her hand, "if it is Sorrel Sparrow we need, then it is Sorrel Sparrow we shall have."

It would be days before Sorrel even noticed the letter as the Nursery prepared for its own reawakening in Granite Point. Then it took some more time before she was nudged into reading it. In fact, it was her sister Nettie who finally read it aloud as Sorrel sat at the kitchen table trimming improbably robust asparagus spears toward the end of March. These were from the Sisters' own garden behind Ivy House and, like the Sparrows Sisters Nursery on Calumet Landing, this garden did not play by the rules. The angry townsmen who blamed the women for everything that had gone so terribly wrong less than a year before couldn't breach the Sisters' private spaces, and for some reason the wild weather of that nasty summer had passed their garden by. The numbness and exhaustion of that time were only a memory in the relative calm of Ivy House.

The thick, pale blue envelope sat in the silver tray by the front door for almost a week along with the bills that were still a bother to pay after the poor high season of the last year. It was Nettie, in fact, who picked it up and, weighing it in her palm, carried it into the kitchen.

Nettie handed Sorrel the envelope and stood behind her chair.

"It's postmarked days and days ago, sweetie," Nettie said, nudging her sister. "It's from England."

"I know, I saw it earlier," Sorrel said and leaned her head against Nettie's side. "I just forgot."

"Open it." Nettie sat down. "Maybe you have a secret inheritance worth millions, hidden by dastardly relatives."

"Breathe, Miss Marple!" Sorrel laughed. "Honestly, I've gotten a bit afraid of the mail."

Nevertheless, Sorrel turned the envelope over and slit it open. Inside was a handwritten letter. She passed it to Nettie.

"Here, you read it," Sorrel said.

Nettie took the letter and made a show of smoothing it out and holding it before her as if she needed glasses.

"A letter, on paper, with ink and such penmanship," Nettie said. "I feel a good story coming on!"

She began reading, and as she did, both sisters felt their curiosity rise. When she finished, Nettie looked at Sorrel with one eyebrow raised.

"Well, he's confident, I'll say that," Sorrel said. "I haven't agreed to anything and he's got me all Sherlock to his Watson."

"How great would it be, Sorrel, if you did take him up on the offer? I mean, an adventure of this sort doesn't come along often, not for us anyway."

"Yeah, but it's no unexpected fortune," Sorrel said as she took the letter from Nettie.

Nettie slapped the table. "Close enough!" she crowed. "Jackpot, Sorrel! Go forth and garden!"

The Sisters spent more days discussing "Sorrel's Grand Adventure," as they called it. Everyone weighed in with the pros, no one with a single con. Fiona Hathaway brought over a picture of her brother, Graham, in knickerbockers and a beanie hat, jam on his face and a teddy bear in his hand. "In case you are concerned that he's a bit grand," she said. "And to reassure you that he is often silly, in the nicest way."

Sorrel did not so much make a decision about the trip as get pulled into it by her sisters and friends. Henry Carlyle offered his well-worn Michelin guide to London from 1994, Ben Avellar made Sorrel promise to try eel pie (she would not), Charlotte Mayo gave her a beautiful leather passport case and a packet of wet wipes; Charlotte was a new mother and overly cautious these days. Simon Mayo, who after Patience's trial found himself unreasonably prone to tears, gave Sorrel a pile of old-fashioned, nearly transparent blue aerograms left over from his postgrad year at Oxford.

"Please keep in touch," he said with a sniff.

"Oh Simon," Patience barked. "She's only going to be gone for a couple of months, and it's not as if you see each other every day as it is."

But in a town as small as Granite Point they pretty much did. So now, when all was said and done, and the Sisters were standing together, straight-backed and smelling of cedar closets and lavender, it was a bit of a shock to think that Sorrel would

be on her own for the first time, more so as the Sisters leapt into getting her ready for her trip. There was no way around it; Sorrel was flying the nest and as much as her family and friends might wish to keep her close, they also wanted her to find her wings.

LEAVING IS NOT *the same as running away,* Sorrel thought as she smashed shut the lid of her suitcase. Like her sisters, she was an infrequent traveler so her luggage was not, unlike that of the rest of the world, on wheels. It was, in fact, her mother's suitcase and was made of leather, worn smooth and shiny not from use but with storage. Sorrel had had a devil of a time finding the thing in the attic and then dragging it down the back stairs and across the hall to her room. She could have asked Patience or Nettie for help, but then she would have had to listen to their opinions again. She realized that a big reason that she had accepted the invitation was that she was tired of being one of three, or *just* one of the three Sparrow Sisters. Sorrel needed to be herself, *just* herself, and now she would.

It was the cusp of May, and Sorrel Sparrow had tidied away everything she could at work. The Sparrow Sisters Nursery had suffered that last summer just as much as Patience had. It had taken weeks of cleanup and an awful lot of careful attention for the flowers and fruits, the vegetables and herbs, to recover from the weather and the hurtful feet and hands that had come through tearing and grinding, stomping and ripping until the Nursery looked not so much like a paradise as a dark

hell. Now, with the soil steaming in the early morning sunshine, Sorrel moved with the speed of necessity as she set out flats of Shasta daisies, dusted peat moss from the dahlia bulbs before setting them into a bed, mulched the roses and the peonies whose deep red stems were leafing out, their tips hinting at the fat buds to come. The sisters were all gifted gardeners so Sorrel wasn't terribly worried about her beloved flowers. Patience's herbs were in fine form, Nettie's fruits and vegetables were well on their way, and now Sorrel's blooms would have the best start they could without her capable hands to see them into June. With detailed instructions and many conversations, all that was left was for Sorrel to move forward.

Sorrel's younger sisters were both in the pleasant middle of relationships that would grow and flourish over time. But that wasn't what turned Sorrel away from her home. Really, she loved seeing her sisters in love. Their happiness poured a kind of soft golden light over everything they touched, including Sorrel. The way Henry Carlyle and Patience always stood canted toward each other, even as they rose to sing the closing hymn in church on Sundays, made Sorrel smile. And when Nettie put her small hand in Ben Avellar's great paw, well, that made her laugh with pleasure. Truly, it gave Sorrel some relief to know that her younger sisters were finding their way toward wholeness again. No, Sorrel was not jealous of their newfound happiness. She had always been the sister most capable of taking joy in that of another, of folding that warmth around her like a cloak, snuggling into the feeling that all was well with

the people she loved. This place, Granite Point, was graced, that's what everyone said, and that grace could be found at its most abundant in the Sparrow Sisters Nursery.

Sorrel always thought herself happy in the little village by the sea. She was content among her flowers and specimen trees, the extraordinary roses and lilacs, sweet peas and hydrangeas that bloomed—somehow simultaneously and for months beyond reason—in the Nursery. She found great pleasure in picking the pears, cherries, and apples for Nettie's tarts, the tender young peas and beans, the lettuce so green it glowed, and the nasturtiums and violas that her sister used in her salads. She was grateful for Patience's remedies on the rare occasions when she felt ill. But Sorrel's hands were happiest deep in the soil and curled around the stems of the flowers she grew and arranged. It was said that if Sorrel made your wedding bouquet, the marriage was all but guaranteed happiness. Her overflowing vases at all three churches in town were so fragrant and colorful that congregants often lost interest in the sermons and instead began to dream of their hearts' desires, of the love they gave away, the moments they treasured most. At the news of her trip, two couples postponed their weddings, and one young family put off a christening so that Sorrel's flowers could bless the events. As she stood among the chickens listening to their chuckling clucks, she was pressed to imagine a simpler, more solid life. But, after what the girls had begun calling the "darkling summer," the oldest Sparrow Sister felt the ground had shifted and she was the only one who didn't have a hand to steady her.

If you had asked Sorrel last spring if she would ever use her long-held, always-current passport to leave Granite Point behind, even temporarily, she might have tried to remember where she'd put the damn thing. But here she was, tucking the frayed lining of her mother's valise under her clothes, snugging the belt across the trousers and sweaters, wedging her gardening clogs, clapped clean of dirt for once, into the sides of the case. Henry took it downstairs and out to the street before kissing Patience and going back to his patients, and Ben swung it into the truck and covered it with a worn moving blanket. The drive to Boston wasn't long, and with Patience at the wheel Sorrel was sure to be far too early for her flight. One last glance as the Sisters rounded Calumet Landing, one last breath of sand and sea, and Sorrel was away.

"YOU'D THINK THAT if we're playing 'name that mystery plant,' Sir Blatherington-Smythe would have contacted me," Patience said as she took a curve on two wheels—again—and Sorrel's suitcase slid across the truck bed.

"Kirkwood, Lord Kirkwood of Kirkwood St. James," Sorrel said and checked her purse for her passport—again. "And, I may be wrong here, but aren't you still skittish about leaving the Nursery?"

Patience frowned at her sister, and Sorrel marked the new lines around her mouth, the pallor that had stolen over Patience when Matty Short died last July and now refused to lift no

matter how long she worked in the sunlit gardens. She leaned into Patience's shoulder.

"Eyes on the road, P," Sorrel said.

"You know, I was so sure *I'd* make the big break," Patience said and shifted gears with gusto.

"Me, too," said Sorrel. "Now there's Henry, and he's a tie I don't think you should loosen right now. Besides, it's not like I'm leaving Granite Point forever. I'm going for eight weeks on his Lordship's dime, 'ta' very much, so I'll be back before the summer rush."

"Well, then, tally ho!" Patience pulled up to the departures curb with a jolt.

"Tell Nettie that the primulas have to be put in the small pots and the hydrangeas into the large before Mother's Day if we're to get the decorators' trade," Sorrel said. "Don't let her cut all the marigolds, either; there's a Colt family reunion in August so I need them for wreaths. The wisteria needs some fishmeal, and the clematis will bloom early so don't let it fall off the trellis. Oh, and the roses by the shed need staking if we want them for the July Fourth parade."

Those roses, their blooms as big as saucers, would flower right into December. How the Sisters managed to grow the flowers—long-stemmed, creamy white, red as blood, pale pink, sunny yellow, and every peachy tone in between—always thornless and as fragrant as a summer day even with snow on the ground, did not bear questioning. If their rare gift had nearly brought them to ruin that last summer, it was

welcome again now that the town had recovered its head and its heart.

Sorrel and Patience got out and stood with the suitcase between them.

"Don't stay away, Sorrel," Patience said. "Please come back to Granite Point."

Sorrel put her arms around her prickly sister.

"I couldn't stay away, Patience," she said. "You and Nettie are home to me."

CHAPTER 2

Lark's Heels

Stella Kirkwood was the most sensible of women, which could put her at odds with her impulsive husband. Still, her slightly dreamy appearance, the way she moved as if on air through the great house, everything about her lovely aspect, in fact, could set a man's thoughts to ballads. But that soft smile, pale hair in a glossy chignon, cashmere shawl across her shoulders and always, always a long string of pearls looped around her neck, belied the strong backbone and stronger heart that beat beneath her silk blouse. She loved her husband and her family, and she loved her brother Andrew with a kind of sturdy vigor that made everyone in her orbit feel safe and cared for.

It was just this kind of care that Stella applied to her attempt at restoring the Shakespeare Garden. When it became apparent

that her efforts made not a bit of difference and, further, that she felt absolutely awful, Stella stopped and allowed her husband to call in the local GP. Graham stood anxiously as the young doctor ministered to Stella in their bedroom.

"I told her that garden is cursed," Graham said. "It's legend, the death in that garden."

"Like the plaque says?" the doctor asked as he fished through his bag for a thermometer.

"Obviously we don't actually believe it's a curse," Stella said, shooting her husband a sharp look.

"No, obviously," Graham said.

"You know, when I was growing up, it was a badge of honor to sneak in and run around in the place," the doctor said. "We were certainly convinced it was haunted, if not outright cursed."

Graham looked at his wife. "There," he said, pointing at the doctor. "Is it any wonder my family's tried so hard to fix the damn place?"

"I hardly think the garden is the root of Lady Kirkwood's malaise," the GP said. "In a village this small bugs get passed around pretty easily."

It was determined that Stella had some kind of virus; in fact, within a week the entire first form of the local school fell ill. The only thing for anyone was rest and fluids.

"And to stay out of that blasted garden," Graham added as he walked the GP out. Then and there he'd decided that the only way to keep his family from harm was to get someone

else to distract the cursed garden from his family. Not that he believed in curses.

Once he convinced Stella that Sorrel Sparrow was an absolute necessity, it took Graham more than a week to craft the letter he wanted to send. It was a delicate task— sharing just as much as was needed to pique her interest while holding back some of the more difficult aspects of the job. There would be plenty of time to explain the rather unsettling legacy of the Shakespeare Garden. Plus, the estate demanded his attention now when the spring was all but sprung. Kirkwood Hall was surrounded by acres and acres of land that had been giving its people the finest sustenance for hundreds of years. The formal gardens that marched elegantly out from the manor were fertile and fragrant, and the fields beyond gave the horses, sheep, and goats feed, summer and winter. The sloping hills would be rampant with bluebells in a matter of weeks, and the three rills that wandered back and forth across the estate were quite simply perfect for walks and romps for man and beast. To say that Kirkwood Hall and the parkland were picture perfect and beloved by all was just too obvious.

So then, to hear Lord Kirkwood say that he was looking for a gardener made no sense to most people. There wasn't an inch of land in the park—fields, flower gardens, or maze—that wasn't tended with great expertise. People came from far and wide to see the Italian Gardens and buy a honeycomb or damson jam in the farm shop. The wool from the sheep and the cheese from the

goats drew buyers in a queue the day they were ready for purchase. In June the pick-your-own strawberry fields were filled with children carrying baskets of berries, their lips stained red with sweet juice. In August the dahlia fields were so flush with color that the cloudy days seemed brighter, and in autumn the apple and pear orchards were woven through with ladders and littered with overflowing bushel baskets. A raft of stable hands, gardeners, landscape architects, greensmen, and woodsmen made sure that Kirkwood Hall looked as beautiful as it must.

There was no spot in need of care and certainly not from an outsider. Except for one: the ancient Shakespeare Garden. Behind its walls it was as empty of life as the other gardens were full. The silence that hung over it was not broken, ever. Not by birdsong or bee buzz or fox call. It was this place that preoccupied Graham, as it had his father and mother before him, and generations before them. *Joke all you like,* he thought, *that spot is a blight and a blot on my world, and I will make it right, curse be damned.*

Graham had no wish to have Stella sucked back into the garden, to be troubled and haunted by its emptiness and saddened by her failure, for she had failed as had all the others. The fact that her health was fragile and that she still rested most afternoons made finding help essential. So when his sister spoke to him from her home in Granite Point, a small town on the edge of the sea in New England, he heard the promise in her voice and dared let the excitement travel down the line to him in Wiltshire.

Stella was the last person to entertain superstition. Unlike her husband, she was troubled not by the fallow garden's lack of life, although that was eerie, but by the potential it held that simply would not be fulfilled. It was like a recalcitrant child who refused to obey, except that this child was stronger than its caretakers. *Never mind,* Stella thought, *we'll have an adventure with this Sorrel Sparrow, curse be damned.*

Stella did feel a little deceptive when she roped her brother, Andrew, into the plot to resurrect the Shakespeare Garden. She couldn't deny that her being unwell this season had unsettled her brother, too. The fatigue that fell over her like a fog, the low fever that came upon her some evenings, and the concern on Andrew's face as they sat over tea, had lessened, but Stella's unease remained. And her energy was still at an ebb. So she leapt on the opportunity to enlist Andrew as Sorrel's official welcoming party in London and a minor partner in the garden, to make the spring and the delicious slide into summer a new beginning for them all. This Sorrel Sparrow (whose beauty Stella could see even in the newspaper photos from the trial) might prove a most promising distraction for a man who seemed determined to remain snarly and unwelcoming to pleasure. Andrew had always been such a joyful man. Now he trudged about the estate like a surly teenager. Stella felt for her brother although, to be fair, she was rather glad his life was changing, even with the heartache. So, yes, a jolt of the new, that's what he needed to help him forgive and forget.

Since Graham would be in London when Sorrel arrived,

the house in Chelsea would already be open and welcoming. Stella suspected that once her daughter Poppy learned of the plans, she'd be sure to be in residence as well. All in all, Lady Kirkwood felt quite satisfied with her organization. She would rest at Kirkwood Hall confident in the knowledge that all the cogs would turn smoothly. And turn they did.

ANDREW WARBURTON PULLED into the terminal and parked his car exactly in the middle of the strip that said NO STOPPING. He sat and scrolled through his phone: sympathetic texts from friends he really should answer and a message from his sister, whose gentle voice informed him that the plane he was here to meet was forty minutes late. That was a call he wished he'd answered. As it was he had another twenty minutes till the Boston flight landed and at least that much time again until this mysterious Sparrow person was expelled from immigration. He spied army security, just a boy really, in his heavy bulletproof vest, an M16 cradled in his arm. Andrew met his eye and silently dared him to make him pull off. But the policeman looked at the CLERGY ON DUTY card on the windscreen and strolled on.

That's right, Andrew thought, *temporarily churchless man of God sitting here in my Morris Minor, and I'm not moving.* He was actually a little surprised it worked, the card. But since it did, he got out, leaving his hazards blinking, and went into the airport for a coffee. He had only the barest sketch of whom he was meeting and knew less than that about what made this

gardener so very important. Andrew plucked at his balding corduroy trousers. Perhaps he should have smartened up.

As the plane came into Heathrow, it struggled through the heavy cloud cover, juddering as it descended. Sorrel woke from a dream, her eyes wide, a breath caught in her throat, her sisters' faces before her.

Lord, what have I agreed to? she thought.

Sorrel turned to the window, watching the formless clouds press against the plane. When it finally broke through, fog and rain swept away the oddly peaceful cocoon. The Thames snaked through London below, flat and gray as pewter. She scrabbled for a brush and wrestled her long black hair into a knot at the base of her neck. The white swath that ran straight beside her part from crown to tip had surely widened over the terrible summer. *Ah me,* she thought, *what's done is done and this Sparrow has taken flight.*

After the late landing and the slog through immigration, Sorrel walked out into the terminal and looked around for some kind of welcoming somebody. She saw her name on a bent card held by a rangy man who was scanning the crowd. She had been told to expect a driver. She didn't relish any more hours sitting, but that's what seemed in store. Sorrel approached him with a small wave.

"That's me," she said.

"Hullo," the man said as he held out his hand for Sorrel's suitcase. His smile was tight and his nose was crooked, just

a little. This couldn't be Fiona Hathaway's brother: he bore no resemblance to the minister's wife and he certainly wasn't lordly, or how Sorrel imagined lordly looked. His hair was black and messy, and his eyes were green as moss, wide and dark. There was a shaving nick on his chin and a thoroughly tatty scarf around his neck. He was tall enough so that Sorrel had to tilt her head back to take him in. Her own eyes were squinty and dry from the flight and against her will she felt the impulse to straighten her sweater and tuck her hair behind her ear.

"Andrew Warburton, Stella's brother," the man said. "I'm here to collect you."

"Oh, lots of brothers to keep straight. I'm Sorrel Sparrow," she said and they shook hands. His was warm and Sorrel's was cold, and for a moment she just wanted to keep holding on until the warmth spread. Instead, she cleared her throat and hefted her bag higher on her shoulder.

"I guess we're going to Kirkwood Park, Hall, um, Manor?" Sorrel asked.

"Oh, not yet," Andrew said, beckoning her to follow him out of the terminal. "Graham thought a few days in London might acclimate you, and he's arranged for some time at the library in the New Globe so you can gather your ideas. You'll also consult with the head of the Chelsea Physic Garden, and it seems that I am to be your minder." He stopped when he noticed that Sorrel was still standing where he'd found her.

"What is it, Sorrel?" he asked. Her name rolled around in

his mouth before it tumbled out. *Good God,* Sorrel thought. *Henry Higgins.*

"I don't need a minder, thanks and I assumed we'd go straight out to Wiltshire. I don't have all that much time if I'm to get the garden in," she said.

"Yes, well, you'll find that Graham and Stella Kirkwood make plans that, however surprising at the outset, usually work for the best." Andrew suspected that such a plan had already happened to him. He fished in his pocket for the keys. "Shall we?" he asked.

Sorrel followed his broad back to the car, an odd, lumpy dark maroon thing that looked as if it had been parked there unmolested at the curb since the Beatles broke up. He threw open the trunk and placed the suitcase in among Wellington boots, a plaid blanket, several worn leashes, a leaning pile of books, and a box of dog treats.

"Come on then," he said as he opened the wrong door for Sorrel. Of course, she reminded herself, it wasn't the wrong door, just the English one. The inside smelled of gorse and heather, wild rosemary and leather, and Sorrel missed her gardens so far away.

The ridiculous car started up with a growl that made the Nursery truck sound like a kitten. And from the moment Andrew pulled away, Sorrel knew that he'd gone to the Patience Sparrow School of Driving, international branch.

"Nimble little thing," she said, fumbling for her seat belt.

"Indeed, she's a 1971, Austin motor, in fine nick, really."

"Really," Sorrel said. There was rust flaking on her door, and the wing mirror was held on with silver duct tape. With every gear change the car shuddered and thumped. She didn't think even Patience would take a roundabout at the speed with which Andrew whizzed past a taxi.

"So, you'll stay in Gray and Stella's house in Chelsea while you settle and then on Thursday we'll drive to the pile."

"The pile?" Sorrel asked.

"Kirkwood Hall," Andrew said. "It'll either become your favorite place in all England or a muddy nightmare, depending on your mood and the weather."

"That's encouraging."

"Sorry," Andrew said (without an ounce of sorry), looking at Sorrel. The car swerved alarmingly. "Stella and Gray are the kindest people I know. You will be happy with them; they will insist on that."

"Eyes on the road, Andrew," said Sorrel and was instantly homesick.

THE HOUSE IN Chelsea where Sorrel would spend the next days was smaller than her own Ivy House, which sat tall and white above the harbor. But like the Sparrow Sisters' home, this two-hundred-year-old brick cottage was both a historic spot and a real haven. Sorrel could see that from the yellowing children's collages framed along the hall, the piles of cricket bats and field-hockey sticks that leaned against the mud room wall, the drift of books and lists and keys that filled the wooden bowl

by the door. A deflated rugby ball, well-handled brown leather flecked with mud, sat at the foot of the stairs. Echoes of family life were as clear as in Ivy House. But here, instead of the salty breezes that drifted in from the Atlantic in Granite Point, the air was heavy with the lush green scent of ancient churchyards and mossy cobbled lanes. Here, in a chic little village at the heart of London, the Kirkwood family had lived for generations at the very banks of the Thames. Wandering through the rooms of the house on Cheyne Row while Andrew built up the fire and set the kettle, Sorrel understood the kind of comfort this house held too. Later, she'd discover all four bedrooms, a low-ceilinged kitchen dominated by a red Aga, three "reception rooms," as they were called, and a surprisingly large back garden. It was a charming and cozy home in the middle of a sophisticated city. Sorrel knew Fiona Hathaway, of course, her crisp accent, the happy jumble of children and adults that filled the rectory after services, but she now saw exactly how she'd spent her early years in London. It didn't surprise Sorrel that Fiona came from such a solid unit; she had built just that kind of nest in Granite Point.

Andrew took a call from his sister, and Sorrel could hear his grumbly rumble reassuring her that Sorrel had survived the flight and the drive. This left Sorrel to poke around, running her fingers along the old swayback sofa, warming her hands before the tiny fireplace and scouting the shelves and shelves of books in the study. Photos crowded nearly every flat surface. Some were of the Hathaway "colonists" and

their lives in America: the church John oversaw, sailboats, Fiona's garden. Others ranged from Graham and Fiona as children—all white, smocked dresses, Peter Pan collars, and short pants—to elegant, festive pictures of people in wide-brimmed hats and morning coats. It all felt terribly, terribly formal, upper-crusty, and English. Sorrel thought of Nettie and how much she would love this world.

Andrew brought the tea in on a tray and sat opposite Sorrel as he poured.

"I forgot to thank you for the pickup," Sorrel said. "Do you need to head back to work, now?"

"Ha," Andrew laughed, although to Sorrel it sounded more like "Har." He put his fingers to his neck. "I'm on sabbatical," he said.

"You're a teacher," Sorrel said.

"Oh, no, I'm a priest," Andrew said and fiddled with the teapot.

"Ah," said Sorrel with nothing left to add.

"Anglican," said Andrew. "Church of England, sort of like your Episcopalians."

"That's a relief," said Sorrel. "I mean it's good, nice, helpful."

Sorrel didn't know whether it was a relief that Andrew *wasn't* a Catholic priest or that he *was* a minister, like Fiona Hathaway's husband at home. A civilian is how she thought of it. There was no relief in how silly she sounded.

"Well, I try to be. Helpful, that is," Andrew said.

"Do you have your own church?" Sorrel asked.

"Not exactly. I was a rector at Christ Church, just round the corner until"—Andrew stopped—"until recently." He offered the plate of cookies to Sorrel. "Biscuit?"

She took one and had to admit after a bite that she might have to take some back to Claire Redmond at Baker's Way Bakers.

"Christ Church is a special place," Andrew continued. "I wasn't giving it my best of late."

"Oh, I see," said Sorrel, who didn't see anything at all.

She'd talked with Fiona about her brother Graham and what to expect (which would turn out to be understated in the extreme), but Andrew was something else. She knew absolutely nothing about this guy. If Patience were here, she'd sniff around and come up with an answer to the hint of hurt that set his jaw so tight. She might even have sensed the reason for his sabbatical. Sorrel suspected his story wasn't entirely as he told it. Still, one thing she knew right away, Andrew was oddly dashing in his slightly frayed way. That wasn't something she associated with a local reverend. Sure, John Hathaway was attractive in that kind of wind-burned "I'm wearing a fleece under this cassock" and "man the sails" kind of way, but he wasn't an Englishman with hair black as night and a small, half-moon scar through his right eyebrow.

Sorrel tried to imagine this Andrew Warburton in his priestly garb and couldn't. She tried to hear his voice in her head calling together a chapel full of hopeful congregants, but all she could hear was that low voice talking about Morris

Minors and their tidy engines. This reverend with his pilled sweater and striped socks seemed a bit more . . . irreverent.

"It's very kind of you to take me on," Sorrel said.

"I owe Gray and Stella a great deal. It's a small thing to collect you." Andrew took the last biscuit. "Besides, Stella would have my head if you disappeared between here and there."

Andrew gathered the tea things before Sorrel even finished her cup.

"Now, if I were you, I'd gallop straight up those stairs and have a kip. I've got some errands, and Gray will roll up for supper so you'll want to be rested for that. He's very enthusiastic about you." Andrew put an emphasis on the *he's* that made Sorrel blink. He stood and took the tray into the kitchen without another word.

Sorrel might have found him rudely abrupt, but she could barely contain her pleasure at the thought of a nap, all niceties aside. Patience had given her some remedies for jet lag, but compared to a bed draped in fern-sprigged eiderdowns piled high with pillows, the little bottles of leopard's bane and club moss were just pretty clutter. On the other hand, the bottle labeled HEART'S EASE was a mystery. Perhaps it was for heartburn, from which Sorrel suffered each time she ate green pepper. No matter, all she needed now was that nap.

Someone, it must have been Andrew, had placed her suitcase on the bench at the foot of the bed. Sorrel threw her traveling clothes on top and shook out her hair. A flannel dressing gown hung from one of the four posts and as soon as Sorrel

wrapped herself up, she found she absolutely could not keep her eyes open. The linens smelled of lemon and old-fashioned starch but Sorrel wouldn't notice that until hours later when she woke.

The sun was low when Sorrel startled back to life. She was shocked to see that it was after five. It had been a dreamless sleep and now she wasn't sure if the muffled peace that enveloped her came from all the duvets and down or was just the doze that clung to her as she moved slowly into the small yellow and white bathroom. The showerhead drip-dropped like a particularly irritating rain and the waffled shower curtain barely reached the lip of the tub. Sorrel thumped the pipes and shifted around trying to get wet enough to wash her hair. She'd always thought it was the French who had bad plumbing. Now, the heated towel rack, that was a bit of all right.

The sound of voices, cello music, and a delicious smell drifted up the stairs as Sorrel dressed. Suddenly she was sure she'd never been hungrier in her life. She followed her nose down the hall to the kitchen where Andrew leaned against the big Aga and a second tall man stood at the counter opening a bottle of wine.

"Sorrel!" Graham Kirkwood sang out. "Sorrel the sorceress, the siren, the Sparrow Sister herself!" He held out his arms, still holding the corkscrew. "Come, my dear, come in for a proper hello." And a puncture wound.

If this was how the titled classes behaved, Sorrel couldn't imagine how the English ever got a reputation for chilly reserve. Then again, there was Andrew. She moved toward

Graham and was captured in an embrace redolent of wood smoke and damp dog, an altogether pleasant feeling. Sorrel laughed into Graham's woolly vest.

"I am grateful for your invitation," she said, cursing the stiffness she heard in her own voice.

"Welcome to England!" Graham said and poured Sorrel a glass of the clearest ruby-red wine she'd ever seen. "Here's to muddy boots, well-oiled loppers, and dirty gardening gloves!"

Do all his sentences end in exclamation points? thought Sorrel.

Graham poured a glass of wine for Andrew and one for himself. "Andrew has made shepherd's pie for us, and it is a thing, let me tell you," he said and sat at the kitchen table, a long, scarred, well-loved cherry slab covered with mail, magazines, and more books. At one end there was a platter of cheese and grapes and chunks of brown bread studded with walnuts.

"Sit," Andrew said. "Supper will be ready soon."

"Just in time for Philippa," said Graham and pulled out a chair for Sorrel.

"Philippa?" asked Sorrel at the very moment the front door slammed and a cheery voice called out.

"Dad?"

"Kitchen, Petal," Graham said with a grin.

In walked what could only be called a creation. She was small, easily a foot shorter than the men and a good three inches under Sorrel. Her brown hair was cut in a bob with a heavy fringe that just tipped her eyebrows. Her tights were maroon,

her Doc Marten boots black velvet, and her dress, really just a sweater that stretched to her knees, was argyle. She looked as if she'd mugged a grandpa on her way to the house.

"This changeling, this spritely bit of fairy dust, is our daughter, Philippa," Graham said.

"Poppy, Father," she said and kissed her father's cheek in greeting.

"The oldest and most interesting Kirkwood sprog," Poppy said and held out her hand. Her smile was every bit as charming as her father's, and it became apparent to Sorrel that this young woman was not silly at all.

"And you are Sorrel Sparrow."

"I am," said Sorrel. "Hello, Poppy."

"See, Dad, Sorrel got my new name right in one." She poured herself a glass of wine.

"Petunia, Pippa, Peanut." Graham laughed. "You are my daughter and I shall call you as I like. Sorrel, you'll miss the other Kirkwood offspring this trip. Rupert and Sophia are off somewhere making trouble, I'm sure."

Graham pronounced Sophia "Soph-eye-a" which made the name sound exotic.

Poppy laughed and served herself some cheese. "Sophia is sequestered at school in Sussex, and Rupes couldn't make trouble if you gave him a recipe. Speaking of, Uncle Andrew, is that your shepherd's pie?"

Andrew opened the Aga. "It is and nearly ready, I think." He slid a bright blue and yellow casserole dish out of the oven

and onto the counter. He slipped a table knife into the center of the dish and then touched the knife to his lips. "Not quite," he said and put it back in the oven.

Nettie did the very same thing when she cooked lasagna, checking her nourishment with the tenderest part of herself. A wave of homesickness rose, and Sorrel took a too-big sip of her wine.

"Sorrel, you are going to love London," Poppy said.

"And Kirkwood Hall," Graham said.

"Yes, but London to start," Poppy said and pulled an overstuffed notebook out of her bag. "I've made some suggestions for you," she said, opening the notebook and pressing it as flat as possible. Lists and stickies and bits of paper spilled onto the table.

"First, a little tourism," she said. "I'll give you tomorrow to have a wander and then on Wednesday you'll hit the Physic Garden and the Globe with Andrew, yeah?"

"Other way round, I think," Andrew said. "Globe, then garden."

"And me stuck behind a table listening to another lecture," Poppy said.

"Poor Poppet," Graham said. "She's back at uni and none too happy, I can tell you."

"Dad, I am happy. Happy that it's my last year," Poppy said.

Poppy Kirkwood hardly seemed like the college students Sorrel saw around town back home. She was confident and charming in a thoroughly engaging way, for one, and she

seemed completely at home chatting away as if her best friends surrounded her.

"Where do you go?" Sorrel asked.

"University College London," Poppy said. "Close enough to come home for Uncle Andrew's dinners, not quite far enough that Mum can't show up at the dorm every now and then unannounced."

"Listen, you," Graham said, "if Mum didn't check in here and there, you might disappear again." He looked at Sorrel. "Our Poppy took quite a hegira before she settled down with art history," he said. "She spent far too long traveling before we managed to bring her home, and only then because her mother stopped writing checks."

"I had an extended gap year—two years," Poppy said. "'Hegira' implies I was fleeing from danger, Dad." Poppy laughed.

"Well, perhaps you were, my lamb. You know we never did like that boy. What was his name? Harcourt, Hugo, Horace?"

"Nice try. It was Hector, and he broke my heart."

"You recovered," Andrew harrumphed as Poppy patted his shoulder.

"Who looks at a baby and names it Hector, I ask you?" Graham hooted.

"The same sort who looks at an infant daughter and names her Philippa," Poppy said.

"Ah, but your name honors your grandfather, the marvelous man who reared the wondrous Stella Warburton Kirkwood, your mum."

Sorrel began to feel at home in this kitchen with the chat and laughter, the teasing and poking. Andrew seemed softer somehow in the warmth. She looked at the window over the sink and saw them all reflected there: a little company of friends and family. This kind of ease was not what she had expected when she left her sisters behind. Sorrel took a bite of the shepherd's pie and actually moaned as the buttery mashed potatoes and savory lamb melted on her tongue. Her three hosts turned as one to look at her.

"I'm so sorry," Sorrel said with her hand over her mouth. "It's just that I've never tasted anything like this. My sister Nettie does most of the cooking at home. She's extremely accomplished but"—she paused and licked her lips—"the richness!"

Andrew bowed his head in thanks. "I've been instructed to feed you up before you fly away." He looked at Sorrel in a way that made her wonder if Andrew Warburton hadn't flown away himself once upon a time.

When the dishes were cleared and the wine finished, Poppy took Sorrel out for a walk. Not a word had been said about Sorrel's brief; no further garden talk, no tapestry thoughts. She wondered when she'd learn the full extent of her work. In the moment she didn't particularly care; as unfamiliar as England might be, Sorrel felt a pleasing sense of calm. The night was studded with clouds against the dark, and Sorrel was surprised to find that there were stars to be seen in the London sky. Great chestnut trees swept over the embankment and were just now budding out, some a deep pink, others white.

Before them the Albert Bridge rose up over the Thames like a great pastel roller coaster dotted with bright round lights. As they climbed onto the pedestrian path, Sorrel stopped to read the warning posted on one of the girders. ALL TROOPS MUST BREAK STEP WHEN MARCHING OVER THIS BRIDGE. She looked at Poppy.

"It's like Joshua and Jericho," she said. "The vibrations from so many feet marching as one could loosen the bolts and bring the bridge down."

"Seriously?" Sorrel asked, taking a step back.

"Oh, who knows?" Poppy laughed. "That's what my father always told me."

Houseboats bobbed along the Embankment, and seagulls wheeled overhead, miles from the ocean. Sorrel followed their flight with longing, their cries a pale echo of the ones she heard every day back home.

"Would you like company tomorrow or do you want the time on your own?" Poppy asked.

"Don't you have class?" Sorrel asked.

"I do. Not that I wouldn't skive off at your request."

Sorrel shook her head.

"Right, on your own it is. You've no plan, which is just how one should discover a new city. I suggest you get on the number 11, 19, or 52 bus and see what you see."

Sorrel had already forgotten the bus numbers as she nodded somewhat witlessly at Poppy's rapid-fire instructions.

Halfway across the bridge they stopped to look out over

the river. The lights strung like Christmas bulbs sent bobbing glowworms onto the ripples. The Thames tide is so extreme that at certain times boats and moorings sit stranded in the mud, and tendrils of moss and duckweed flow down the Embankment walls like ivy. But tonight the water slapped at the boats, setting their brightwork jingling.

"Uncle Andrew is one of Dad's closest friends, despite the age gap," Poppy said. "He's been with us in Wiltshire for a bit, you know, finding his way."

Sorrel chuckled and thought that Andrew Warburton seemed quite sure of his way, even if he drove there with little regard for the Highway Code.

Poppy tapped Sorrel's arm.

"He's pretty great, you know, Uncle Andrew, just a bit on the dour side of late. We think he needs the kind of care that London can't give him right now. You'll see when you get to the country. The house has a way of clarifying things just when one needs direction."

Sorrel wondered if Poppy could tell that she was in need of a map herself. She acknowledged the gentle and genuine care Andrew gave this family and resolved to get to know that particular Andrew.

The two women stood on the bridge as heavy clouds rolled in, the sky so low Sorrel felt the rain pressing down before it fell. And then it did, with a rumble of thunder.

"Oh dear, more talk will have to wait," Poppy said. "Let's make a dash. We can dodge the worst of it."

Sorrel didn't think she could move fast enough to keep up with Poppy, whose boots slapped through the puddles ahead of her, throwing spatter up her tights. If it weren't for the prospect of the bed, oh the bed, she might have ducked under a tree to wait it out.

Graham was sitting before the fire when they came in. Poppy shook the rain out of her hair, and Sorrel left her shoes in the hall. They plopped down in the sitting room and Sorrel stretched her toes closer to the grate.

"Did Poppet tell you all our secrets?" Graham asked.

"Just a crash course in public transport," Sorrel said and looked around for Andrew.

"Gone, my dear," Graham said. "Our Andrew must be exhausted by his charm offensive."

Sorrel thought charm was a bit of an overstatement.

Poppy stood and hugged her father and then Sorrel.

"It's time for me to go to bed. I've got an eight o'clock seminar."

Graham and Sorrel sat for a minute or two watching the fire die.

"Andrew is a complicated fellow, with his own story to tell," Graham said. "As are we all, really."

"I guess," Sorrel said. "Although I'd like to think that the important stuff is pretty simple. Honor, love, kindness."

"Yes, let's keep that thought," Graham said. "But I suspect you too are complicated, remade by what happened to your little world." Graham stood and offered his hand.

Sorrel opened her mouth to say something, anything to send the conversation away from a topic she hadn't thought of once in these happy hours in London, but Graham kept on as he pulled her to her feet.

"I am so very glad that you agreed to come and grow with this family. It is important that, as we remake ourselves, we also give the world around us a chance to follow along. Kirkwood Hall has a varied history; some bits are worth celebrating, others not. It's the reason we work so hard to make it a place of comfort and joy today. I think the house deserves your magic, Sorrel, and you deserve hers."

CHAPTER 3

Narcissus

In all his approachable glory, his jolly, game attitude, Graham Kirkwood still kept secrets. That evening with Sorrel and his family gathered by the fire, he only hinted at the mystery of the garden or Stella's most recent failed attempt at restoration or her troubling illness. He said not a word about the tapestries hung in a climate-controlled room on the third floor of Kirkwood Hall. He didn't much like thinking about them beyond ensuring that they were kept safe in all their priceless, pristine, dreadful beauty. It wasn't so much that they were fragile, which they were; it was that the subject matter had always unsettled the Kirkwoods, particularly the tenderhearted Graham. Out of sight had helped to keep them out of mind over the years, and there hadn't been one of those years that Graham hadn't

wished they'd never been found. But with the decision to bring Sorrel over, it was essential that she have all advantage on her side, including access to the wretched tapestries. So, yes, he had mentioned them in his letter to the Sparrow Sister, although he had been discreet on the visual punch they always gave him.

Stella had never been one to sidestep a difficult situation so it was she who had come to know the tapestries best. When she and Graham had been married some years with Poppy a babe in arms, he told her of the Hunt of the Innocent, as the series was named. She took it upon herself to come to grips with both the story and the Kirkwood family's connection to it, and there was nowhere better to start than the grand Kirkwood library. There she began to see the outlines of a history that, for good and ill, shaped her family.

It was hard to believe that the warm and caring Lord Kirkwood could have ever sprung from the warring family who built the estate. It was nearly impossible to reconcile the love-filled house of today with the cold place it had once been. But that was exactly how Kirkwood Hall was born: out of a greed that led men of the same name to tear through a small but treasure-laden monastery, grabbing up everything of value and casting aside the monks and their faith like ninepins. It was a horrible time when the church and the state played a hateful, bloody tug of war over the loyalty of the people and the spoils of their conflict, and the winners were whoever had the monarch's ear.

Unlike the present Kirkwood scion, the head of the manor

in those times was less interested in the beauty of his estate and more in the riches and standing it could bring him now that those pesky priests were out of the way. A prodigy house is what Kirkwood Hall would become, built and maintained in the event that the monarch might visit on his perambulations through his kingdom. And he did, for King Henry was quite fond of the area with its rolling hills and fields of green. So Lord Kirkwood, as he became upon being given the title and even more land, kept the estate in fine shape, stocked with deer for hunting, fine swans on the lake beyond the chapel, and geese, ducks, and chickens for the table. He raised his sons to take the same kind of care. As unpleasant and frankly violent as the birth of Kirkwood Hall was, it endured, and while civil wars swirled around it, there was a sense of relative calm that cloaked the estate. Some attribute the prosperity and peace to the march of Lord Kirkwoods who, to a man, were a driven lot. Certainly there were no recorded uprisings of disgruntled peasants, servants, or farmers, no angry landowner from a neighboring estate who felt he might be better suited to the Kirkwood manor, and finally, no shortage of sons to keep the fairy tale of a beneficent lord and his happy dynasty going. Inside the family and its home there were, over the years, plenty of disagreeable Kirkwoods who imposed their will and their way. And outside, there were plenty of people who held their tongues.

Stella compiled an extensive historical library of her own as her family grew to include a son and another daughter. She

spent less and less time in London, finding the air in Wiltshire clean, and the long walks she took across the estate, when her neck cramped from close reading, invigorating. Eventually, she took over a small room on the third floor near the tapestries and filled it with proper shelves and filing cabinets to store her research. She was pleased with her work, if not always with the characters and events she uncovered.

It happened that every generation or so a particularly hateful Kirkwood took the reins. This was what defined Thomas, who was Lord Kirkwood in the years that Queen Anne, last of the Stuarts, held the throne. His management of the estate was without peer, as was his temper, a fact that made it into history by way of village records that detailed his harsh treatment of anyone who dared to disobey him. He was an unpredictable bully, and his family and attendants lived in a state of almost unbearable tension. When Thomas, Lord Kirkwood exploded, no one was safe, and those explosions could be triggered as easily by an overcooked roast as by a run of fly strike in the sheepfold. His wife, Elizabeth, an accomplished woman of great beauty, kept a diary; there are references to how exacting her records were on the running of the household and gardens, any travels undertaken, the births of her children, and every single painting of her showed her holding her book close. The diary itself was nowhere to be found amongst the village or estate papers even though Stella dug away and pestered the town clerks about this frustrating gap in their otherwise impressive records. It might have proved most helpful to Sorrel

and Stella, for it was Elizabeth, Lady Kirkwood who planted the first walled garden at Kirkwood.

If the documented history of the Kirkwood family was easily found in the dusty books and dustier local records of the area, the true stories needed to be teased out of those archives without the aid of Elizabeth's book. And this is where Stella's curiosity blossomed and took on the energy of a quest. This too would become Sorrel's unexpected mission, to learn the secrets of the Kirkwood legacy of beauty and beasts. It would become the way to save the garden, and the family.

On her first morning in London Sorrel rose with the sun as she often did back home in Granite Point, although it took some upward swimming to leave the ocean of bedcovers. Birdsong surprised her in this city of unexpected comfort, but she still missed her sisters. Nettie would be poking around in the bean patch by now, picking the edible flowers, tying up the grape vines of the tiny, only a bit illegal, vineyard hidden beyond the orchard. Patience would be back at Baker's Way Bakers for another muffin and a cup of coffee before she pulled mugwort for her lucid dreaming sachets. Sorrel could almost smell the sweet peas Nettie promised to tend for Sorrel, the juniper berries, sharp and piney, that Patience used in her digestive tinctures. For a moment she thought she might not be able to stay away from her sisters and their nursery after all. She questioned why she had ever thought to leave in springtime. But other gardens were waiting, so Sorrel dressed for the unpredictable weather

and went downstairs. It was still quiet in the early hours. She made toast and tea and looked through the A to Z guide Poppy had left on the table with a note.

"I assume you are phoneless at the mo' so this little book will be your best companion. Look up the street you need in the back pages and you'll find it on the map by the coordinates: very old school but utterly reliable. Use the Oyster card on all buses and tubes."

Sorrel was relieved, for she'd wondered whether Henry's tattered green guide would be of much use twenty years on, and now she had another worn but trusty handbook. Slipping it into her bag, Sorrel set off on foot. She crisscrossed Chelsea and Knightsbridge, walked through Kensington into the park and gardens that rolled gently away from the palace. The warm red brick and the upright yew hedges worked their way into her mind, and Sorrel began to think about the Wiltshire garden ahead. Walls, yes, she thought, but also boxwood, pea gravel paths, a mossy mound with a sundial, and a chamomile lawn. A roughly drawn plan began to form in her mind.

Just as Patience read the people in Granite Point, searching for the troubled bits in their bodies or hearts, and Nettie collected the harvest and composed meals that sustained the very same parts, Sorrel wove her plants and flowers into a tapestry of her own, first in her imagination, then on paper using watercolors and ink to bring a garden to life. Then, when everything was ready, each bulb accounted for, each tender sapling and fragile seedling, Sorrel poured that knowledge, and her

body and heart, into the fertile soil. What sprang forth was as precious to all the Sisters as any child. And here, so far from home, Sorrel began to feel the rising of her gift again. It felt right and so very good after a time of fruitless anguish.

Sorrel approached the Long Water, the river that flows through Kensington Gardens to become the Serpentine in Hyde Park, and paused. She was suddenly surrounded by children and looked over their bobbing heads to see a statue of Peter Pan. Sorrel too was drawn to the boy who never grew up. She thought of Matty Short, whose death had ignited her town, of Patience and Henry, who found each other under fire. They mourned him still, the little boy who struggled so in his own childhood and now would never grow beyond it.

Sorrel bought an utterly tasteless and strangely satisfying ice cream from the Mr. Whippy truck near the Albert Memorial and sat on a bench with the pigeons and the old ladies who fed them. It could easily take months to get a handle on the crooked streets and swaths of green flowered parks in London, months more before a visitor could afford to stop staring at her A to Z map. But she didn't have months or even days, so, recalling Poppy's advice, she got on the 11 bus, which took her practically to the front door of the house on Cheyne Row.

It hardly seemed possible that the day was nearly gone. There had been no rain; in fact, the sun had stayed warm and high all day. Now, though, there was a chill coming off the Thames, and the light had gone gold and low. The house was empty and still, but the kettle sat on the Aga, and Sorrel found

that there was nothing she wanted more than a cup of tea. *I've gone native already,* she thought. Waiting for it to boil, she looked in the cupboards for the biscuits Andrew had fed her. Jaffa Cakes, they were called, an odd name but a decidedly delicious cookie covered in chocolate, filled with bittersweet orange marmalade.

Sorrel sat at the kitchen table with her laptop and returned to her research on Kirkwood Hall, her tea steaming beside her, her third Jaffa Cake nothing but crumbs on a chalky gray Wedgwood plate at her elbow. There the house was, with its very own page on the National Trust site. Spreading across a park-like setting, Kirkwood Hall seemed part castle and part farm, which, she supposed, was how it had all begun. It was open to the public at certain times of the year, the gardens as well, and Sorrel realized that when she was finished, her as-yet-to-be creation would be a part of history too. This was pleasing to Sorrel; she was happy that the Sparrow name would live on in the English countryside even though the Sparrow Sisters were the last of their line in America. She pulled her plate closer and used her thumb to gather the crumbs.

"I cannot bear those plates," Poppy said as she threw her bag on the table. She shook two biscuits out of the box and ate them together, like a sandwich. "The texture, scratchy and dusty," she shivered. "Bah, makes my teeth itch." She swiped at the chocolate on her lip. "How was your wander, Sorrel?"

"So wonderful," Sorrel answered. "This city is like a nest-

ing doll, one unexpected treasure inside another. I wish I had more time."

"Perhaps you'll come back, or at least whiz in while you're working on the gardens in the country. Me, I can't stay too long out there or I go a little mad. Mum almost never comes into town anymore unless it's for Andrew or the season."

"The season?" Sorrel asked.

"We still have a 'season,'" Poppy drawled. "You know, parties, dinners, the occasional orgy, just kidding. Most of my set has been raised not by wolves, but by overbred show dogs." She laughed. "While the fathers mint money in the City, the mothers gather in the conservatory to embroider themselves a better life. Then everybody gets drunk on Dubonnet and gin."

"Not really, not this family," Sorrel said. "I mean you certainly don't seem like a cartoon out of *Punch*."

"*Punch*! Excellent, Sorrel," Poppy said. "No, we are the Kirkwoods, bastions of sensibility and honor, charming eccentricity and also, goats! You'll see." Poppy picked up her tea and another biscuit. "Sadly, the oxymoron of the tragic hero in classic Greek literature calls. I'll be in the library if you need me."

Sorrel showered and repacked her suitcase for the trip to Wiltshire, leaving out only what she'd need for her visits the next day. As she did so, she found herself wondering if Andrew would be back for dinner that night and if so, what he would cook. Sorrel caught herself. Andrew had a life, and a fine one at that. Surely he had better things to do, better people to be with than this motley bunch; a slightly shell-shocked garden

lady from New England, a clever college girl, and a bear of a lord whose warmth was enough to melt the ice in everyone's gin and tonics. *Wait,* she thought, *we're a perfectly pleasant crew on a spring evening. Why wouldn't Andrew want to join in? Then again, if he brought the grumpy along with the groceries, was it worth it?* Perhaps his story would unfold in time. She wished Nettie and Patience could see her in this cozy house, try the shepherd's pie and the Jaffa Cakes. She could just hear Nettie cooing over Andrew's forlorn edge and Patience cracking up at Poppy's snark.

As it turned out, Andrew came for dinner and with it, too. And, yes, he came trailing grump. Sorrel was intrigued by the hints her hosts dropped about Andrew, and truth be told, by the sadness that hid in those dark eyes. But she knew from her own experience that secrets and stories only revealed themselves when you weren't looking for them.

It was unclear to Sorrel what Graham did all day long but whatever it was, he arrived just before Andrew, full of his customary good cheer. What he did, in fact, was sit in the House of Lords and irritate all the other peers who wished that the modern age had never arrived. Graham Kirkwood was the burr beneath the saddle of the English aristocracy, a role he relished. While it was true he was clever with the Kirkwood fortune and enjoyed the privilege it afforded his family, he was also generous. He and Stella were patrons of so many charities and supported so many causes the tabloids called them Lord and Lady Give-a-lot. Graham's true passion lay in the land,

and not just his own: he charmed additional monies out of his colleagues for important preservation work.

If they were regulars in the glossy pages of *Tatler,* it was only because the flash of a camera came along with the writing of a check.

Poppy burst forth from the library as soon as she heard her father's voice. Sorrel loved how affectionate they were with each other, how freely they laughed and teased. She couldn't remember her father, Thaddeus, as ever having been so open or easy. Poppy rummaged around for silverware and glasses and tossed pressed-smooth damask napkins in a pile on the kitchen table. Sorrel noticed that she set out four of each and felt an unreasonable delight. Soon after, when Andrew came through to the kitchen with a canvas bag in each hand, Sorrel hastened to help him. Carrots, celery, a sturdy green and white leek as long as a cutlass, a net bag of potatoes, a tangled bunch of herbs, and a knobby stalk of brussels sprouts tumbled out onto the table. Andrew pulled a chicken wrapped in butcher paper, four perfect pears, a block of French butter, and a pint of cream out of the other bag. Sorrel whistled.

"I so hoped you'd be back to cook," she said.

"And why not?" Andrew asked. "I've nothing to eat in my flat, and certainly no company."

"Gee, I feel so special," Sorrel said.

"Listen," Andrew started and then stopped. "Someone get the wine for us, yeah?"

Poppy and her father exchanged a look that Sorrel knew

very well. When Patience was at her most prickly, everyone tiptoed, and now Sorrel was going snip for snip with Andrew. Unreasonably, her eyes burned and her lip threatened to tremble.

Graham and Poppy began shuffling papers and books around to make room for dinner, getting the wineglasses out of the cupboard. It was a scrum of affection and purpose and served to move everyone away from further tetchiness. There was a flurry of activity; Sorrel pulled the cutting board over and began chopping while Andrew made a great show of checking the Aga, opening and closing the heavy iron doors with much clanking and slamming. He peeled the pears and filled a heavy Dutch oven with red wine, anise, and cinnamon sticks and set it simmering with the pears. Poppy pulled out the roasting tin, and Graham dug around in a glass-fronted drinks fridge for some wine.

"Let's hear," Graham said. "Tell us all about your day, Sorrel."

Sorrel told her wandering story again and got approving nods from Graham.

"Buses!" he said and clapped his hands. "Nothing better to give you the lay of the land. And tomorrow you shall have your own personal guide."

Andrew was peeling potatoes over the sink but even with his back turned Sorrel could see the stiffening in his shoulders.

"I hope you didn't have other plans, Andrew," she said.

"Hardly," Andrew mumbled without looking up.

Poppy set the chicken on top of a bed of vegetables in the

roasting tin. She rubbed butter and salt and pepper over the skin and threw thyme all around it, slid it into the hottest Aga oven chamber, and set a timer. Then she filled a pot with water for the potatoes.

"Uncle Andrew," Poppy said, "what does the day look like for you two?"

"Well, while I still don't quite know how I got sucked into this adventure, we will begin at the Globe," Andrew said. "We've an appointment with the curator who's opened the archive to us. Sorrel can look at some of the contemporaneous materials that might give her clues to the gardens in the tapestries so she can suss out her own ideas." He tipped the potatoes into the pot, wiped his hands on the towel tucked into his belt and came to sit at the table with everyone else. "Then to the Physic Garden so she can see some of the oldest botanical specimens."

"A reluctant tour guide, but a good one, I promise," Poppy said.

"Onward," Graham said and raised his glass. "To our intrepid explorer!"

"To Sorrel," everyone said while the woman herself hardly knew where to look or what to say.

The dinner was, if possible, lovelier than the night before. Andrew portioned out the roast chicken, mashed potatoes, and vegetables into wide, shallow bowls so that the rich sauces pooled invitingly all around. Graham poured more wine, and Poppy and Sorrel pulled the wishbone, a tradition the Kirkwoods found hugely endearing

"Tell us your wish, Sorrel," Poppy said.

"Only that I can fulfill your expectations and, somehow, repay you for your kindness."

"Sweet Sorrel," Graham said and patted her hand, "We really do feel that you've been delivered to our doorstep like a much-anticipated parcel. We can't wait to see what's inside that magical gift of yours!"

THE NEXT MORNING Andrew arrived to find Sorrel, wrapped up like the present Graham had described, sitting on the low brick wall that marched around the house on Cheyne Row. The weather had turned sharp, so she'd borrowed Stella's loden coat and was folded into one of her cashmere shawls. They set off together in Andrew's ridiculous little car with a grumble and a backfire.

Andrew was nearly silent, only briefly pointing out the occasional landmark or swearing under his breath at his fellow—far more polite—motorists. Poor Sorrel might have coaxed him out of what was a familiarly unpleasant mood if she hadn't been so focused on willing the car to stay on the road.

"Almost there now," Andrew said as they took some air over Blackfriars Bridge. "Tate Modern," he waved at a giant old power station. "Nice views of St. Paul's."

"No doubt," Sorrel said with her eyes closed.

SHAKESPEARE'S GLOBE WITH its plaster and timber façade and its thatched roof like a heavy halo, was as captivating in the twenty-

first century as it must have been in the sixteenth. Visitors milled around the pit and the galleries just as they had in Shakespeare's time. Andrew let Sorrel gape a bit (like the penny groundlings before her) before leading her toward the museum beneath the stage.

"There are candlelit concerts indoors in the off season," Andrew said. He paused for a moment and looked at Sorrel. "You would like them." He moved off before she could comment.

Sorrel followed Andrew, who seemed thoroughly confident as he wove his way down the stairs, around the giant tree that sprang from the center of the below-ground space, and through a door marked STAFF. He held the door for her and said, "The Kirkwood Foundation is a major donor. The curator is an old friend of the family, and she's been very generous with her time."

"I'll be sure to thank her," Sorrel huffed.

Freya Millen and Andrew greeted each other with handshakes and murmured hellos. *Seems he's not the only grump in town,* Sorrel thought.

After they were settled into a corner of the small meeting room next to Freya's office, she brought them three archive boxes and two pairs of white cotton gloves.

"I don't need to tell you how precious these things are," she said, looking straight at Sorrel. "The first one includes an annotated list of all the plants mentioned in the plays. The second is a collection of woodcuts and other art that illustrate some of the scenes and botanicals, and the third is just a load of photos

fans have sent in of their own Shakespeare gardens." Freya left them, calling over her shoulder, "Come find me when you've finished. I can make copies of the documents you want to take away with you."

"Divide and conquer," Andrew said and pulled over the box of photos.

"You don't have to stay with me, Andrew," Sorrel said. "You must have other duties."

"Not today," he said shortly. "This is my duty."

"Great," Sorrel muttered and reached for a box herself.

"Why don't we just make copies of everything?" she asked. Then she opened her box and drew in a breath. Nestled between archival tissue and protected by nearly transparent paper were woodcuts and engravings of such detail and delicacy that Sorrel was afraid they'd lift right off the page. With a glance she could see and name many of the plants: lavender, of course, primula, bay laurel, viola, yew, box, holly, and roses. She had to grip her gloved hands together to keep herself from running her fingers over the papers.

Andrew sifted through the photos: lush, sprawling gardens of herbs and flowers, others dotted with crabapple trees, woodbine, and hawthorn—not that he could name anything. Sorrel leaned over and picked up several photos. Her long, loose braid fell over her shoulder and brushed against Andrew's hand. He shivered and pushed it away. For a moment he thought that the gardens in the pictures had come to life as Sorrel's scent drifted over him. She smelled of summer and sea with a whisper of

something he couldn't name, familiar and strange at once. He didn't know that Patience Sparrow had concocted special cologne for Sorrel's trip. It was made of privet blossom, new green grass, lime, and the smallest hint of patchouli and had been the last thing she packed.

"We can't have them thinking you're some kind of new age, new world dippy hipster," Patience had warned as she used a tiny pipette to add not even a full droplet of strong patchouli oil to the mix. The bottle was no bigger than the half ounce of scent it held, and the stopper was attached to a thin glass wand the length of a thumbnail. "Seriously, Sorrel, try to de-witchify us if you can in the old country," Patience had said and nestled the linen-wrapped bottle into a corner of the suitcase. As it turned out, the scent was thoroughly bewitching to Andrew, which was not in anyone's plan.

"Your scent," he said. "I've never smelled anything like it."

"Ah, a gift from my sister Patience," Sorrel said.

"It's enchanting," Andrew said and almost smiled before he turned back to his work.

Sorrel bent her flushed face to the photos in Andrew's box. She spread them out and compared them to the list of plants. She took notes in a cloth-bound blank-page book. Andrew could see that her handwriting was clear and graceful. He marveled at the straight lines of text as they spooled out of her pen. Sorrel used a fountain pen, which charmed him. He gave a quick headshake to clear his thoughts and went back to his pile.

An hour, then two, flew by with little conversation as Sorrel and Andrew catalogued the pieces they wanted to copy and compared the original plants in each Shakespeare play with the ones Sorrel had been using for years. Andrew provided a list of the plants Stella had identified in the tapestries, and Sorrel folded it carefully into her notebook along with the dried and pressed samples from the Sparrow Sisters Nursery. Each was stowed in a glassine sleeve so that Sorrel could see every leaf and blossom without disturbing them. There was no need for labels; Sorrel knew precisely what she held. Beneath the tattered lining of her mother's suitcase Sorrel had slipped tiny envelopes of seeds from the Nursery as well. She'd worried as she went through airport security: What would the scanners make of the wild sweet pea pods, the spiky marigold, and dame's rocket seeds? But no one had noticed, and Sorrel now added those seeds and others into the garden mix taking shape in her head.

At last Freya presented them with their requested copies, and the amateur researchers made their way to Andrew's car.

"Next," Andrew said, and they drove off from one end of London to the other, crossing Southwark Bridge to wind their way along the north side of the Thames. Sorrel watched the Embankment race by and when Andrew took the roundabout at the foot of Westminster, she slapped her hand on the dashboard and urged him to slow down.

"I need to see this," Sorel said. "It may be old hat to you, but it's a once-in-a-lifetime thing for me."

"You're right," Andrew said and tapped his brakes. "I forget you're a tourist, sorry." He slowed the Minor to a pootle and gestured for Sorrel to look out her window. Andrew almost enjoyed the sights; it had been so long since he'd really looked beyond his own troubles.

Andrew pointed out the Elizabeth Tower, Big Ben, the Houses of Parliament, and the towers of Westminster Abbey as he drove three times around. Then he turned off and showed Sorrel Whitehall, Pall Mall, and St. James's Palace and got back on the Embankment at speed to tear by the Jewel Tower.

"That one's as old as the original Kirkwood Hall," he said as the honeyed stone towers flashed past. "You should really spend more time here."

Sorrel agreed, but what was she to do? With just eight weeks to research, select, and plant the early stages of the Kirkwood garden, to cheat the soaking rain that swept through weekly (not to mention look at a bunch of dusty tapestries that might tell her nothing more than she already knew from her own research), Sorrel barely had time to register the face of London or what it would be like to know the stories.

The drive brought them back to Chelsea, and Sorrel watched pubs and cafes come and go with some longing. She was tired, jet lagged-loopy, and hungry, but Andrew pressed on. He took a sharp right, and a surprising vista opened up: the Royal Hospital set like a graceful ship in the center of its gardens. A scattering of people strolled the grounds; old men in

red wool coats festooned with gold braid and medals, tricorne black hats set on their gray heads.

"Chelsea Pensioners," Andrew said. "Retired army, three hundred of them, fed and cared for. They live here almost free until, well, they don't."

"What a wonderful way to spend your last years," Sorrel said. "My sisters and I always joke that we'll have our own little nursing home at Ivy House in the end."

"Ivy House?" Andrew asked.

"It's our place in Granite Point. It's been home to Sparrows for a couple hundred years," Sorrel said. "Not as long as this one, I'm guessing."

"Christopher Wren built it in the late sixteen hundreds," Andrew said. "So, yes, older than your house."

Sorrel wanted to mention that it wasn't older than her town. She was beginning to feel distinctly like the unsophisticated colonist.

Andrew pulled into a side street, reversed out and spun back past the Royal Hospital. Stuttering to a halt, he reversed into a tiny, crooked road called Swan Walk, and Sorrel wondered if it was even meant for cars. It was so narrow she shrank back from her window. Andrew stopped the car and hauled on the brake.

"You can't mean to park here?" Sorrel asked.

"It's fine. I know the residents."

They each had to slide out the narrow gap of their open doors.

"Couldn't you just park on the big road?"

"No spots. I checked." Andrew gave the hood a pat. "Come on then, deep breath in."

Sorrel squeezed along the brick wall and considered being insulted but then Andrew crooked his elbow and she slipped hers through. This courtly gesture might be simply the product of good breeding, but it was lovely on a chilly day to be arm in arm with someone whose coat smelled of cedar and tea, no matter how aloof his disposition. After all, a man who cooked such a thing as shepherd's pie must have a warm heart.

They stopped in front of an iron gate set into another brick wall. It was so overgrown with clouds of purple clematis and climbing roses that they both had to duck to enter. At the little ticket booth Andrew leaned in and spoke quietly to the attendant, who then used a phone that looked as old as the Morris Minor to call their host.

Andrew handed her some pamphlets. "This is one of the oldest apothecary gardens in Europe," he said. "Planted in 1673 by"—he paused and looked at the pamphlet—"the Worshipful Society of Apothecaries, not surprisingly."

"You've read up," Sorrel said and laughed.

"I have," Andrew admitted.

"So you're not such an unwilling tour guide after all."

Andrew looked at her. "Perhaps," he said. "Graham insisted on the homework."

Their guide arrived, a small man in Wellington boots and a waxed jacket, pockets bulging with notebooks, rough twine,

and a pair of secateurs. He handed them both a map and a pages-long list of Latin names.

"I'm terribly late," he said, reminding Sorrel of the White Rabbit. "I'm double-booked for a meeting and I'm afraid I'll have to leave you to it." He shook their hands and scurried away.

"Well, that wasn't the plan," Andrew said. "I thought I'd seen the last of unknowable plants with impenetrable names."

"We're here now, and you've done all that homework," Sorrel said. "Let's just explore." She handed Andrew her papers and pulled out the notebook. "Come on, then," she said with a smile. "Deep breath in."

Andrew tamped down his irritation and tucked the papers under his arm. Nothing to do but just get on with it.

Together they walked the gardens one by one, for there were many distinct areas, each with its own character and purpose. There was the Garden of Medicinal Plants, the Pharmaceutical Garden that was arranged by affliction—here Sorrel took a flurry of pictures for Patience—the Garden of World Medicine, the Garden of Edible and Useful Plants—more pictures here—and on and on. Sorrel consulted her map and list, making notes, ticking off several of the plants in each of the gardens. When they came to the rock garden, Andrew paused.

"That's a curious old thing," he said and looked at his pamphlet. "Made of stones from the Tower of London, oh, and Icelandic lava, it says here."

"We use lots of Icelandic lava in our nursery. Who doesn't?" Sorrel said and swore she heard Andrew chuckle.

"Listen," said Andrew. "It's been a fascinating day, but I could murder a cup of tea. Let's go back to the house. I have the head gardener fellow's email—or perhaps it's more like Morse code given his age. You can consult with him throughout the project whilst you're in Wiltshire."

Sorrel suspected that Andrew had entered what Nettie called "The Fog of Flora." This was a state that often crept over a Nursery visitor when Sorrel lost herself in her plants. So she agreed to put away her work for the time being and head off.

Andrew asked Sorrel to wait while he pulled the car out to make room, which was a relief and maybe even a sign of a thaw in his mood. *Or perhaps the fog is lifting,* Sorrel thought as she climbed in with ease. It was only a matter of minutes before they were home and just minutes more before Andrew had the kettle on and was building up the fire in the library. Sorrel settled into the sofa and shivered. Andrew took a worn blanket and tossed it to her.

"Thank you," she said. "I feel a bit like an invalid aunt."

"You are hardly that." Andrew almost smiled as he walked out.

Sorrel sat for a moment with her mouth open. It had to be acknowledged that Andrew was a pill, but was it his mysterious backstory or Sorrel who brought out the clipped speech, the way his eyes slid away from hers, the moments when he seemed distant and alone even in the midst of his family? Then again, there were moments when they were almost, almost comfortable together.

In the kitchen Andrew stood over the kettle and tried to

figure out just how and why he seemed to be enjoying himself. He thought he'd lost the impulse to look after anyone. In the beginning, with February's stubborn chill a match for his state, he'd hardly looked after himself. Stella came to him in London and stayed for a full week, setting Andrew up in one of the Chelsea bedrooms as if he were a child home sick from school. Only for her brother would Stella spend that much time away from Kirkwood Hall. Andrew knew his story wasn't as awful as some, not even tragic, really, but it was *his,* and that was enough to derail him. Sabbatical, such a gentle word for what was, in Andrew's case, nearly a leave-taking from his faith as well as his job. Because Stella insisted, he had begun to hack away at the thorny sadness and anger as he worked on the chapel grounds and fine-tuned the look and feel of the restored building. She wasn't wrong in her belief that as the architects went about their delicate work, Andrew would benefit from a more physical attempt at his own restoration. Her quiet hope that the chapel could become something more than just a curiosity on the grounds of the estate rested with Andrew as he reexamined his calling along with his heart. And now here he was, making tea for someone, placing biscuits in a crescent on the plate, warming the milk, and shaking out sugar cubes into a bowl. Quotidian pleasures he almost didn't recognize, graciousness he'd forgotten he possessed.

Andrew came in with a tray. The tea and cookies—different ones, Sorrel noticed—and cups rattled precariously as he set it down.

It was over this tea, and many chocolate digestive biscuits (even better than Jaffa Cakes) that Andrew began to understand the Sparrow Sisters. He learned, from words that only Sorrel could say, all about their trials and their town. He did not share, as Graham had pointed out, the story that was only his to tell. Instead, he let Sorrel's tale wash over him, the beautiful and the horrible, and found in her voice a kind of consolation, an understanding that Stella was right. Hard is hard—there is no measuring stick—and sadness too often comes right in as the shadow kin of joy.

Andrew wondered at the fairy-tale nature of Sorrel's little world. He heard the softness that crept into her tone when she talked about her sisters, and he watched her long fingers, her capable hands, gesture as she described the Nursery.

"You would enjoy my town," she said. "Now that it's shaken off the crazy."

"I think I would," Andrew said. He moved to the window and looked out at the back garden. The sturdy black mulberry tree was blossoming as it had for centuries. Legend had it that the tree was planted at the same time Elizabeth I planted the one in the garden next door. The weather was meant to warm, which was helpful, he supposed, for Sorrel—unless she didn't need outside help, calling instead on the secrets of the Sparrow Sisters to bend nature to her will.

"I have to ask, do you believe there is magic afoot in Granite Point?" Andrew asked. "Not magic, magic, surely, but something unique to your town and your presence in it?"

That was the question, of course, that swirled around the Sisters all their lives. It hovered over the Nursery; it trailed the Sparrows wherever they went and whenever they used their gifts for making their world just a bit better, whether it was to grow a garden, soothe a fever, or feed a hungry friend.

"I'll tell you this," Sorrel said, neatly avoiding any opinion. "If you can't believe in a little magic, then life is a much grimmer thing. And anyway, it's not just me, or us. Lots of people say the whole town of Granite Point is graced with all sorts of charms."

"Enchanting in an entirely different way than what we have," Andrew said and waved out the window.

"Oh, I don't know," Sorrel said. "I am quite taken by the charms here, and I think I needed a different garden to plant. I just didn't realize it."

"I wonder if I might need a fresh start myself," Andrew said. "There are pieces of my life that I wish I could release. There are many nights I would give anything to look out at a different sky."

Sorrel remembered the nights she had spent sitting with Patience on the window seat in her room, how neither one of them could sleep and neither one of them had ever been so tired. She completely understood what Andrew meant. Patience, who had been given an unexpected happiness with Henry, and Sorrel, whose roots ran so deep in Granite Point, wondered if it wasn't time to walk away from all the trouble.

Andrew Warburton was a terrible sleeper. He'd always been

restless, but now he'd begun waking before dawn even if he'd only been asleep for an hour or so. In the hours ahead of him, before first light, Andrew could do nothing more than stare at the walls and remind himself that broken hearts and reputations could be repaired and that he had time now to rebuild his own. In the same way that Sorrel and her sisters couldn't help where their gifts led them, Andrew reckoned that relearning how to be of some use to others who were despondent was the only way he might be of use to himself. With the chapel he found that he was remembering how to live in the world again without doubt and regret as a constant companion. And now Sorrel, with her own kind of loneliness and her own sort of ministry—might she show him how to grow again?

He turned back to Sorrel. "I am unexpectedly interested in being a part of your project," he said, surprising himself into a laugh. "I wonder, can I do that?"

"I would welcome your help," Sorrel said and gave Andrew her first true smile. "I really would."

CHAPTER 4

Woodbine

Nettie Sparrow unpacked lunch as she watched Patience write labels in her careful hand. A row of small linen pouches lined the worktable in the Nursery shed, and a glass mixing bowl filled with dried herbs and flower petals sat at her elbow. The air was suffused with scents both soothing and invigorating, a combination that only the Sparrow Sisters Nursery could create. Nettie thought perhaps they should have gone home for lunch. She wasn't sure what remedies Patience was creating, but she was beginning to feel so relaxed she wondered if she might fall off her stool. Patience, on the other hand, was never affected by her own remedies and went about filling each pouch with precisely measured scoops.

Nettie set out a loaf of sourdough bread from Baker's Way

Bakers, a wodge of runny Camembert, and a container of left-over lamb, rich with garlic and rosemary, nestled on a bed of spicy arugula from the home garden. She'd plucked two sharp green apples from one of the trees in their tiny orchard, and she placed a waxed bag of caramel shortbread beside them. Patience moved her work away to make room for the wide plates and heavy cotton napkins Nettie pulled out of her bag.

"What do you think Sorrel is doing today?" Patience asked.

"I am positive that she is elbow deep in soil . . . in her head if not for real," Nettie answered. "Although, did you notice a certain—oh, I don't know—lightness to her yesterday when we talked?"

Sorrel had contacted the Sisters on her computer in London, and the three had huddled around their screens watching each other on the spotty video feed, laughing and talking for an hour. The Granite Point Sisters were given a brief tour of the house as Sorrel carried the computer from room to room. Nettie was fascinated by the big red Aga, but Patience began to feel a little dizzy as Sorrel swung around to show her the library. Truth be told, Patience did hear a change in Sorrel's voice, a lifting of her tone, and she certainly made note of her easy smile.

"I thought she was just happy to see us," Patience said, "but you're right, something is up."

"If only we had smell-o-vision," Nettie said.

Indeed, a moment's inhalation would have told Patience exactly what was up. Part of her gift was that Patience Sparrow could read people, particularly the ones she cared about. She

was able to sense everything from lost love to envy to the onset of a migraine simply from the scents that only she could detect. Sometimes it worked the other way around, too, but only with Patience. The town of Granite Point had learned years before that what floated into the air from Patience Sparrow's heart and mind was a faultless indicator of her mood.

"At any rate, Nettie, whatever changes are being wrought by England, they feel good, I think."

"Oh, absolutely," Nettie said. "Sorrel looks content somehow, less lonely, right?"

"That's it," Patience said, thumping the table, which made the remedies quiver in their pouches and Nettie's fork clatter from her hand. "She's found someone!"

She hasn't!" Nettie squealed.

"She doesn't know it yet," Patience said. "Neither does he."

If Patience had come through the summer intact, although forever altered, it was due to her sisters and to Henry Carlyle, who healed her in ways beyond doctoring. And if Nettie had grown stronger out of trouble, Ben Avellar was certainly her not-so-secret helpmeet. But Sorrel had stumbled through the darkness alone, and at the end of the summer she did not have anyone to hold her hand, to lead her safely into the light again.

So when Patience guessed at the possibility of Andrew, if not the fact of him, she was as surprised at her certainty as Sorrel was by her own contentment so far from her sisters. As for Andrew, he knew nothing at all. And really, neither did Sorrel.

"Do we tell anyone?" Nettie asked.

"It's not our news to tell," Patience replied. Stories, news, past heartbreak, future happiness, all these were to be shared by the person at the center of the tale. This the Sisters knew as well as Lord Kirkwood. "We'll just have to wait until Sorrel comes home."

"What if she doesn't want to? Come home, I mean?" Nettie asked.

Patience sat for a moment and let her hands rustle through the leaves in the bowl. She tilted her head to one side and then the other.

"She'll be home," she said. "But she might not be alone."

CHAPTER 5
Gillyvor

Graham Kirkwood stacked the photos of his tapestries on the boot bench by the front door so he wouldn't forget to bring them to the country. Each one showed only details of the whole; close-ups of flowers and plants, leaves and colors, to give Sorrel the visual clues she needed to begin her work. He hadn't wanted to muddy their cheerful waters with the tapestries until he had to, so they sat in their envelope hidden from everyone's sight, just as his father had hidden them from him. Graham reckoned that Sorrel would want to study them at her leisure instead of having to stand before the hangings in the chilly chamber every time she needed to identify a plant. In fact, he was almost certain that lounging around in front of the fire in the great library with a bit of busy work, surrounded

by the dogs, perhaps sipping sherry and nibbling Marcona almonds with Stella, was the absolute tip-top activity available at Kirkwood Hall on a late spring afternoon. He hoped that Sorrel would join them and in this way feel further settled. Should Andrew wish to use his time in the same manner, why, who was Lord Kirkwood to question? Besides, Stella was never happier than when she had a house full of the people she loved. No doubt Sorrel would soon be among them.

The old Land Rover Defender was packed with Sorrel's suitcase, several cases of wine, Poppy's book bag, and Graham's briefcase. He felt particularly pleased that Poppy was in such good humor with Sorrel. It felt a bit like the old Poppy who loved Kirkwood Hall and all its history. He dared to think that his daughter might bring her skills and her degree back to the family for good. Graham returned to the house for the photographs and carefully slipped the folder into the backseat.

Andrew pulled up in his car, and the two men went in for coffee while they waited for the rest of the crew to emerge.

"I can't help but wonder if Sorrel really knows what she's in for with you lot at Kirkwood Hall," Andrew said as he warmed the cafetiere with hot water and measured out the coffee.

"Who ever knows what to expect with this family?" Graham said. "Truly, there isn't a thing better than tumbling into a house filled with dogs and children and, one hopes, a proper lunch. We'll all be in fine form soon."

The men leaned against the counter in comfortable silence

as they drank their coffee. They could hear Poppy thumping around in her room and Sorrel coming down the stairs.

"But you know what," Graham said, "I think that whatever Sorrel finds, in the garden and in our home, she will be the better for it. I know we will."

Andrew was a little startled by Graham's certainty. Surely neither of them knew very much about Sorrel and how she would change and be changed by the land. And if Graham wasn't being thoroughly open with her about the state of the Shakespeare Garden or the history buried there, how could anyone guess what Sorrel might feel once she saw it?

"Coffee before we leave?" Andrew asked Sorrel as soon as she appeared in the kitchen.

He handed her a mug already rich with cream and sugar. It was just as Sorrel liked it, and she nodded to show Andrew her thanks. She plunked her notebooks and papers on the kitchen table along with her laptop.

"I think I've got a good foundation for the garden," she said and turned a wide sketch pad around so that Graham and Andrew might look. Sorrel had stayed up late the night before capturing inspiration while it was fresh. A fine-lined pencil rendering of what the men could already see was nothing less than a fairy-tale garden spread over the page. Each minute plant and flower was labeled with Sorrel's tiny, clear print. The beds were set out in a careful geometry that guided the visitor from "room" to "room" in a garden that would have been perfectly at

home centuries earlier. Several benches were drawn beside the gravel paths, a small greenhouse sat along one side, outside the wall, and Sorrel had even sketched in a very little sundial at the center. As soon as she had time to study the existing garden, Sorrel would use her paints and pastels to flesh out the plan. It was ambitious, but she let her imagination point the way.

"Oh, this is remarkable!" Graham cheered. "I am incandescent with anticipation!"

"What is Dad waxing all lightbulb about now," Poppy said as she came into the kitchen dragging a drawstring sack behind her. "Laundry," she said to Andrew's raised eyebrows and reached for a mug. "Honestly, the man cannot just say what needs to be said without a flourish." Poppy laughed. "Feel free to tease him, Sorrel. We all do."

"I will ignore your sarcasm in this moment," Graham said. "Look at this and try to remain unmoved! Gaze in wonder at what our sweet Sorrel has magicked into being!" Graham guided Poppy to the table.

"Oh, Sorrel," Poppy whispered. "It's perfect!" She reached for Sorrel's hand. "You've really done it. Wait till Mum sees."

"Was there ever any doubt?" Andrew asked and gave one of his rare smiles.

"Just mine," Sorrel said and lifted her mug to hide her own smile.

After much milling about and shuffling of bits and bobs, the little party made its way to the cars. Poppy threw herself into

the Land Rover leaving Sorrel and Andrew to the Minor again. Graham roared off with a wave and a final challenge.

"Race you to the pastoral idyll," he shouted.

For two days Sorrel had heard tales of Kirkwood Hall. She couldn't imagine that it would live up to her expectations, and yet her excitement was such that she bounced her leg continuously as they drove. Andrew filled her in on the more historical particulars of the estate as they negotiated London traffic. It had been in the family in one form or another for over six hundred years. Before that, Saxons had battled across the land, Danes had attempted to settle down, and Normans had conquered. There had once been a Benedictine monastery on the grounds. Now all that was left was the chapel, empty and unused since the nineteenth century, and soon it would be filled again. Right and proper that was as the very name, Kirkwood, meant church wood even if nasty Lord Thomas hadn't a speck of Christian charity in his soul.

"I think that Stella always loved the idea of having the house and the land for their family," Andrew said. "The Warburtons are an old family as well, but we grew up in a pleasant suburban house in Wimbledon. The Common was our playground and it could be a wild and wonderful place. I think that's where Stella began to feel most comfortable in a grander landscape than our back garden. There were only the two of us, and ten years between us at that, so I spent a lot of time marching around behind Stella as she made up complicated games involving meadows and woods and windmills. I think Stella

wanted her children to have the same kind of happy childhood we had, as Gray and Fiona did, one foot in town, the other in the country, hands and knees dirty and hearts filled with nature."

"And she has, hasn't she?" Sorrel asked.

"Oh, that she has," Andrew said. "All three of the kids are as much at home mucking around in Wiltshire as they are at a formal dinner in London."

Fiona and Graham had spent summers and school holidays running around the hundreds of acres and tearing through the huge house, filling it with laughter and mud, dogs—and once a pony—in the great hall. Sorrel had no trouble imagining those scenes; after their father's death the four sisters had defied their housekeeper at every turn, dragging sunflowers with their drifting pollen through the hall, tucking an abandoned bird's nest into the Christmas tree one year, stowing a foundling chipmunk in a padded shoebox by the warm stove the April it snowed a foot, and experimenting with their garden compost mix in the pantry sink. Sorrel knew how a well-loved house looked and sounded. She already had fond feelings for Kirkwood Hall.

"Well, we never brought a pony into our house," Sorrel said, "but one time Nettie and Patience convinced our housekeeper that a baby raccoon was the neighbor's kitten."

Andrew snorted. "I suspect that housekeeper had her hands full with you all."

"Mrs. Batlett, as Patience called her, was a saint," Sorrel

said. "Four parentless girls and a house with plenty of places to make trouble."

"Wait till you see Kirkwood Hall," Andrew said. "More places and more acres to make trouble in than a carnival, and I suspect it has always been that way."

WHILE AT FIRST the estate had been more of a family retreat for the current Kirkwood clan rather than a full working farm, the stables still kept horses, including a great draft horse that was used by all the locals on the days that Christmas trees were cut from the Kirkwood Hall forest. An organic orchard planted the year Sophia went away to school had begun to pay off in heirloom apples and pears for the tonier London markets. Then cashmere and milk goats joined the sheep, and both provided wool and cheeses to those same clients. Preserves made from Damson plums, golden raspberries, and scarlet wild strawberries could be found on the shelves of Harvey Nichols and Harrods, as well as on those of the farm shop. As for the unexpected profits, they were funneled through the Kirkwood Trust for Children and Animals. Graham Kirkwood always said that children and animals were so interconnected that it made sense to ensure that his charity benefited both. So it was that the estate became nearly as active as it had been when entire villages existed simply to serve the land. It was certainly a good deal happier. It was no surprise to Sorrel that the Kirkwood legacy was becoming as defined by the care and nourishment it provided today as it was by its past.

The drive out took over two hours, so there was plenty of time to get a feel for what was waiting for Sorrel in Wiltshire. The first hour, though, was spent just getting out of London. Then quiet descended as they each sank into their own thoughts. Within miles of the last sprawl of pebble-dashed houses, worn caravans, and garden gnomes, there was a great opening up. The downs swept away on either side of the motorway, some green with rye, others carpeted with the golden yellow of rapeseed. And everywhere sheep grazed in random puffs of white. Since the thirteenth century, the sheep had stood as sentries around the hills and dales of Wiltshire. The Salisbury Plain stretches for hundreds of miles, broken only by Stonehenge and Salisbury Cathedral itself—monuments to faith past and present and the site of British army training in the fields once painted by John Constable.

"So, Sorrel." Andrew's voice surprised her. She was lost in the rumble of the little engine and the rattle of the wind through the loose windows. "What do you think will happen in your village now that the world has been let in and you've been let out?"

Sorrel assumed that, given his job, Andrew was probably most attentive to the fear and distrust that had consumed Granite Point to the point that any faith-based kindness was swallowed up by anger. And, naturally, how anyone pulled their hearts back to the light. But Sorrel was tired of her town, tired of explaining the strange events and their aftermath. Why else would she be here, as far away as she'd ever been from home

and from her sisters? Sorrel was more interested in how Andrew might accept her abilities, acknowledged or not. Graham Kirkwood had clearly hired Sorrel because he knew her carefully constructed landscapes were precisely what he was looking for. His sister, Fiona, must have told him more than just the summer story. Her host must suspect that Sorrel was bringing more than her green thumb to England. Sorrel imagined that it was his fascination with the extraordinary grace the Sparrows brought to everything they touched that led Lord Kirkwood to fold her into his family with such obvious pleasure. She feared that Andrew might not share that affection once he heard that the girls simply accepted their gifts for what they were: gifts. After all, if you hadn't spent your life watching the Sparrow Sisters weave enchantment through your town, you might well wonder just what these women were. Then again, even if you had, the Sisters remained a mysterious thing.

"The death of a child is a tragedy beyond measure," Sorrel said at last.

Andrew nodded. "It is the darkest of grief."

"It can poison even the sweetest memories." Sorrel stopped. This was as much as she wanted to say.

"How did you recover?" Andrew asked. "How did you manage to stay on in a place that made you all so unhappy?"

"If you're asking how we forgave the people we have lived beside all our lives, the people who became more venomous than anything Patience could dream up, well, I have to say that I'm still struggling with that. Perhaps I should ask your help."

"Oh, I wouldn't be of much use there, I'm afraid," Andrew murmured. "I've my own forgiveness to find. Still, it's good that you are away. Perspective can be a healing thing, and it can only be gained through distance, I know."

"And you? Is perspective what you need, too?" Sorrel asked. "Isn't that the point of a sabbatical? Or are you fleeing a sorrow of your own?"

At this Andrew stiffened, and Sorrel regretted that she'd pressed.

"Perhaps you should keep to bringing forth fruit from the gardens," he said. "I am, at this moment, not for tending."

"I didn't mean to pry," Sorrel said.

"Yet you did." Andrew shook his head. "We're here now anyway."

Andrew turned the car into the long pebbled drive of Kirkwood Hall. As Sorrel looked around at the huge manor and gently sloping lawns, she couldn't help but contrast it with the spare lines of Ivy House in Granite Point. The white clapboard and gray shingles of her town seemed positively primitive next to the soaring stone façade. Andrew pulled around the clipped yew plantings in the center of the carriage drive, and the car thumped to a stop.

"Brace yourself," Andrew said. "The affection level is about to spike."

"Thank God," Sorrel said, relieved to hear that a bit of warmth had crept into his voice.

She stepped out of the car just as the mistress of the manor hurried out to greet the travelers.

Tall and graceful, Stella Kirkwood was the very picture of an English rose in full flower. Even now, slighter than usual and tired, Stella's skin was soft and creamy, in this moment highlighted with cheery spots of bright pink on her cheeks. Her smile was as wide and genuine as the goofy grins on the hounds that swirled around her legs. She reached to fold Sorrel into her long arms.

"Sorrel Sparrow," she cooed in her ear. "I can feel the garden sprouting at the very mention of your name!"

"Reverend Warburton!" Stella said as she broke away.

"Lady Kirkwood," Andrew answered with a little bow.

Then they collapsed into each other's arms, and Sorrel's shoulders relaxed a little as she watched Andrew soften in his sister's embrace.

"Did we beat Gray out?" Andrew asked.

"You did not. He's just gone with Poppy to see Delphine," Stella said. She turned to Sorrel. "Delphine was Fiona and Gray's au pair long ago. She came from Belgium when she was sixteen just for a summer, and I'm afraid they kept her. Now she and her husband run the Queen's Hart in the village. Gray always takes the chance to visit."

"And have a pint," Andrew said.

Stella pulled her brother closer. "There is nothing better than a proper sibling hug," she said.

Sorrel agreed, which only made her sisters seem farther away.

There was no time to wallow as Stella and Andrew swept Sorrel into the house. A tall gray-haired man in high leather boots and a muddy quilted jacket appeared out of nowhere and got the bags and boxes out of the car. The dogs fought to move through the massive front door together, and the man shooed them out of the way as he wrangled everything inside.

Sorrel had just turned to look again at the vista when a smallish, sleekish, roundish bundle threw itself against Andrew's legs.

"Wags!" Andrew crowed and gathered the wriggling dog in his arms.

"This little butterball is Wags," he said. His eyes were shining and his voice light with pleasure. Sorrel reckoned Andrew couldn't be all frost as she watched him cuddle his dog. This was an Andrew she wished she saw more.

"That explains the paraphernalia in the car," Sorrel said, laughing.

Wags turned at the sound and cocked her blocky head. The dog was the size of a breadbox, shiny brown and white. Sorrel couldn't quite place the breed.

"Pit mix," Stella said. "She's a funny little thing, Andrew's soft-hearted rescue, but we do like it when she comes to stay with us."

"My current, and only, pastoral-care assignment these days," Andrew said as he put the dog down. "Found her at Battersea Dog's Home some years ago."

"She's been super practice for your return to the care of the

lost and downhearted, sweetie," Stella said. "Now we've got Sorrel here to rescue us."

Kirkwood Hall may have seen more lustrous days, say in the eighteenth century, but it was awfully impressive. A wide staircase wound up from the main hall, and paintings crowded the walls. A fire roared in a hearth big enough for Sorrel to stand in, and the dogs splayed themselves in front of it with groans of pleasure. Wags stayed close to Stella.

"Sorrel, I've put you in the blue room." Stella headed up the stairs. Sorrel hesitated, looking at Andrew with raised eyebrows. He stood where he was, jerking his chin up toward the stairs. "Go," he said. Andrew turned to the man who still held her bags.

"Hello, Gabe," he said. "How are you?" As he spoke, Andrew's hands flew in the gestures of sign language. Gabe answered silently, his own hands moving quickly. Andrew turned to Sorrel.

"Gabe says since Kirkwood Hall became part of the National Trust there are far too many Americans wandering around the grounds," Andrew said as he signed to Gabe again. "Careful, we've got our own American right here." He pointed at Sorrel. Gabe looked unperturbed. He moved up the stairs with the bags, and Sorrel hesitated beside Andrew and the dogs in front of the fragrant fire.

"Gabe knows more about Kirkwood Hall and the land than anyone, including Graham," Andrew said. "They've known each other since they were kids, and there is nothing Gabe

can't tend. He'll be helpful if you can get in his good graces. Now, up you go," he pointed to the stairs.

She caught up with Stella in the room that would be hers for the weeks to come. It was just as promised: Wedgwood blue and white with a bed so high there was a step stool at its side. Heavy silk curtains tied back with sashes surrounded the bed, and more sumptuous duvets lay in wait. All in all, it was a storybook room fit for a princess rather than a muddy-heeled planter.

"Sorrel, sit." Stella pulled her over to the toile-covered chaise by the window. Wags was already settled on the feather cushions that whooshed as they sat.

"Graham tells me you are not just a master gardener but a heartfelt one, too." She smoothed her skirt, her hands long and graceful, but definitely working hands, calloused and strong. "This garden, this"—she waved toward the tall window—"project may look like a folly to you but to us, it can only be called a mission, really."

Sorrel understood the drive to make things grow. She knew the gentle quaver that set up in her chest when she saw the first tender shoots of the sweet peas in spring, the nearly transparent new stalks of the dahlias in summer, and the sway and feather of the wildflower meadow on the edge of the Sparrow Sisters Nursery.

"Our Shakespeare Garden, so long dormant, is more than a challenge to rebuild, Sorrel," Stella said and took Sorrel's hand. "Graham feels very strongly that this garden is central to

restoring the heart of the estate itself. We've been searching for the right soul to tend it. Come down once you've unpacked, and we'll tell you the story beneath the soil."

This Sorrel understood, too. The Nursery had to recover in order for the Sisters to reclaim their lives, and the process was still underway back home. So, with that link between the two families, Sorrel was determined to help this one find its way to peace.

Stella stood, shaking off the brief moment of intimacy. She whirled and walked out of the room, clapping for the dog and calling down to Andrew, "Kettle on, brother mine!"

Sorrel turned in a circle trying to gather both the sight and the scent of the room. A fire was already snapping in the hearth, the high ceilings climbed to ribbed coffers painted with the clouds and sky of a summer day, and the leaded glass windows, diamond upon diamond, looked out toward the stone horse stalls, the carriage house, a long wooden barn wreathed in wisteria vine, and the fields beyond. An armoire stood, doors open, waiting for Sorrel's things. The bath was painted in lightest blue, the tub, shower, and all fixtures chrome and modern yet utterly at home in the light-filled room. A bathrobe, softer if possible than the one in London, lay across a small slipper chair in the corner. Sorrel was already planning a bath and a nap.

Downstairs Andrew and Stella sat in the study. Their heads were bent toward each other, and their voices were lowered.

"Tell me, do you think Sorrel even guesses at the true state of the garden?" Stella asked.

"Good heavens, Stella, you make it sound like you believe it's cursed, too."

Stella tipped her head. "Well, there are some . . ." she said. "Perhaps we should send Sorrel to Delphine. She remembers more than I do."

"She's forgotten more, too," Andrew added. "Is that why Gray went straight to see Delphine with Poppy? Is he drawing her into this adventure?"

"We could hardly leave Delphine out, plus I know he wants Poppy to be a part of the project. He's worried. Poppy seems less connected to us somehow, and Gray thinks the garden can bring her home as well."

"He's not wrong, but only if he leaves her be for a bit," Andrew said. "Poppy isn't a child anymore and she can't be jollied into being Gray's little girl. Let her have her 'bolshie' rebellion; she'll be the wiser for it. Besides, she honestly likes Sorrel; they can be a good team."

"We all can," Stella said.

SORREL CAME DOWN at the same time that Graham and Poppy arrived at the house. The three collided sweetly in the great hall, Poppy shaking the new rain from her hair and Gray hopping around on one foot as he tried to remove his boots.

"Ah, the gang's all here," he said just as one boot flew off and he stumbled into Sorrel. "Jesu! I hate getting older!"

Sorrel steadied him, and Poppy kicked her clumpy boots away as the dogs leaned into her, a single mass of joyful wriggling fur.

"My darlings!" she crowed.

"Come through, you lot," Stella called. "Tea!"

"Tea?" Gray asked. "I need whiskey to warm these creaky bones."

"Though it must be said that Delphine's barman pulls a damn good pint," Poppy added.

Everyone settled into one or another of the squashy sofas before the fire with sighs and murmurs while the dogs snuffled and groaned as they calmed. Sorrel felt the silence as a comfort. The shelves that faced every wall were crammed with books and pictures, silver cups and porridge bowls, and small blue and white Chinese pots. The firelight flickered off the wavy glass windows. Platters of cold meats, cheeses, fruit, and crackers had been set out on the table by an invisible hand, and a bowl of the estate's apples sat at her elbow.

"I'm going to get right to it," Graham said. "Sorrel, if you are who we think you are, the garden beyond these walls has been waiting for you for a very long time."

The silence lost its comfort as Sorrel digested the full meaning of Graham's words. It seemed that this lord of the manor believed he'd hired himself a sorceress as well as a gardener.

"If you think I have some kind of superpower," Sorrel said, "I'm afraid I left it in my other cape." Her voice was sharper than she had intended. And the look on Graham's face proved

that her fragile peace with her town's accusations was just that, fragile. For a moment she wondered if she'd actually shouted.

Andrew rose and moved to the decanters arrayed on a side table. He poured a glass and handed it to Sorrel.

"Let's not overreact," Andrew said. "Sherry." He nodded at the glass.

"Yes, let's pause," said Stella. "Don't think for a minute that you have been engaged as a hedgewitch."

"Christ, Mom," Poppy said.

"Well, that came out all wrong!" Stella said.

"It certainly did," Sorrel said. She took the sherry and drank it in a gulp, which sent her off into a splutter. "My sisters and I had a really bad time because we are gardeners," Sorrel said. "We are part of our gardens, born and bound, but we are not witches or magic, or even very special."

"Now look," Graham said. "All I'm trying to say is that given your gifts in the garden, your work in the Nursery and your recent troubles, we naturally thought that you could bring something to that godforsaken garden that we cannot."

"As Gray said rather inelegantly"—Stella reached for Sorrel's hand—"there are your surface abilities about which we are very confident"—she paused and looked at Andrew—"and then there is what is in your heart as well as your hands. Can you understand what I mean?"

Sorrel felt the fight go right out of her because of course she understood. She knew what she and her sisters could bring to an empty place. It's just that no one at home had ever said such

a thing to Sorrel's face. No one, that is, until everything fell apart and the Sisters' gifts had been turned against them. And now, these people she'd only just met were talking as if there was nothing odd about her, as if they needed her, just her, not all the Sisters, not Patience to heal or Nettie to feed, just Sorrel to make things grow, to make things right again. And this was fine.

"I hope you don't think my sister and her husband have lost their way," Andrew said.

"Just that they've lost their minds," Poppy said. "Really, what were you two thinking bringing Sorrel here without full knowledge of your silliness? And me, Dad, did you think you needed me to distract her, to trap the nice American lady in Kirkwood Hall, hostage to the haunted garden, the creepy tapestries?"

"Don't be so dramatic, Poppy, it doesn't suit you." Graham sounded peeved.

"It suits me just fine," Poppy said. She turned to Sorrel. "You know they've been fixated on that place for years. They think I don't know that something's wrong in that garden, something more than bad soil and poor light. It's been fallow for a bigger reason, and Dad believes it's the curse, you know he does."

"Poppy!" Stella snapped. "That's just silly. You make us sound mad as March hares."

"What? You and Daddy are the world's worst secret-keepers. And you *have* always been a bit mad in the nicest way,

but I think too long in the countryside has made it permanent March and all those hares are breeding. Andrew, you're the sane one. What are you doing here?"

"I would do anything for this family. You know that, Poppy," Andrew said. "Besides, it's not as if I've got a full docket just now."

Sorrel put her glass down and waved her arms like a referee.

"Enough," she said. "I have hard-won expertise in places that, for whatever reason, don't thrive, so I get why I'm here. But before you all become caricatures of yourselves . . ."

"Too late," Poppy said.

"Probably." Sorrel laughed. "Why doesn't one of you show me the garden while there's still a chance I won't leave on the next train to London?"

"I'll take her," Stella said before anyone else could. "Poppy, meet us at the Shakespeare Garden in twenty minutes. I'll fill Sorrel in on all our secrets, and you can reassure her that we're not dangerous at all."

THE RAIN HAD stopped, but the damp of the day hadn't lifted. The sky was featureless and gray, and everything under it was as well. Stella had pulled on boots and offered Sorrel an extra pair. As they squelched down the gravel path that led around the back of the house, a path that stretched for a good thousand feet, Stella apologized for her family.

"We aren't nearly as barking as that conversation made us sound," she said.

"Really?" asked Sorrel.

"Ha, really! We are only as cracked as we need to be to live here."

A ghostly silence built around them the farther they walked. Behind the stable buildings and the carriage house facing the forecourt where lords and ladies had once alighted from their mounts came the Shakespeare Garden. It announced itself with red brick walls that should have been lined with espaliered apple and pear trees or perhaps draped with clematis and wisteria. Instead, the brick was shadowed with dry brown lichen that fell away in Sorrel's hand when she touched it. Stella led her to the gate in the center of one wall.

"Don't touch anything else," she said. "Not that it's dangerous, exactly. Still, it's rather nasty in here."

Sorrel and Stella entered the opening of the garden; the gate screeched in protest, catching on broken branches and clumps of shriveled roots. How it was ever called a garden was beyond Sorrel. Of course it made her think of the Nursery last summer, after the men had come through with their shovels and axes, after the rot had set in and the plants had fallen, defeated by so much hate, and the greenhouse glass had been broken by rocks. Only here there didn't seem to be anything left at all. Here were ruined parterres defined by wide gravel paths, all set into a precise rhombus. Any flowers or fruit, any shade trees or ornamental shrubs were long, long gone. The soil itself stirred under Sorrel's boots like powder sending up puffs of fine grit and the iron tang of rust and decay.

"Good God," Sorrel whispered.

"Indeed," Stella agreed. "Although I suspect God has left this place altogether."

"What happened?" Sorrel asked. "This can't just be age and neglect." She picked her way down the center path, the pea gravel breaking into dust with each step. "Was there a toxic event? Was it intentional, like ours?"

"No and no, or yes and yes. It all depends on how you look at it." Stella took Sorrel's elbow. "Let me tell you a story. But first come with me to a place more welcoming."

Stella led Sorrel out of the garden, and they each shook the brown dust and clinging grime from their clothes. They walked in silence to the churchyard. It was warmer there, as if a veil had lifted as soon as they left the garden. The grass was still green, mown long and scattered with buttercups and purple clover. Headstones, some looked as old as the church, leaned this way and that, their inscriptions all but worn away by time. A wooden bench circled an oak tree, and Stella drew Sorrel to sit. Birdsong settled around them and for the first time since she'd come outside, Sorrel's breath came easy.

"Kirkwood Hall has a long and illustrious history of which we can all be proud," Stella said. "But it also has a darkness that gathered force centuries ago and burst out in the most awful way in the sixteenth century when the riches of the Catholic Church and the politics of the time brought forth the very worst in the family. That sinister vein lingered, resurfacing

every now and then, as ugliness does. Graham would tell you that he feels personally responsible for his relatives, and Andrew would tell you that history is not made nor told without blood, but I will tell you that, in the case of the Kirkwoods, it is both." She pointed at one of the headstones.

"Now here we have Cosima Kirkwood, gone too young, completely harmless in life, known mostly for her collection of Venetian glass, which I've given to the Victoria and Albert. As you can see, she is one of the newer residents, post–World War I, I believe. Spanish influenza I think." Stella patted Sorrel's hand. "Graham and I are undecided about where we wish to be buried. He's quite set on being scattered somewhere on the estate, but I'd rather like to have visitors at my grave."

"Stella," Sorrel said, "when do we get to the story of the garden?"

"Right, right. Here it is, or as much of it as I have been able to tease out from books and records and Graham. Also, the tapestries have been invaluable, as you will see. After the money had settled in and the poor monks were long-forgotten, the Kirkwoods polished up their reputation by creating an estate of both beauty and wealth. For some time that wealth was spread about to create a healthy little economy in the region. In the early seventeen hundreds the grounds were the pride of Thomas, Lord Kirkwood. Actually it was his wife, Elizabeth, Lady Kirkwood, who planned and planted the Shakespeare Garden. Thomas, it

seems, was a thorough shit," Stella said with some gusto on the epithet. "At any rate, the garden thrived for some years and grew to include not just specimens from Shakespeare's plays and sonnets but also from Anne Hathaway's cottage."

"You mean actual plants?" Sorrel asked.

"So the stories say although I can't believe she would travel to Stratford-upon-Avon. Apparently Elizabeth never went anywhere without her secateurs."

"That is terrific," Sorrel said. "Our mother was not above a little neighborhood nocturnal pruning herself. Our most productive lilac started from a cutting she took near the little train station one year."

"My kind of girl!" Stella laughed. "The garden was a wonder and was known throughout the area. Eventually, Elizabeth consulted with locals about some medicinal botanicals she wanted to add, and that's when Thomas got involved. He was not happy about his wife's forays into the village, I suspect because he'd been making his own visits to dip his wick, so to speak."

Stella looked at Sorrel to make sure she understood what was meant. Sorrel did.

"Lovely thought," Sorrel said.

"Indeed, Thomas Kirkwood took what he wanted when he wanted it and, as it turned out, he took the garden into ruin, at least that's what I have gathered."

The truth was that nobody at the time really knew why the garden began to fail. And Stella's research had uncovered little

more than rumors and ghost stories, legends and fantasies about curses and hauntings.

"How did he do that? I mean, did he physically destroy it?" Sorrel asked.

"That's what we think happened," Stella said. "I can only imagine that he had it torn out as a kind of punishment for Elizabeth because she found life outside his walls. Then he marked the garden with a plaque that threatened anyone who dared to enter or cared to replant it. That's the curse Poppy mentioned, but of course, it's just a story."

"Could the garden have recovered given the right care?" Sorrel asked. She'd already dismissed Graham's hapless conviction that a curse was even possible.

"Who can say?" Stella answered. "Elizabeth died soon after the garden failed, and at Thomas's nasty order, no attempts were made to salvage it then. Any more recent attempts, including mine, have been unsuccessful."

"So how does anybody know even this much of the story?" Sorrel asked.

"Gossip mostly and the archive that lists births, deaths, mercantile exchanges, land grants, surveys, that sort of thing. We know when the garden was planted and when it failed, when the estate passed from Kirkwood to Kirkwood. The rest is detective work on my part and an obsession on Graham's. There are clear hints at a diary that Elizabeth kept in the history and if I had that, I am sure I could practically hand you the garden

on a silver salver. But it's gone with the years, that book, and all its secrets with it."

"And now?" Sorrel asked. "You all think I can bring this place out of ruin?"

"We do, and with any and all help you require, we hope it will be done before the solstice."

"About that," Sorrel said. "I will need to be home for my high season, which doesn't give me much time. Why didn't you come to me earlier?"

"We didn't know you, did we?" Stella asked. "And as it turns out, you hadn't been tested in your own life yet. I suspect that is required for a woman of substance to change her world. As for waiting another year, to give you a full season, I guess we just couldn't. I was poorly this February and made no headway within the walls. Graham was frightened, I think, that I might be seriously ill and that the garden was the cause. That's why he started searching for an outsider. Then Fiona came through and here you are, late but not too late, I hope."

"So my health is of no consequence to your husband?" Sorrel asked. This was a side of her host she couldn't quite accept.

"The Thomas Kirkwood 'curse' is quite clear," Stella said with an eye roll. "Only his subjects were threatened, and since he considered even his family subjects, no one dared cross him. And of course, it's all just superstitious nonsense."

"Okay, but Graham almost seems to believe it, which makes him not just superstitious but also kind of uncaring," Sorrel said and wondered if she'd overstepped.

"It does," Stella said. "Or it would if my silly husband were even sillier." She took Sorrel's hand. "Graham has the softest heart of us all," she said. "He couldn't hurt a soul, and it is just that softness that drives him to restore the garden for everyone. His ancestors may have been real shits, but this Lord Kirkwood is determined to cancel them out. Please believe that."

Sorrel thought for a moment. She remembered the misguided people of Granite Point when they turned on the Sisters, the fear that spiked their hate, and the return to sense that came when the fear faded. She knew what a curse looked like, real or just imagined and she wasn't going to let this ancient one change her one bit.

"Well then, I guess I need to dig in, even if this family probably needs a keeper more than a gardener," Sorrel said and stood, offering her own hand to Stella, who seemed drained by the story. Together they walked back with an occasional stop for Sorrel to pluck a blossom or touch a leaf on the path.

Sorrel left Stella at the stables surrounded by steaming horses and the scent of warm hay and oats. Three baby goats followed her as far as the tall, crenelated yew hedge before leaping in a circle to return to the barn. She pulled her jacket closer as she crunched along the path back to the garden to meet Poppy. The rain had changed to mist now, and the sky had lightened to the west as afternoon came on. The sedge warblers and mourning doves began their songs as they might in Gran-

ite Point, and Sorrel began making lists as she approached the garden walls where Poppy was waving her on.

"You've not run away then?" Poppy asked.

"Not even after your mother told me about the curse," Sorrel answered.

Sorrel and Poppy followed the wall around until they were at the very back of the garden. Neither woman felt the need to go back into it, particularly after Stella's story. They stood and read the sign in silence.

"It's not a curse, clearly," Poppy said. "It's just an ancient scary story, and my father is just being a bit of a tit."

"It says right here that it's a curse," Sorrel said and pointed at the nearly featureless iron plaque. "Also, this is a plaque. People don't make plaques unless they are informing the viewer of something important. In this case, a curse."

She bent low to read the worn letters aloud. LET NO ONE ENTER THIS GARDEN WITH THOUGHT TO PLANT. LET NO WOMAN BRING FORTH FRUIT OR FLOWER LEST SHE GIVE HER LIFE FOR IT.

"Right, but it's not real is my point," Poppy said. "We've all known about it for yonks, but no one pays any attention. Really, the whole thing is more like the toxic uncle the family keeps in the spare room because he can't be trusted in fine company. He's not dangerous, just embarrassing." She looked at Sorrel with something very like fear. "Please, you've just got to stay. Otherwise I swear my summer will be cursed for sure!"

Sorrel laughed. "I don't believe in curses, Poppy," she said. "I've had far too much experience with the destruction that

comes when people think they can blame misfortune on something or someone 'other.'"

"Well, that's settled then," Poppy said. She was relieved, not just that Sorrel dismissed the curse but that she wasn't going to run screaming into the night now that she'd seen the full scope of the Kirkwood madhouse. "The curse won't stop the Sparrow."

"There is no curse, Poppy."

"Of course not."

CHAPTER 6
Laurel

Now that Sorrel had seen the garden with her own eyes, she indeed began to wonder if she was on a fool's errand. She'd assumed that the site was simply fallow from neglect so the idea of resurrecting a Shakespeare Garden in a green and pleasant land had given her new purpose. Then, after meeting the Kirkwood family, each member more charming than the last, she'd thought that leaving Granite Point and her sisters was going to be easier than it had any right to be. But now, as she washed her hands and watched the sandy, sooty grit swirl down the drain, Sorrel was having a hard time recalling the easy pleasure that this project had once promised. The grime beneath her nails spoke not of growing things but of hopeless ones. She wondered if the privilege so evident in the Kirkwood family

had numbed them all to the possibility that this project might be doomed. She sat down at the desk in her room and emailed her sisters, a poor substitute for throwing herself on Patience's bed with a deep, satisfying groan. No instant advice would be forthcoming from the girls, no laughter as she mimicked Graham's fluty tones and florid language or Poppy's acid remarks. And certainly no one was going to tell her the thrill of fear that ran through her blood at the sight of the garden was just a chill.

It was clear that no matter the short season, the Kirkwoods would have their Shakespeare Garden. Sorrel was engaged by the challenge of time, if not by the creepy nature of the land itself. If nothing else, she could grid the plots, get the bare root roses in, maybe find some peonies, alliums even, and certainly the herbs would be simple enough. Still, the thought of scrabbling around inside the crumbling walls, hauling out the spent soil, and carting in the fresh, marking with string and chalk each square, storing her seedlings and young plants in the greenhouse—after first getting the greenhouse repaired—left her overwhelmed and anxious. She decided to go looking for distraction in the long halls, the wide rooms of Kirkwood Hall. If she shook off her disquiet, she might earn her bath.

It was silent as the grave when she stepped out of her door. Was there an English equivalent of an afternoon siesta? Had everyone simply up and left once they realized she wasn't some malleable toy shipped in from the colonies? Sorrel went down the stairs and back into the library where a snoring pile of dogs

lifted their heads as one and regarded her with a moment's interest before wheezing back to sleep. She paced the bookcases, rolling the ladder before her, and tried to understand how the volumes were shelved, hoping to find some kind of guidance. Nothing made sense: Agatha Christie next to the letters of Abigail Adams, Boris Johnson's book on Churchill cheek by jowl with a study of Flannery O'Connor by Brad Gooch. The books were shelved in layers two deep, resting sideways, top in or out in some places. Sorrel had no idea how she was meant to access the historical resources Graham had promised her if she couldn't even find a volume of Shakespeare.

"What are you up to in this, the lunatic's library?" Poppy stepped onto the ladder and rode it a few feet.

"I'm not doing much because I don't see much of a system," Sorrel said.

"Ah, yes. Mr. Dewey would have a hard time finding a single decimal in here."

"How can I start my research if I can't locate anything?"

"Well, as I am a highly disorganized sort, like my father, I can tell you that these shelves speak to me." Poppy waved her arms through the air as if incanting. "Yes, I'm getting something." She turned to Sorrel.

"The volumes are arranged by author's first name," Poppy said with a triumphant bow.

"That's ridiculous," Sorrel said and leaned in, tipping out one book and then another to see the spines. "Oh for garden seed," she said. "You're right!"

"Indeed, so what are you looking for first?" Poppy set herself rolling again, one socked foot pedaling her along the longest wall.

"Shakespeare," Sorrel said.

"To the W's, then." Poppy nudged Sorrel away and took off. "You know Mum has a wicked hidden library." Poppy looked at Sorrel as she hefted down a book. "She didn't tell you?"

"Not yet," Sorrel said.

"Well, then let's go on a reccy!"

"A what?" Sorrel asked.

"A reconnaissance mission," Poppy said and hopped off the ladder. "Third floor, next to the hall of horrors tapestries room."

"Jesus, you people are just full of weird," Sorrel said and took the book from Poppy.

They climbed the stairs and walked past Sorrel's room, several additional closed doors, Poppy's room, and her parents' suite at the end of the hall.

"Where is everybody?" Sorrel asked.

"Mum is resting. Dad will, no doubt, be reading in the chair next to their bed, and Andrew, I reckon, is walking with Wags—you know, getting his gloom on." Poppy put her finger to her lips and tiptoed as she approached the second flight of stairs. "Perfect timing for us, but watch the seventh step, it's wonky."

This staircase was narrower, carpeted in sisal and lit by

modern sconces along the wall. No ancestral oil paintings here, just frame after frame of architectural drawings of Kirkwood Hall. Some looked nearly as old as the house, and others were clearly from the renovations undertaken through the last years. The hall itself was also narrow, and Sorrel realized they were in one of the four corners of the house, not exactly towers, more large square blocks with a room on three sides, a door to a connecting hall and a landing at the center.

"Right, let's hope Mum hasn't taken to locking up." Poppy turned the knob on a worn wooden door, which opened easily. "Hey, presto," she said. "History at your fingertips."

An upholstered bench piled with books nestled below a wide square window, the glass wavy with spent rain. A desk flanked by two old gray filing cabinets sat against one wall, and a low bookshelf ran along another. It was filled with glossy coffee-table books, their covers bright with colorful gardens, simple stone country cottages, castles, and reproductions of paintings. On top were three silver pitchers overflowing with blowsy roses, their petals falling in a drift. There was a mounted magnifying glass on the desk, fuzzed with grime. The air itself was suffused with dust and pollen, and a confused lonely bee bumped against the window.

"Has your mother been in here recently?" Sorrel asked.

"Doesn't look like it," Poppy said. "I guess she really was pretty out of it." Her face clouded. "Flu, Dad told me. I do wish he would be a bit more forthcoming, you know?"

"Yeah, I do," said Sorrel.

"Well, where do you want to begin?"

"Look," Sorrel said. "Let me get your mother's permission before I start poking around, okay?"

"If you *must* be polite, but at least you know it's here," Poppy said. "Come on, let's go sneak into the hall of horrors! You really must see the tapestries to get the full 'pretty' of my father's cheery ancestors." She pulled Sorrel out of Stella's office and across to the only other door. It opened easily into a dark, cold room. Poppy fumbled for a light switch along the stone wall. To protect the panels and help keep the temperature uniform there were no uncovered windows in this room, no natural light or air. Finally, Poppy found a pull cord.

"This will either illuminate the room or flush a loo somewhere," she said. "Can't remember. I haven't been in here in ages."

Whatever explorer bravado Poppy and Sorrel possessed fell away as pin spots came on around the room. Across every wall hung a tapestry, jewel tones and faded glory picked out by the sharp light from the spots. More breathtaking in their beauty than Sorrel could have imagined and more pristine than Graham had promised. Still, what made both women literally gasp was the subject matter. There were six panels on these walls, each one so very like the famed unicorn tapestries in the New York Met Cloisters museum that Sorrel peered closer, looking for the mythical creature. But, whereas the Cloisters' panels detailed the hunt, capture, and slaying of a unicorn, these depicted something strangely more real to Sorrel: A chase of men and

hounds ranged through a forest, a field, through a maze and past castle barricades until, in a walled garden, they gathered around something before them. Graham was right: Never did the viewer see what or who was being hunted. There was a flutter of cloth in one panel, a hand grasping a cluster of plants in another, and in the last, a bloodied leg stretching out as if in midstride, just visible between the boots of the hunters. Surely a final panel would have revealed all, as it did in the unicorn tapestries, but without it, Sorrel could only think that this was the story of another kind of innocent altogether. Why anyone would wish to capture such ugliness for all time with silk thread, vibrant dyes, and stitches so fine the only way to know they were there was to run one's hand across the surface, was a question. But there they were: six panels of such terrible beauty that Sorrel couldn't decide whether to move closer or run from the room.

Poppy had her hand to her mouth, and Sorrel held the other as they stared.

"Yeah," Poppy said. "They're just as disturbing as I remembered."

A faint rustle made them both wheel around. Gabe stood at the door; his eyes wide with shock and what looked to Sorrel like fear.

"I'm sorry," Sorrel stammered, "I was just exploring, I didn't want to wake Stella, I didn't want to . . . Poppy and I . . ." Sorrel ran out of babble at the same moment she realized stupidly that Gabe probably couldn't read her confused lips.

"Hello, Gabe," Poppy said calmly. "We were just leaving."

"Yes," Sorrel said, "we'll just go now."

They sidled past him, Sorrel still apologizing. His face was guilt stricken as if it was his fault that an outsider had wandered into the Kirkwood family secret, or at least one of them.

As soon as they were down the stairs, Poppy started giggling.

"Ooooh, all that schoolgirl terror! Honestly you'd think you got caught smoking by the headmaster!"

"He scares me," Sorrel said. "Or he did just then."

"Gabe—a little power is a dangerous thing," Poppy said. "I love him, but he does take his duties awfully seriously. He practically came with the house, you know. He and Dad are about the same age, and when Gabe lost his hearing while Dad was at uni, it was Dad who learned sign language first."

"Does he speak at all?" Sorrel asked.

"Only to Dad. They understand each other like brothers."

"Why was he so upset with us?" Sorrel asked. "I mean, aren't I supposed to study the tapestries?"

"No one ever goes in there if they can help it, and only with Dad or Mum," Poppy said. "Dad considers the tapestries proof positive of his ancestors' barbarism."

"What are they chasing?"

"Theories abound: a thief, a possessed child, a witch."

"*Now* you tell me," Sorrel said. "I understood that the tapestries would be useful in planning the garden, but I see that your father left out another very important detail. First the family curse and now the hall of horrors." Sorrel stopped at the door to her room. "Is he always so cagey?"

"Yes, a master at withholding essential info," Poppy said. "So, now that you've seen the artistic rendering of the origins of our family's black thumb, let's see what magic you brought from America to fix it." Poppy opened Sorrel's door and walked in as if it were her room.

"What, exactly, did Dad say when he invited you here?" Poppy asked and threw herself onto Sorrel's bed. "Like, word for word."

"I can show you the letter," Sorrel said, digging in her suitcase. "But basically he hired me to re-create the Shakespeare Garden as it originally was. He thought the tapestries could be helpful, a template and a botanical reference. He said he knew my work through Fiona, and he mentioned that he knew about my sister's trial and intimated that it would be good to have a project as therapy in a way."

"Nothing about the Kirkwood weird and not-so-wonderful history? Nothing about the absolute worst Kirkwood ever, Thomas, the one who commissioned the tapestries? No words about how many landscape gardeners have tried and failed to restore the Shakespeare Garden, not to mention that every few generations or so some Kirkwood maiden gives it a go and promptly succumbs to, well, the garden, I reckon?"

Sorrel considered for a moment. Graham had written that his family had experience with the kind of chaos a witch hunt produced. And Stella had given Sorrel a taste of Thomas Kirkwood and certainly piqued her curiosity about Elizabeth.

"Surely there was enough all-purpose illness to go around

over the years," Sorrel said. "Plague, pox, flu, childbirth? Plus, I don't suppose your dad had all the history at hand when he wrote me," she said.

"Let me tell you something," Poppy said. "My parents have delved deep into this family. There is very little they don't know about the Kirkwoods and our house. If Dad left things out of his letter, it was for a reason, and that reason was to get you here before you twigged to the eccentricities of this bunch."

Poppy hopped off the bed and looked at the bottles on Sorrel's dresser. She held one up. "And this is?"

Sorrel looked up. "Um, my sister Patience sent me off with a bunch of her remedies."

"Cool," Poppy said, reading the labels. "Jet Lag, excellent, Sleeplessness, useful, Calendula oil—so very you, Sweet Marjoram Tincture, and Heart's Ease. Tell me about that one." She held up the bottle.

"Yeah, that's for indigestion, I think," Sorrel said. "She didn't give me instructions. Patience has a way of anticipating need, so I suspect I'm going to eat green peppers at some point."

"Riiich." Poppy laughed. "Now why didn't she give you some truth serum? That would be useful with just about everyone here." She slipped the bottle into her pocket. "Shall we leave this in the kitchen for easy access? Andrew won't do the cooking every night and if Dad has his way, he'll make paella and we'll all need it."

Sorrel wasn't paying attention because she found Graham's letter along with her seeds. She handed it to Poppy, who read it with much hooting and huffing.

"So like Dad to dole out just the bits he needed to suck you in. If we're to unravel all this mystery on our own, we'd better get going."

"We, who?" Sorrel asked. "This is my assignment, and you've got school. Besides, your parents hired me. I answer to them."

"If you wait for my father to give you what you need to build this garden, to really know the stakes, you'll never break ground," Poppy said. "Now me, I've explored every inch of this old place, and I am desperate for an adventure. Let me help you. We'll be like the Secret Seven!"

"More like the Terrible Twos," Sorrel said.

"Come on, then," Poppy said. "Might as well put my art history study to work. Let's grab some wine and start with Lord and Lady Kirkwood's last portrait."

THE KITCHEN IN Kirkwood Hall was an efficient, homey amalgam of ancient and modern. The flagstone floors were scattered with worn Moroccan rugs, a professional, pull-down faucet on a spring topped the wide apron sink, and the huge range had two ovens and a grill as well as its own faucet for pasta pots. There were three refrigerators, one glass-fronted and filled with wine and other drinks. White dishes, mugs, and bowls marched along a stainless steel shelf that was mounted over a

low Gustavian buffet, pale gray and blue and waxed. Pitchers of roses much fresher than those in Stella's office clustered on the heavy white oak table in the center of the room, and a sponged blue bowl was filled with Comice pears.

Andrew walked out of the larder holding a basket. He was wearing jeans and boots and a rough linen apron that reached below his knees, like some kind of manly pastoral forager. Wags followed, a soggy rawhide chew in her mouth.

"You look guilty," he said to Poppy.

"Oh, not yet, Uncle, but soon!" Poppy said and reached into the fridge for a bottle of wine and into the buffet for glasses. She grabbed a bag of potato chips while Andrew turned in circles trying to follow her.

"What's up?" he asked. "You know I don't trust you, especially when you have a new partner in crime."

"Wait," Sorrel said. "I am thoroughly blameless in all this. I'm just tagging along to be polite."

"Liar." Poppy laughed. "Sorrel and I are on the hunt for clues to the Kirkwood curse."

"There is no curse, Poppy," Andrew said without humor. He set down the basket, which was filled with tender young herbs, basil, coriander and flat-leaf parsley.

"That's what they'd like us to believe," Poppy said. "Murder and mayhem lurk beneath the crumpets, mark my words."

"Stop it," Andrew said rather more sharply than was necessary. "This house and this family have been terrifically generous to me, and I won't have you playing at things you can't un-

derstand at the expense of the peace and pleasure my sister has built here." He pushed past them without another word.

"What an old fart," Poppy said. "I'll leave him a glass of this excellent wine to soften his hard heart." She poured a glass for Andrew. "Hey, what if Heart's Ease is for affairs of the heart, you know, to ease?" she asked Sorrel.

"Not likely," Sorrel said. "Patience never gives a remedy that isn't needed."

Poppy tipped two drops of Heart's Ease into the glass with one eye on Sorrel. She was her father's daughter after all, clever, canny, and a bit secretive. She put her provisions into the basket and hefted it over her arm. "Come on then, I'll try to explain Uncle Broken-hearted on the way."

Sorrel followed Poppy back up the stairs.

"Andrew doesn't seem to like me very much, or maybe he doesn't like anyone," Sorrel said as soon as they were away.

"Pfft," Poppy said. "He doesn't like himself most of all. But Andrew wasn't always like this, and I devoutly hope his poor outlook isn't permanent."

She came to a door at the opposite end of the wide second-floor landing.

"This leads to the public wing," Poppy said. "My grandfather was the one who turned parts of Kirkwood Hall into a museum, an attraction, really to raise money to keep restoring the estate and because he believed in sharing history. The house used to be open every year from April through October.

Lately, though, Dad keeps it to strawberry and rose season and the solstice, a hayride or three and then the farm shop stays open through Christmas."

"That's what Gabe meant when he said there were too many Americans around," Sorrel said.

"Yup, crawling with tourists, garden clubs, school trips," Poppy said. "This wing is restored as it was in the seventeen hundreds, only cleaner and better lit. Sophia and I used to plant Rupert's little green army men all around. We thought it was a riot to see someone point and whisper about 'artifacts.'"

The door swung open into a shadowy hall, the mirror to the one the family lived on. More portraits, beautifully lit, hung on the walls, and the long runner was deep red and bordered with woven lions rampant, a nod to the long-ago Queen Anne.

Poppy moved with purpose to a velvet bench halfway down the hall. At its center was an embroidered unicorn wreathed in a golden collar and trailing a chain. There was a cord across the seat, which she removed with a flick of her wrist. Sorrel hesitated in front of the bench.

"Go on," Poppy said. "Sit down. It's what it's made for after all."

"But it's so old, what if we break it?"

"Repro, silly," Poppy said and patted the seat beside her. "Some Kirkwood or other sold off a bunch of the good stuff between the wars."

Sorrel sat and held the basket while Poppy opened the wine and the potato chip bag.

"Food of the Gods," Poppy said around a mouthful of chips. "Prawn cocktail crisps, like crack in a bag, only saltier."

Sorrel had to agree. The chip was, at first, screamingly fake, lip-chappingly salty and covered in a thoroughly unconvincing shrimp-y pink dust. But as it fizzed on her tongue, she found herself reaching for another.

"Wine," Poppy said and handed her a glass.

Sorrel looked up and down the hall and then let her eyes stop on the huge portrait directly across from them.

"The man, and woman, really, of the hour," Poppy said. "Thomas and Elizabeth, Lord and Lady Kirkwood as painted by the less-than-famous Flemish artist Jan Josef Horemans the Elder." She pointed at the signature on the canvas. "I looked him up and, according to Mum's research, the portrait was begun on a Kirkwood family tour of Belgium and France. Maybe they were looking for good beer and pâté."

Sorrel laughed. "Or better weather."

The frame was tilted slightly downward so that the viewer felt almost as if she were in danger. And, from the look on Lord Kirkwood's face, she was. He was a tall man, particularly for his time, and that was clear from the way he towered over his wife. Of course, that perspective could have just been the work of a sycophantic portrait artist, but somehow Sorrel believed his stature to be true. His hair was swept back in a glossy mound and tied with a satin ribbon. It was not powdered as was the fashion but black, shot through with silver. His brow, while no doubt noble, was lowered over his dark eyes, and there had

clearly been nothing the painter could do to make his subject smile. His mouth turned slightly down at the corners, in fact, and one hand was fisted on the pommel of a tall ebony stick. Meanwhile, the lovely Elizabeth stared out at the viewer with clear blue eyes. Her hair was powdered and coiled in a precarious pile of curls. Somehow she didn't look silly but rather as if all of her was a confection topped with a dollop of meringue. Her dress was white silk satin, sprigged with what Sorrel could see were cornflowers. The bodice seemed punishingly tight, if flattering. Elizabeth held a posy of flowers in her left hand. Her right hand rested proprietarily on a stack of books on the table beside her. She was beautiful and as pale as milk.

"So this is our original gardener," Sorrel said.

"Indeed, and *he* is, if not the original Kirkwood asshole, certainly the most well-documented one." Poppy handed Sorrel a glass. "I think that these two are the keys to the Shakespeare Garden and its failure."

Sorrel was thrilled. Never had she been given such an assignment, obviously, and never had she had such rich materials from which to draw inspiration. Her fingers twitched to take notes as Poppy talked.

"Your mother gave me a peek at this couple, and I'm with you," Sorrel said. "I think that if we can trace back everything about the garden all the way to these two, we'll have found something."

"I knew you'd get it," Poppy said. "On to Andrew."

"I don't think you should be telling me Andrew's story,"

Sorrel said. "If he's got one that has anything to do with my work, I'm sure he'll tell me himself."

"He won't, you know. He's become such a bear lately."

"Exactly why I wouldn't want to poke him." Sorrel took a sip of the exceedingly good wine. Or maybe the chips had made her unreasonably thirsty.

"Exactly why you should," Poppy said and drank her wine as well. "Mum lets him get away with all sorts ever since Miranda."

There she is, thought Sorrel. There's the woman and the reason she must keep her heart to herself, as always. She gazed at the painting in silence and refused to look at Poppy.

"Come on, ask me who Miranda is," Poppy said.

"None of my beeswax," Sorrel answered, then drank more wine and shoved three chips into her mouth. "Couldn't be less interested," she mumbled.

"Oh, you are absolutely interested," Poppy said. "I wouldn't be telling you any of this if it weren't so, so clear that you and Andrew might be friends."

"Would you just stop," Sorrel said.

"I won't because I think Uncle Andrew has as much to do with rescuing this old place as you do. And furthermore"—Poppy poured wine—"I think it's your turn, and his, to have some proper fun."

"Jesus," Sorrel said, "put the brakes on, Petal!"

"Fine, fine," Poppy said. "Let me just say this: Miranda and Andrew were the golden couple until they weren't. And Miranda, well she didn't just break his heart, she broke his sense of him-

self. If there was a way to hurt him, she did and all we could do, the people who really love him, was watch."

"Yeah, okay, now you've done it," Sorrel said.

She longed for Patience and her gift. She felt totally unsuited to this conversation and only wished that her sister was with them to scent the air, to divine the source of Andrew's troubles. But here she was, alone with a girl who seemed determined to not just pique her interest in a thoroughly unsuitable man but drag her into his murky orbit without the benefit of Patience's clever nose.

"Yes," Poppy said, "I can see that you're powerless to resist the challenge. Andrew, battered but not defeated by Miranda—who is no longer in the picture, by the way—waits, nearly hopeless but still rich with promise, for the only woman who can make him whole again."

"Oh, for God's sake, Poppy," Sorrel said. "Cart before the horse!"

"Right, right you are," Poppy said. "Let's turn our heaving bosoms to the unhappy couple before us."

"Leave me hanging, is that the plan?" Sorrel asked.

"For now, I'll parcel the story out like a bread crumb trail until you two reach each other in a great crescendo of soaring theme music."

Sorrel laughed and shook her head. "Love is more complicated, I'm afraid, than some romantic movie."

"Don't be so sure," Poppy said.

Sorrel and Poppy stood and moved to the canvas. It was

actually harder to absorb the picture the closer the viewer came, but one thing that did come clear was the top book under Elizabeth's hand. Sorrel pointed it out to Poppy.

"All those years in the English school system," Poppy said. "I can read Latin and that book, right there, the title is *A Mistress's Handbook*.

"The diary!" Sorrel said.

"What diary?" Poppy asked.

"Your mother mentioned it earlier. It's lost or destroyed or simply gone, I guess," Sorrel said. "But look, there it is, big as life."

"Bigger," Poppy said.

And it was: a leather-bound book, not particularly beautiful in itself, even in the idealized portrait, crack-spined and leafed out with untidy papers. Its covers were brown, the title stamped in gold and worn, the edges deckled and beside it, a scattering of herbs and flowers. No clearer picture of Elizabeth's gift could be found. And, to Sorrel's eye at least, no clearer argument that the Shakespeare Garden was worth saving.

"I'm sure Mum would have led you to this eventually but we are now way ahead," Poppy said.

"Does this painting exist in an art book somewhere?" Sorrel asked. "And the other ones, anything that has this book in it."

"Probably. We can dig through her study."

"Or you could just ask me."

"Mum, you're up." Poppy wiped her hands on her jeans. "We were just detecting."

Stella came forward and put her arm around Poppy.

"I'm glad," she said. "It pleases me to see this project capture you both. But it is time to make a plan for dinner, unless that is, you've already filled up on crisps."

The three women left the painting and the hall in darkness and Sorrel decided she finally had time for her bath.

CHAPTER 7
Primula

Stella and her daughter sat across from each other at the kitchen table. Poppy had rinsed Andrew's herbs and was patting them dry, and her mother was leafing through the book she'd brought down from her study. It was a large, glossy coffee-table book commissioned by the Kirkwood family when Graham was invested with the title. Page after page of photographs showed the estate in every season, and every important ancestral portrait had been reproduced: exactly what Sorrel needed.

"It seems that you've forgiven us for our madness, Poppy," Stella said. "Have you been seduced by the mystery of the garden or by our American visitor?"

"Both, and I'm sorry I was shirty with you and Dad," Poppy

said. "You two have such a strong bond it's hard for me to get through sometimes."

"Darling, that bond includes you, it is *made* of you and Rupert and Sophia."

"I know that, Mum. It's just that when you guys get onto something on your own, we're left waving at the sailing ship."

"Well, we're all in this one together, even Andrew," Stella said and stood to kiss the top of Poppy's head. "Where is he?"

"Brooding, moping."

"Now, now, patience, Poppy."

Just then Wags came skittering in.

"Ah, the bumptious harbinger," Stella said as Andrew came through.

He seemed cheerier, clear-eyed and flushed from his walk. He stroked Poppy's hair and kissed his sister.

"I am calling a rain delay on my unpleasantness, not that I plan to burst into song or anything," Andrew said. "I have decided to make an effort if for no other reason than that I am exhausting myself with my brooding."

"Told you," Poppy said to her mother.

"Niece," he said, "I will let that comment slide if you tell me you haven't finished that most excellent wine."

"Who are you and what have you done with my brother?" Stella said. "What has prompted this change of heart, darling? Wait, before you start to analyze, let's just enjoy this for a moment. Come and help me with dinner."

Whatever change had come over Andrew, how long it

would last was Stella's main concern. She'd seen him pull himself together before only to get a call late into the night from her thoroughly discouraged brother looking for answers. But this change seemed promising if only because he'd announced it with such gusto. And, to be hopeful in the extreme, Stella suspected that Sorrel Sparrow was already working her magic with them all.

While Sorrel and Poppy were sleuthing, and Stella resting, Andrew had returned to the kitchen to apologize for his behavior, but the women were already gone. He eyed the glass of wine and the small pile of chips Poppy had left him.

"Bribery," he murmured and finished both before calling Wags for a walk. In fact, it was the wander with Wags, a walk that led him eventually to the abandoned Shakespeare Garden, that began another kind of journey altogether for Andrew. Actually it was Wags who brought him to the walls of the garden as she snuffled whatever it is dogs snuffle.

"Wags, come," Andrew said, but the dog continued to worry at the wall, digging and snorting.

"Wags, enough," Andrew said and stepped up to grab her collar. He pulled, and the dog dug in, stiffening her legs and whining. Finally Andrew scooped her up in his arms and walked away, but Wags turned her head over her shoulder to watch the garden recede. He had to carry her all the way to the kitchen garden, out of sight and smell of the other before he could trust her to stay by him. When he put her down, he pulled a long

strand of black hair from her collar. *Sorrel,* he thought, *she's really here and what will that mean for us?*

As he walked back between the healthy raised beds of Stella's perfect kitchen parterres, he wondered if Sorrel's magic would be enough. He'd known the Shakespeare Garden was in a sorry state, but the chill he felt as he stood calling Wags, the leaden quality of the light that seemed unique to that space, and the way his dog had bared her teeth, scrabbling and keening at the wall, made Andrew think that this was a place of deep and powerful darkness. Surrounded now with such nascent bounty, Andrew felt as if he'd escaped some ugly fate and found himself in the mood to protect Sorrel from the same. He tucked a bit of mulch around the tomato plants, the lovely rows upon rows of lettuce, spinach, and arugula, and sat for a minute on the wooden bench by the larder door. The last of the sun had come through the watery clouds and was warm on his face. Wags sat by his feet, peaceful now. Andrew was tired of being sad and angry. The idea of Sorrel's commitment to the garden made him eager to be of service again. He thought of the Sparrow Sisters and how they had brought not just their gardens but themselves back to life. He understood that it was time he did the same. Andrew suspected that he needed to be alert and present for the months ahead if he was to be of any use to Sorrel or the garden. Truly, he needed to pay attention to his head and his heart if he ever wished to return to his church and be any use to his congregation. Perhaps Stella was

right, perhaps a return to caring for someone else could heal him after all.

Sorrel was having something of the same talk with herself as she bathed. The tub was deeper than the one at home so that the water came right up to her chin. She'd piled her hair on top of her head to keep it dry but after a while she let it down and sank beneath the scented water. The hollow quiet stole over her as she held her breath until she sat back up and blew it out with a whoosh. It was as if that act, sinking, waiting, and bursting forth again, was the mirror of her own state. Breaking away, letting go, taking wing, whatever Sorrel called it, she was beginning to feel almost giddy with freedom. Even the ghostly garden wasn't going to dampen her newfound high spirits. And certainly bad-tempered Andrew wasn't either. Although, it had to be said that a man whose heart had been tested, whose own spirit seemed to be as fragile as a sweet pea seedling, had a certain appeal. After all, Sorrel was awfully good at making things grow.

It was as if the dinner hour burnished the Kirkwoods in all their varied ways. Stella, just bathed and smelling of roses and lavender, stood on a small stool in the kitchen to reach plates and bowls on the shelf over the buffet. Poppy was wearing skinny jeans and an oversized woolly sweater that settled around her neck like a cloud. She sat at the table reading aloud from the Kirkwood book, her floppy-socked feet stretched out

toward the fire that flickered in a wood-burning oven set into one honeyed stone wall. Graham was rummaging in the larder for cheese and butter; everyone could hear him nattering to Wags as he poked about, and Andrew was at his post before the stove stirring a pot that steamed a delicious aroma. Sorrel stood for a moment in the doorway, taking it all in and letting it sift over her newfound state of determined, directed cheer.

Yes, she thought, *this is where I belong just now, no matter what happens next.*

"Darling," Stella cooed as she stacked the dishes before her. "Come here and wonder at the marvels that Andrew has made for us this evening! Let's gather and discuss our adventure."

Andrew turned from the stove with the first effortless smile Sorrel had seen on his lips. In fact, it was a lovely smile, tentative but real and wide enough to show the overlapped front tooth that had endeared him to many a parishioner. He stepped forward to put a shallow bowl of steaming, lemony artichokes on the table.

"Please," he said, looking at Sorrel. "Let's take a breath before we all start planning."

His words seemed almost a call to prayer or grace, and Sorrel found herself sitting with her head bowed. Soon enough the smell of the artichokes and the sound of Graham's voice and Wags's tickety-tick toes as she came into the kitchen made her look up and return Andrew's smile.

"I've decided that," Graham said, a stack of wrapped cheeses balanced in one hand and a roll of the estate's butter

in the other, "as of this evening—only what, six weeks after the spring equinox, in case you hadn't noticed—all Kirkwoods and Kirkwood-adjacent, that means you and you"—Graham pointed at Sorrel and Andrew—"shall be renewed in body and spirit." Graham looked at his wife. "I feel extremely optimistic, Stella mine."

"Of course you do, dear," Stella said. "Optimistic is your default setting."

They sat around the table pulling leaves off the artichokes, butter dripping from their fingers until the bowl beside them contained a teetering tower of leaves and the hearts were all that was left. Andrew sliced them into pieces and everyone popped the last bites into their mouths with sighs.

"Asparagus by next week," Andrew said. "I saw the first of the spears this afternoon."

Graham poured more wine, and Poppy filled glasses with fizzy water as Stella set the table. It was as warm an evening as any of the little group had had, and with Stella nearly back to her old self and Andrew behaving as if he just might be ready for his own spring, it felt as if Kirkwood Hall itself had shaken off the long winter for good and all.

And so Sorrel's first day at Kirkwood Hall drew to a close. After the dishes were done, the last of the minestrone put to cool in the larder, and the dishwasher started, Andrew and Sorrel took Wags out for her final walk of the day. They let her off her lead as they strolled toward the chapel, which meant that the dog disappeared into the darkness as if the very hounds

of hell were at her heels. Andrew seemed unfazed even if Sorrel was certain they'd seen the last of her.

"She's after a rabbit," Andrew said. He looked at Sorrel's face, which was alarmed. "Don't worry, she'll never catch it."

He was right; as they approached the churchyard, Wags came bounding back, tags jingling, tongue lolling, and completely empty-mouthed. She sidled up to Andrew and matched her pace to theirs.

"I am sorry I've been such a dark thing of late," he said. "I've been alone so much in recent days that I think I almost forgot how to be human."

Sorrel put her hand on Andrew's arm, and he slowed.

"Tell me why," she said. "Why are you alone, why are you so angry, or sad or captured by whatever it is that haunts you?"

"Ah, you want my story then," Andrew said.

"Only if you want to tell it." Sorrel remembered how Patience had had to tease Henry's story out of him, how his reluctance to reveal his pain had nearly halted their journey toward each other, and she hoped that Andrew wouldn't close up just as she was beginning to see him.

"I lost my wife," Andrew began.

"Oh God," Sorrel said, "that's just awful."

"Oh no! Nothing like that . . . I suppose you could say I was left at the altar."

"Oh, well, that's . . . wait, what?" Sorrel asked.

"Yeah, it was rather a jolt," Andrew said.

"My non-wife? Ex-fiancée? Shit, Miranda is her name,"

Andrew began. "We were at university together, a bit of a fling, and then I went on to seminary, she went into the law. We lost touch, as you do, and then reconnected when her sister was married in St. Luke's, where I was a junior vicar. She'd been called to the bar a few years before and was quite successful—a barrister with chambers in London. Anyway, I was happy at St. Luke's in Chelsea; it's the sister church to the one I serve now. The ministry gave me great pleasure, and I loved being near Stella and the children. And then I added teaching to my duties and I liked that even more. No surprise that being around kids made me think of our future, and we decided to marry. Once we were engaged, Miranda seemed more determined than ever to establish us as a 'social entity.'" Andrew drew quotes around the words.

"And you weren't interested?" Sorrel asked.

Andrew shook his head.

"Miranda always thought I was a bit poky. Even Christ Church was a bit of a Chelsea backwater to her. She was sure that if I only applied myself, you know, met the right people, went to the right parties, then I could rise through the Anglican ranks and have a prominent post of my own, or, at the very least enjoy the niceties that could be had at the higher levels."

"That wasn't for you, was it?" Sorrel asked.

Andrew tilted his head. "It's so hard to know, now that it's all over. Miranda worked mad hours trying to prove herself to her firm, and she was exhausted. I was finding my feet as a minister and a teacher, which was less taxing, really, than what

Miranda was up against. I mean, I had to prove myself too, but I didn't have a herd of misogynists riding me. Still, I knew inside that I was happiest as a parish priest."

He whistled for Wags, who'd gone to the graveyard gate.

"In hindsight, I'm not entirely sure why I proposed," Andrew said. "Of course I am so pissed off at her now that it's hard to have any perspective. And then, you know, am I so shite that a woman would leave me days before the wedding?"

"I'm sure I couldn't say," Sorrel said. Inwardly she wanted to laugh, not at Andrew exactly but at the whole idea that he could be so clueless as his engagement unraveled, such a poor judge of Miranda's character, so hesitant to claim his own.

"At any rate," he said, "the Sunday before the wedding, Miranda and I had an awful row. It began stupidly, as fights so often do, arguing over the fact that my church was too small and the guests would be budged up in the pews. It escalated in an embarrassingly public way, a shouting match on the church lawn, in full view of dozens of people with mobile phones, some of whom belonged to Christ Church."

"Surely a lovers' quarrel is hardly news. Why would they care?" Sorrel asked.

"Because I was wearing my full vestments and swearing like a sailor. Clearly Miranda was already out the door in her head, and this was just the excuse to break it off. A picture of me, surplice and stole flapping, arms waving, in the *Daily Mail* was just the thing."

"Oh, that would be a scene," Sorrel said.

"Yes, it would. It was, and my bosses were none too happy," Andrew said. "Hence the scurrying away to Wiltshire to lick my wounds and give the bishop time to forgive me and my parishioners time to forget me."

"Okay, this might sound harsh, and I completely understand the feeling of being stared at and whispered about, not to mention being ditched, but *this* is the trauma that has so destroyed you that you've terrified your family into tiptoeing around you?" Sorrel asked. "All this stormy moping and simmering distress is because you got dumped?"

"Why, thank you for your sympathy," Andrew said.

"Look, I'm sorry Miranda broke your heart and then stomped on it," Sorrel said.

"Ouch," said Andrew.

"I know how it feels to have the rug pulled out," Sorrel said. "I know exactly what it's like when everything you thought was real and true turns out to be false."

Andrew stared at Sorrel for a moment, his head cocked and one eyebrow raised.

"What makes you such an expert on loss and love and everything in between?" he asked.

"Oh, you have no idea how expert I am on matters of the heart!" Sorrel snapped. "I am the product of every kind of loss you can imagine, and I am stronger and smarter for it so don't you dare question me."

This was a very different Sorrel than the one who had trailed

Andrew around the Globe or sat before a fire sipping tea. He realized he'd rather like to know this Sorrel better and felt, for the first time since her arrival, optimistic about her promise to grow something out of nothing.

"You're right," Andrew said. "A little blunt, but right. Most of my wounds are self-inflicted, and my ego is probably as broken as my pitiful heart."

"I can be opinionated," Sorrel said, already regretting her outburst. It's just that she'd seen tragedy and regret up close, too. And she'd seen what it could do to someone like Rob Short, who had no hope left and was made transparent by his loss and afire with despair.

"I won't let you give yourself over to desolation, Andrew," Sorrel said. "If I did, I would be ignoring all the hard lessons I learned last summer, and what kind of friend would that make me?"

"You've certainly got the courage of your convictions." He turned to Sorrel and in the darkness she could see that tears stood in his eyes. "What kind of man am I then? I mean, it's my job to guide people through their darker times, and here I am completely gutted by a woman I loved. Why couldn't I save something I thought was precious?"

"Oh, Andrew." Sorrel took his hand again. "You can't save something that doesn't want saving." She thought of her father, his slide into alcohol-fueled fury at the loss of her mother. She remembered the nights the sisters would sit in her room, hud-

dled on her bed listening to Thaddeus Sparrow stumble into the house, swearing and crying out for his wife, Honor, shouting for the girls, cursing God himself.

Wags began to whine at Andrew's feet. He knelt down next to the dog and stroked her gently. Sorrel let the silence fall around them, waiting for Andrew to resurface.

"Thank you, Sorrel," he said finally and stood, wiping the back of his hand over his eyes.

"For what?"

"I suppose for listening, for pulling me up short, for, I hope, forgiving me."

"It isn't my place to forgive you, Andrew," Sorrel said. "You're grieving the loss of something you thought was a certainty, and there is no blame to be laid at your door for that. Besides, you've done nothing requiring forgiveness from me except, I guess, being shouty and rude and generally unfriendly."

"Oh, Lord, you are so right," Andrew said. "I've gotten too used to being judged a failure at—well—everything lately. I haven't been fit company and I certainly haven't been worthy of this family's love. But you have my word, I will turn over a new leaf, no pun." He laughed weakly. "Please, let me prove myself to you and that garden. I know it's what Stella wants, and I owe her any chance I have at a fresh start. Will you let me help?"

"Oh, I wish you would," Sorrel said, and they walked home together under the stars.

UNDER THOSE SAME stars and a moon that was no more than a silver slipper, the garden stirred in the night air. The place where Wags had dug and nosed lay in the shadow of the wall. A tiny, curling tendril of green reached upward. The spot on the wall where Sorrel had brushed at the browning lichen was damp with night dew, the lichen slipping off in thin strips to the ground beneath. Inside, Sorrel's footprints began to fill with clear water, the pea gravel swelling and the dusty soil soaking up the wet. One could argue that the afternoon of rain had seeped into the benighted garden, and the mild evening had simply fed a growing that was long overdue. But that was not what was happening, not at all.

CHAPTER 8
Rose

Sorrel woke late. Her head ached and it felt as if every limb weighed a thousand pounds. *Shit,* she thought, *I'm getting sick.* She pulled herself out of bed and into the all-singing, all-dancing modern shower. The water was hot, and the pressure so much better than in town. By the time she toweled off, Sorrel felt more herself. She dressed for a day in the garden: jeans, a navy sweater of indeterminate age, and her clogs, which had once been thick black rubber and were now worn into soft, gray, gummy blobs. As she made her way to the kitchen, she passed the dog pile in front of the great hall fireplace. She reached into the warm mass of bodies for a pat and the comfort of velvety muzzles and furred bellies. But the dogs roused and shuffled away from her hand.

"Hey, guys, it's just me," she said as she straightened with a little groan. *I hope someone has an aspirin,* she thought. Then, *why didn't I bring a Patience remedy for the creeping crud?*

In the kitchen Sorrel found Poppy and Graham sipping coffee and eating toast with what looked like black sludge spread across it.

"Morning," Poppy said. "You look complete crap."

"Thank you," Sorrel said and poured herself a coffee.

"What I meant to say was . . ." Poppy continued. "No, I was right, you do look complete crap. Are you ill?"

"I think I'm coming down with something," Sorrel said.

Graham's head came up.

"Oh dear, that's not good," he said unnecessarily. "You've work ahead and besides, we can't have you ill after I have declared all and sundry renewed by spring!" He stood and came around to Sorrel's chair. "Is it a fever?" He bent to stare into her eyes. "Stomach, throat, grippe?"

"Dad, stop it," Poppy said. "You sound like you want to call a witch doctor."

Sorrel stuck her tongue out at Poppy and laughed. But the truth was that she didn't like the look in Graham's eye as he continued to stare at her. It was an alarmed and, somehow, calculating look that she hadn't expected from such a cheery man. It did indeed make him seem as superstitious as the biggest idiot in Granite Point.

"I'm fine," she said. "It's probably just the last of the jet lag."

"Or the last of that wine last night." Poppy laughed. "We

Brits are champion drinkers, and sometimes we forget not everyone has the training on board."

It was true that Sorrel had probably had more fine wine in the last few days than she'd had in the month before. A hangover, how embarrassing.

"Have some toast and Bovril," Poppy said. "Breakfast of said champions and a surefire cure for when you're feeling tired and emotional, also known as hungover."

Sorrel looked at the shiny smear on the toast Poppy held out for her. It smelled beefy and malty and altogether unpleasant.

"And what is it, this foul paste you offer me?" she asked.

"Only meaty extracts and yeasty bits, you know, the muck at the bottom of a beer barrel." Poppy fought a grin as she watched Sorrel's eyebrows disappear into her hairline.

"Stella, ever the wise one, stocked up before the makers stopped using beef in an overabundance of caution, if you ask me," Graham said with renewed good humor.

"Mad Cow and all," Poppy said, and Sorrel dropped her toast.

"Well, I am a cautious sort," Sorrel said, which she was not or she'd never have come to Kirkwood Hall in the first place. "So, no thanks."

Croissants were scared up, jam was found, and Sorrel had breakfast without danger of infection. And so she was ready to begin. Her fingers twitched and she checked and rechecked her pockets for her gardening gloves, worn, nearly bald suede,

rubber-tipped things so old they were the color of the soil Sorrel worked.

"I'm heading to the Shakespeare Garden," she said. "Wish me luck."

"I'll do more than that," Poppy said and pushed her chair in. "I'm coming along."

"Poppy, no!" Graham snapped.

"What is the problem?" Poppy asked.

"Your mother has plans for you today. She wants you with her in the library." Graham patted Sorrel's arm as he shooed Poppy away. "Plenty of time for mucking about once Sorrel has had a spell on her own with the place."

Because Sorrel didn't know Lord Kirkwood all that well yet, she didn't register the guile in his voice, nor the look on Poppy's face as she followed her father out of the kitchen. She didn't notice that Graham couldn't get Poppy away fast enough and, in fact, couldn't wait to have Sorrel, only Sorrel, behind the garden walls.

"WHAT IS *UP* with you?" Poppy asked as they climbed the stairs to Stella's library. "The secret is out, the garden is dodgy in the extreme, and you are the only one who thinks the Kirkwood legacy includes a supernatural hazardous waste site."

"Absolutely not," Graham said. "I am confident that we've moved off that particular theory. I really did promise Mum you'd give her a hand with some research this morning. You're welcome to join Sorrel later if you like."

"Dad, you are stranger than usual, and that's saying a lot," Poppy said and joined her mother in the library.

SORREL MADE A list of what she needed just to begin: shovels, excavator, rototiller, compost tea, mulch, and stakes, chalk lines, organic matter, sterile soil. She also needed a couple of strong backs and stronger arms. There was no doubt that all the groundskeepers would be roped into service at some point, but Andrew had promised his help today so Sorrel stuffed her pocket with a banana and a bottle of water and went in search. She found him at the chapel with a mug of tea and a cigarette. As she approached, Sorrel took a moment to observe Andrew in what she thought of as his natural habitat. He stood looking at the chapel, his sweater tied around his waist and his shirt-sleeves pushed up over his elbows. He rolled his neck and shoulders, took a last sip of his tea and drag of his cigarette and turned to see Sorrel.

"Ach, don't tell Stella," he said as he stubbed the butt out on a rock and slipped it into the gap between shrubs. "I'll be back for this," he said pointing at the butt.

"I won't say a word," Sorrel said. "Patience thinks we never knew she smoked, but we did. We just decided that the less we bugged her, the quicker it would lose its allure."

"And did it?"

"Pretty much."

"Come, I've got a couple of chores inside then I'm all yours." Andrew beckoned Sorrel toward the chapel.

"Just to be clear," Sorrel said, "telling me about Miranda, about your . . ."

"Breakdown, nervous collapse, episode of self-inflicted madness?"

"No," Sorrel said. "Your grief and general shit show of guilt."

"Oh, much better, those are American technical terms then?"

"Please, I just want to be sure that you are comfortable with me, working on the garden, taking time away from your own stuff." Sorrel stopped. "I don't want you to feel like you're trapped."

Andrew took Sorrel's hand and turned her toward the chapel.

"This *is* my stuff," he said. "This chapel and the people who may wish to find solace here. Like the Shakespeare Garden, this little church was left to fall if not to complete ruin at least into disuse. It had become more of a curiosity than a place of contemplation and worship. Bringing it back to life and value is important to this village. I honestly think helping you is very much a part of that. Until I'm ready to go back to London and Christ Church, Kirkwood Hall is a perfectly fine place to regroup."

It seemed impossible that only days had gone by since Sorrel's arrival. It was true that she had begun to feel a natural part of the family, but she could still feel "other" in the face of this tight-knit unit. Each time she thought she'd pinned down what was expected of her, something shifted, or some new bit of history surfaced, changing the way Sorrel thought about her job and her employers. Here she was standing in

the churchyard surrounded by headstones and a carpet of waning bluebells. The young roses that climbed along the church walls and the bushy stands of rosemary at the door were as familiar as old friends. Wisteria, heavy with buds, twisted and clambered over the pergola. Sorrel was surprised to see passionflower scaling the low iron fence surrounding the graveyard. Beloved plants—chamomile, lily of the valley, nigella, even dandelions—grounded her.

Inside the chapel, sunlight scattered through the windows, picking out the gleam of polished pews and the still water in the font. Andrew walked quickly down the aisle and went to his knees just to the left of the altar. Sorrel stopped halfway along in case Andrew was about to launch into some kind of prayer. He took a long staff from beneath the pew and pulled himself up with it. He turned and saw Sorrel.

"Daily ritual," Andrew said, and his voice echoed through the chapel. "It won't take a moment."

"What are you doing?" Sorrel asked.

"The church sits on part of a flood plain. For all these centuries the verger has had to check the water level like this." He pointed to his staff. "Come here. I'll show you."

Sorrel joined Andrew, and they both stared into a grated hole in the chapel floor. He slipped the grate aside and lowered the staff. It had a tatty sponge tied to one end and as he withdrew it from the hole, a single drop of water fell.

"We're not in trouble this day," Andrew said. "The waters will not be taking us over just yet."

"Good news," Sorrel said.

"Indeed. Let's move on to the next challenge, shall we?"

"Listen, I have a bunch of stuff I need before I can even think about design and planting. Right now it's all about clearing the garden, digging out the old soil and replacing it, feeding it with organic matter, so what I really require is a little bulldozer thingy."

"And will you be operating this heavy machinery, Sorrel?" Andrew suppressed a laugh.

"As a matter of fact, I am quite capable, thank you, Andrew," Sorrel said.

"Well, shoot," he said. "I've always wanted to run a backhoe."

"If we can get one, I will give you a go, promise."

Behind the chapel, out of sight of any visitor or wandering Kirkwood was what could only be called a ramshackle builders' dump. Stella had insisted on erecting a wooden fence to mitigate the tumbledown view. Inside, along with a JCB backhoe perfectly suited to Sorrel's purpose, were a sawhorse, several wheelbarrows, and a stand of shovels of varying degrees of usefulness. Buckets stacked high leaned against a little cement mixer and a decrepit gas mower. Several empty pallets were piled beside bags of cement and crates of extra paving stones.

"Jackpot!" Sorrel said. "How do we get the thing out?"

"I believe we will have to drive it."

Together, Andrew and Sorrel pulled debris away from the backhoe and made a path out of the yard. Andrew found a

petrol can and filled the tank. Sorrel dried the seat with her sleeve.

"I have to say that this seems rather a blunt instrument to use in a delicate garden," Andrew said. "And I do wish you'd let me drive."

"Wait your turn."

The backhoe started up with a roar, and Andrew leapt out of the way as Sorrel rocketed toward him.

"Lift the bucket!" Andrew shouted. "Up, lift it up!"

Sorrel slammed a lever forward and the boom swung away. Andrew waved his arms until Sorrel turned the excavator off.

"This isn't going to work," Andrew said. "We'll never get it through the Shakespeare Garden gate."

"Could we take some of the wall down and then rebuild it?" Sorrel asked. "I don't know how I can clean up all the toxic stuff without a machine."

Andrew shook his head. "Those bricks are Tudor era even though the walls are not. I'm not sure we could even get permission."

"What if the wall was already broken through and we just took advantage of the gap?" Sorrel asked.

"But it isn't," Andrew said. "And if we start demolishing historic sites, we've no hope of turning this whole thing into an amusing backhoe anecdote we can tell our friends."

"Let's go see how big the opening needs to be," Sorrel said and took off.

Andrew and Sorrel walked the perimeter of the garden with

Wags leading the way, nose to the ground. When they came to the gate, Sorrel found what she was looking for.

"Look here," she said, pointing at the join between iron gate and wall.

The bricks were laid in a sturdy cross bond pattern that created diamond upon diamond along the wall. But, as Sorrel could see, the bricks that enclosed the gate were damaged and chipping, the mortar around them crumbling, several missing altogether. She tapped the toe of her clog against the lowest brick line and watched as red dust, black rot, and decaying mortar showered her foot. Wags began to whine and nudge Sorrel away from the wall.

"She was doing that yesterday, too," Andrew said.

"Imagine the smells she's finding," Sorrel said. "But I wouldn't let her eat anything around here."

Wags was nosing along the wall again so Andrew bent to pull her away. She already had something in her mouth and Andrew felt a moment of fear.

"Sorrel, pull that out, will you?" Andrew asked as he held the dog by her collar.

Sorrel reached in and hooked her finger around what looked to be a stem. It was green and fresh as spring, and Sorrel bent close over it, turning it toward the sun.

"Rue," she murmured. "It's rue."

Andrew dropped the dog's collar and came closer.

"I don't understand," he said. "This garden has been completely fallow for three hundred years."

"The whole three hundred?" Sorrel asked. "It never had a comeback at all?"

"That's why this little sprout is so remarkable, Sorrel," Andrew said. "It's the first live thing since Thomas Kirkwood effectively cursed the place with his temper."

"So I've heard, but that's a bit dramatic even for me," Sorrel said. "And I know a lot about plagued gardens."

Sorrel pulled the rusted gate wide open and stepped into the garden. Behind her several more bricks fell away from the hinges, leaving the gate hanging crookedly and shedding rust flakes onto Sorrel's hand.

"See," she said, "this wall obviously needs shoring up. It's a good thing we have that backhoe!"

Andrew came in just behind Sorrel. He was the first to notice that the path before them shimmered with puddles. Each watery patch was like a step forward, leading Sorrel and Andrew deeper into the garden.

"Did it rain all that much last night?" Sorrel asked.

"No, it was clear," Andrew said. "Maybe the flood plain is affecting the garden?"

"All of a sudden?"

"Right . . . no, I mean . . . seems unlikely." Andrew suppressed a shiver. "I don't think you should mess about with this until we figure out . . ."

Sorrel was already scooping water with her hand, peering into it, confirming what she knew in her bones: this water was fresh, clear and sweet and absolutely astonishing.

"No rogue irrigation system under here?" she asked as she squatted over a puddle, scraping away the gravel until she came to soil. "No leak from the chapel, village pipes, anything?"

Andrew shook his head. "You know, this is the first time I've come all the way in here, ever."

"And why would you?" Sorrel said. "It's a graveyard, not a garden."

And that was the challenge; one that Sorrel already knew she could never turn away from. In fact, her enthusiasm rose like sap, and she stood up with a whoop.

"This is going to be wonderful," she said. "I am going to transform this garden and you, Andrew, you are going to join me."

"I know very little about horticulture and even less about hands-on gardening," he said. "I'm not even very good company these days, although I am trying."

"I do like a challenge, Mr. Warburton," Sorrel said. "Game on."

By mid-afternoon Gabe had cleared a path for the little backhoe. His mood was no better than before, and it was clear that he thought he should be in charge of the JCB, so Sorrel left Andrew to direct him. Each time she glanced their way, Gabe seemed to be scowling right at her. *Give it a rest,* Sorrel thought. She collected all the hand tools she needed and spent some hours scraping down the last of the lichen from the outside of the garden walls. It fell away easily and seemed to melt into the dirt.

"Let's take a break before we go at it," Andrew said. "I'm starved."

"You're always starved," Sorrel said.

"I am!" Andrew grinned.

He whistled for the dog, and they walked back to the house.

"Are you really going to be friendly now or is your good cheer temporary?" Sorrel asked.

"I will do my best," Andrew said, and his smile faded. "I'm sorry that I told you my story now because you'll just look at me as Stella does."

"How's that?"

"Oh, darling brother," Andrew said in a falsetto, "we must save you from yourself."

"Ah," Sorrel said, "I've had a similar lecture from my sisters."

"And did you save yourself?"

"Well, I'm not entirely sure that's what I required," Sorrel said. "Perhaps I needed to get away from everything that made me find out if I'm worth anything at all."

Andrew thought that Sorrel was worth a great deal. In fact, as he watched her work, pulling wadded leaves and rot away from the garden gate, starting up the yellow JCB with fearless gusto and laughing as Wags tried to climb onto her lap in the excavator, Andrew was certain that this particular American tourist was very precious indeed.

It was hardly eleven, but already the kitchen was in full swing. Several dogs were sitting under the kitchen table with

rawhide chews, and a tiny woman stood kneading a great pillow of dough. She wore a linen apron that came nearly to the tips of her terribly chic boots, and a sky blue scarf wrapped around and around her neck in a complicated yet somehow effortless cloud.

"Delphine," Andrew cried as Wags threw herself around the floor in a spasm of joy. "Sorrel, this is Delphine Vermeil, Delphine, Sorrel Sparrow."

"Hello, little gardener," Delphine said. "You are here to change the fortunes of this family, yes?"

"Oh, well, I'm here to change the garden, I hope," Sorrel said.

"*La même chose,*" Delphine said as she tipped half the dough into a large green bowl and threw a towel over it. "The same thing, believe me."

"*Hetzelfde,*" Andrew said.

"Close enough, Andrew," Delphine said. "Sit while I finish off the bread."

Once a month or so Delphine came by to top up Stella's sourdough mother and sometimes leave her with a loaf or two of warm bread. As soon as she heard that Sorrel had started in the garden, Delphine made sure that her husband, Arthur, had things in hand at the inn and hurried over to meet the American.

"You know that I have been a part of this family and this village for more than forty years," she said. "And for all those

years that Shakespeare Garden has lain fallow. Worse, it has been a dark presence because of the absence of life in it. You are here to fix that?"

"Is that a question or a command?" Sorrel asked.

"Graham has made a study of you and your sisters," Delphine said as she peeled a pear and arranged the slices on a plate along with some cheese. "He thinks that you have never met a garden you cannot coax into blossom."

"You're right, I haven't," Sorrel said, and simply acknowledging that gave her confidence a bounce. "I am not going to let this one ruin my record."

"So, tonight you will come to me for supper and I will tell you about what I know of the tapestries Graham hates so much." Delphine looked at Andrew. "Yes, you will come, too." She stood and wiped her hands on her apron. "He has some light back in his eye. This I give you, Sorrel."

While Sorrel blushed and ate pear slices as if her very life depended on it, Delphine punched down the second ball of dough, instructed Andrew on oven temperature and proper use of the lame and set out a baking stone.

"Diagonal slashes, yes"—Delphine pointed at the bread with the tiny razor—"then, tell her our tales, Andrew. Be bold," she said and swept out of the house.

Andrew went about his bread making, shaping the dough, placing each boule gently between two damp towels, slicing the tops with the sharp tool as Delphine had instructed.

"Delphine taught me to cook," he said as he looked up

from his work to see Sorrel staring at him with interest and, he hoped, affection.

"Well?" she asked. "The tales, please."

Andrew began as he carried the loaves to a warm spot on the counter and made them both a pot of tea. He explained to Sorrel how it was that Delphine knew so much about the Kirkwoods and their tapestries. As he talked, Sorrel put her chin in her hands and closed her eyes. There was something soothing in Andrew's voice, and she found that now she *could* imagine him giving a sermon, she could see him teaching children about, well, she wasn't sure what he taught, but Sorrel decided it was some kind of magical combination of faith and fairy stories. Which, of course, it wasn't; along with religious studies, which for the little ones were indeed filled with stories of a certain kind of derring-do, Andrew also taught literature with its fair share of enchantment. At any rate, his tale of Delphine and the tapestries was compelling enough that Sorrel stopped daydreaming and started really listening.

It was pure serendipity that had brought Delphine to the Kirkwoods that first summer. The agency was meant to send a Parisian girl to teach Graham and Fiona French and oversee Fiona's eleven-plus exam preparation while her brother, already accepted at boarding school, ran wild through the estate. Instead, Delphine Vermeil arrived, French (and Flemish) speaking, yes, but not terribly interested in schoolwork. Delphine was happy to speak only French with the children, happy to show them how to find their way around a kitchen, particu-

larly when it came to anything made with butter and sugar, and happier still to play hide and seek through the countless rooms of Kirkwood Hall. She did the very minimum of study with Fiona and even less with Graham, who couldn't take his eyes off the spritely au pair. She was lovely, no doubt about that, but she was also so full of energy that both children soon learned that if they had longed for an adventure through the cold winter and gray spring, here it was and they'd best leap and hope the net appeared.

Delphine was a skilled and enthusiastic seamstress and embroiderer, and while she may have been a bit loose with her attention to homework, when it came to art history and the stacks of books Fiona had to consult as she revised, Delphine was fascinated. Eventually, as she got to know Kirkwood Hall better, she became so captivated with the treasures she found, as well as the children she shepherded that unseasonably warm and sunny summer in the countryside, that while she went back to Brussels to complete her education at the lycée, Delphine would never call that city home again. She returned the following summer and stayed for good. She worked for the Kirkwoods through the year, traveling with them to London and helping Lady Kirkwood, Graham's mother, run two complicated households; over one particularly harried year, she earned her chef's certificate at the revered Leiths School of Food and Wine. Soon enough an invitation to the Kirkwoods of London and Kirkwood Hall was most coveted, and Graham and Fiona, both at boarding school by then, required less and

less of Delphine's attention. They remained, however, her dear friends despite the age differences, and to this day Fiona kept all of Delphine's early letters in a sweets tin in her house in Granite Point. The box lived in the kitchen because Delphine always included recipes along with her stories of parties and outings in London while the children were away. In fact, her letters were still coveted by both Graham and Fiona, and Stella wouldn't have dreamt of entertaining without her guidance.

All this talk of Delphine's accomplishments made Sorrel wish she'd stayed to tell the stories herself. But once Andrew settled in beside her on the long cushioned bench under the kitchen windows, bread baking serenely in the oven, Sorrel decided that perhaps it was a fine thing that Delphine had hurried off. She leaned her head back and let the story wash over her.

At twenty-two Delphine fell in love with Arthur Burden, whose family owned the shabby but comfortable five-room inn and pub in the village. Together they refurbished the place themselves after his father retired. They did this through hard work, late nights, and early mornings, and with anonymous financial help from the Kirkwoods (Delphine thought that Arthur had a heretofore undiscovered trust, and Arthur thought the same of Delphine). It was while she was pregnant with her daughter (a secret she had not yet told Arthur and one that gave her such a thrill that her cheeks were a permanent rosy pink) that Delphine and Graham made their discovery. Graham, a dashing and, he thought, sophisticated university student in his last year and his last June half-term break, found the Kirkwood

tapestries rolled and stacked like old rugs in a storeroom on the third floor. Delphine had agreed to tutor Graham for his French finals—her mother tongue had settled into Graham's bones, and he continued to study it right through university. Both of them had remarkably short attention spans when it came to homework and had decided to take a breather by reliving their explorer days. It was chucking down rain, so any kind of outdoor adventure was out. The two decided to have a wander on the third floor, which was shortly to be restored to its former glory and so was a bit of a hoarder's mess at the moment. Eventually it would become part of the public rooms after the house was opened as a museum, which wouldn't happen until years later, as it turned out, shortly before Graham took over the estate.

It would not be telling tales out of school to say that Graham had always had a bit of a crush on Delphine. She was five years older than he, but those years had only added to her allure when she was au pair to Fiona and her older brother. Now, although she was a married woman and a business owner, Delphine could still work her significant charms on Graham. She could always make him laugh, and when a pastry accompanied an unpleasant task, both Graham and Fiona were helpless before her. On that afternoon, she put these wiles to good use as soon as she realized that the dusty, filthy "rugs" were in fact tapestries woven by Belgian artisans. Graham, for his part, felt a chill the moment Delphine began to toe the first tapestry open. He had heard the stories of the series commissioned by Thomas Kirkwood upon

his return from the trip to France and Belgium. His arrogance knew no bounds as he instructed his agent in Brussels to ensure his tapestries would rival the La Rochefoucauld family's centuries-old unicorn hangings at their chateau in Charente. After seeing them, dragging Elizabeth from panel to panel, even as she cringed, he insisted that only fifteenth-century recipes for the dyes be used, that the methods and appearance of his wall hangings would make them look as close to the unicorn tapestries as possible, as ancient as a family of great and old wealth deserved. Perhaps the brutality of the La Rochefoucauld hangings, their mixture of Christian and pagan iconography appealed to Thomas's own ruthless drive for dominion over his world. Inventory of the Kirkwood treasures listed seven panels in the early eighteenth century but the tapestries were never mentioned again in any of the documents Stella found. Graham's father Richard had always told him they were lost, and his mother had cautioned him that this was a story a Kirkwood shouldn't share. But here he was watching as a chattering Delphine knelt beside a panel that startled him with its color and depth. He was powerless to stop her as she flitted from one image to the next, running her hands gently over stitches so fine they all but disappeared into the whole. When she saw his pale face and the look of disgust he gave the tapestries, Delphine reached into her basket and withdrew a bottle of fizzy lemonade wrapped in a tea towel and a slightly squashed éclair.

"Come then," she said. "Let's share this and then we will be fortified on our quest for the truth of the tapestries."

Graham found himself with sticky chocolaty fingers and no way to refuse Delphine.

"Wait, wait," Sorrel said, putting her hand on Andrew's arm. "Graham's father hid the tapestries, Graham found the tapestries, is revolted by the tapestries, restored the tapestries, hates the tapestries, and now keeps them in a Mrs. Rochester room upstairs?"

"That does sound odd, but it's what happened," Andrew said.

Delphine convinced Graham and Gabe to unroll the tapestries and hang them from dowels in that same storeroom so at least the worst of the dust and grime might fall away. Gabe was unenthusiastic at best, and his silence and scowls were enough to rattle even Delphine. Still, up they went and there they stayed for close to five years behind the lock Gabe installed. Delphine held the key to the room and spent those years studying the tapestries, carefully cleaning what little she could, tacking up the decaying linen and muslin backing, tucking in frayed threads and making sure no harsh light got to them other than her little anglepoise lamp. The truth was that Delphine knew she had no business tampering with the weavings so, after getting reluctant permission from Richard, Lord Kirkwood, she called in a textile team from the Victoria and Albert Museum to restore each panel. There was an agreement signed, a confidentiality contract that ensured no one would speak of the subject matter but only of the restoration project itself. "Let people think we've found ourselves another set of

unicorns," Graham's father said the day the museum restorers arrived to transport the tapestries.

As the rolls, lined with archival tissue in huge sheets and laid upon cotton shrouds, were brought down to the truck, Delphine wondered as she watched the six panels being loaded if, like the unicorns in France, there was a seventh panel in the Kirkwood series as well. But, Graham was adamant that six was more than enough to brand his ancestors barbarians; no need to go looking for anything more. The truth is that Graham's father had whisked a seventh panel away before he'd had the rest shoved unceremoniously into the storeroom. He had seen it, shrank back in horror and then determined that the ultimate unpleasantness would never come to light on his watch. This was the panel that could have so easily solved the mystery of the victim's identity. But since it was nowhere to be found and Graham was becoming angry with her persistence, Delphine kept her suspicions to herself and decided that, in her story, the purported witch escaped through the Shakespeare Garden and went on to live a long and happy life far, far away. Had that been the case, there would have been no tale to tell all these centuries later.

"Delphine based the new altar cloth at St. Mary's on the plants in the tapestries," Andrew said. "Her embroidery has only improved with time."

During the years Delphine built up the inn and spent her spare moments on her own needlework, she also raised her daughter, Mathilde who, everyone agreed, was as lovely as her

mother and as mischievous as well. If Delphine and Graham were intrepid explorers with the tapestries as their greatest find, Mathilde was a friendlier, smaller version of a conquering army. She swept through garden and field at Kirkwood Hall, gathering wildflowers and unnameable herbs to weave into crowns, place in jelly jars throughout the inn, and scatter in her sweater drawers to discourage moths. She spent time learning how to bake at her mother's side and how to ride the smallest horse in the stables with Graham. She was fearless and twice broke her wrist climbing the oldest, tallest oak on the estate. Graham often looked at Mathilde with a real sense of longing. To have a daughter as wild and game as this girl would be a fine thing, he thought. And so he would, although Poppy and Mathilde were never to meet.

But first, Graham and Fiona finished university, fell in and out of love several times each, and eventually found their soul mates and hearts' desires. Fiona and John Hathaway took off for America, and Graham and Stella took over Kirkwood Hall when his father chose to retire to the South of France with Graham's stepmother and a herd of small, nasty dogs. Graham's mother had divorced his father for the curator of the Hans Sloane collection at the Natural History Museum in London. The entire tumultuous, gossip-fueled event was so unexpected that no one had the time or energy to be angry.

"I don't believe that for one minute," Sorrel said.

"No, it's true," Andrew said. "I was in the picture by then,

and I can tell you that while there was some sadness, and Fiona refused to come to her mother's second wedding, for the most part everyone just got on with things."

"See, that's the problem with you people," Sorrel said.

"What people?"

"People who are so privileged and overbred that they can't even feel anymore."

Sorrel's eye's sparked and Andrew saw what temper looked like on her. It was beautiful. Before he thought, before he let his own overbreeding stop him, Andrew leaned in and kissed her. It was a tender kiss, small, cautious, but not without passion. Sorrel stopped moving and while Andrew held her shoulders, she couldn't seem to find the strength to lift her arms. He withdrew and searched her face for a reaction.

"I'm terribly sorry," Andrew said. "I can't explain what just happened. I really can't."

"I think you just kissed me and I sat here like a lump," Sorrel said. The she put her hands on Andrew's chest and kissed him right back. This time there was no hesitancy, and both parties were fully committed to the experience. It might have gone on—and further—had the distinct odor of burning bread not found its way out of the oven.

Andrew leapt up. "Bugger, shit, shit!" He hissed and grabbed oven mitts. "Delphine will have my balls."

Sorrel began laughing and kept at it until she thought she might pee her pants. Andrew brought out the bread and found

that it wasn't quite as bad as he feared. Only then did he turn back to Sorrel who sat with her legs folded under her and a grin on her flushed face.

"That was some kind of language there, Reverend," she said.

"I know," Andrew said. "It's one of my skills, swearing with gusto. I'm afraid I picked it up in boarding school and never did shake it." He walked back to Sorrel with his arms out. "I am eager to take up where we left off, now that I'm certain I've not set the house afire."

"Listen, Andrew," Sorrel said. "This is . . ."

"No, don't," Andrew said. "Don't say it was a mistake or you weren't thinking or you think you're a distraction for me because that's just bollocks."

Sorrel opened her mouth to say that, in fact, she hadn't been thinking, at least not clearly, but that it was no mistake and that she hadn't felt so delicious—that was the only word for it—in years. But Andrew seemed to be on something of a run and the only thing to stop him was to stand up, walk over and kiss him again. Which she did. Andrew put his arms around Sorrel, his oven mitts meeting low on her back.

"Ach," he said and shook the mitts off. He pulled back and rested his chin on Sorrel's white streak. "Please don't let's regret this."

"Never," Sorrel said. "I've regretted a few things in my past and I can safely say this will not be one of them. Besides, how do you know you're not *my* rebound?" As she spoke, Andrew's

chin bobbed along and he began to laugh a rumbly, grumbly chuckle that tumbled out of his chest and into Sorrel's heart.

"Well, then," Andrew said. "Where were we?"

Naturally at that moment there was a great thunder of paws and boots as the dogs and Graham came in from the barns, and Sorrel and Andrew sprang apart.

"What ho!" Graham said with the kind of robust good spirits only found at Kirkwood Hall or in a pub on match day. "I see you're taking a break in the action?"

Andrew explained that he'd been filling Sorrel in on Delphine's history with the family and the tapestries. While he gestured with one hand, he kept the other behind Sorrel's back and lightly stroked her spine.

"Ah," Graham said as he picked at the crusty bits of the warm bread. "Now you know that I am, apparently, the scion of a family with deep, dark roots in stamping out the occult, or rather the innocents we believed were purveyors of such. Perhaps you should all hate me. I know I do every time I think of those damn things."

"Oh, Graham," Sorrel said and reluctantly, covertly extricated herself from Andrew's touch. "How could we hate you?" She put her arm through Graham's. "You've given me a purpose I haven't had for a year now and you opened your home to me with such affection. What's a little witch-hunting between friends?"

"Little Sparrow," Graham said and patted Sorrel's arm. "I do believe we have helped you spread your wings." He turned

to leave. "I'm going to release the girls upstairs from their den of inquiry, and we can all have something savory on that bread of yours, Andrew. You two"—Graham pointed at Andrew and Sorrel—"may go back to the delicate exploration of each other's snogging skills."

Sorrel and Andrew froze.

"Carry on!" Graham threw over his shoulder as he left. They could hear him laughing all the way to the stairs.

CHAPTER 9
Hyssop

It would take Gabe and three men two full days to dig out the spent soil in the Shakespeare Garden, time enough, as it turned out, for Sorrel to reflect on Delphine's dinner and its aftermath. Sorrel couldn't get into the garden while the team worked because each day she tried, Gabe came to the gate, now carefully widened to fit the JCB, and waved her off. They all wore kerchiefs over their mouths and noses, and Sorrel supposed she might have to do the same. As they dug and scraped and offloaded the powdery soil, great billows of dust and rust and popping fluffs of mold blew into the sky and settled over the walls. Delphine had warned her that the garden was trouble at dinner the night after Andrew and Sorrel kissed over burnt bread, but there was no way Sorrel could imagine the dark grit

that seeped into her clothes and lay in cracks in her garden-hardened hands.

"I used to believe that garden could come back," Delphine had said as she spooned out goat cheese soufflé. Andrew and Arthur passed the plates around, and Sorrel served a spinach salad bathed in garlicky, lemony dressing. Andrew's second, more successful batch of bread sat all crackled crust and airy crumb on a slatted board in the center of the table.

"And now you don't?" Sorrel asked.

"After Mathilde," Delphine said and looked at Arthur. "I lost heart."

"We didn't talk about Mathilde," Andrew said. "I didn't have time and I didn't feel free."

Sorrel looked around at the three faces, each as downcast as the next.

"What have I missed?" she asked.

Delphine turned as if to leave the room but instead she sat and began to talk as the soufflé cooled before them.

"Mathilde is my daughter," Delphine said. "When she was little, she was convinced that gremlins had gotten into that garden. She made houses out of twigs and painted cardboard and placed them all about in the hopes that they would attract the *les fees,* fairies, yes? They would, naturally, chase away the bad. Those tiny houses were such a pleasure to Mathilde. Even as she grew she still treasured them." Delphine's voice had become almost mechanical as she explained that her daughter contracted meningitis, perhaps at boarding school, perhaps

from a visitor, who could say. After the initial illness and terror it brought to the little family, Mathilde seemed to recover and came back to the village to rest up before her return to her studies. Only a month after her release from the hospital she suffered a seizure and died in the same hospital she had only just left.

"When Mathilde died," Delphine said, "I felt as if any beauty or care these hands could make was tainted by my failure to keep her safe." Arthur took his wife's hands and held them without saying a word.

"Oh, Delphine, I am so sorry, and there isn't a word I can say that will help you," Sorrel said. "Please, know that everything you do is full of beauty. Everyone you love"—Sorrel nodded at the table—"is here because of your care."

"Andrew has been of great comfort to me in the past, you know," Delphine said. "That is why I am glad to see how he is unfolding again." Delphine smiled. "This one is special, this little gardener of ours," she said to Andrew. "Sorrel is so full of hope. Perhaps the land cannot take that from her. Perhaps she might succeed where all others have failed."

Sorrel was not so sure. It seemed as if what Delphine called taint hung in the air around the extended Kirkwood clan. From the history poisoned by Thomas Kirkwood's legacy of hate to Delphine's indescribable loss, there was too much darkness pressing in for Sorrel to approach the Shakespeare Garden with anything but trepidation so soon after her initial joy.

Still, as she and Andrew walked home from the village that

night, Sorrel felt an unexpected ease steal over her when Andrew took her hand in his.

"I should have told you about Mathilde," he said. "I know her loss must remind you of that little boy back home. I wish I had prepared you—not that I could ever make sense of Mathilde's death. It's just that we never got a moment alone again and it seemed such a sad tale to leave you with."

And that was true: First Graham had come in with the dogs, and then Poppy and Stella had arrived to slice the burnt loaf and make sandwiches of warm ham and melting cheese and pickle. In the general commotion there hadn't been a minute for Sorrel and Andrew to think, let alone reflect on their kiss. If Sorrel had known about Mathilde, she couldn't imagine that she would have thought about anything else.

After lunch everyone had scattered again. Andrew and Graham went to check on the lambs and kids, and Sorrel spent time at the little desk in her room marking out parterres and calculating square footage. In the silence and warmth she found herself irresistibly drowsy so she took her drawing pad to the bed and settled into the pillows. She woke with a start; the light had changed so she knew she was running late for Delphine's dinner. She'd wanted a moment with Andrew, oh hell she wanted more than a moment, but again there was no time so Sorrel winged down the stairs and met him in the hall. Together they walked into the village, along with Poppy, who was meeting a friend for a drink at the pub.

"So," Poppy said, "did you move some earth?"

Andrew heard "did the earth move" and he spluttered and coughed and thought, *not yet.*

Later, with dinner done and the quiet settling over the land, Delphine's sadness lifted from them, and Sorrel and Andrew had their moment.

"I'm hoping that you haven't had a chance to regret our kiss?" Andrew asked.

Sorrel shook her head.

"I don't think I have ever felt so awkward in my life," Andrew said.

"No? I may have you beat," Sorrel said. "Actually, I suspect the only cure for awkward is this." She reached up and ran her knuckles along Andrew's cheek before gently pulling him close enough to kiss. Sorrel felt his quick breath and the heat rising from his neck. He sighed and pressed into her; there was no sound but the rustle of field mice in the hedgerows and the call of an owl somewhere over the field.

When they came apart Andrew took Sorrel by the hand and led her quickly through the darkness to the small Tithe Barn beyond the carriage house. He opened the door with a key the size of a teaspoon and without turning on any lights led her to the back.

"I stay here so that Stella doesn't feel compelled to look after me all the time, or keep tabs," he said.

The ceiling was vaulted, each carved wooden arch bending into the next, the soffits whitewashed and curved. When the farmers brought their wheat to the monks, the sheaves

would have nearly filled the room to the high ceiling. Now it was divided so that a bedroom was tucked away facing the fields beyond and a wall-wide window let in the starlight. Andrew's bed was beautifully made, which surprised Sorrel. It was draped with white sheets, a pale gray duvet, and pillows striped like ticking.

Andrew reached around Sorrel and unpinned her hair. It fell over her shoulders, the white swath like a reflection of the moon on water. He stroked her hair away from her face.

"When did this happen?" he asked, letting the streak fall through his fingers.

"When my sister died."

"Ah, grief is a transformative thing, isn't it?"

Sorrel took his wrist and kissed the inside where a vein tapped against her lip. "I don't want to think right now, Andrew," she said. "I just want to let you wash over me. I want to feel only this, only you just for a little." She unbuttoned her shirt and let Andrew slip his arms under it and around her waist. He pressed it away from her shoulders and let it fall behind her. Then he slipped each camisole strap down until the silk pooled just above her breasts.

"May I?" he asked as he reached for the hem.

"Oh, please," Sorrel said. She was left standing in her low-slung jeans, which she began to unzip.

In that moment Andrew thought he'd never felt such truth. This woman and this still night were as close to prayer as he

had come in months. Wanting Sorrel was a pull stronger than his own fear so he placed his hands on the bones of her hips and slid her jeans off.

Sorrel reached for Andrew as he hauled his sweater and shirt over his head in one move. He dropped them and let Sorrel unbutton his own jeans.

"I'm a little, well a lot, out of practice," Sorrel said as she fumbled with Andrew's buttons.

"Let me help you," he said and took her hands between his own. He kissed her knuckles before letting go. "Come with me," he said and moved toward the bed.

Sorrel's hand shook as she let him lead her across the room.

"Are you cold?" Andrew asked as he put his arms around her.

"No," she said. Andrew's chest was warm against her, and his skin smelled of vetiver and deep woods and possibility.

"Don't be afraid," he said. "We shall be brave together, at least tonight."

Andrew lifted her onto the bed and pressed her down into the pillows. Her hair was dark as the sky and smelled of the sea. As he brushed his lips over her collarbone, he tasted rosemary and salt. Her work-roughened fingertips spread against his back, her thumbs pressed into his ribs, her breath whispered at his ear, and Andrew was lost.

Sorrel shivered as Andrew moved over her. Her thighs trembled against him and she worried that he might stop. His touch was cautious, more than gentle, yet it reminded her how

empty she had been, even in the midst of plenty. She felt tears building and let them fall as Andrew bent his forehead to hers.

"Don't cry, little gardener," he whispered. "I'm here."

Andrew woke to find Sorrel at the window, one palm pressed against the glass that was now weeping with rain. The stars were gone and the night was dark under the clouds.

"Are you all right?" Andrew asked.

Sorrel turned, pulling Andrew's robe tighter around her.

"You Brits have the best dressing gowns," she said.

"You've made a survey, then?"

"A very small control group: one flannel, one cashmere, and this."

Andrew's robe was dark blue poplin with red piping. The pockets were baggy and on Sorrel the hem nearly brushed the floor.

"That old thing followed me from university. I can't seem to let it go," Andrew said. He sat up. "Will you come back to bed?"

"I should probably go back to the house," Sorrel said. "There'll be talk."

"No doubt it's already started. It's past midnight. Poppy will have a water glass to your wall by now."

"Graham will have the hounds out," Sorrel said, laughing.

"Gabe is leading them with a flaming torch," Andrew added.

Sorrel poked around in her head looking for regret, sharp as

a sore tooth, or at least a bit of shame at her wantonness, but she simply couldn't find anything but pleasure. She walked back to the bed and sat on the edge next to Andrew.

"What are we going to do with this?" she asked reaching over to stroke Andrew's hair away from his eyes. He took her wrist and kissed it, as she had his.

"I think that we will savor this night. We will sleep in each other's arms and let the world spin on without us," Andrew said.

"Is that possible?" Sorrel asked. "Can we trust tonight, believe it, keep it?"

"Keep it?" Andrew asked. "I plan to repeat it, to build on it, turn it into days and days together."

"Andrew, you're new, I'm new, we're both bumbling around here."

"Bumbling, is that what the kids are calling it these days?" Andrew pulled Sorrel onto the pillow beside him. "Fancy a bit o' bumbling, darling?" he whispered into her neck, then murmured, "Stay with me, please."

In the end, Sorrel gathered her things and dressed in the bathroom. She pinned her hair back up, feathered her fingers across the bruise Andrew's thumb had left on her shoulder and washed her face with soap that gave her skin a scented memory to sustain her on the way home.

The dawn was a golden thread on the horizon as Sorrel made her way back to the house. She'd had to be sharp with Andrew to keep him from coming along and now she was go-

ing to have to find her way to her room without a hand to hold. There was no one to see her as Sorrel slipped up the stairs, no one to hear her laughing into her pillow.

THE NEXT DAY, and the one after, Poppy dropped so many hints that Sorrel thought she might trip over them. It was only once Sorrel promised she'd make a full accounting in private that Poppy gave in and stopped prying. Since Gabe wouldn't let her into the garden until all the soil was replaced, Sorrel and Andrew spent the mornings at the nursery in Middle Wallop. Naturally the name tickled Sorrel and she felt compelled to give Andrew a gentle shove every time he said it. Together they strolled through the tidy rows of plants and seedlings. Sorrel pointed and called out names that reminded Andrew of his boarding school Latin lessons. Three clerks in coveralls followed behind making notes and tagging each plant she selected. Andrew found himself smiling goofily as he watched Sorrel.

"This is absolutely brilliant," he said as he juggled two flats of creeping phlox onto a trolley already loaded with hybrid tea roses and alliums not yet blooming, their flower heads tight green balls on long bobbing stalks.

"Honestly, I can't remember when I've felt quite so useful," he said as he tripped over a hose.

"Glad to hear it," Sorrel said, her hand already waving at a stand of columbine. "We'll need dockweed and elder," she called out, "the nettle, too. Birch and yarrow, hawthorn and holly."

"You are optimistic, aren't you?" Andrew asked. "You seem

very sure that the garden will be ready, and willing, to accept all these plants."

"If I don't get these plants in my hands now, it won't matter."

"Right, clearly," Andrew said cluelessly.

"It's too late for daphs and hyacinths, narcissus and violets, too. I'll have to move fast with the sweet peas."

Sorrel continued to steam through the rows until she came to the five-gallon pots of foxglove. There were no blooms yet, just a cluster of leaves and stems.

"Not this," she barked and moved on to the monkshood and delphiniums.

"What's wrong with that one?" Andrew asked. "I mean other than it looks like spinach run amok."

"It's poisonous and invasive and besides, it doesn't show up in any of my research." Sorrel's voice was shaking as she lied. She hadn't counted on seeing the plant that had been at the root of the Sisters' troubles, and she certainly didn't want to explain her aversion to Andrew.

"Hullo, you sound unsettled," Andrew said, tapping her arm to slow her march.

"Pressed," Sorrel said. "I'm feeling pressed for time."

He stepped in front of Sorrel and bent his knees to come face to face.

"Sorrel, talk to me," he said. "I'm not with you just for the bumbling."

Sorrel burst out laughing, startling the nursery helpers who, it has to be said, were more than a bit afraid of her.

When she calmed, she told Andrew about foxglove, how its deadly beauty had brought tragedy and rancor to her town. Matty's death was more than haunting; Andrew saw that to lose this boy to a Sparrow Sisters flower designed to mend hearts was sadness wrapped in awful irony.

The return to Kirkwood Hall was silent but for the Minor's growl, and Sorrel went straight up to Stella's library with only the smallest smile at Andrew. She found Poppy sitting on the floor sifting through photographs.

"Ah," she said, "have you come to regale me with tales of love and languor?"

"No, my mind is reeling with plant names and square centimeters, not Andrew," Sorrel said and then slapped a hand over her mouth.

"Gotcha!" Poppy crowed. "I told Mum that there was something thoroughly *coup de foudre* happening between you two."

"Coo de what?" Sorrel asked with her hands covering her burning face.

"Thunderbolt, love at first sight, fate, Kismet, lust!" Poppy leaned in and took Sorrel's hand down. "Be happy, this is good stuff—for everyone. And if you ask me, even the garden will be pleased."

"Would you stop," Sorrel said. "We're just finding our way, it's all very new, like days new, so don't start writing me into a fairy tale."

"Ooooh, perfect segue," Poppy said. "Look what I found

in a shoebox, well, strictly speaking a boot box. Here." She pushed the box over to Sorrel.

Sorrel lifted one of the photos; it was faded but clear, as was the subject: a tiny house of twigs and moss studded with chamomile blossoms and a single four-leaf clover.

"Mathilde's fairy houses," she said and reached for more. Picture after picture of houses, each different, some made of popsicle sticks, others of slate chips or pebbles, all covered with leaves and flowers, herbs and moss. They were, if not truly occupied by fairies, absolutely magical.

"I never knew her, but Dad always said I'd have liked Mathilde. Apparently she was both an adventurer par excellence and, as we can see from these houses, something of a lovely dreamer."

Sorrel scrabbled, looking for a picture of the girl herself, but there were only more houses and the occasional snap of a squirrel or robin. She would have loved to see the face of such a charming creature.

"She must have brought in all the materials from outside that blasted garden," Poppy said.

Of course, that made sense. Sorrel could just see the dark grit behind the houses, the gray dust and bareness that served as the backdrop.

"Well, if Mathilde's enchanted fairy houses couldn't call goodness back to the garden, I am in real trouble," Sorrel said and stood, slipping a couple of pictures in her pocket. "Let's

have some lunch and then take a look at the gruesome tapestries again."

They brought mugs of tea back upstairs with them and settled in for an afternoon with Thomas Kirkwood's ugly legacy. They dragged two spindly chairs in from the portrait hall and sat like schoolgirls before the panels.

"Right," Poppy said. "What are we looking for?"

"If I call out the names of each plant I can identify, can you write them down on this pad? I want to check them against the invoice from the nursery. There are a lot of specimens I can grow here but not back home with the salt and wind."

Poppy stayed seated while Sorrel paced from panel to panel, saying the names and spelling the ones Poppy didn't know. It was oddly pleasant if you didn't look too closely at the snarling dogs or sneering hunters. In the sixth a clump of green was woven into the bottom right edge of the panel, and Sorrel had to bend over and come nearly nose to nose with one of the hounds to see the shape of the leaves.

"It looks like woodbine but without a bloom it's hard to confirm," she said. "And this brown behind it is clearly not a plant, but I couldn't say what . . ." Sorrel stopped.

"Couldn't say what, what?" Poppy asked and got up.

"Turn on the flashlight on your phone," she said, sounding very much like the commanding Sorrel at the nursery earlier, and Poppy handed it over.

Sorrel focused the beam onto the panel. "Look at this," she ordered.

"It's a bush and a book," Poppy said. "It's a book in a bush. Holy Mother of Pearl, it's Elizabeth's book!"

"Yes, it is!" Sorrel cried. "It's Elizabeth's diary smack dab in the middle of a—let's just call it what it is—a witch hunt."

Sorrel brushed the tapestry with one finger. The diary seemed to spark under her touch. She crouched down and gently turned the panel over at the corner, as if more information, more of the book, might reveal itself on the other side.

"We need a seventh panel, it must exist," she said to Poppy. "Or, failing that, some kind of sketch for it? Some study? A mention of it in the histories? I mean, it's too much to ask for the book, the diary to turn up, right?"

"Right. No one's seen it since . . . well, since this." Poppy pointed at the tapestry.

"What do you think Delphine knows?" Sorrel asked. "She's the one who found them. Surely she's got a theory about a last panel?"

Sorrel stood and walked the length of the wall again. "Here," she said pointing, "and here, this is our Shakespeare Garden, I know it. It's all of a piece, this mystery, the dead garden, the loss of the diary, it's all the same thing."

"I'm glad you said 'our,' Sorrel," Poppy said and slipped her arm through Sorrel's. "Not to sound too crystal ball-y but I think you belong here, at least for now."

Sorrel gave Poppy a hug and agreed. "Let's find Delphine. We can pass by the garden on our way and see if Gabe is still playing gatekeeper."

He was. Sorrel picked her way through the tools and tarps to the gate to find Gabe magically waiting for her, his hand already up in a stop sign. When he saw Poppy, he began shaking his head fast and hard.

"Gabe, you old so-and-so," Poppy said, "we just want to have a wee look."

Gabe signed no and drew his hand across his own neck. His hand moved again, and Poppy huffed out a breath.

"Apparently while you are to be granted access after all the shit's been dug out and the better shit put in, I am forbidden entrance, ever."

"By whom?" Sorrel asked.

Gabe tilted his head and looked at Poppy.

"Darling Daddy, naturally," she said. "For heaven's sake, Gabe. It's not like I can break anything."

She took Sorrel by the arm. "We're going to interrogate Delphine, Gabe, and you're not invited."

Gabe's eyes widened, and he watched the women follow the long path back to the house. He took out his phone and began texting.

Sorrel and Poppy rode bicycles into town, which made Sorrel wonder why she didn't bike more back home in Granite Point. By the time they got to the Queen's Hart, they were both flushed with good cheer and the warm sun that followed them all the way. In fact, it was Sorrel who suggested they get a drink and convince Delphine to sit with them in the little beer garden.

All three women took their shandies and sat at one of the

tables in the shade of a lilac now in riotous bloom as May settled in. The scent was both nostalgic and invigorating to them all; grandmothers' hankies, pastel purple soaps in aunties' bathrooms and, for Sorrel, the memory of her own garden just beyond her kitchen door perfumed the air.

The drinks were delicious, and Delphine presented, seemingly out of thin air, three perfect rosemary flatbreads glistening with olive oil and sea salt.

"They're still warm," Sorrel said.

"They're really only good warm unless you have some *saucisson sec* to eat with them," Delphine said.

Poppy explained why they were there, and Sorrel saw Delphine's face grow smooth and expressionless. She seemed to be not so much listening as absorbing their story, and Sorrel wasn't sure if that meant she was ready to help or about to send them away with a flapping tea towel.

Finally, after Sorrel laid the two pictures of Mathilde's fairy houses on the table between them, Delphine broke her silence.

"Where did you find these?" she asked.

"Mum had a box of the pictures, every house Mathilde ever made in the garden. Are they yours?" Poppy asked.

Delphine shook her head. "No. When she died, I wanted nothing to do with any of her games. I was, unjustly I expect, certain that her illness was a result of her adventures, the way she tore about the estate in all weather collecting pebbles and feathers and bits of things no one saw any use for. I made Gabe throw all the fairy houses away. I asked him to burn them."

"I am so sorry," Sorrel said as she scooped up the photos. "I can understand."

Delphine stopped her hand.

"I was wrong to close the door, the gate if you will, on my daughter's imagination after her death. I suppose it was her magic, like the flowers are yours, little gardener." She looked more closely at the pictures. "She was such a force: the heart of a lion and the touch of a lamb."

Poppy sniffed, and Sorrel wiped her eyes with the back of her hand.

"So, will you help us?" Poppy asked.

Delphine nodded.

THAT NIGHT THE garden was filled with mist from the coming weather. Heavy air settled over the new soil, which gave off its own fog, a mixture of the heat from the day and the rich compost. There was a whispering in the wind, and insects returned to the garden. Along the walls rock cap moss crept between the bricks, and damselflies appeared, drawn to the damp. Spring peepers around the distant pond took up their song again, confused into mating calls by the scent of green shoots and earthworm castings. Life was returning to the garden.

CHAPTER 10

Spear Grass

It was Delphine who showed Sorrel the blood drops woven into the tapestry. There were three, two on the book and one on the leaf beside it. The delicate bare foot and ankle, all they could see of the hunted, were spattered as well, and two of the hounds' muzzles were bloodied. Sorrel just knew that if there was a seventh panel, as Delphine believed, it would show the death of the woman no one knew, and while that image frightened and disgusted her, she also knew that somewhere in that panel she could find a clue to the death of the garden as well.

Graham gave Delphine the photographs of the tapestries originally meant for Sorrel. In this way Delphine could study them, not that she didn't know the images in her sleep, and share her thoughts with Sorrel without leaving the inn to

run itself. Truly, Graham hoped to distract Delphine's continued hints at a seventh panel by immersing her in the six at hand.

On the day Sorrel planned to finally get into the garden, it rained as if Noah were their neighbor. Even Gabe stayed away, and the groundskeepers took the day to maintain their tools and trucks. Stella and Graham had gone into London with Poppy, which left Sorrel and Andrew happily lolling about in the Tithe Barn. They read and slept and made love and then took a shower together in the tiled wet room, filled with steam and the scent of green tea shampoo as Sorrel washed her long hair. Andrew asked if he could brush it so Sorrel sat on a chair by the window while Andrew ran a wide-tooth comb through the heavy locks. He said nothing because he was afraid to startle her from such intimacy. Finally it was hunger that drove them out of the bedroom.

"I didn't realize how little I'd miss those pesky Kirkwoods until they were gone," Andrew said. He spoke into the disturbingly empty fridge. "I seem to have kept their larder full instead of mine."

"Not even an egg?" Sorrel asked.

"Nil," Andrew answered and shut the fridge. "Shall we swim over to the big house and make dinner there?"

At the word "dinner" Wags bobbed up from under the couch cushions and barked.

"She really does smell like an old stuffed animal and I don't know what else," Sorrel said.

"Shoes," Andrew said laughing. "She smells like wet shoes, always has."

Wags groaned and slid off the couch.

"Won't she have to go out soon?" Sorrel asked.

"Not in the rain. She'd rather explode than suffer a downpour."

Just then there was a crack of lightning followed by a window-rattling roll of thunder.

"Right, that's it," Andrew said as he grabbed a sweater and his jacket. "I'm heading to the village where I will pick us up a takeaway curry from Malabar."

"Be careful, Andrew," Sorrel warned. "If that car of yours hits a puddle, it'll die for sure."

"Perish the thought," Andrew said. "The old girl has seen worse."

He left, letting in some rain and wind and several tender green beech leaves ripped from their branches.

Sorrel went to stand at the window again. She loved looking out across the land and sky, but tonight it was so dark and the storm was so brutal that she stepped back from the panes. The rain threw itself at the glass, plastering leaves and twigs over it, and the wind pressed against it with determination. Sorrel saw her reflection, hair sleek as an otter, her arms crossed over her chest. Another flash and the lightning lit up the landscape. Sorrel jumped. And then she saw someone. At first she just assumed it was Andrew, but why would he be there? No, too small for Andrew, too small altogether. A child, thought

Sorrel. She ran for her jacket and out the door, swinging wide around the side of the Tithe Barn, sliding in her clogs, slamming her shoulder into the side of the house.

She wiped the rain out of her eyes and cursed the dark and the wind. She could see nothing, hear nothing, and suddenly she felt foolish standing in a storm looking for a will-o'-the-wisp. *Of course there's nothing out here,* she thought. *Except for a half-dressed idiot.* She turned and stumbled back inside, cold, dirty, and shaken. Wags met her at the door whining and quivering, but Sorrel had no comfort to give her.

Andrew came back to find Sorrel in his dressing gown, now settled enough to be holding Wags in her lap on the couch.

"What is it, what's happened?" he said as he dropped their dinner and knelt in front of her. "Is it your family?"

"Oh, Andrew," Sorrel said, "how wonderful that your first thought was my sisters." She reached out and brushed his wet hair away from his eyes. "I thought I saw someone outside and, foolishly, I ran out to see who it was."

"Good God, you look as if you'd barely escaped a serial killer! I was ready to leap into some kind of manly action!"

"I'd pay money to see that," Sorrel said. "Seriously, I did think there was somebody out there, a kid actually, and with the lightning I got nervous."

Andrew picked up the bags and put them in the kitchen. When he came back, he had two Cobra beers in hand.

"This may sound a little therapy-y," he said, "but do you think hearing about Mathilde has sparked memories of Matty?

And, with that in mind, your grief has resurfaced, taken shape here tonight?"

Sorrel thought for a moment. "Probably," she said. "Add the foxglove at the nursery the other day, and I am ripe for a crazy-lady episode. All I need is a cat."

"No cats. Wags does not approve," Andrew said. "I'll get the food; you poke the fire."

They sat eating mildly spiced butter chicken (Andrew didn't know how adventurous Sorrel might be) and *balti* and *dhal*. They used their fingers and warm naan to sop up every bite, fresh coriander scattered over everything, and tart yogurt in a small bowl beside the dishes on the table.

"My sister Nettie makes a lovely Thai fish soup, springy and fresh."

"I should like to taste that," Andrew said and scooped a dollop of *dhal* into his mouth.

They fell silent. Sorrel did not want to encourage Andrew's enthusiasm for all things Sparrow. It would only lead to disappointment when Sorrel returned to Granite Point after the summer solstice. In her head if not her heart, she knew that Andrew was temporary—lovely, more delicious than any curry—but temporary. If he made her feel as if he might actually find pleasure in being by her side day by day, Sorrel understood that here was a man who'd forgotten how intoxicating new love felt. Perhaps he'd never known to begin with. Certainly he was silly with it; even Sorrel could see that and it was charming, but it couldn't last.

"So tomorrow then," Andrew said when the silence was too heavy to bear.

"Yes," Sorrel said, "we get into the garden tomorrow."

"Will you require my services?" he asked.

"Um, well, I think Gabe and the guys who have been on site will be with me."

"Oh, fine, yes, I see," Andrew said. But it wasn't fine. "It's only that I would very much like to see what's happening there, you know, behind the wall you tore down."

"I did not tear down that wall," Sorrel said and laughed. "It fell over."

"Ah, just like Humpty Dumpty."

"Exactly like that only we'll put it back together again without any king's men or horses."

Andrew cleared the dishes away, gesturing for Sorrel to sit and finish her beer. Wags followed him, hoping for a little spillage, which she got. He returned with a bowl of Pan Masala, a fennel seed and jeera candy mixture.

"*Digestivo,*" he said, mixing his cultures.

Sorrel ate some. It was sweet and sharp at once, so like the moment.

"Shall we go back to bed now?" Andrew asked. "I'm exhausted by the act of eating and feel inexorably pulled toward that tangle of blankets and pillows, don't you?"

"I do," Sorrel said. "I am compelled by a force I cannot understand."

This was true in some strange way. Sorrel felt swoony and silly at once, and perhaps they were the same thing, but she recognized that she should be wary. Still, there was something about this new Andrew, something hopeful and light that swept away all her good sense, so she took his hand and let him lead her off.

"Perhaps we have been overtaken by a mysterious alien virus," Andrew said as he untied the dressing gown. "It might be wise to self-quarantine to save the others, hmm? Just stay here until we feel our sensible old selves again."

But Sorrel didn't want to be her old self, not then and not ever if she was honest. It wasn't until Andrew made that comment that she realized how relentlessly sensible she had been all her life. As the oldest of the Sisters, it had been down to Sorrel to take up the slack between their grieving father and their loving but distracted housekeeper. It was Sorrel who explained the birds and the bees to Nettie and Patience (in the garden naturally) and Sorrel who found her mother's old debutante dress and re-purposed it for Nettie's senior prom. Patience, the youngest and the one who had never known a mother's love, was such a fierce little girl that Sorrel almost never had to soothe her, and she certainly never had to find a ruffled dress for her. Patience wouldn't be caught dead at the prom, and Sorrel never went to her own because she couldn't leave the girls alone with their father. Simon Mayo and Sorrel had always had a sneaker for each other but neither ever acted. It would

have been fairly shocking all around if Simon had suddenly stepped up and offered to take her. No, instead he escorted Lucy Titcomb, an appropriate choice made by his mother.

So here was Sorrel not just throwing caution to the winds, but flinging it into the eye of a hurricane. She and Andrew twined together in a way that neither of them ever thought they'd experience again. Even Wags gave up trying to come between them under the covers.

The next morning the skies had cleared, the sun was warm, and steam rose from the fields behind the stable block. Three horses stood in the distance, silhouetted against the woods beyond. When Andrew opened the front door, he found an enormous bundle of lilacs wrapped in butcher paper with a note from Delphine that read: "Saved from the storm for our little gardener." Alongside was a blue striped box tied with twine.

"Breakfast," Andrew said and handed Sorrel the flowers. She bashed the stems and put them in water and wondered how it was that Delphine knew just where to find her.

ANDREW WAS DISAPPOINTED not to join Sorrel the first time she entered the garden with its new and fertile soil. He'd set a meeting with Marcus, the verger, at the chapel with his young family to test the refurbished church bells, and while the lure of Sorrel in a garden was strong, the charms of three small children and a puppy were a fine substitute. Andrew was happily rolling about on the lawn with a brindle

pup of unidentified lineage and the boys within minutes of his arrival. Marcus Everlane, who had spent countless hours shoulder to shoulder with a much more dour Andrew as they worked on the chapel, couldn't guess what accounted for this extraordinary change of heart, but he certainly welcomed it. When Andrew and Marcus began their work it was mostly harmless ferrying of bags of rubbish and rubble out of the chapel once it was determined that there was nothing of historical value in the wheelbarrows. Marcus remembered how Andrew's temperament at the time seemed uniquely suited to the bashing and slamming about. Now that they were on to the finishing touches for the little chapel; sanding down the restored pews before protective varnish was applied, polishing brass and stone and choosing the bibles and hymnals that would become a part of the building and her visitors' lives, Marcus was glad to see Andrew using a lighter touch. With the bells in place and the roses just blooming, the two men shared a gentle thrill at the fruit of their labors and an overarching sense of optimism about the weeks ahead.

Sorrel, for her part, would not be rolling around in the Shakespeare Garden any time soon. Several truckloads of rich compost had been spread throughout the garden along each gritty pathway and right up to the side walls where the dwarf apple trees would be espaliered. Now the whole thing awaited Sorrel's marking and plotting. The earth was soaked with the rain, and the smell of manure rose up to float over the estate like the Victorian miasma. Even in the village people lifted

their wrinkled noses and hurried back inside. Sorrel couldn't have been happier, if a bit drier. She squatted down and took off her gloves so that she could feel the soil between her fingers. It was heavy, wriggling with earthworms, blobby and perfect. She wiped her hands on her jeans and picked up her long waxed tape measure, a fistful of stakes, and her chalk line. Sorrel pinned her garden map to the handle of the wheelbarrow and consulted it as she measured and staked. Over and over she tied the chalk line to a stake and snapped it, leaving a white line the length and width of each parterre. A satisfying puff of chalk hung in the still air above the soil with each snap, and Sorrel looked around her with pleasure. *It's begun,* she thought. Just then the tentative chime of the chapel bells floated over the wall. Sorrel washed her hands and face with the hose and wandered over to see Andrew and, perhaps, ask him to make lunch. She was sweating and a bit disoriented from being walled in all morning; it would be good to feel a breeze.

On her way to the chapel Sorrel passed the big pallets loaded with her plants. They were lined up in the greenhouse. Clear plastic covered the broken panes, and the air was heavy with moisture. The lavender worried her a little; it was budding out too fast and the blossoms could be damaged in the planting. She ran her hand over the swaying tops, whispering, "Not yet, not yet." The climbing roses, on the other hand, were struggling. "Come now," Sorrel murmured. "It's your time." The plants leaned into her hands as if they were listening.

CHAPTER 11

Wormwood

"I have to say I'm anxious to get back to the country," Stella said as she sorted through the post.

"You always are, darling," Graham said and closed the newspaper.

"Indeed, but with the weather cleared and Sorrel properly in the garden I am missing more than just the estate." Stella stood. "Let's head back early."

"No," Graham said sharply, and Stella raised her eyebrows. "What I mean is that Sorrel should have unmolested time with the garden. We will only be a distraction and"—Graham grinned and rubbed his hands together—"I do believe Andrew has found in Sorrel a distraction of an entirely different sort."

"Just as I hoped," Stella said and bent to kiss her husband's

leonine head. “You are right, of course. We’ll leave your gardener and my brother to find their pleasure together.”

“Come with me, Stella, let’s walk by the river before I head to Westminster.”

As they walked, Graham made several false starts at coming clean about his lingering fear of the Shakespeare Garden. Certainly hiring Sorrel Sparrow was the tip of the spear, but what he had not shared with his wife was how much danger he really suspected lay beneath even the richest new soil. Finally, he drew Stella to a bench beneath the flowering chestnut trees and cupped her cheek until she had no choice but to look deeply into his worried eyes.

“I am afraid I have not been totally honest with you, or with Sorrel,” Graham said. “I realize now that my actions have been selfish, but you must understand that everything I have done, every plan, every move, has been to keep my family safe.”

“Gray, what is the matter?” Stella asked. “Why are you so unsettled? Have you done something regrettable?”

“I may have,” he said. “But only because I saw no other way.”

And so Graham confessed to how calculated his plan really was. To be fair, when his sister, Fiona, had first told him about the Sparrow Sisters and their trials in Granite Point, he’d barely listened. This new world Fiona had chosen over Kirkwood Hall had always felt like something of a fairy tale anyway, so hearing the story of the enchanted sisters only provided a vaguely interesting bauble at first. But with time he began to wonder about the Sparrow women. If they were, in fact, as gifted as Fiona

believed, surely one of them could bring her gifts to his world. And if such a thing happened, a special gardener like Sorrel Sparrow might be immune to the darkness of the garden, if there were such a thing as a garden with that kind of power.

"Graham, are you saying that you have some knowledge that the blight in that garden is actually physically dangerous to humans?" Stella had a moment's thought that her beloved husband had lost the plot before she briefly considered some sort of illegal toxic waste dump.

"I have no real knowledge, my love," he said. "I haven't had the soil or bedrock tested. But surely you have made the connections?"

"Clearly not."

"Long ago Elizabeth's unexplained death, the death of the garden, Cosima, Mathilde, your illness . . ." his voice trailed off. "I know it's mad, but I can't help but believe that something happened in that place that poisoned it in ages past and does the same to every woman or girl who attempts to revive it."

"That is mad," Stella said. "What is madder is that if you believe this theory, then you have deliberately put Sorrel in harm's way."

"I know, I know," Graham said. "What was I to do, Stella? You were so ill, and I was so afraid I'd caused it all with my curse. It does seem to be limited to Kirkwoods, mostly."

"Good God, Graham, you can't be serious."

"Well, obviously I am," he said. "I called a stranger into our world precisely because she is not a Kirkwood. I won't let

you back into that garden until and unless Sorrel does what she promised."

"You mean if she doesn't get sick, too. And if she fails or breaks trying?"

"Now, Stella, I could hardly ignore family history. And look, Sorrel is perfectly fine, isn't she? Please don't be angry with me for trying to save the garden and ourselves."

"At what expense, hmm, the health of a newly precious friend, a perfectly lovely woman who has brought nothing but joy to people all her life? Is that the price, Gray?"

Stella was more than angry. She was frightened. All her research now seemed nothing but a dilettantish folly, or worse. She'd fed Graham's obsession and never made the connections he did. Women and men died throughout the Kirkwood family tree, this is what history is, but now Stella could glimpse the patterns that Graham was so sure of. First, Elizabeth, whose death so soon after the garden's demise now looked very much as if it was linked. And then, the midwife who delivered Elizabeth's children in the eighteenth century disappeared from village records shortly after the last of Thomas Kirkwood's sons was born, the same year that Elizabeth made the first recorded attempt at reviving the garden. Stella could only assume she had died or moved on soon after Elizabeth succumbed to what was most probably pneumonia—although *that* was in question now, too. And Cosima, dear harmless Cosima, dead at forty only months after she oversaw a team to work on the damn garden. Then again, the world was a

dangerous place all those years ago. Even with every ounce of sense firmly in place Stella wondered, *Who else, who next?*

"Now you listen to me, Graham," Stella said. "I am going straight back to Kirkwood Hall. This minute, in fact."

"You can't, we've only got the one car. Wait for me, please," Graham said. "We'll leave first thing in the morning, I promise."

"I *can* leave and I will," Stella said. "I'm driving. You may take the train. I'll have someone collect you tomorrow while Sorrel and I are in the garden. I won't have her in there alone."

"I forbid you," Graham roared. "I forbid it; do you hear me?"

"Silence!" Stella snapped. "You have no right to forbid me—or Andrew or Poppy for that matter."

"Oh, please, not Poppy, not our girl!" Graham was tearing up, and Stella had no wish to comfort him. She did love her husband, but this man was someone else entirely.

"Get a grip on yourself, Gray, or I will have to slap you."

While Graham slumped on his red leather bench in the House of Lords, Stella whipped through the Chelsea house packing what little she needed for the country. As soon as Poppy returned from class, they would make their way to Wiltshire. How much she would tell her daughter about the roots of Graham's selfish, wild scheme Stella was unsure. Poppy had to know that the Shakespeare Garden, while not off limits, must be approached with caution, and then Sorrel must be told as well. Stella knew that she would probably forgive Graham in time; after all, he was of good heart if not sound mind. Still,

how would the others react when they learned that the lord of the manor believed that a centuries-old evil really was afoot, if not in the form of a curse, then certainly in the very soil beneath their feet? Indeed, what would her family say once it learned that Graham was so cavalier as to sacrifice Sorrel to the garden? The more Stella went around and around in her head, the madder it all sounded and the more abstracted she became so that when Poppy walked in, she found her mother standing in the middle of the front hall with one shoe on and a market basket full of leftovers on the floor beside her.

"Are you running away from home, Mum?" Poppy asked.

"Something like that," Stella said. "I'm taking you with me."

"That isn't usually how it works, you know."

"It's what we're doing, so get your things," Stella said and looked around for her other shoe.

"Hey." Poppy took her mother's arm. "What's happening here?"

"I'll fill you in on the way, darling," Stella said. "We have work to do at Kirkwood Hall and very little time to do it."

Poppy wasn't sure who was barmier, her father for his nonsense about a malevolent force or her mother for believing him enough to take action. Of course, she had to admit that she had always thought the Shakespeare Garden was just wrong somehow. And there was that plaque which, for all her teasing, did leave Poppy with a shiver. As for Sorrel, whatever her parents planned, Poppy knew that her friend mustn't suffer for it.

"Fucking garden," Poppy growled.

"Indeed," Stella agreed.

"Fucking Dad," Poppy spat.

"That's a fuck too far, sweetie," her mother said.

"So what's the plan?" Poppy asked.

"I think we present all we know to Sorrel and see what she makes of it."

"She's going to run for the hills, and not our hills either," Poppy said.

"I wouldn't blame her, but think about it," Stella said as she turned into the long drive that led to Kirkwood Hall. "This is not the first time that Sorrel has encountered the unexplainable, or what would we call it—the darkness beneath the light?"

"Oh boy," Poppy said. "Isn't that why she came here, to escape the dark?"

"Well, that's not working out terribly well, is it?" Stella asked. "Never mind what we call it, let's just make sure that our precious gardener learns what she's really gotten herself into."

Gabe stood at the front door as if he'd been waiting for them.

"How does he always do that?" Poppy mumbled.

"Where is everybody?" Stella asked.

Gabe pointed in the direction of the garden. His frown said more than any words.

"Take this, Poppy," Stella said, handing her the basket. "I'll be back with Sorrel."

"Wait, I'll come with you."

"No you won't," Stella said. "Let me do this part. Your father doesn't want you near the garden."

"Oh, now you're following orders?" Poppy huffed, but she took the basket and followed Gabe into the house. She was surprised when he tapped her shoulder and beckoned her up the stairs. When they stopped in front of the tapestry room, Poppy was thrown.

"What is it, Gabe?" she asked.

He opened the door with his key and flicked on the lights. Nothing had changed: The panels marched along the wall, the hunters chased, the dogs tracked, and the mystery remained.

Gabe went to the last panel and pointed at the book.

"Yes, I know, we saw it, too."

He traced his hand up, past the bloodied foot, past the woodbine, and beyond the line of linden trees to a particularly faded section at the edge of the panel.

"Pretty," Poppy said. "Those trees are long gone."

Gabe shook his head and took a small penlight from his pocket. He trained it on the worn spot, which was a pale green and white, with a hint of sky still visible.

Poppy was becoming impatient. "Just tell me, Gabe. I'm too short to get up close to that section."

Gabe turned around and began to sign. Poppy was able to follow simple sentences, but Gabe was moving too fast for her. She was ashamed that she'd always counted on his lip reading, unlike Andrew, who'd made a point of learning to communicate with Gabe in his own language.

"I'm sorry, Gabe," Poppy said. "I'm not getting this."

She swore that Gabe growled before striding out of the room and into her mother's library. He riffled through a stack of books until he found what he wanted and flipped through the pages. Finally he opened the book wide for Poppy. He pushed it toward her and jammed his finger onto a page.

"It's the chapel," she said. "Hold on! Stay right there."

Poppy scattered papers until she found her mother's giant scrapbook. She knew there were pictures of the tapestries in it, perhaps not as good at the ones Delphine now had but good enough. She flipped the book open and began leafing through the pages.

"There," she said. "There's the panel." She grabbed her mother's smudgy magnifying glass and peered through it at the picture. The tick, tick of her mother's desk clock was loud, and the sound of her own breathing filled the room beneath it. Poppy could hear the tension Gabe held in his silence. Finally, she looked up.

"Oh Gabe, you clever, clever man!" she cried and lunged to hug him.

Gabe stood stiffly as Poppy squeezed him.

She beckoned him over to the scrapbook.

"You're right. It's here, just as you tried to tell me," Poppy said, keeping her face turned to Gabe.

And it was. With proper lighting by the V&A team, the faded area came into clearer relief. The Kirkwood chapel stood at the end of the linden tree path. The façade was pristine, not

tumbled down as it had become, and the pale threads picked out a rustic stained glass window on the side facing out. It might have been a rendering of the Virgin Mary or some other female saint sitting in repose with a sacred text. But with a larger rendering of the window and an interpretation of its contents on the facing page, Poppy saw the image for what it was: a key. At the woman's feet were blossoms and leaves, flowers and greenery of all kinds. Even Poppy could see the waving Solomon's seal, and she recognized lily of the valley and rosemary, spiky and tall. The rest was a mystery for Sorrel to solve.

"Thank you, Gabe," Poppy said. "You have no idea how you've helped us."

Gabe nodded and for the first time since Sorrel had come to Kirkwood Hall, Poppy saw him smile. She skittered down the stairs in triumph.

Left behind, Gabe turned off all the lights and locked the door behind him. He was relieved to have shared this secret at last.

Of course, all Poppy wanted was to race off to the garden and show everyone what Gabe had uncovered; she might have, too, if Andrew hadn't come through the front door with an armload of wood.

"Slow down there, cheeky monkey," he said and steadied Poppy with his shoulder.

"I've got something, something real and useful and completely amazing," Poppy said.

"If it's not the cure for the common cold, I'm afraid I'm unimpressed," Andrew said and dropped the wood into the copper tub beside the fireplace.

"Oh, this is so much better than that!" Poppy crowed. "Where's Sorrel? And Mum?"

"I've not seen Sorrel since this morning," Andrew said and blushed.

"Yeah, yeah, old news, you and Sorrel, got it." Poppy held up her mother's scrapbook. "I have the key to this whole garden, witch hunt, Elizabeth's diary extravaganza!"

"You found something?"

"Actually Gabe found it. I've just purloined it," Poppy said. "Let's go tell the others."

"Slow down. Can I just bring us back to the old news portion of the program?" Andrew asked. "What do you think you know about me and Sorrel?"

"Look, Dad shipped Sorrel in for the garden," Poppy said. "Mum shipped her in for her morose brother. And I stole Patience's remedy for a broken heart and dosed you."

"Jesus," Andrew said. "I'm such a pawn."

"Actually, Sorrel is the real pawn, and we think she's in trouble so if you want to continue this affair of the heart, let's make haste to the cursed garden and save the damsel, shall we?"

"You know, sometimes I think your father's high drama has rubbed off on you," Andrew said.

"Let's hope not or next I'll be playing his game." Poppy pulled at Andrew's jacket. "Come on then, deep breath in."

Poppy gave Andrew a précis of her father's deceit as they walked. His face got tighter and tighter until the skin around his lips went white. The Graham Poppy described was unrecognizable to Andrew. With or without completely sharing in Graham's questionable supernatural theory about the garden, or even the poisoned-ground one, Andrew had heard enough that his anger at his brother-in-law threatened to spill out onto Poppy.

"Let's just replace 'cursed' with 'toxic,'" Andrew snapped. "What kind of asshole sends someone into Chernobyl without telling them so?"

"That would be Dad," Poppy said. "I don't believe he's malevolent, I really don't. Just blinded by a misguided desire to protect us."

"But not Sorrel, no care for her?" Andrew said. "That's just plain selfish. And while I'm handing out labels, why on earth would you feed me some unknowable syrup de witch. I could be dead by now or, you know, have boils."

"Or you could just be in love," Poppy said, and Andrew shook his finger at her. "Now let's not be judgy; Patience is Sorrel's sister. She'd never send her off with something harmful."

"We're not done," Andrew said to Poppy as they neared the garden.

All was quiet when they arrived save for the insects that rode the warm breeze. When Poppy stepped over the pile of disassembled bricks, Andrew stopped her.

"Just to be safe, you'll stay out for now," he said.

"Jesus," Poppy said. "You and Gabe are almost worse than Dad."

Andrew entered and stood just inside the ruins of the threshold. He'd expected to feel the shiver he'd become accustomed to, but in that moment he was too taken by the sight to feel anything but awe. Thin white lines of chalk traveled the loamy soil, turning the abandoned garden into a disciplined grid, unspoiled by even a single footprint. Sorrel must have raked her way backward out of it. He inhaled, scenting for the smell of mold, the sooty smell of the desiccated lichen. Instead, the aroma of manure and healthy decay rose up, the fragrance of promise, of potency. But no Sorrel and no Stella.

"They're not here, or they've been consumed by the monster garden," Andrew said when he came back to Poppy. "Where to next?"

"The chapel," she said with such a gleam in her eyes that Andrew could only follow her, shrugging his shoulders.

"So you aren't going to tell me anything about your really useful 'thing'?" he asked, pointing at the messy folio under Poppy's elbow.

"It's a group presentation," Poppy said, shifting her mother's scrapbook from one arm to the other.

"Not including your father?"

"Ha, like he deserves my brilliance."

Andrew had locked up the chapel after he and Marcus tested the bells, so he fished for his key as they walked.

"Where's Wags?" Poppy asked.

"She doesn't behave around that garden, digging and whining, rolling around like she's found a dead thing. Too difficult to control her."

"That's what I'm talking about," Poppy said. "Even Wags is getting the bad vibes."

"Maybe," Andrew said. "But when I went in just now, I didn't get the bad vibes, and, I'll confess, the place usually chills me."

"Sorrel's magic!" Poppy said.

"For the love of God," Andrew moaned. "Enough."

They found Sorrel and Stella sitting on the bench in the churchyard. Poppy had expected to find an angry Sorrel and a contrite Stella, but instead the two women were laughing, eating from a bowl of early sugar snaps and sharing a bottle of water.

"What ho!" Poppy called. "No drama? No crack of thunder? No raging or blowing from Sorrel?"

Stella looked at Sorrel and then at Andrew.

"It seems that our Sorrel thinks that Lord Kirkwood might well be off his nut and that we needn't worry," Stella said.

"That's not exactly what I said," Sorrel nudged Stella.

"What *did* you say, Sorrel?" Andrew asked with frost in his voice.

Sorrel's head snapped around at his tone.

"Hey, what's up?" she asked.

"You first," Andrew said.

"Fine, I am less concerned about the nature of, let's say,

the afflicted state of the garden than Graham is. Remember, I've seen damage like this before and I've felt the venom of frightened, angry people as well. This garden is a catastrophe for sure, and the history that brought it to such a sorry state is awful." Sorrel stood and walked toward Andrew. Right there in front of the Kirkwood women and God she took his hand and kissed his rough knuckles. Andrew gawped.

"Andrew, I am safe and I am well. I will make the Shakespeare Garden safe and well too."

"But, Dad's fraud, his . . ." Poppy spluttered, "fuckery! Doesn't that change anything?"

"Oh, I'll have a conversation with your father about that," Sorrel said. "But let's be clear, none of us believe that Graham is a bad guy. I am certain of that, so it makes it a little hard for me to fit him with a black hat. Deception is intolerable. Let's be clear on that too."

At this Poppy grimaced and looked at Andrew. "Yeah, sorry about that whole heartbreak-remedy thing," she said. "I can be a bit impulsive."

"Oh, Poppy," Sorrel said. "What have you done?"

CHAPTER 12
Thistle

It was remarkable how the excitement Poppy felt about her discovery melted away when Sorrel whirled around and pinned her with those sharp eyes.

"Look, it was just a little experiment," she said. "What's important is what I found with Gabe."

"What's important, Poppy," Sorrel said, making the name Poppy sound like shrapnel, "really important, is that you are fooling around with something that could backfire."

Poppy thought that was exactly what Sorrel was doing, actually. And her father, come to that. And, oh, Andrew as well since he'd plunged headlong into a romance with Sorrel. She was about to point that out when she recalled an important detail.

"Hey," she said, pointing at Sorrel. "You said it was for heartburn."

"For all I know it is," Sorrel said. "Or Patience has made me something else entirely, so what were you thinking sneaking off with it?"

"Is this true, Poppy?" Stella asked. "Did you nab this remedy, whatever it is?"

Andrew saw his opening.

"Excuse me, but we're not talking about someone nicking the last piece of cake," he said. "Sorrel has hinted at how powerful her sister's remedies are, and now it appears that I am to find out for myself."

Sorrel was just preparing her answer when Andrew began to laugh.

"I wish you could see your face, Sorrel," he hooted then he looked at Poppy. "Oh come now, I am unchanged," he said. "No, hold on," Andrew put his hand on his stomach and considered, "My digestion has been quite efficient, but that's about it."

The three women looked at Andrew with a mixture of concern and, in Sorrel's case, dismay. She was the only one who knew exactly how effective Patience's remedies were. If Heart's Ease was what Poppy assumed, then anything Andrew felt for Sorrel was suspect. If, on the other hand, it was indeed a heartburn soother then, well, then Sorrel had no idea why she was so afraid.

"If I promise to stop channeling Lucrezia Borgia, can I tell you all what I found?" Poppy asked.

Andrew reached to stroke Sorrel's hair, to tell her with touch that if he'd been enchanted in some way, he was grateful, but Sorrel shook her head.

"Go on then, Poppy," she said and stepped back, leaving Andrew's hand in midair. "Show us what's in that book of yours."

Something that seemed very like the garden chill stole over Andrew when Sorrel withdrew. And then he felt the rising of his old bitterness. For a moment he felt the shameful pleasure of believing that he was right all along: There was no one who could make him care again and he was a fool to have even let Sorrel try.

For Sorrel's part, she required some time to measure Andrew's feelings for her, to weigh them in her hands and heart and calculate whether what had sprung up between them was enchanted by Patience or by each other. And then she had no idea what might happen. But right now Poppy was talking, and Sorrel needed to listen so she turned her attention away from Andrew and let the murmur of the words resolve into a story.

Poppy held out the scrapbook. "You see, this is what Gabe steered me to. And look"—she pointed up at the chapel windows—"Is that where it was, the stained glass? Did Thomas the Hateful destroy it because it told a story he didn't want told?"

"Or did the weavers, the nuns, I presume, just make it up on their own?" Stella asked. "I've seen no mention of it anywhere

in the records. A Kirkwood, certainly not Thomas, must have communicated with them. This is all making my head ache."

"It's a stealthy way to tell the true story, the victim's story," Sorrel added. "If you ask me, the only one who could have shared that story was Elizabeth. Let me see what's in that vignette."

Poppy handed Sorrel the book. "Can we go back to the house with all this?" Poppy asked. "I'm feeling peckish."

"I have never met such hungry people," Sorrel said.

"It's a Kirkwood thing," Poppy said.

There was no resisting, so Sorrel tucked the scrapbook under her arm and everyone walked back to Kirkwood Hall.

Of course Sorrel could identify all the plants in the stained glass with ease and she knew their meaning, and that is where the story lay. She spread the book out on the table.

"Anemone: forsaken," Sorrel touched each plant as she described it. "White rose: innocence, secrecy; purple hyacinth: sorrow, forgive me; edelweiss: courage and purity; freesia: innocence and trust, and here"— she tapped the page— "monkshood: a deadly foe is near."

Andrew listened to Sorrel's voice and let it become music that soothed him. Surely this feeling was stronger, better than his earlier disappointment? There had to be a chance that theirs was nothing more, or less, than a love story.

"I do feel a bit dim that I didn't parse the truth out of this illustration when I first found it," Stella said and moved the

book to the center of the kitchen table. "What we've got here," she said as she whisked eggs and cream in a bowl, "is some crafty nuns who wanted to be sure the truth came out about this witch."

"Alleged witch," Sorrel said.

Andrew snorted.

"And then there's the book," Poppy said and pointed at the page. "If it is Elizabeth's diary, what's it doing with the alleged witch unless Lady Kirkwood was trying to right a wrong before she died?"

"I can't stand another minute of this frivolous speculation," Andrew said and left.

"Let him go," Stella said when she saw Sorrel rise from her chair. "Today has been a bit of a shock to the system."

"I am rather enjoying this whole mysterious thing we've got going," Poppy said.

"The point of all of it is to gain some insight into the Shakespeare Garden," Sorrel said. "Let's keep that as our focus, Agatha Christie, OK?" She stood and took a plate over to the stove where Stella was stirring the eggs and toasting bread in a vaguely steampunk contraption over the wood fire. "While I am sorry that this garden has such a sad and complicated history, and I can't imagine the pain that was Elizabeth's end, my job is to restore it as best I can and then leave you all to enjoy it."

Poppy watched Sorrel walk off with her plate and wondered if she hadn't just schooled them all in the art of grace under fire.

Andrew was on the couch in his living room with Wags sitting on his feet when Sorrel came in. He hated himself for it, but the smell of the food on the plate she held made him lick his lips.

"I come bearing buttery, chivey eggs," Sorrel said. "I am irresistible if only as a conveyance for food."

Andrew slid sideways on the couch. "I am helpless before you . . . and your eggs," he said.

Sorrel knew it was past two, but somehow the velvety eggs sprinkled with chives and parsley and tumbling over toast made from one of Delphine's boules were precisely what she found herself hungry for too.

"You haven't put anything in them?" Andrew asked.

"Very funny," Sorrel said and took a huge bite.

"Step away from my eggs!" Andrew said and sat up, reaching for the plate.

"We could share."

"We could," Andrew said, "but I don't really want to do that."

"Selfish boy," Sorrel said and sat down with him.

Together they cleaned the plate, and poor Wags watched with such longing that Andrew jumped up and got her a piece of clearly moldy cheese.

"This has been a ghastly day," Andrew said. "I seem to have let all that anger and ill temper back out to play. I mean, what was Gray thinking? Are you feeling well or should I get the leeches?"

"You know what," Sorrel said, "let's go over. I think we can dispel some of the poor attitude if you see that it is nothing but an irritable garden waiting to be told how to behave."

While Andrew agreed to come along, he reminded Sorrel that she had once thought the garden was disturbing, and she reminded him that he, in a matter of an hour ago, had made fun of her sister's ability to take plants and turn them into remedies that some people called magic.

"Neither one of us can have it both ways, you know," Andrew said. "Either we believe in all the tales from the crypt and your ability to change nature or we don't."

Sorrel had no answer for that, so she just kissed Andrew and made him forget what it was that he meant to say next.

After Sorrel's ministrations the garden was already feeling less unsettled, but the enormous pile of spent soil that had been taken out was festering not far from its walls. Sorrel took a stick and poked at it, sending up grit and a faintly coppery smell. There was something bothering her about this drift of waste. There was the problem of how to get rid of it, but she supposed Gabe and his men would take it away and dump it somewhere far from the house. Still, Sorrel worried that the spoiled soil might somehow sully wherever it ended up. Of course, that was a possibility only if one believed Graham's stories and, no matter what Sorrel told Andrew, the shadow lingered.

Andrew wondered anew at the orderly plots, dark composted soil mounded between crisp chalk lines. It had a beauty to it that was akin to the rows of polished, empty pews in his

chapel. He understood that this was Sorrel's church and this was where she found both peace and direction. With a start he realized that he missed his own church. Maybe not the one in London but certainly the rewards of walking his congregation through the Anglican rituals, of leading a lost parishioner back to faith. He needed to feel his faith again and, standing beside Sorrel, Andrew understood that he could never really turn away from service.

"Will you begin planting today?" he asked, thinking that perhaps it was the perfect time for him to begin to tend to his own seeds so carelessly tossed aside in the wake of the breakup and ensuing mess.

"Tomorrow," Sorrel answered. "I want to give it a little time to adjust. It's like bringing a new baby into the house. Everything and everyone has to find a new way of being."

"A new way of being," Andrew mused. "I think that is exactly what I need as well. You can't do all the work yourself, surely?"

"The heavy lifting I'll leave to Gabe and his guys but all else, yes, I do it myself, alone with the plants." Sorrel looked at her hands. "It's essential that I touch everything that will live here."

"I would like to help."

"I don't mind a visit once I've found a rhythm," Sorrel said. "Why don't you come later in the day tomorrow."

"Thank you, Sorrel," Andrew said. "Your faith in this process is inspiring."

With Graham due the following morning Sorrel guessed

there'd be a lot of heated talk before the Kirkwoods let cooler thoughts prevail. Andrew might well need the peace of a garden afterward. He'd certainly need to consider that Graham's less than honest performance of late came from a harmless place in his heart if not a completely harmless spot on his land.

"Come back to the Tithe Barn?" Andrew asked.

"I have some research to do," Sorrel said.

"Do it with me. I'm terrific at research," Andrew said as he took her hand and brought it to his cheek. "It has recently come to my attention that I rather like sitting with a beautiful woman poring through papers."

"Computer research."

"I actually have Wi-Fi, you know. I may live in a former wheat depository manned by chanting monks in hooded robes, but it has all the mod cons. Also, Wags." Andrew smiled uncertainly. "Are you sure everything is all right, Sorrel?"

Everything would be once Sorrel had a chance to consult Patience. She might play off everyone's concern about the Heart's Ease remedy but what if, what *if*? How real was Andrew's infatuation, or hers for that matter? Sorrel had seen how Patience's remedies had a ripple effect and Sorrel did not want to be the ripple in this case. She wanted to find her heart's ease without her sister.

"Where are you?" Sorrel asked.

"At the Nursery," Patience said. "Where are you, Castle Hedgerow Warthog?"

"Since when do we have Internet at the Nursery?"

"Since Ben Avellar decided the Sparrow Sisters Nursery needed to be introduced to the twenty-first century," Patience said. "How are you, Sorrel? You look a little peaky."

"I am piqued, that's for sure," Sorrel said. "What did you pack in my suitcase?"

"What did *I* pack? You packed it," Patience said and looked away from the computer.

"Nice try, Patience," Sorrel said. "I found the Heart's Ease."

"Oh, that," Patience said.

"Yes, that," Sorrel said. "What is it? What's it meant to do?"

"Well, now that's entirely up to who takes it, isn't it?" Patience said. She was sitting at the tall counter in the Nursery, and Sorrel could see a row of bottles just like hers lined up beside her sister.

"And if I take it?" Sorrel asked.

"Hmm," Patience stalled.

"Spill," Sorrel snapped. "There's some crazy shit going on here, and I need to know if you started it."

"ME? I'm like a million miles away, Sorrel," Patience said. "What kind of crazy shit?"

"First, there's some seriously bad blood buried in this garden and it will be a struggle to save it."

"That's not good."

"Yes, thank you for that science of the obvious," Sorrel said. "I think now that I've dug it out and replaced the soil I can fix it, but I'll only know when the plants go in."

"And I have something to do with the hoodoo in the garden?" Patience asked. "Because I'm really pretty done with that kind of situation."

"No, Patience, you have something to do with the hoodoo you hid in my bag."

"Did you take it?"

"No, as a matter of fact, someone else did."

"Whoa! Who?" Patience leaned into her computer, distorting her lovely face.

"Back up," Sorrel said. "You look like a nightmare clown."

"Sorry," Patience said. "So whose life have I changed this time?"

Sorrel told Patience about Andrew. She skated around the more intimate details, but she knew that she couldn't hide her growing feeling from her sister. Even separated by a screen, and an ocean, Sorrel could tell that Patience was reading her face and voice.

"So here is a terrific guy who seems to find you quite wonderful and you are doubting every move he makes?" Patience asked.

"I am because he's the one who took the Heart's Ease so, again, what is it for?"

"It does exactly what it says on the bottle, Sorrel," she said. "Like Alice in Wonderland."

"That is not comforting, Patience," Sorrel said.

"No, no, wrong reference," Patience said. "OK, here's what's in it and why I made it."

Patience picked up her tattered notebook and leafed backward through it for a minute.

"Don't you remember what you put in it?" Sorrel asked.

"I do. I'm making sure I give you everything. Show me the bottle, will you? I just want to see how much is left."

Sorrel realized that she didn't have it. Clearly Poppy did and just as clearly she'd been dosing Andrew for days.

"Poppy has it," Sorrel said.

"Poppy? Do we have a secret English sister?"

Sorrel hadn't thought of that, another flower name, another woman gathered into the Sparrow circle. She explained Poppy as best she could to Patience, which only served to excite her sister even more.

"That girl is definitely one of us," she said. "Who else would slip a remedy to someone? I don't think you need to worry too much. I mean look at Henry. I threw my whole arsenal at him in secret and he still loves me. This could be good, right?"

"Patience, what is it and what is it made to do?" Sorrel was losing patience, and the little thrill of anxiety that had been living in her chest since Poppy's confession began to grow.

"Clematis, star of Bethlehem, Sweet Chestnut, Melissa, and hawthorn berries," Patience rattled off the ingredients. "I made a strong tincture; just a drop or two daily in any liquid will do it."

"Do what?" Sorrel asked.

"Look, after Matty and the trial, and then all the relief of bringing the Nursery back to life and Nettie and Henry and me . . ."

"Patience, get to the point."

"I sensed an emptiness in you, Sorrel. I felt that even though you were happy for all of us, happy for Simon and Charlotte, there was still this, I don't know, thwarted feeling coming off you."

"Thwarted? Terrific, you make me sound all Miss Havisham."

"Not like that," Patience said. "You smelled of carnation, you know, cloves, pepper, and too intense, which is what caught me."

"Patience, I was happy, I am happy, for all of you," Sorrel said. "I never begrudged you a single moment of joy."

"Of course you didn't, Sorrel. You couldn't. But what I sensed made me want to make sure that your heart softened, opened to someone else, someone who isn't us."

"Oh, Patience," Sorrel said. "Now there's Andrew."

"Exactly," Patience thumped her hand on the counter. "Now there's Andrew."

"But is it real? Is it Andrew Warburton or is it Patience Sparrow?" If Andrew were simply under a spell... Sorrel shook her head. *Not a spell,* she thought.

"Sorrel, listen to me," Patience snapped. "Love, lust, attraction, whatever you want to call it, it can't be mixed up in a bowl or distilled from the garden. You know that, or you should."

"Right, tell that to Andrew," Sorrel moaned. "You've got to stop looking for my knight in shining armor, Patience."

"You don't want the shiny knight, Sorrel, you want the dented one who's actually had to fight for something."

"Andrew went through a fairly cataclysmic relationship rupture," Sorrel said. "I'd label that a battle, and it certainly accounts for the darkness at his center and his shaky faith."

"Then if I opened his heart instead of yours, I am not the least bit sorry," Patience said. "And if you are responding to that as well, then the only magic at work is what your heart is telling you. Attend to that, Sorrel, and stop looking for an excuse to seal yourself away."

Patience ended the conversation, fumbling to find the right key on her computer just long enough for Sorrel to see the smile stealing onto her lips.

"I AM EXHAUSTED," Sorrel said into her room. "I am confused and tired and"—she looked at the bed—"I am lying down and no one can stop me."

She woke to Stella's gentle hand on her shoulder.

"Sorrel, darling, do wake up," she said.

"What's wrong?" Sorrel asked. "What time is it?"

"Nothing's wrong, dear. Delphine's come by and I knew you'd want to talk with her."

Delphine had arrived with a box of homemade savory thyme shortbread and a bottle of elderflower cordial. When Sorrel came into the library, she was handed a glass and told to sit by the imperious Delphine, something she was getting used to.

"So, little gardener, here is what I have discovered."

Sorrel thought that if someone handed her another discovery, she just might hit them over the head with it.

"The seventh panel of the tapestry is in the chapel," Delphine said and raised her glass.

"No it's not." Andrew walked into the room. "No one has ever confirmed there *is* a seventh so we don't know if it's a *thing* period."

"But it is a *thing*," said Delphine. "And the chapel is the only possibility, the only place it must be, I am certain."

"Delphine, I have seen an awful lot of that chapel during the renovations and if there is a giant meters-wide and long, richly woven and embroidered, ancient tapestry of a dead or dying witch or thief or unicorn languishing in some hidey-hole, I'd have found it."

Every woman in the room rolled her eyes. Of course there was a final tapestry.

"The panel is well hidden, and you were not yourself when you began the project," Delphine said with a sniff. "You wouldn't even know where to look. The nuns were resourceful."

"The nuns were never here," Stella said. "The tapestries were commissioned by Thomas and woven in Belgium. If anyone oversaw their installation, it would have been Lady Kirkwood."

"Who was, sadly, sick or dead by then," Sorrel added. "As we know now."

"Yes, but if we assume that Elizabeth had a hand in the

weaving then she wouldn't need to be alive when they were installed to be sure the story was told." Poppy clapped her hands. "You see, Thomas was an ass, he'd never figure out the 'fuck you' that was really in the tapestries, he'd have celebrated their brutality. Only later would any Kirkwood be embarrassed by the subject matter!"

Delphine took this as proof that she was right. "Perhaps hiding it was someone else's secret, then. So, we go to the chapel, we bring out the tapestry, we solve the mystery for Sorrel, and all will be well." She stood and looked around at the gathering.

"Why are you not moving?" she asked.

Sorrel slumped over, Stella smoothed her skirt, and Andrew up threw his arms.

"Fine, I'll take this one," he said. "*Allons-y,* Delphine."

"I do believe that Delphine might have grabbed us all by the ears if Andrew hadn't volunteered," Stella said.

Sorrel snorted. "She is persuasive."

"And determined," Stella agreed. "So, Graham will arrive tomorrow, and I want you to know that if you feel compelled to give him a good dressing-down, I will cheer you on. And even though you have assured me you won't leave us, and I hope you haven't reconsidered, I would take you to the airport myself if that is what you asked."

Sorrel wasn't going to upbraid Graham; there was no real call for that. He was a bit of a kook, but he wasn't mean-spirited. Besides, if she had to lecture people who thought of their own

concerns first, she'd do nothing else. And she certainly wasn't going to run home like a scared child. For the first time in a long while Sorrel knew exactly what she was doing. The minute she breathed the still air in the Shakespeare Garden, the minute her fingers felt the crumbling moss and powdery soil, Sorrel knew this was a garden built on skeletons. Perhaps she hadn't expected the truth to be quite so literal, but she also couldn't blame Graham for his single-minded drive to save a family he thought in peril. As for the garden being actually bad for her health, well, that remained to be seen once Sorrel really dug in. And now that she'd alerted Patience to the situation, Sorrel suspected there'd be a package at the tiny post office within days. Not that she'd need it, not at all. It wasn't as if she was about to step onto the moon without a spacesuit.

SORREL WAS WAITING for Andrew in the Tithe Barn when he returned from his Delphine-induced scavenger hunt.

"Well, Indy, did you find the idol?" she asked.

Andrew bent to take his boots off, and Wags flew in from the bedroom and slammed into him.

"Ooof," he said and fell back on his butt. He was dusty and there was an angry scratch on his cheek.

"Oh dear," Sorrel said. "What happened?"

"A losing skirmish with a bramble." He touched his cheek. "Have you got anything for it, my little wiccan?"

"Only this," Sorrel said and leaned down to kiss him.

"Nicely done," Andrew said and pulled her onto his lap.

Wags danced around them until she gave up and settled with a sigh before the fire.

"We should talk about it," Sorrel said.

"It's only a scratch," Andrew said. "Isn't that what all the heroes say?"

"No, we need to talk about Patience's remedy and how you've been feeling and, I guess, how I've been feeling."

"Are you ill?" Andrew said and turned her face to his. "I knew it, that damn garden."

Sorrel sighed and pulled his hands away. "Come here," she said and led him to the couch. The fire was dying and there was a bite in the room now that the sun was low.

"I spoke with Patience this morning and she explained Heart's Ease," Sorrel said.

"The remedy, inverted commas, right?" Andrew said gesturing with his fingers.

"Right. Now, before you crack any more witch jokes, let me tell you that Patience and her boyfriend, who is a medical doctor, by the way, are both considered Granite Point's most effective healers." Sorrel ran her thumb over Andrew's scarred eyebrow. "Between the two of them there is almost nothing they can't at least treat if not fix."

"Lucky town," Andrew said and caught Sorrel's thumb. "And you? Do you consider Patience's work useful?"

"I do," she said. "As for this particular remedy . . ." Sorrel hesitated. She didn't want to seem like a lovelorn maiden. "This was made for me."

Andrew couldn't imagine why Sorrel would need any help with her heart or her ease. To him she was as clear and cool as spring water, smooth as silk, full of life and perhaps the most sensual person he'd ever met. Everything she touched, including him, seemed to blossom under her hand, and he honestly didn't think any souped-up tincture could make her any more desirable.

"I've told you Patience can divine things about the people who come to her. She sees the world in a highly scented way and, somehow, those scents speak to her."

"And you can make anything bloom, anytime and anywhere, right?"

"Let's hope so," Sorrel said. "My point is that Patience detected a sadness in me that should have lifted once we all got on our feet again. She said I was thwarted."

"That's an ugly word."

"Yeah, it is but, essentially, she was right." Sorrel folded her feet up under her and shivered.

"I'll build up the fire and you can talk without my overweening scrutiny," Andrew said.

So Sorrel told him how everyone in her little world found their way after the summer settled down. She told him about Henry and Patience, how they seemed to cleave together in the forge of her trial. About Nettie, who found her voice and then her love in Ben Avellar, and about Simon and Charlotte, whose new baby had turned both of them to mush. Which left Sorrel, alone.

"I'm fine alone, you know," she said. "I mean I've had to get used to it since Marigold's death. Sometimes I wonder if being the twin left behind has made me a half instead of a whole."

Andrew poked the fire once more before he came and knelt in front of Sorrel.

"I cannot even think of the loss of a sibling, let alone a twin," he said. "I am adept at helping people through their darkest hours, or I was once, but I won't use that skill now. You see, Sorrel, you are not alone, not anymore. I am here and, since I would never consider you half of anything, together we can be more than whole."

"You are so lovely, Andrew," Sorrel said as she stroked his hair. "You are kind and funny and full of all the things I value above all."

"But?" Andrew said.

"Not a but, just," Sorrel stopped. "Andrew, what if this isn't you? What if this is Patience's gift, her remedy turning you into someone you're not? What if in a week, or next month or tomorrow, even, you wake up and realize that whatever you feel for me isn't real at all?"

"I love you, Sorrel Sparrow," Andrew said. "I don't know how or why such a startling shift has come over me, and I don't particularly need an explanation. Until you came along, only weeks ago, I was loathed and loathsome. If your sister's concoction has released me from that unhappy state, well then, marvelous. If you have somehow punctured my swell of despair, and the remedy is nothing more than a digestive aid, then

fabulous. The result is the same, give or take a little gas. I love you and I would very much like to know if you love me."

Andrew had never made such a speech in his life. It compelled him to realize that he'd never, never felt this way about Miranda. The lightness in his spirit, the goofy humor that had resurfaced, the smiles he'd nearly forgotten how to make, all of it was part of an Andrew he hadn't known was still alive.

"That was some barnburner," Sorrel said.

"You mock me."

"I wouldn't dare," Sorrel said. "Because I love you. There I said it."

"It didn't hurt, did it?" Andrew smiled.

"Not nearly as much as I thought." Sorrel smiled too.

CHAPTER 13

Pansy

Sorrel was in the garden by dawn. She stood at the very center, where she planned to set the sundial, and surveyed her surroundings. The beds were well wetted even though the watering system had not been turned on yet. It smelled good: loamy, earthy, and ready. Most gardeners would plant parterre by parterre, but Sorrel Sparrow knew that she would choose each plant and the order in which she'd dig them only after she had touched them all. So she wandered from pallet to pallet, brushing her hands softly over leaves and buds. She leaned in to smell the apricot-tinted rose whose petals had just unfolded into a ruffled cup. The scents of lemon, myrrh, and peach floated up, and Sorrel once again wondered why anyone would name a rose Jude the Obscure. Next she adjusted the

bamboo stake in a peony bush and checked to be sure the ants had found their way to the buds. There was more wandering, more touching until finally Sorrel had visited every pallet. She pulled the wheelbarrow over and began to fill it with bounty. Once in the garden she knelt and began to place seedlings, plants, and root balls in place. She never wore gloves at this stage; her fingers had to feel every ridge in a stem, every vein in a leaf, and the nap of velvet on a petal.

As the hours passed, Sorrel lost herself in the work as she always did. She went back and forth to the pallets to refill her barrow and stopped now and then to look out over the garden. Occasionally she shifted a grouping from one parterre to the other. The time for that was now before the final mulch was spread and the low box hedges went in. There seemed no rhyme or reason to her planting. In the early stages of any garden Sorrel only listened to the plants; even her beautiful watercolor plans could change if she sensed the need. Tonight, for instance, she might well go back and draw all over the plan that had so entranced Graham Kirkwood. Never mind, she'd make a new one when she was finished.

That is how Graham found Sorrel, on her knees, elbows deep in mulch, rose petals in her hair and dirt on her cheek. She felt him before she saw him: the subtle shift in the air around her as another body entered the space. She turned.

"I am so very sorry, Sorrel," Graham said. "Can you ever forgive me?"

"You are in the garden, Graham, as am I. What do you think?"

"Well, I could certainly understand if you wanted to throw a sod clod at me."

"Do you think that because I am in this garden I have any good humor about your secrets?" Sorrel asked.

Graham spluttered and then sat down on an overturned bucket.

"No, no indeed. There is very little humor to be found at Kirkwood Hall at the moment. Of course, it is my fault, my shortsighted, misdirected, ill-considered plan to save a family, a legacy, my wife, and my daughter in one stroke. You have to know that I truly believe the garden is only a danger to Kirkwoods." He stopped. "I haven't any words for my regret."

Sorrel let Graham sit in silent misery for a moment or two while she hosed the dirt off her hands and grabbed a towel to dry them. She walked over until she stood over him—loomed was how she saw it, and she hoped he saw it that way too. Her height could be an advantage and with Graham hunched over on his sad bucket, she felt satisfyingly looming.

"Come with me," Sorrel said.

Graham looked up and let out a breath as if he'd been spared execution.

"Absolutely, right behind you," Graham said as he stood.

Sorrel led him through the garden, pointing out what she'd planted, what she'd changed, what she would do next. She

stood him at the center of the four paths and told him how the sharp-edged gravel walkways would all lead to a sundial, that a chamomile lawn would roll away from the external walls on each side; dwarf apple and pear trees would espalier over one internal wall while the others would be home to climbing roses and clematis or perhaps woodbine if she knew it could be controlled. She sketched out the willow teepees she planned to install so that sweet peas would fill the air with scent.

Graham followed her in a fog of relief and gratitude. He was surprised at Sorrel's gracious pardon. Of course, he hadn't been terribly good at keeping his concern to himself so Sorrel had, at least, been cautious in a healthy fashion. And now, with the garden underway, he felt reprieved and optimistic once again. Stella was another matter. He wondered if Andrew had softened his sister in his absence. As befuddled as he could appear, with a shambolic, good-natured mantle he could and did put on when necessary, Graham was sharp as a razor and missed nothing. He knew that Sorrel and Andrew were ensconced in a pleasing love affair, but he had worried that Andrew's own protective bent might have swayed Sorrel away from her task. Today he felt his mood lifting and was already imagining a jolly lunch, perhaps on the terrace overlooking the formal gardens. Yes, that was the way forward: pink wine, cold roast beef, Delphine's bread, his cheeses, and tender leaves from the kitchen garden. *Such an idyll,* he thought. *All is well.*

Sorrel brought him up short.

"Graham," she said, "you need to know that what you did

was wrong and that while I am determined to make this garden as rich and lasting as Shakespeare's work itself, I do not excuse you. I was brought here without full disclosure, and I can't forget that."

"I am undone by my deceit," Graham said.

"Hardly," Sorrel said. "But you'd better hope that no one else is."

DELPHINE AND ARTHUR joined the family for lunch. Graham was subdued, but clearly it took an effort. Every time he tried to leap to his feet or envelop someone in a bear hug, Stella put a hand on his arm.

"You really must contain yourself," she whispered in his ear. "It's unseemly given your recent revelations." With the omission of the endearment "darling," Stella made it clear that she still harbored some robust resentment.

Graham took Delphine aside at one point to apologize.

"I am sorry that I never told you of my suspicions, however unfounded, that the garden was a thing of, well, a thing not to be trifled with," he said. Graham could see Arthur eyeing them with a fierce look.

"You did not need to tell me, Gray," Delphine said. "I knew, somewhere, I knew. When we found the tapestries together, all I could think about was how exciting they were. I let my spirit run away from my wits."

"I think we were a team in the witless department," Graham said.

"Still"—Delphine pinched between her brows and looked up at Graham—"Mathilde, do you think she . . ." Delphine couldn't finish.

"Oh, no, Delphine!" Graham couldn't pretend he hadn't had the same thought over the last few years, hadn't in fact included Mathilde in his late night worries when he decided to look outside for garden help. Still, he pushed forward. "If for one moment I had thought she was in real danger, I would have stopped her forays instantly. You must believe me." And that was true, all those years ago.

"I do," Delphine said. "And now, this Sorrel, this little gardener you have imported, how will you protect her?"

"Unclear," Graham said. "She doesn't believe that she needs protection. Sorrel doesn't believe in the curse at all. And perhaps she's right, or at least safe because she does not bear my name. I must have been a bit mad to be swept up in such a ridiculous tale to begin with."

"We shall see," Delphine said. "Perhaps Sorrel is immune through her own sorrow."

"Or through her new happiness," Graham said and kissed Delphine's temple. "Thank you, for all you are and all you do. You became family the moment you set foot in Kirkwood Hall, and you are under my protection henceforth!"

Delphine rolled her eyes and went off to reassure her husband that she was not about to fall prey to the Kirkwood family curse, or its charms.

Poppy had been curiously silent as she drank her wine and

ate the first of the white asparagus. Sorrel sat beside her and snagged a spear, which she dipped in lemony butter and carefully lowered into her mouth.

"Careful," Poppy said. "Kirkwood butter is notoriously difficult to get out in the wash."

Sorrel was wearing a white poplin shirt with a high collar. Her mother's string of lapis lazuli beads lay against her chest where the sun had already turned her skin golden. Her hair was up, the white stripe stark and striking against the black. After she left the garden with Graham, Sorrel had showered and, instead of slipping into her customary jeans and tee shirt, she had found herself grabbing something less "garden-ish." She was beautiful.

"Poppy, I'm not angry at you, not now at any rate," Sorrel said. "You did what you thought was kind, and I get that."

"Well, bugger all," Poppy said. "You couldn't tell me—oh, I don't know—last night?"

"You needed to stew, to have a time out before I forgave you," Sorrel said. "Also, I needed to talk to Patience to be sure you hadn't poisoned the man who seems to be the love of my life."

"Oh my God! This is news! Who knows? Who can we tell?" Poppy cheered, "Oh, wait, we all know. You two are utterly transparent, which is something I can't say about Dad."

"Great," Sorrel said. "I do love being the subject of gossip."

"Sorrel, not gossip, just general jubilation. Andrew is back to himself, you are about to make some miracles, Dad seems to

have regained his senses, and Delphine brought mille-feuilles and éclairs for dessert."

Lunch was just as Graham had pictured. Even Gabe passed through and took the plate Stella offered. He stood in the shade of a newly leafed-out willow some yards away and ate. Several dogs gathered at his feet hopefully, and not even Gabe had the heart to shoo them off. He watched the people he cared for group and regroup as they ate and drank. It was a pastoral painting come to life, and Gabe felt more keenly than ever the need to protect them. He was a part of Kirkwood Hall, the land, the dogs, and the gardens. Since he was a boy he'd watched over these people. When scarlet fever overtook him at nineteen, Graham's mother called the doctor out in the night to attend him. The antibiotics worked but not before near complete deafness set in. Lady Kirkwood never quite forgave his father, and it was she who took up sign language and painstakingly taught Gabe over that long winter. The care went both ways from that time onward. It was a durable thing that had held fast through the years. The boys not only signed at speed, but also developed their own kind of code so that they could still keep secrets together. But now the world had intruded, as it does for everyone.

At first, Gabe had feared the changes that Stella brought with her when she married Graham. Then, as he saw her gentle ministrations to both the land and the animals and then to her growing family, Gabe softened and accepted that everything around him would continue to shift over time but that he, at

the center, would not. He would be the rock for this generation as he had been for the last.

It might have seemed out of character for Gabe to have revealed any clue to the Kirkwood secret, particularly to Poppy, who was still young and dreamy beneath her sharp wit. But once he had watched Sorrel for a week or two, he understood that he needn't be alone as keeper anymore. Sorrel seemed to have the same kind of eye as Gabe. She noticed the tiny dragonfly hovering over the mock orange and smiled at the iridescent wings, she saw the hornet's nest that hung hidden in terrible beauty under the Tithe Barn eaves and approached it without fear. She was the only one who could lure the skinny barn cat away from her kittens long enough to feed her scraps. One day as Gabe was overseeing the dredging at the pond, he saw her carefully, gently collect a fallen hatchling and reach high into the hedgerow to replace it in a nest. At first Gabe scoffed, prepared to dislike her just a little bit more for not knowing that she'd doomed the fragile thing with her touch. The mother bird would never accept it, and it would starve before it fledged. After Sorrel returned to her work, Gabe watched for the mother with a grim certainty that he'd have to keep the hounds away from the dead chick by afternoon. Instead, the mother returned and fed her nestlings without incident.

Gabe let his knowledge out bit by bit over the weeks it took for Sorrel to settle in and undertake her work. First he left the tapestry room door unlocked and let Poppy and Sorrel spend just enough time in the room to be frightened. Now he wasn't

sure if he meant to drive Sorrel off or draw her in further. He hadn't expected Poppy to be so engaged in the matter of the Shakespeare Garden. Poppy had been distant of late, growing up and away, Gabe reckoned, and that was probably just as well. Soon enough Rupert would need to be made wise in the ways of the estate so that there would be a seamless transition when he inherited the title. Rupert clearly had his eye on taking over from his father, and a fine lord of the manor he would be. It was Poppy who seemed unable, unwilling, really, to take up her duties as Lady Philippa, a courtesy title but a powerful one. She had yet to choose a charity patronage, spent little time with her godmother, the Princess Royal, and rarely took advantage of the perquisites of inherited wealth. Still, her attention to Sorrel and the work of returning not just the garden but also the family to peace was encouraging. Seamless, that is what satisfied Gabe, no bumps, no hiccups, and certainly no outsiders to throw his world into chaos. Yet, here was Sorrel and instead of upending things, she seemed to be smoothing them over, for everyone.

Gabe had planned to show Sorrel the connection between the tapestries, the chapel, and Elizabeth's book, but it was Poppy who had barged in with her mother in a state. Being a skilled lip reader was more than just an everyday necessity for Gabe. He picked up enormous amounts of useful intel simply by going about his business in the presence of others. Eavesdropping on Poppy and Stella as they took off their coats and greeted the dogs gave Gabe enough information about Graham's weeks-

long dissembling that he knew he had to act quickly. As soon as Stella headed out to the garden, Gabe had taken his chance and given his next secret over to the girl. Now, as he watched Poppy and Sorrel laughing together, he felt less guilty about exposing Poppy to the secrets. Together the two women were more powerful, Gabe was certain.

When Delphine too agreed to help Sorrel, Gabe began to feel almost optimistic. He'd known Delphine as long as she'd been with the family and he had, naturally, fallen a little in love with her right along with Graham. He'd watched how the two explorers began to unravel the secrets in the house, how they approached their adventures with great exuberance, and each little mystery they solved was another cause for celebration. He couldn't remember now why he hadn't stopped them that rainy day so long ago when Delphine found the tapestries. It had seemed of little concern because Graham wasn't particularly enthused by the tattered rolls so Gabe imagined it would all just go away. But it didn't and after Delphine revealed she was pregnant Gabe began to worry in earnest. The subject matter was unsuitable for anyone, but when he thought about the true magic happening inside Delphine and how delicate she appeared as she struggled through the early months, Gabe knew the tapestries had to be removed and he needed to make that happen. Richard Kirkwood had already "disappeared" the disgusting seventh panel; it was down to Gabe to find a way to take the others far away for as long as possible. At least Delphine would be free of their pull while she waited for her baby to be born.

One of Gabe's daily chores was collecting the post in the village. He could have given the job over to one of the young workers who seemed to be multiplying as the estate began to come into its own, or he could have asked one of the business staff. But Gabe found the daily trip a pleasant break so he continued, always stopping for a cup at the teashop and the racing form at the newsagents. It was on one of those trips that a solution to the tapestries presented itself. Graham's mother, Helena, Lady Kirkwood was a patron of the Victoria and Albert, an honor held by Lady Kirkwoods going back to Cosima, whose Venetian glass collection was on permanent display at the museum. Gabe was wrangling the letters and bills, circulars and magazines out of the Kirkwood box when he came upon a shiny catalogue raisonné for a V&A exhibit of Elizabethan textiles. Here was an answer, and it was just the place for a load of old tapestries to find a home. It was of no interest to him whether they sat in a storeroom in London for the next three hundred years or ended up in a dumpster. Honestly, he'd have preferred the dumpster. Besides, he was uncomfortable with the fact that Delphine spent her spare time poking away at them with her needle and thread, her magnifying glass and her tissue paper squares to hold the fragile hems. Gabe feared what so much time before such ugliness could do to a spirit.

The next time Delphine was at Kirkwood Hall, Gabe handed her the catalogue without explanation and strode from the kitchen before she could say anything. For one thing, Gabe was still nervous around her, more so now that she was so

clearly pregnant, and for another, because he found it next to impossible to read her lips. She spoke too quickly and her mouth formed words differently in her Belgian accent. Gabe had retained a form of spoken words because he had practiced in front of the mirror in secret from the very start of his deafness. It was important to him to know that he still had a voice, even if almost no one ever heard him. He and Delphine most often used pen and paper to share their news. This time there was no need for a note: Delphine came to the same conclusion that Gabe had and in a matter of days she believed that it was all her idea to ship the tapestries off to London. It took almost no convincing to make Lady Kirkwood see things her way, but Lord Kirkwood had several back-and-forth negotiations with the museum before he convinced them (by way of a substantial donation) to keep the tapestries away from prying eyes and their owner anonymous. The curator was certain that, given time, he could convince Lord Kirkwood that giving them outright to the V&A was a fine idea. Gabe so wished that the curator had been right.

Away they went for the moment and Graham was able to return to his studies, Delphine to preparations for her baby, and the rest of the Kirkwood estate to the business of being stately. Over the coming years Gabe never regretted his or Richard's undercover machinations, never mentioned the seventh panel, nor its hiding place. When the restored tapestries returned to be hung in their own special room, Gabe held the only key and never opened the door. Graham unexpectedly approved of the

secrecy too and so Gabe found his purpose and contentment in the public and private role of caretaker to Kirkwood Hall and all its denizens.

When Mathilde was born, Gabe left a full set of Beatrix Potter books on the inn's doorstep. They were wrapped in rose-printed paper and tied with an organza ribbon, but there was no card; Delphine would have recognized his hand straightaway. To this day she did not know who had left them. Years later they would be well worn from reading and then dusty with disuse. They still sat on a shelf in the hallway between the dining room and the library, behind the thrillers and romances left by guests over the years. There was no one to read them anymore.

Gabe pushed off from the willow with his empty plate and tried to escape before one of the cheery lunchers wanted to chat. But Sorrel noticed. She grabbed a pastry and followed him. Gabe was headed for the small maze that lay at the center of the formal garden. *This could end badly,* Sorrel thought as she surveyed the tall hedges. *Minotaur or meaningless death by starvation after the Napoleon is gone . . .*

"Hey," Sorrel said as soon as she came to the entrance of the maze. Pointless shouting as Gabe had his back turned. Sorrel reached to grab his sleeve. He turned, and she said again, "Hey." She was overwhelmed by the smell of healthy boxwood. There were some who thought box smelled of cat piss, but Sorrel was not one of them and for a moment she was stilled by the wave of scent, green, damp, rampant.

Gabe too was stopped. He was not immune to this brief season of electric green, of newness and possibility and limitless future. As he looked at Sorrel, he lowered his guard. He knew who and what she was, and if he was ever to fulfill his purpose and ensure that the Kirkwoods found their rightful place in history, Gabe needed to stay and heed.

"I'll talk slowly so that you aren't thrown by my accent, is that good?" Sorrel said standing as close as she could without spooking Gabe.

He nodded and reflexively snatched a cluster of box leaves and held them to his nose.

"I know," Sorrel said. "It is the smell of both age and youth isn't it?"

Gabe nodded.

"Here's the thing," Sorrel said. "I am like you."

Gabe made to turn away.

"No, stop," she said and touched his sleeve. "I am of the land and the soil and all the elements that make things grow. So are you."

Gabe closed his eyes. If this woman made her way into his head, then the Shakespeare Garden would never be saved. She would see what he knew, what he feared, and she would run away from all of them as fast as she could.

Sorrel tapped his chest and Gabe jumped.

"Look at me," she said, and Gabe nodded, acknowledging that she hadn't asked him to listen to her.

"I can fix this," Sorrel said. "I can resurrect this garden, I

can heal this family and remedy the poison of their history. No one I have met here deserves to be cursed by the past."

Gabe shook his head and pointed to his own chest.

"Oh no, you don't," Sorrel said. "You are the clear water that runs through a blighted landscape, Gabe. You are the one who, for whatever reason, has taken this family on and you are part of what will fix it, all of it." Sorrel waved her arms around as if the maze itself were closing in. "I am the hands that will plant the new garden over the old. You must be the heart that stands with me."

Gabe began to cry silently. He drew a giant handkerchief from his pocket and mopped his face.

"Yeah, I knew you'd get it," Sorrel said. "Come on then, lead me out of here before I eat your éclair."

CHAPTER 14
Harebell

Planting was slow, precise work for Sorrel. If the weather co-operated, she would be finished in a week, or maybe two. And then she would watch and wait to see how the garden received her plants. In the weeks since her arrival, May had crept toward June, and everything on the estate, with the exception of the Shakespeare Garden, surged into bloom. The orchards were a froth of apple and pear blossoms, the last of the lilacs had been cut and could be found all over the house, and the peonies in the formal garden needed constant staking to support the giant blossoms. Sorrel was given permission to cut some of the flowers as they unfolded. She knew exactly how to select the best blossoms while leaving the formal beds unspoiled. She made arrangements of early delphinium and bells of Ireland

and white lilac for the chapel and filled Andrew's house with bouquets of Queen of Sweden and Lady of Shalott roses from the cutting garden. Each time she gathered the flowers, she worried over the late planting of the Shakespeare Garden.

Gabe met Sorrel every morning that she worked with a paper cup of tea and just the right amount of organic matter in piles. He had laid a tarp down in the center of the garden, and each day he tipped the mulch and compost onto it, ready for Sorrel's needs. He never stayed, though. He knew she planted alone, but sometimes he climbed to the top of the tool shed to watch. He couldn't hear her murmurings, but he could see her mouth moving and the way her head tipped as she seemed to listen to each plant. He also watched for any sign of poison. But Sorrel moved with determined grace, pausing only to adjust a bed here or settle a peony ring there. Gabe winced when she pinched off the first growths of the herbs and cut back the first marigold buds. He knew she was right, but he'd always had a bit of a soft heart when it came to pruning.

Sorrel loved the pattern of her day: the moment with Gabe at the start when the light was new and the dawn chorus just fading away, the solitary time among her plants that no one dared interrupt, and the time when she stood, twisted the kinks out of her shoulders, and left the garden for a while. After a few hours Sorrel always took a break. She cleaned off a bit but not so much that she'd hesitate before going back to the soil. Often she grabbed a snack from the main house and went to sit on the bench in the shady little churchyard. If she was lucky, Andrew

might be messing about in the chapel and together they'd lean against the old oak and rest in contented silence. Once she fell asleep with her head on Andrew's shoulder. She dreamt of a white stag and a hare with a crown before waking with a start. Andrew laughed at her horrified face as he dabbed at the drool on his shirtfront.

"Were you dreaming of me, my love?" he asked.

"Only if you are really a giant stag with antlers or a rabbit with a tiara," Sorrel said.

"Ah, you've found me out, then," Andrew said. "This shape-shifting of mine has got to stop."

Sorrel nuzzled his shoulder, still logy from her brief sleep.

"Listen, I have to go into London tomorrow," Andrew said.

"Oh."

"I've been called to a meeting with my bishop."

"Is this a good thing or a bad thing?" Sorrel asked.

"It's a review, really. In theory, my time in purgatory—to mix religious canons—will end with the summer solstice. Reopening the little chapel on that day was Graham's idea, a rebirth for us all I suppose, and a return to myself in a sense. Of course the boss needs to give me the once-over to be certain I'm not going to go off the rails again."

"Is that what you want, to return to your London church?"

"Unclear," Andrew said. "A few months ago I would have told you that I had left my faith"—he paused—"rather that it had left me. Now I'm not sure."

Sorrel remembered what it was like when the Sparrow Sis-

ters Nursery fell into ruin. She felt abandoned by her faith in a way, too. But hers was built on the soil and what it nurtured, on nature and her ability to work inside it to create things that some called miraculous. So she was glad that Andrew was at the very least looking at his work again. Examining it in the light of his newfound happiness might restore his spirit in a way even she couldn't. Sorrel didn't, wouldn't look any deeper at what Andrew's return to London meant for them. No, she could not bear to think beyond the walls of the Shakespeare Garden. Once it was complete, the gate returned with the bricks and mortar, Sorrel would be without purpose to the Kirkwoods. It would be time for her to return to *herself.* So, instead of counting down the days Sorrel chose to drink them in, and she hoped that Andrew would join her.

"You know," Andrew said. "I do believe I am capable of care again. I think that I might even be better suited to the calling than I was before."

"And that makes you happy?" Sorrel asked.

"It does," Andrew said. "When the days were at their darkest, I couldn't imagine believing in light again. But as with all natural things, I suppose, my faith is returning, and I find that my heart and my head need to be put to use again."

"I can't imagine being so certain in my belief," Sorrel said. "I'm jealous, I suppose, of yours."

"Don't you understand, Sorrel? Faith is belief in the absence of proof."

"And?" Sorrel asked.

"Your faith couldn't be much stronger, my little gardener, you just don't give it a name." Andrew looked a little surprised at the way the two devotions were suddenly one.

"You'll leave in the morning?" Sorrel asked.

"Yes, but I'll be back in two days' time." Andrew took Sorrel's face in his palms. "What shall I do without you?" he asked.

"You'll be busy," Sorrel said.

"What will I do when you have quite disappeared from our lives, Sorrel Sparrow?" Andrew asked. What would he do when this faith, this love of his that he had never prayed for, never expected, went away?

Sorrel had no answer because she had no idea.

THAT NIGHT THE lovers ate dinner at the Tithe Barn. Poppy and her parents were at the Queen's Hart, which left Andrew and Sorrel to cook—Andrew to cook, obviously. He made pasta with Kirkwood's own sheep's milk blue and soft goat cheese, mascarpone, marjoram, and asparagus from the kitchen garden. They drank white wine on the little terrace and put napkins over their shirts as they twirled the long strands of *tagliolini*. The horses milled in the distance, fog lay low on the land as the air cooled, and the pastures gave up the last of their warmth.

Andrew was melancholy. "I'm already nostalgic for us," he said.

"Let's not borrow sadness," Sorrel said. "It's beautiful. We've got three more weeks until solstice and the official opening of

the garden, the dedication of the chapel, your reinstatement as, what *do* they call you?"

"Father, Reverend, Sir, Darling, the usual."

"Darling!" Sorrel laughed. "Darling Warburton!"

"Well, they could call me beloved but I'm saving that for you."

Sorrel took a piece of focaccia and swiped up the sauce in her bowl.

"When did Delphine teach you to cook?" she asked, moving away from the chink in her guarded heart.

"After Stella married Graham, they often invited me out for weekends and summer break; I was still a teenager when they started seeing each other. When Arthur renovated the pub and opened the kitchen up to the bar area, I used to sit and watch Delphine cook. Eventually I drifted back, behind the bar and into the kitchen. I think I learned more just by observing than from any recipe she gave me."

"I'm awfully glad you did," Sorrel said. "Nettie is a very modern cook in some ways. She uses everything out of the Nursery and our garden: herbs, flowers, foraged bits and pieces. Her food is very beautiful, very clean."

"I'm afraid mine is more about filling you up with buttery, cheesy goodness," Andrew admitted. "I could learn a lot from Nettie."

"Oh, Andrew, would you ever come to Granite Point?" Sorrel hadn't dared to ask before. She didn't have parents to impress, but asking Andrew to visit Ivy House and meet her sisters

was still an intimate proposition. When Henry and Patience first got together, they used to sneak in and out of the house as if the Sisters hadn't guessed at their connection, hadn't scented the air for the desire that floated off Patience like perfume. She didn't think she could possibly do that, the subterfuge, the fumbled kisses in a darkened hallway, not at thirty-eight, not now that Granite Point felt less and less like home.

"I would," Andrew said. "I would come. Please ask me."

As the light left the sky, Sorrel and Andrew finished their wine and picked at the berries he'd bought at the market. He'd scattered mint over them and the lightest sprinkling of sugar. They released their juices, turning both their lips rosy. It was the happiest either one of them had been in so very long that neither wanted to break the spell with further talk. Spring had suddenly given way to summer, and Sorrel's time at Kirkwood was winding down just as quickly. They rose without a word, left the plates where they were, and went to bed, a line of daylight still touching the horizon.

Andrew found himself in the grip of an urgency he hadn't felt with Sorrel before. Grown-up, that's how he thought of them: too sensible, too experienced to flail about tearing clothes off one another. But tonight that was exactly what he needed, exactly what he did. And Sorrel matched his hunger as she pulled the tee over his head and he grabbed at the buttons of her shirt. His hands were trembling as he watched her kick her linen trousers off, leaving them in a wrinkled mound at her feet. Sorrel tugged Andrew closer with her fingers in

his belt loops and he had to push her hands away to unzip his jeans.

"Good God, I am unmade by you, Sorrel," he whispered into her hair. "I am restored and I am changed altogether. I hardly know myself and I will not stop knowing you."

Sorrel pressed her temple into his hand but said nothing.

"Do you hear me, little gardener? I am yours now, please, please say you are mine?"

Could she say that? Could she let go of every careful tie with which she'd bound her heart, every blinder she'd donned over time so that she wouldn't lose sight of her sisters? Simon Mayo flashed through her mind. They'd lost each other before they'd been found because neither one of them was willing to give up a piece of themselves to be part of the other. Sorrel would not make that mistake again.

Sorrel threaded her fingers through Andrew's choppy hair and pulled him toward her. She laid her forehead against his. He smelled of the rye grass in the pasture, the rosemary by the chapel door, and the lemon zest he'd grated earlier. She could feel him take a deep breath and knew that if she didn't speak, he would release her, not just on this night but forever. So she matched her breath to his and spoke.

"I belong to you, Andrew," she said. "I have never been so sure of anything in my life."

"That was my prayer," said Andrew and lifted her in his arms, carrying her to the bed, which now lay in a stripe of clear blue light as the night fell and the moon rose.

The Forbidden Garden

IN THE MORNING Andrew and Sorrel woke together, he to drive into London and she to work in the garden. She could tell he was nervous by his return to clipped speech and short one- or two-word responses.

"I hope your meeting goes as you want," Sorrel said uncertainly.

"Hmph," Andrew said and picked up an empty garment bag. He looked at Sorrel. "What?" he asked. He was cross because he was nervous, and crosser still that he couldn't control his nerves.

She pointed at the bag. "Just wondering about that," she said.

"I need to collect my vestments while I'm in town," Andrew said.

Sorrel nodded. "Do you go to a special shop?"

"No, Harrods," Andrew said.

"You're kidding!" Sorrel said.

"Yes, I am," Andrew said without laughing. "The dry cleaners."

He kissed Sorrel and then drew her into his arms.

"Sorry I'm distracted," Andrew said. "Keep an eye on Wags, will you?" and he shouldered through the door.

Sorrel heard the car start up with a growl. She sat back down and finished her coffee, aimlessly running her foot over Wags's smooth back. Andrew's departure jarred her more than she had expected, and she found herself unenthusiastic about the garden this morning. There was nothing for that but to dig in so Sorrel gave Wags a last pat and headed out.

Gabe was sorting the Tudor bricks on a large tarp when Sorrel arrived. He looked up with a small smile and handed her the paper cup of tea.

"Morning," Sorrel said, "How's it looking in there?"

She walked past the wall and stood drinking her tea as she gazed out over the beds. Everything still looked so new, raw even. Sorrel had hoped her plants would be a bit more committed to growth by now. Back at the Nursery she practically had to jump out of the way the minute she got a seedling in the ground. Of course, here there was so much healing going on that it was no wonder the plants were a little slow off the mark.

Sorrel began her wander through the pallets planning and plotting as she touched each plant. With Gabe right there she decided to erect the willow frames for the climbing sweet peas rather than wait till the beds were more organized. She could see, and smell, that the sweet peas were on the very brink of exploding into a riot of blooms, late but still lovely, and she didn't want that to happen without something for their delicate tendrils to climb. So she directed Gabe to carry the frames in and set them up at the corners where any rogue stems could clamber up the bricks and drape over the wall. Sorrel was not used to working with other people's seedlings. There was a part of her that didn't trust anything grown, no matter how skillfully, by someone other than a Sparrow.

Once Sorrel began, her uncertainty left her and she forgot about everything but the garden. Elbow deep in the soil Sorrel

could feel the growing and the coursing of life, of her particular magic, being exchanged between her hands and garden. She put away the mystery of the tapestries and the book, the ridiculous superstitions surrounding this place, even Andrew's enchanted renewal, and his return to faith. His anxiety of the morning would abate, his certainty would return and, if they were very, very lucky, their paths would meet as neatly as the gravel ribbons in the garden. With that thought Sorrel focused anew until all she saw were the plants she settled, the flat of seedlings she'd started from her own garden back home, the sparkle of dew on a spiderweb in the sun. By noon the carpet of green had expanded under her touch, and the parterres began to look as if they too were becoming as content as Sorrel.

Poppy watched from the gate as Sorrel tamped down a lump of soil here, gently spread a curled leaf there. She marveled at the veil of scent that hung over the garden. It was captivating, and Poppy wondered how anyone would ever be able to take it all in when the garden was finished. She'd brought along her notes about the tapestries and Elizabeth, but they hardly seemed necessary in the face of so much life coming into being.

Gabe saw Poppy poised just inside the gate and walked over, trying not to rush, not to show her that he was still concerned that the garden was unsafe. He didn't want to be the last irrational man standing, but he couldn't help himself. He tapped Poppy on the shoulder.

"Oh, hello Gabe," she said. "What fresh secrets are you uncovering for us today?"

Gabe nodded toward Sorrel and then back at Poppy. He pointed toward the chapel.

"Should I get Sorrel?" Poppy asked.

Gabe nodded again.

Poppy stepped further into the garden toward Sorrel, but Gabe stopped her.

"Fine," Poppy said. "Sorrel," she called, "Gabe needs us."

Sorrel looked up, surprised that anything existed outside the garden. But Poppy's smile cheered her, and she cleaned her hands and went to her.

"Gabe wants us to go to the chapel with him," Poppy said. "I'm almost afraid of what he's got for us now."

"You know, as this garden is taking shape, I am less and less interested in all the historical high jinx," Sorrel said.

"Yes, well, Gabe seems pretty determined, and Dad is still pretty wrecky so we might as well keep digging."

"I prefer my kind of digging to yours," Sorrel said.

"Where's Andrew?" Poppy asked.

"He's in London."

"Ah, how did he seem about that?"

"I think he's a mess," Sorrel said. "Didn't he tell you he was going to see his bishop?"

"Sort of," Poppy said. "He seemed his old cryptic self though, so who can say?"

"Maybe you need to rethink your remedy dosage," Sorrel said a bit sharply.

"Now, now, I left that little miracle bottle safely in the larder behind the dog biscuits," Poppy said. "I've hung up my apothecary apron."

Sorrel wasn't sure if that meant Andrew's ardor was real or that he was on a slippery slope to despair again.

Gabe had walked ahead of them to the chapel so that by the time the women caught up, he had already unlocked the door.

"Any thoughts as to Gabe's mission here?" Sorrel asked.

"Not a clue, but if I were to guess, I think Delphine's certainty that a last panel is here somewhere has infected him."

Sorrel didn't tell Poppy about meeting Gabe in the maze. She was as certain as Delphine that whatever Gabe was doing, he meant only to help. Still, Sorrel felt a little sneaky coming into Andrew's space without him.

Gabe led them behind the altar to the ancient crypt. During the restoration year, Andrew had hovered over the architect and the builders as they shored up the crypt, watched as every elevation drawing and ancient sketch was consulted, carefully wiping down the stone sarcophagi and the marble and brass grave plaques that lined the floors.

Poppy shivered as Gabe pulled the gate open and turned on the builders' lights.

"Right, this isn't creepy at all," she said. "I don't care if my ancestors are all having a party down here, I'd rather not attend just yet."

Gabe took out his flashlight and beckoned them over to a

pair of sarcophagi side by side in the center of one of the low-ceiling crypt rooms. On the lids were life-sized statues of their occupants, Thomas and Elizabeth, Lord and Lady Kirkwood.

"If I were Elizabeth, I'd have asked for better accommodation," Poppy said. "Or at least a spot further from Thomas."

"I don't suppose she had much choice," Sorrel said. "At least she brought a book."

Elizabeth Kirkwood lay in repose, her tiny pointy-shoed feet resting on a dog that looked remarkably like Wags. Her husband's effigy was arrayed beside her, clad in chain mail, and, Sorrel thought tellingly, his full helmet. In his hands he clasped a scabbarded sword point down. At his feet was not a beloved pet but a curling snake.

"Well, now," Poppy said, "that serpent has clearly found a mate."

Sorrel moved closer to Elizabeth. There was a slight smile carved into the effigy's face and although her eyes were closed, her hands were holding an open book. At first Sorrel only thought how clever Elizabeth had been to bring a book along for all eternity, and then she noticed the carving.

"Gabe," Sorrel said and turned to face him. "Is this what you want me to see?"

Gabe nodded and signed briefly.

"I understand," Poppy said, all humor gone. "Gabe wants me to read the Latin inscription. It's probably a Bible verse." She turned to Gabe. "Hand me your torch," she said.

"Wait!" Sorrel snapped. "What if it's . . ." she didn't finish.

"A spell? Another curse?" Poppy looked at Gabe. "You wouldn't let us fall afoul, would you, Gabe?"

He shook his head and gestured at the carved book. "Read," he whispered in a gnarled voice that had not been used in public.

Poppy and Sorrel gaped.

"Read," he repeated.

Poppy turned back to the effigy. "First, this is really old and worn and second it's, you know, Latin, which I had hoped to forget before I had to use it again."

She bent over the book and ran her fingers across the letters for some moments, murmuring and backtracking before she stood up.

"What lies beneath is more than what is written on these pages," she said. "I think. I mean that's the closest I can come."

"So what? She's pointing out that her body is buried here?" Sorrel asked.

"I don't think Elizabeth had anything to do with her grave. That would have been Thomas, and he'd hardly leave a cryptic message for future grave robbers," Poppy said. "It was not unusual for a noble's effigy to contain something of value to the dead person. There's Thomas's sword. Eleanor of Aquitaine's effigy is holding a book, too, and married couples were often pictured with clasped hands in death to indicate their eternal bond."

Gabe shifted behind them. He came forward and patted the book. Then he waved them away. He bent and gave an almighty shove. The carved book scraped away from the tomb with a grinding screech.

"Jesus, Gabe, what the hell!" Poppy yelled.

Sorrel stepped forward and peered into the hole. "It's the book," she whispered.

"Yes, I can see that, and now it's cracked and Dad is going to have our heads."

"No, Poppy," Sorrel said. "It's THE book, the diary. My God, it's been here all this time." She turned to Gabe. "How long have you known about this?" she asked. trying to speak slowly and clearly so Gabe wouldn't have any doubt what she was asking.

Gabe spread his hands and turned to Poppy. He signed, also slowly, hoping she would be able to follow.

"Hold it," Poppy said. "Can you talk this part?"

Haltingly and with great effort Gabe began to, something he only did with Graham.

"I found it during the building," he said softly.

"Well, clearly someone wanted to hide it," Poppy said. "Thomas, no doubt, but why not just destroy it?"

"Maybe it was one of her children," Sorrel said. "I'd like to think someone cared to leave it with her."

"Should we touch it?" Poppy asked. "Should we wait for Andrew or maybe Mum?"

"Yes," Sorrel said. "Let's find your mother."

Within the hour Stella and Graham were standing in the crypt staring at Lady Kirkwood's effigy. Stella reached out and stroked Elizabeth's face while Graham stood by her side,

his face as white as the stone. Slowly she reached into the opening beneath the stone book. With a cloth she lifted the book out. Stone dust and centuries-old dirt sifted away as she drew it to her.

"I don't know what to say, Gabe," Graham said, signing as he did. "This is remarkable and more than a little unsettling."

"Obviously we'll get the historical people in," Stella said. "But before we do I think Sorrel and I need to have a wee look."

"I won't have it," Graham said. "What if it's contaminated or something?"

"Cursed, my love?" Stella asked with a small smile. "I think we can safely say that this book may be the only thing that can lift that curse you are so afraid of. Or do you expect Sorrel to poison us from our own garden?"

Graham spluttered and felt that spluttering was all he was good for of late.

Stella wrapped the book in the cloth and led the way out of the crypt.

The sun was near blinding as the little party stood at the church door. It was as if they had all been lofted out of the darkness together, blinking and squinting at a brave new world.

"I say we get Delphine in for supper, and Gabe," Stella said, looking around. "Yes, there you are, Gabe, you must come, too."

"Please Stella, let's not race into some kind of grand escapade without guidance or thought." Graham was wringing his hands like some kind of Edwardian fop.

"Oh Graham, it is much too late to worry about that," Stella said. "Besides, Gabe is our guide, Delphine is our thought, and Sorrel is our enchantress. I think we're quite safe together."

THERE WAS NO Andrew to reassure Sorrel as she finished up in the garden and showered for dinner. There were no Sparrow Sisters to offer advice, even remedies, as Sorrel dressed back in the blue room. She felt uneasy in the Tithe Barn without Andrew. It was as if she didn't wish to examine the veracity of her happiness there without the tranquil influence of Andrew's touch.

In the kitchen all was activity. Graham was decanting wine, Stella setting the table, Poppy shooing Wags back to the hall fire with the hounds and at the center, an oasis of calm as Delphine assembled her *mise en place*. Sorrel watched fascinated as Delphine set out a row of glass bowls and filled them with all the ingredients for her meal. On one wonderfully scarred baking sheet she placed all the chopped and minced vegetables she needed: carrots and celery, onions, shallots, and leeks, mushrooms and minced garlic. On the next she arrayed two cut-up chickens and on the third were beakers of wine and stock, saucers of softened butter and herbs, stripped and cleaned from their stems. Finally, a mortar of finely ground salt beside two bowls of coarse ground pepper and flaky Maldon sea salt.

"Coq au vin, only with white wine," Delphine announced. "It is too warm for red, and we are too busy to be made drowsy with heavy food."

Whatever was in the future, and it might be hard indeed, Sorrel was at peace in this moment, content in all ways save the absence of Andrew. As if she read her mind, Poppy brought out the missing puzzle piece.

"How do you think Uncle Andrew is faring in London?" Poppy asked.

"I imagine he is finding his way with the benevolent overlords," Graham said. "Surely he will be welcomed back given his"—Graham looked at Sorrel and raised his glass—"recent return to life and love, sense and sensibility."

Sorrel blushed and lifted her glass. There was no denying the relationship, no hiding the brazen way she'd simply shifted herself from the comfort of the blue room to the passion of the Tithe Barn.

"I am grateful to you all for welcoming me and for accepting that Andrew and I seem to have found common ground."

The laughter was full-bodied and immediate.

"To common ground," Graham toasted as soon as he'd regained his composure.

Stella leaned into Sorrel and whispered, "I couldn't be happier for both of you."

"Can I say something?" Sorrel asked.

Of course she could, and five pairs of eyes turned to her.

"Not so long ago I sat around a kitchen table in my home. My sister, and by extension all of us, were accused in the death of a little boy. Patience was carved away by the sadness of her loss, and Henry, our doctor and her lover, were as uncertain

about what had happened as the vitriolic chorus from the town was sure. But on that evening we gathered with our friends and champions and made a plan to save Patience, to save all of us, really. Tonight I believe we are here to do the same for this family."

"Hear, hear," Graham said. "Let it be known that as ridiculous as our quest may seem, as silly as I may appear—all too often—my motives are pure, my trust is complete, and my dedication to all in this room, and to Andrew, of course, is unwavering."

Poppy uncharacteristically held her tongue, for she heard from her father the kind of declaration suitable to the eighteenth rather than the twenty-first century. Truly, the mission was more antique than modern, and the means were clearly as old as time as Sorrel went about saving the garden, but Poppy was struck by the vigor of her father's statement and in that moment her resolve found its footing and she knew that, however mad it might seem to the rest of the world, she was in.

After dinner Stella brought out the diary, and she and Sorrel carefully leafed through it, both using tissue paper to turn the pages. At first there was nothing unexpected, notes on guests at the estate, what was served, which linens were used, household matters that were of no particular import to the current Kirkwoods. Then, there was a section on Elizabeth's work on the formal gardens. Clearly they had been added to over the years, but it was Elizabeth who first set them out. It seemed that this

success piqued her interest, and by the time her fourth child was born, she had taken a cue from the French and planted a kitchen parterre. Then Elizabeth began the Shakespeare Garden. This was what everyone was looking for, and Sorrel dipped closer and closer to the pages as Stella deciphered the faded writing.

"Yes, she began making her lists here and here," Stella pointed. "Then by spring she was putting in the first bits of the garden."

"When was it finished?" Sorel asked.

"Hard to say, but here you can see that she was sketching out the knot garden a year after the original planting."

"My knot gardens are mostly herbs," Sorrel said. "Patience has her own garden for remedies, but much of it is repeated in the knot gardens."

"Right, let's see if great minds think alike," Stella said and gingerly flipped to the next list of plants.

Sorrel immediately saw that these plants were medicinal. If they were of a Shakespeare Garden, they didn't all appear in her research. They did, however, play a part in Patience's work.

"This garden is an apothecary garden," Sorrel said. "And a good one, too."

"Show me," Stella said.

Sorrel recited the plants and herbs with such ease that Poppy was reminded of music.

"Shepherd's purse, motherwort, and mallow," she read, "boneset, horehound, red clover, skullcap, all used in remedies.

Wolfsbane and trillium for labor, blessed thistle for milk. Many of these are used in midwifery."

"Elizabeth wasn't a midwife," Stella said.

"With four children she must have needed one," Poppy said.

"A lot of these I'd have to check with Patience on, but I think they are for various common ailments," Sorrel said.

Stella pointed out that the garden only lasted two years, and Elizabeth just two more.

"All this helpful stuff and nothing to save her," Poppy said. "Nothing to control Thomas either."

"Go to these entries." Graham pointed. "Gabe thinks they might be useful."

Sorrel looked at Gabe, who hadn't left the comfort of the fire. "What do you know, Gabe?" she asked.

Gabe shook his head and simply gestured for her to continue.

Stella began to read, haltingly at first until she became accustomed to Elizabeth's hand.

Anna assures me that Thomas will not divine that my newest herb garden is something more. If I can supply her with all she needs, then I can rest easy in the surety that no woman will suffer in childbirth, not even the ones who must deliver a bastard.

"Good God," Graham said. "She knew about Thomas. She must have known about his by-blows from wenching."

"Seriously, Dad?" Poppy said. "Is that even a word?"

"Indeed it is, or was in Elizabeth's time."

"Well, it's ghastly," Stella said. "Anna is the midwife but is Anna the witch?"

"Honestly, darling," Graham said, "Isn't there a better word for the poor woman?"

Stella ignored her husband and continued to read, and it became clearer still that Elizabeth's Shakespeare Garden, while lovely and a pleasure for the family, also hid a substantial physic garden within its walls.

"I need to go back to Middle Wallop," Sorrel said. "The herbs and plants in this diary need to be in our garden, too."

"Our garden, how encouraging," Stella said and patted Sorrel's arm. "Tomorrow will be a full day for all of us. Let's put Elizabeth to bed and do the same."

Delphine had been silent throughout the reading and discussion. As everyone gathered themselves for bed, she pulled Sorrel and Gabe into the larder on the pretense of collecting some cheese for the inn.

"Do you think the herbs in the old garden could have poisoned it forever?" she asked. "Graham says no, but Mathilde spent so much time in there . . ." She trailed off. "I am not looking to blame, you understand, it's just that no matter how unlikely, there is that chance that she got into something. And I cannot speak of this with Graham again. He is already too remorseful."

"Delphine, from what I have read, there weren't any dangerous herbs in Elizabeth's garden. Not even the accidental variety," Sorrel said. "And to expect anything to be left after all those years, well, no, I don't think there is any chance at all."

Delphine looked relieved and took Gabe's arm. "Come

then, you and I will walk back to the village together, and I will give you tea and a piece of my raspberry clafouti." Delphine snagged a small crock of Saint-Marcellin as she led Gabe out through the kitchen garden.

Stella took the diary up to her study. She'd have much preferred to sit in her bedroom by the fire and carefully turn the pages until she understood what was missing, what Elizabeth was telling her with the words she had not written. But sitting under the bright light at her desk, Stella found it was easier to see and knowing that she had only a day, at best, before the book was scooped up by conservators, she bent low and went to work.

What Stella needed was some clue to Elizabeth's state of mind after the garden was destroyed. What she'd love was the story of Anna's disappearance. Surely when a village midwife goes missing, every pregnant woman notices? Did she flee Thomas's wrath at her meddling? Or, and this would be a lovely story, did Anna fall in love and make a life of her own far from the Kirkwoods? Of course, with the tapestries in her mind Stella had to discount that fairy tale. Surely Elizabeth would have been distraught at the loss of her friend and mentor, no matter how she left. Stella went to the very end of the diary and worked backward. Then she started from the section where Elizabeth obliquely described the death of the garden.

Thomas announced to one and all that nature is a cruel mistress the day after my garden fell to ruin. I know that from experience, but it is Thomas who is cruel to use those words now. Crueler still, he has or-

dered the youngest children and me to London and then on to Brussels to hurry the nuns along, to Antwerp to chide Horemans about our portrait and lastly Delft to collect the pottery. Days away from solstice I cannot think of worse places to be when the sun is high, or worse errands to fill. And, who will champion the garden while I am gone? Who will mend the damage and start anew? Without my remedies, how will I care for my children? Without Anna, how will I bear my life?

That Elizabeth was learning from Anna was clear. Anna was gone, perhaps dead, as Stella suspected, perhaps only scared off by Thomas, and with Elizabeth in London, he would have no impediment to finish what he'd started, the complete destruction of the Shakespeare Garden.

After some entries about her trip abroad, an inventory of the blue and white pottery, an approval of the portrait and a single sentence on the tapestries, *Awful, but I have corrected the worst of the mistakes*, Elizabeth returned to Kirkwood Hall and took up the garden narrative again. Thomas had, in fact, ripped the entire thing out, leaving a walled desert in its stead. He forbade Elizabeth from attempting to revive it. There was an entry telling how the villagers and staff were particularly anxious and timid around Lord Kirkwood and a mention of the death in childbirth of the butcher's wife; then there were several weeks without a word. When Elizabeth picked up her story, she was already ill and there were only three entries before she died. None of the entries made much sense; in fact, Stella found the text disjointed, nightmarish even, and assumed that fever had stolen Elizabeth's thoughts until she came to a

scrawled section nearly at the end of the diary. Here Lady Kirkwood made reference to the chapel window, which as Stella suspected, never existed. *It will tell the story I cannot*, she wrote, *it will be my epitaph*.

With a mixture of horror and awe Stella understood that Elizabeth had damned her husband and told Anna's story in the only way she could by weaving clues into the tapestries themselves. That it took hundreds of years for the truth to surface was heartbreaking but now that it had, Stella prepared to spread the word.

She rewrapped the diary and placed it in an archive box and turned out her desk light. In the room's darkness the stars were stark in the sky through the window. Stella thought, not for the first time, that those stars had seen the truth play out beneath them, all the truths of Kirkwood Hall for centuries, and now they kept the secrets even better than her husband.

CHAPTER 15
Carnation

Andrew packed up his vestments and shoved some shorts into the side pocket of his garment bag. His meetings had been uncomfortable; he felt as if he'd been called into the headmaster's office after fulfilling a particularly harsh detention. It wasn't that his overlords weren't benevolent, exactly; it's just that they so obviously both pitied and were embarrassed by him. There would be a place for him in service, of course, they insisted, if he felt he was ready. Only the picture of Sorrel waiting for him at Kirkwood made the muddle of his thoughts tolerable. His bishop (a man only a few years older than Andrew and already Bishop of Kensington and father to four boisterous children whose pictures rebuked Andrew as he sat in in the office) had been mildly empathetic when he assured Andrew

that the past was past and, perhaps in a veiled bid to convince Andrew to stay in the countryside and out of the tabloids, he promised to attend the solstice service in Kirkwood Chapel himself. Andrew suspected that his boss wanted a day out and a chance to hobnob with the landed gentry and the Bishop of Salisbury. Still, the consecration and dedication ceremony, the first in over 150 years was something to celebrate. There was no set in stone service for the consecration of a disused Anglican church; each diocesan bishop was free, within the constraints of the faith, to create his own. Andrew had planned to watch the Bishop of Salisbury preside and then face up to the next step away from Sorrel. He'd expected to feel put out by his boss's suggestion that he bide a wee more at his sister's home, but as he thought about it, Andrew dreamed of Sorrel and began to wonder if Kirkwood Chapel might be where he belonged after all.

This visit to London had grated on him; even Christ Church seemed cloying, smelling of candle wax, and furniture polish instead of Sorrel's phlox and delphinium. He had spoken the truth when he told Sorrel his confidence was returning, his certainty that he was of use to a parish again. But he suspected that the venue was about to change. Would Sorrel find this good news?

Andrew's step was light as he left his flat. He hadn't called Sorrel at all and as he threw his things into the car, he knew he didn't have time if he wanted to arrive while the day was still fair. Better to apologize in person and he'd see her soon enough. *I've been given another chance,* he thought, *let's not bol-*

locks it up. What he needed now was to have his time and his love back. What might transpire beyond that he couldn't think, so he shifted his bag over to make room for Wags's new bed. The car started with a wheeze.

"Damn," Andrew said and ran back into the flat. He went into the bedroom and opened his bedside drawer. Poppy would never be recruited by MI6: Andrew had found the remedy in the pantry soon after she hid it. The little blue phial rolled to the front, and Andrew pocketed it. He was on the road minutes later.

ANDREW ARRIVED BY midafternoon, and the first thing he did was go to the garden. He thought that if he didn't have Sorrel in his arms in the coming seconds, he might just explode. But when he got to the gate, he was so captured by the fact of her after the hours of dreaming of her that he stilled. She was on her knees in one of the beds; her sundress spread out around her like petals and her hair was tucked under one of Stella's wide straw hats. A bird came to rest on the handle of the wheelbarrow beside her. It watched Sorrel as intently as Andrew, fearless and focused. Andrew shook himself just as the bird ruffled its feathers, both resurfacing from the spell Sorrel cast over the garden. He took only a few steps on the newly laid gravel before she turned and saw him. Her smile was instant and, given how crisply they'd parted, very warm.

"You're back!" she called and stood, wiping her hands on a towel.

"I am, and I don't think I can stand another moment without you right here," Andrew pointed at his chest and then held out his arms as he approached.

Sorrel moved just as quickly, tossing her hat aside, and found herself pressed up against Andrew's starched shirt. He smelled of soap and petrol fumes, and Sorrel breathed deeply. For his part Andrew sighed and rested his cheek on Sorrel's warm hair. There was a new herby smell to her, something green and fresh that he couldn't name.

"Can you take a break and perhaps consider a bumble?" Andrew asked, already laughing. "An apology bumble for my abrupt departure."

"Oh, to bumble again when summer is near," Sorrel crooned. "But I can't. I need to get these herbs in now so that they have time to catch up to everything else."

Andrew looked past Sorrel at the small knot garden she'd carved out of the corner lawn. It was no more than four feet across and was already jam-packed with tidy whirls of what to Andrew looked an awful lot like leafy sticks and patchy grass tufts with a few tatty flowers thrown in.

"Is that it?" he asked. "Because, if I may say, it looks a little tired. Kind of like I feel at the mo'."

"Listen, Mister," Sorrel said, "that tiny patch will become our very own physic garden as per Lady Elizabeth's diary, so watch yourself."

"OK, first, it's Reverend Darling to you and second, what have you kids been up to?"

Sorrel had already gone back to her knees, so Andrew joined her, landing prettily on his ass when his footing failed.

"Look away, look away," he said when Sorrel glanced over at the thump.

Sorrel snorted, offering her elbow, which Andrew refused as he crawled closer. As she worked, she told him about the discovery in the crypt, and as she talked, she was again struck by the near impossibility of all of the puzzle pieces coming together.

"Without Gabe," Andrew said, "it wouldn't have mattered how many pieces you had, you'd never have made them a whole."

He was right, and that morning when Sorrel and Delphine had gone to the nursery to pick out the apothecary herbs, Delphine had said as much. She was, however, not as self-satisfied as the rest of the Kirkwood clan.

"You know," Delphine said as Sorrel handed her peat pots one by one, "we cannot be distracted by the diary from finding the tapestry."

Sorrel demurred. The last thing she wanted was to keep picking at that scab.

"Perhaps," she said, trying to sound interested but not terribly, "We don't need a last panel to solve the mystery. We certainly don't need it now to plant the garden; Elizabeth has given me the perfect template."

"*Alors,*" Delphine said, her accent thickening along with her temper. "We have no idea why the garden failed, so how will you prevent it from doing so again?"

"Technically, I'm not tasked with keeping the garden healthy, only with giving it the best start," Sorrel said. She was embarrassed that her temper was rising as well. And besides, she planned to make a garden that would not fail.

Delphine looked at Sorrel for a long moment.

"As you say, Sorrel." Delphine turned away. "I will go get a place in the queue. The tills are always busy here."

Crap, Sorrel thought. *It's going to be a long ride back.*

Perhaps that was why she was so eager to see Andrew. Surely no Englishman, no matter how toffee-nosed, could match the condescending sniff of a pissed-off Delphine. Sorrel already planned to make her a beautiful bouquet for the long zinc bar at the inn. If she tucked a single stem of holy basil into the center, Sorrel was sure Delphine's strain would abate. She carefully snipped one from the plant in her barrow and put it in a bucket in the shade until she was finished. She let Andrew collect the little empty peat pots while she surveyed her work. Then they went together to the cutting garden to assemble Delphine's bouquet.

"I am sorry I was unpleasant when we parted," Andrew said. "I am still weighing exactly how much I want to take up my duties again. Or perhaps I should say where to take them up."

"What did your boss say?" Sorrel asked.

Andrew told her of his meeting and how, if nothing else, the reopening of the estate chapel would put him before a congregation again and then he'd know if he could still feel the joy he missed. He didn't exactly lay out that, if all went well,

he might indeed stay. London or Kirkwood Hall, he realized with a dropping heart, neither was any closer to Granite Point and Sorrel.

"What will you say, I mean what will your sermon be about?"

"Lord knows," Andrew said and held out the basket for Sorrel. "And let's hope he really does."

Sorrel gently stacked the delphinium and bells of Ireland. Next she bent to the peonies. Beneath the glossy leaves there were blossoms still unfolding and she carefully cut one or two from each bush without disturbing the round crown of the plant.

"If you aren't totally hypnotizing in your oratory, I'll sit in the front pew and make faces," Sorrel said. "My sisters and I used to get so antsy in church that Mrs. Bartlett would separate us."

"Did that work?"

"Absolutely not. Patience got wise and started slipping sage oil onto Mrs. Bartlett's hankie. The scent was enough to make her drowsy and vague, so we just went on with our shenanigans."

"Please don't mess about when I'm preaching, Sorrel," Andrew said. "It will be hard enough just seeing you before me. I don't want to have to leap off the altar and wrestle you into appropriate respect, or better, inappropriate canoodling."

"I will be the picture of propriety, promise," Sorrel said. She cut some spray roses for Delphine, and they walked back to the big house.

Wags was in the kitchen, and her reunion with Andrew was boisterous and noisy. Sorrel searched in the china closet for a vase large enough for her flowers while Andrew rolled around on the hearth rug with his dog. As she stripped and cut each stem, Sorrel told Andrew about Delphine's insistence that the final tapestry be found.

"We had no luck the first time. Perhaps Gabe has an inkling," Andrew said. "He's the one with the secrets."

"I think he would have spoken by now," Sorrel said.

But Gabe had spoken, just not to Sorrel. He'd confronted Graham that very morning as they surveyed the copper flashing on the farm shop roof. There'd been a run of nighttime thievery; copper was of some value and there had been enough stripped that Graham needed to get in the roofers.

Gabe had turned to Graham as soon as the builder left.

"The tapestry," he signed. "Delphine is pushing."

"Yes, well, she can push all she wants," Graham said. "We are on the brink of a new and healthy era for this family, and dragging that plagued thing into the light will help no one."

"She won't stop," Gabe said.

"Gabe," Graham said, "that panel has been gone forever and I think we can all guess at its subject matter. Whatever power it has comes from people's fascination with it."

"You have seen it," Gabe signed, and it wasn't a question. Signing kept secrets far better than speaking.

Graham turned from Gabe. He looked ready to walk away, so Gabe reached out and grabbed his arm. Graham spun around.

"Do not touch me in anger!" Graham snapped.

"You are hiding it," Gabe signed, his face red.

Graham deflated. "Gabe," he said, "my father chose to hide that tapestry years ago. The only reason I was ever shown it was to warn me never to speak of it. So yes, I know what it depicts, but I don't know where it is. It was not restored, even the Victoria and Albert Museum believes it is lost to time. I cannot let Stella or Delphine, or Poppy for that matter, see the end of that hunt. It is hideous and shameful and will only poison them against the family."

"Keeping secrets will do that too," Gabe signed and walked away.

Graham stood for the longest time looking up at the farm shop roof. He wasn't seeing anything, though. He was blinded by regret and flimsy lies told over the years. Something very like fear overtook him when he thought of Stella's reaction to the truth. Secret by secret, Graham had built a safe haven for his family, and a wall to keep the ugliness hidden. Now, secret by secret, it was all tumbling down.

Andrew and Sorrel drove into the village with Delphine's giant arrangement wedged precariously in the backseat. It was too heavy and too blinding to be carried on foot. Sorrel was reminded of the founder's day bouquet she'd made for Charlotte Mayo the summer before and how she'd sat among her wildflowers and cried for chances she hadn't taken, happiness she hadn't seized and held close to her heart. Today, though,

her happiness was evident in the flowers she'd arranged and even in the bumblebee that had nestled into the very center of a peony and would not be roused. Sorrel felt certain that the love and care she'd built into the flowers would seep right into Delphine's poor mood and lift it.

The bar at the Queen's Hart was quiet and cool after the riot of color in the gardens. Sorrel hefted the vase onto the spotless zinc and looked around for Delphine.

"Halloooo!" Andrew called. "*Viens, viens, un bouquet de fleurs pour Madam!*"

"Impressive, Peppy le Pew," Sorrel said and laughed. "Maybe she's out back."

Delphine was in the beer garden, a sack of lemons at her elbow and a large mechanical juicer on the table in front of her.

"Andrew," Delphine said, pushing down on the chrome lever. Lemon juice spilled out into a pitcher. "I am making *citron pressé* now that summer has arrived."

"It is not official until I say so, in the chapel," Andrew said and kissed Delphine.

"Sorrel, how is the physic garden?" Delphine asked.

"Fine, I think," Sorrel said. Perhaps the holy basil wasn't necessary, as Delphine seemed to have recovered her good humor. "It's a bit raggedy at the moment, but water and sun and time will help.

Delphine mixed fine sugar and spring water into the pitcher of juice and poured it into three glasses. She placed a tiny sprig of lavender in each one and gave them a stir.

"I left some flowers on the bar," Sorrel said.

"*Merci,*" said Delphine. "And allow me to apologize for being a little *en colère* at the nursery. It has been a time of remembering for me with the garden and Mathilde."

"I wish it didn't remind you of your sadness," Sorrel said. "But I understand. After Marigold died, I couldn't even go to the nursery. Nettie had to drag me with dire predictions of choking weeds and waterlogged snapdragons. In the end it was probably the plants that brought me back."

"Perhaps now that our little gardener has made her mark, we can all move forward." Delphine smoothed Sorrel's hair. "You are striking indeed. It is no surprise that Andrew has awoken at last."

Sorrel bowed her head. She felt as if she had awoken, too. To have purpose in your day and then such passion in your night was more than Sorrel had ever thought she'd be given.

Andrew slapped his knees. "I haven't unpacked, so I'm off," he said and looked at Sorrel. "You?" he asked.

"Sure," Sorrel said and kissed Delphine on each cheek. "Please, when you're ready, come to the Shakespeare Garden with me. I think you'll be surprised how much has changed."

Sorrel left Andrew to his unpacking and finished up in the garden. The sun seemed hotter at four than it had at noon. Sweat ran down her chest and every leaf bit and speck of soil made her itch. She found herself irritable and impatient as she looked out over the garden. Yes, it had progressed faster than she thought because the weather was so fine, yet everything still looked unfinished and bedraggled. *One good rain,* Sorrel

thought, *not a storm, a soaker, that is what I need.* She took off her hat and wiped her face. She could already feel tenderness on the tops of her shoulders, the backs of her calves and wished, again, that she'd been more welcoming when Patience tried to give her a fully stocked remedy kit.

The Tithe Barn was cool and inviting with its high ceiling and shaded windows. A suspended fan spun lazily, moving the dust and pollen through the air. Sorrel stopped in the kitchen for water then moved into the bedroom where Wags lay sprawled next to the open doors to the terrace.

"Wags, you clever girl," Sorrel said and lay down beside her on the cool stone floor.

"Oh dear, have you succumbed?" Andrew asked.

Sorrel opened her eyes to see Andrew, upside down in his clergy shirt, dog collar and boxers. She gaped.

"What? I was just checking to be sure everything still fit," Andrew said.

"Everything but the pants?" Sorrel asked.

"My trousers, if you must know, are a bit tight, but I've still got time to slim down a tad."

"I do like a man in uniform," Sorrel said as she sat up. "Come over here and I'll take it off for you."

"I can hardly believe I'm saying this, but let's wait," Andrew said. "You are covered with garden detritus and I am spackled in road grime. Perhaps we should bathe before we throw ourselves on each other?"

"Oh, let's," Sorrel said and peeled away her clothes.

"Have you ever noticed that if we aren't eating, we seem to be in bed?" Sorrel asked Andrew and sat up, pulling the sheet with her. Her hair was still wet and her sunburned shoulders were beginning to sting.

Andrew lay with his hands behind his head. "I have absolutely no problem with that," he said.

"We never just sit around and talk," she said. "No, that's not exactly what I mean."

Andrew sat up. "Tell me."

"We're both on these tracks that will meet on the solstice, but we aren't really working together."

"As I remember, you're the one who kept me out of the garden," Andrew said. "A peek here and there is hardly enough. I can't imagine anything better than spending time there with you."

Sorrel was unused to sharing her work in progress with anyone but her sisters, but Andrew was right.

"Tomorrow, OK?" she said. "Let's do it tomorrow."

Andrew nodded. He felt hopeful, nearly giddy with the prospect of finally seeing Sorrel in her element as she planted. He shifted and put his arms around her.

"I am hugely, enormously, ridiculously happy," he said. "You've done that for me, Sorrel."

Sorrel leaned back against him and nodded.

"But now I am also very hungry," Andrew said. "I brought some wonderful provisions back from Harvey Nicks. Let's get ourselves together and head over to the big house."

"It never ends," Sorrel said.

CHAPTER 16
Rue

Sorrel woke Andrew at dawn. He might have slept on for hours, and the sky was still a milky blue against the big windows, but Sorrel had plans.

"Come on then, you asked for this," she said.

"I haven't had a coffee," Andrew pointed out, "and neither have you."

"Gabe brings tea for me. You can share."

"That sounds strangely charming but if you don't mind, my love, Wags and I will join you after our coffee."

Sorrel was secretly relieved. This moment each morning with Gabe was both a ritual of beginning and a time for both to reorient themselves to the work. She found him sitting on the edge of a large crate. Two cups steamed beside him.

"The sundial?" Sorrel asked.

Gabe nodded.

"That's good. I didn't expect it till the end of the week."

Sorrel wanted to open the crate, but while Gabe had a crowbar right there, she decided to wait, finish the plants, and then have the whole family join in to place the sundial. The image made her smile, and she told Gabe her plan.

"Andrew will be coming by this morning," Sorrel said.

Gabe looked surprised. Sorrel was so self-contained when she worked that he had a difficult time seeing her with any sort of company. Even Gabe didn't dare enter into Sorrel's presence without her permission.

Sorrel drew on her gloves and walked into the garden.

It was overcast and mild, which was just as well, given Sorrel's sunburn. First she walked the paths from one end to the other, all four that met where the sundial would live. Then she examined each bed with attention to insects and black spot. Finally she went back for her wheelbarrow and began to load up the rest of the florae. Trip by trip the plants went in until Sorrel's shoulders pinched, and Gabe returned with water. She beckoned him in, and they stood together, two tall, silent gardeners waiting for the magic to emerge.

Andrew came upon them just that way. Their hands were on their hips, backs long and strong, side by side. They seemed more siblings than cohorts. He wondered if Gabe had ever had this kind of connection before, kindred spirits with the same goal. It gave him a jolt of pure envy for a moment, but he pushed it away and entered the garden.

The scent struck Andrew first, then the color and finally the impossibility. It was a transformed place in the space of a night. Under Sorrel's hands everything seemed to be blooming madly, and at once. What had been spindly and frail now looked lush and inviting. He paused to look more closely at a rose whose blossom was as big as a saucer and whose scent reminded him of elderflower cordial. He bent lower, invited in by the smell and the spiral of petals, and took a stem into his fingers. There were no thorns, not one. Andrew thought that was quite the horticultural invention.

"Sorrel," he called out and she turned, tapping Gabe on the arm.

"Come see how we're making out," Sorrel said.

They were standing before the new physic garden, which only the day before had seemed unfinished in the extreme. Now the tender herbs and flowers were standing at attention, and the soil around them was deep and rich and dark.

"What a difference a day and some compost tea make, right?" Sorrel said. She brushed her fingers over the plants, humming softly. Andrew swore they leaned into her, certain he saw a change in the light as she moved through it.

Gabe watched Andrew. He too saw what Sorrel's touch created but, unlike Andrew, he was pretty sure that it was more powerful than feed or time. Andrew stood with his head cocked and tried to reconcile the abundance all around him with the barren place he'd avoided. He acknowledged that Sorrel was a

gifted horticulturist, for all her self-taught skills, but this kind of radiance brought forth from such thick shadow, such buried rage, this was something he struggled to process.

"I don't understand what you've done here, Sorrel," he said. "It hardly seems conceivable, let alone real, this transformation in what feels like moments."

Sorrel was accustomed to the wonder her gardens engendered, but there was more than wonder in Andrew's voice. There was disbelief and even a hint of trepidation. At once the old sorrow swept over her. Sorrel had heard this tone before in the questions from the prosecutor as he tried to discredit Patience, her gift, and her sisters. She'd felt the fear of the unknown barreling off the men who confronted the Sisters as they tried to reclaim their own garden.

"Hold it, Andrew," she said. "I don't like the sound of your voice."

Gabe looked back and forth between them. Without actually hearing the words he could pick up on the tension. He found himself bracing, as if he might need to defend Sorrel against, well, he wasn't quite sure what kind of trouble was brewing, but he was compelled to protect this woman with all her gifts.

"I'm just saying that it's pretty remarkable, almost indescribable," Andrew said and walked toward Sorrel. "I didn't mean to upset you." He took her hand. "Really, I'm just a fellow in need of a little enlightenment."

Sorrel looked into Andrew's eyes. She didn't see the kind of intimidation and dismissal she expected. Instead there was real curiosity, along with the uncertainty.

"Walk with me," she said. "I'll tell you what I know."

Gabe let out his breath and left the garden.

"Is this what happens in Granite Point too?" asked Andrew. "This explosion of bounty, this inexplicable beauty?"

"It's not inexplicable, Andrew," Sorrel said. "It's always been this way for us, ever since we brought my mother's garden back. My father tore through it after she died, and it was two years before we could set foot in it. And then, with the Nursery, we all found our talents and our rhythms."

"But it's all such a contrast, so fine and flourishing, and a little unnerving," Andrew said.

"Well, I know that at home our Nursery is a very particular spot. I suspect that after I rehabilitated the soil, set just the right plants in the right places, this garden is on its way to being a very particular spot as well."

"Peculiar, that's certain, in a lovely way, of course" Andrew said. "Forgive my glazed look and my reservations," Andrew said. "Let's just say that you are a very particular gardener and for that I hope the Kirkwoods are suitably grateful."

The truth was that Andrew suspected that if he looked too closely at this garden, or dug too deeply into Sorrel's explanation, it would trouble him in a more serious way. Just as he chose not to marvel at how fast they fell for each other, he understood that he mustn't put too much thought, or science, into

how the garden grew. And, if nothing else, Andrew liked being happy and loved being happy with Sorrel. If that meant he looked away now and then—and perhaps restocked his Heart's Ease—then that's what would happen. He couldn't face returning to who he was before, and he wouldn't give up the small measure of bliss he'd been given. Besides, if he took on the chapel as his new church, Andrew would be faced with the mysterious garden every day. Was this the time to tell Sorrel about that possibility?

"I will endeavor to be open to all the miracles you have wrought," Andrew said. "I will put away my far too sensible outlook and allow you to enchant me as well."

Sorrel tried to access her inner Patience and see if Andrew felt, if not exactly smelled, like truth. She stared at him, inventorying his beauty and the persistent sadness that still shadowed him. Andrew stared right back, unsmiling but still hopeful, and Sorrel decided that this fragile, unexpected beginning for them both was precious and worth tending.

"There are all sorts of miracles, you know," Sorrel said. "Why not grab ours?"

Andrew felt a breath he didn't know he was holding rush out. Gabe some yards away inhaled and reached for his shovel. It was time to set the boxwood.

By the first streaks of pink in the western sky half the low hedges were in. The rest stood ready, soaked in their small burlap root balls. Andrew's shirt was sweated through, and Sorrel had long since rolled up her sleeves past her elbows. Gabe was

down to his tee shirt, and all three were streaked with dirt and flecked with oval box leaves, sticky and done in. They parted at the gap-toothed gate, knowing that with another good day's work or so, the Shakespeare Garden would be finished. Then Gabe and his men could replace the ancient bricks and rehang the gate, and Sorrel could finish with ground cover geranium, moss, and creeping phlox to soften the entrance, wisteria to drape the far wall in years to come. When Poppy returned on Saturday, the family could place the sundial and let the garden find its own rhythm in time for the solstice.

Gabe left Andrew and Sorrel and went to his park keeper's cottage to shower. He felt as content as a lonely man can and even stopped in the great hall to scoop up the three-legged hound puppy. Gabe didn't keep a dog because he was never without an eddy of hounds as he worked around the Kirkwood estate. There were the hunting dogs that did little of that now, the two labs and the shepherds, and those were enough. Still, this newer addition, an odd spotted runt with a malformed foreleg that left her to lag behind the others appealed to Gabe's sense of difference. He told himself he wasn't actually taking the little one on as his own, just giving her a bit of extra care, and who couldn't use that?

THE FOLLOWING DAY brought a murky dawn. All the leaves on the birch trees were turned over, silvery in the low morning light; rain was coming. Sorrel pulled on a borrowed mackintosh and wellies and walked quickly to the garden. Gabe was

there with the tea and an extra man and nodded when she pointed at the sky.

"We'll move fast and be all but finished before it comes," she said to both men.

The groundskeeper dug, Sorrel followed with coco fiber soil and fertilizer to line the holes, and Gabe unwrapped the small shrubs, lining them up precisely as Sorrel instructed. Together they planted, as efficient and speedy as an assembly line until the last boxwood went in. Gabe pulled the hose up and down the paths watering in the new plants while Sorrel gathered the burlap and tidied the beds with dark mulch. Now the parterre borders marched away in symmetry, creating an ordered, confident structure to contain the abundance to come.

It was past lunchtime when they stood to survey their work, and Sorrel chuckled as she thought about Andrew surfacing from his sermon-writing fog, no doubt pining for sustenance. Last night they'd piled sliced meats and grilled marinated vegetables, great rounds of focaccia topped with rosemary and olive oil, and a container of new potatoes dressed with mustard and herbs into a canvas sack and carried everything over to Kirkwood Hall. Graham and Stella were in the kitchen, and Graham looked up with relief at the sight of the bag.

"Thank God," he said. "We've managed to let our cupboards go bare and were just about to expire from hunger and distress."

"What have you brought us?" Stella asked as she made room on the table.

Andrew unpacked to much lip smacking, and Graham went scavenging for cheese and wine.

"How is it that you're not all poster kids for high cholesterol?" Sorrel asked.

"Oh, Graham is," Stella said. "It took me months to convince him to take the tablets our GP prescribed. Now he just thinks he's got leave to eat whatever he wants."

"On the other hand, my sister and I are genetically blessed," Andrew said as he held out his arms. "As you can no doubt see."

Sorrel wondered if his parishioners ever guessed at the divine physique that hid beneath Andrew's cassock.

Sorrel filled everyone in on the garden's progress over dinner, and after coffee Stella brought out an ice-filled bowl of Italian cherries. Soon stems and pips piled up in front of each place, and everyone's fingers were stained crimson. Stella swept them into her palm, tossed Wags the last piece of focaccia and announced she was retiring.

Graham and Andrew and Sorrel sat around the table a bit longer. Graham seemed distracted now that the meal had ended or perhaps because Stella was gone. Andrew found himself talking too much, and Sorrel was overcome with exhaustion. When Graham stood abruptly and went up to Stella, there was no reason to stay. Andrew and Sorrel loaded the dishwasher and walked back to the Tithe Barn in the kind of comfortable silence that belonged to friends of many years. They fell into bed; Wags nestled between them and for the first time since their unexpected cleaving, they did not make love. It was a

pleasant revelation for them both, this coming together that only led to dreams.

It was no surprise that Andrew didn't stay with her in the garden on that last planting day, and just as well. It felt right and proper that Sorrel and Gabe finish things together. It felt just so when Sorrel returned to the Tithe Barn after the small grass lawns were mown and the deadheading and tidying done to find Andrew sitting on the sofa with Wags, a pint glass in his hand and a sheaf of papers beside him.

"You are come home to me, your man of letters," Andrew said. "And also to the glossy meatloaf beside me."

"I am," Sorrel said. "I am come home." She ignored the twinge, the truth of the words, and slid the image of her sisters away.

THE WAXING MOON shed little light on the garden that night. A shiver of movement moved over the plants in a wave. It might have been the wind if there were any, but the air was still. In a far corner the poppies that should have been forming seedpods were still open like shallow bowls to lure bees. As the moon drifted behind the clouds, the poppies drooped and the cowslip folded in on itself. The eglantine rose that Sorrel had planted to scent the air in that corner bent forward, crooked and woody unlike any of the other roses. There was a chill in that corner of the garden, a shadow that did not lift even when the moonlight returned. The garden and her plants around it gathered itself, shying away from the darkness that reached out to them all.

CHAPTER 17

Willow

Graham woke with a start on the day Sorrel had chosen to show the family the Shakespeare Garden. She had hinted at the success of her planting, and Gabe had certainly been far cheerier of late, so Graham pushed his anxiety away and crept quietly down to the kitchen. He found the detritus of Poppy's arrival in the hall: an open backpack, a duffle, and her clunky boots now in the possession of the dogs. He smiled and allowed himself a moment of undiluted joy. It was true that Poppy had struggled being the oldest. Rupert and Sophia were more like their mother, easy and gracious in their privilege. Poppy had always chafed against the attention and found the responsibility of her family's position an archaic burden. Her two years off from school, and the Kirkwoods,

had begun in anger and rebellion but had mellowed her in the end. It had also given her perspective. Graham knew that she saw him more clearly, for good or ill. He couldn't bear any more of her harsh judgments, her doubts that age-old entitlement couldn't be transformed into a greater good. And now, with all that had transpired with Sorrel's presence, it was nearly impossible to keep a secret from Poppy even when he most wanted to.

With the kettle on Graham sat down with the newspapers in the kitchen. The warmth of the coming day was just a whisper this early, but he knew it would be beautiful and clear by the time the family gathered in the garden. A frisson of fear sidled up to his anticipation, and Graham pulled his dressing gown closer.

When Gabe came in through the larder, Graham startled.

"I forget that you are such an early riser," he said. "Tea?"

Gabe nodded and got down a cup. He joined Graham at the table and poured from the pot. Gabe rarely spoke; his voice was raspy from disuse, and his words were not so easily understood. But sometimes words were what was needed. Since Graham had known him before he went deaf, he encouraged Gabe not to be silent in his presence. So, even though they could both sign nearly as fast as Andrew, when they were alone, Graham wished for Gabe's voice. In a way Gabe's ability to speak was another of his secrets, and he revealed it only when words were the only way to be heard.

"Sorrel has remade the garden," Graham said. "You see,

Gabe, we have broken whatever curse has shadowed us, and we can all stand in the light again."

"At what cost?" Gabe asked. "What next?"

Graham wanted to snap at Gabe. *What cost?* He thought, *seventy thousand pounds all in, that's at what cost!* But he didn't say anything.

They drank their tea in silence. Graham kept his eyes on the paper, and Gabe stroked the funny little dog that had become his tail of late. Graham had a vague idea that it was one of their hounds and gave it a pat as he stood.

"I guess I should smarten up, eh?" he said to Gabe, who was in his usual worn trousers and boots.

By the time Gabe came to the garden, the sun had warmed. The mulch steamed and the smell of boxwood filled his nose. He was always first in the garden although Sorrel thought she reached it only minutes after he did. The truth was that Gabe was often alone for as much as half an hour before she arrived. Sorrel thought he waited for her every morning before entering, and he did, mostly. Sometimes he stood just inside the gate or a few steps onto the path and watched the garden wake. He, like Andrew, saw what Sorrel had brought forth from nothing, less than nothing, really, and he too knew that what she did with her hands was unlike what any other gardener could do. If Andrew was unsettled by the way Sorrel's plants flourished beyond expectation, or nature's laws for that matter, Gabe believed her abilities were

a gift to them all. To Gabe every luminous green shoot, every unfolding blossom and scented breeze, spoke of life returned, of a past rewritten and a future of promise. He felt lifted up with optimism, such an unfamiliar and surprising feeling that he laughed aloud.

Emboldened, Gabe ventured farther into the garden, brushing his fingertips over the plants as Sorrel did, pausing to see that Andrew was right, there were no thorns on the roses, no aphids on the slender dahlia stems or leaves, no beetles, not a single bit of blight to sully the orderly beds. The box had been placed some inches apart to ensure that they would grow uncrowded, each with just the right amount of space to fill in with time. This sunny morning it seemed that the glossy leaves and sturdy branches had reached toward each other and now presented a deep green ribbon that framed each parterre. The entire effect was of a garden that had spent years becoming and was now ready to be admired like a lady at the top of the stairs before a fine party. He came to the center of the paths where a square hole had been made to hold the sundial. Just before it was placed he would fill it in with enough concrete to keep it plumb and solid for the years and Kirkwoods to come. He bent to settle the canvas tarp over the hole, the last raw spot in the garden.

The bird looked as if it had been laid gently into the ground. Its eyes were closed, and its wings folded against the tiny body. Gabe squatted down by the hole. He was overcome with sadness and a chill had set up so quickly that he rubbed

his hands together. Here it was then, the ruin returned. Was it the first sign of a new darkness or the last of the old? Gabe suspected the former. He felt it like a blow, this little death. He reached in and gathered the bird, nearly weightless, in his hand. With a speed and stealth born of practice Gabe wrapped the tiny thing in his handkerchief and walked swiftly to the tool shed. He stooped to slip it into an old steamer trunk where he kept his own secrets. The lock was newer; he'd installed it himself and kept the key on a chain around his neck along with the St. Francis de Sales medal Delphine had given him when they became friends. Patron saint of the deaf, she'd told him as she folded his hands over it. Gabe didn't believe in a saint of anything. but he wore it anyway and now he looked at it with a kind of affection simply because Delphine *did* believe.

In the trunk Gabe made a nest of his handkerchief for the bird. He knelt down and lifted a little house made of woven willow and long-dried lavender stalks. The scent remained, as did the memory of Mathilde's high, sweet voice singing as she sat with Gabe carefully bending and twisting until her fairy house was done. Gabe replaced the house carefully so as not to jostle all the others he'd placed in the trunk the week after Mathilde died. Delphine had instructed Gabe to burn them all. In her grief and misplaced guilt she'd seen the houses only as reminders of her daughter's absence, of the very day she collapsed in the wildflower meadow gathering bachelor's buttons

for her mother. Gabe saw them as talismans, more powerful than any saint's medal. So he had hidden them away as if they might find their purpose again.

Gabe decided he would not tell anyone about the bird. He'd have to dispose of it soon, but now the estate was stirring and Sorrel would be arriving shortly. He locked the trunk and jogged back to his cottage to make her tea.

The dog was waiting for him at the door. Gabe had finally named her Maggie. It was clear that he would not be giving her up, or she him. She was a comfort, and Gabe found that on this morning he needed comfort. Maggie followed him around the small kitchen as he boiled the kettle and filled the paper cups with strong, sweet, milky tea. He slipped a worn collar around her neck in case she made a run for it and let her follow him to the garden. She never went in; Gabe had taught her to stay by the entrance, and Sorrel had come to enjoy seeing her little face peeping through the gate. The Shakespeare Garden was no place for a snuffling, digging puppy, and now Gabe was glad he'd never let little Maggie in.

Sorrel appeared, smiling with her hand outstretched for tea. She'd brought a baguette filled with butter and jam and laid it in her lap on some parchment paper as they drank.

"Well, here we are, Gabe," she said and handed him half the baguette.

Gabe smiled and held his cup up in a toast. Sorrel tapped hers against it and checked her watch.

"Right, we've got a couple of hours before the family stirs here. Let's give everything a blessing and a water."

Together Gabe and Sorrel walked the garden, straightening a plant here, tucking another handful of mulch around a bush there. The hawthorn tree was small but sturdy, and Gabe was surprised to see it in full bloom weeks after it should have dropped its petals. He pointed it out to Sorrel.

"Well," she said, "we could hardly have it bare, could we?"

They came to the back corner of the garden together, drawn by the bare patch just inside the wall. Gabe held out his arm, barring Sorrel from getting too close. Poppies lay on the ground, their stems softened nearly to mush, and the little eglantine rose was furred with mildew, dusted with thorns. The checkered lily Sorrel had planted because she couldn't resist its dipping purple blossoms looked as if it had been eaten down to the skunky bulbs.

"What the hell happened here?" Sorrel asked. She ducked under Gabe's arm and squatted down beside her failing plants.

"Gabe?" she asked. "Do you know what's causing this?"

That was the question, wasn't it? Gabe didn't want to have an answer for Sorrel, or he didn't want the answer he had. He shook his head and tried to pull Sorrel away, but she was already wrist deep in the soil. It was dry in the spot, the dirt already grainy and gray.

"Shit," Sorrel spat. "It'll all have to come out." She began

pulling the poppies, which gave without resistance, coating her hands in milky ooze.

Gabe knelt beside her, offering his gloves but she waved him away. He dug around the roses with his own hands, feeling for something that might have spoiled this corner. *Grubs,* he hoped, *grubs could do damage beyond their size or numbers.* But there was nothing but knobby roots and ashy soil.

They gathered their dead and carried the pile out of the garden. As soon as Sorrel hipped open the new gate, Maggie dashed in. Gabe couldn't drop his plants; he was too afraid they'd poison the rest of the garden. He could only watch as the puppy headed straight to the corner and began to dig.

"Get her out," Sorrel snapped.

Gabe threw everything over the wall and ran back in. He nearly lifted the dog off her feet by her collar. He held her with both arms and wrestled her out, the sound of her whining as cutting as a scream. He grabbed a length of baling twine and looped it around the stack of pallets by the shed and tied it to her collar, leaving her scrabbling against the weight of the pallets.

Sorrel was standing over the dead and dying plants with her hands on her hips. Dirt and mulch streaked her arms.

"We've no time to replace these today," she said to Gabe. "Can you and your guys put the sundial in now? I want to focus all eyes on that instead of this awful corner."

Gabe nodded.

Sorrel patted his arm. "We'll fix this, don't worry," she said. "I'll clean up and meet you back here with everyone."

Gabe couldn't imagine a fix for what he feared was coming.

THE SOUND OF the shower woke Andrew. He turned over to find Wags on the pillow beside him.

"Big day, girl," he said as he rolled her into his chest.

Andrew waited for the water to turn off before getting up. He found Sorrel staring at the shower drain. It was ringed with silt and leaves.

"What have you brought home, little gardener?" he asked.

"Yeah, that is pretty gross," Sorrel said. "Don't tell, but I've got a bit of a rebellion in one corner of the garden."

She explained about the dead plants with a carelessness that belied her concern.

"I will dazzle the family with the sundial and all the healthy plants and take care of the problem later," she said.

Andrew folded her into his arms. She smelled of shampoo and a lingering sourness that was so unlike Sorrel he coughed.

Sorrel sniffed her own arm and frowned.

Andrew shifted her out of the way and turned the shower back on, tilting the head to sluice away the dirt.

"Get dressed. I'll be out in a minute," he said as he dropped his boxers.

Sorrel opened the wide doors to the terrace and stood towel-drying her hair in the sun. She held a coil up to her nose but it didn't seem stinky. She pulled a violet-sprigged dress out

of the closet and slipped it on. The full skirt fell around her like water, and Sorrel was glad she'd let Patience pack three of her mother's old sundresses. Sorrel didn't often wear such girlish things, but today the soft cotton lawn felt like a blessing. She let the memory of her mother settle for a moment while she braided her hair. On this morning Sorrel was an awfully long way from the Sparrow Sisters of Granite Point, but she felt them beside her all the same.

CHAPTER 18
Ivy

The Kirkwood clan stood in a little cluster halfway down the long path between the house and the Shakespeare Garden. Sorrel and Andrew had come to the big house to walk en masse to the garden and Graham insisted on a photo.

"I do miss Rupes and Sophia," Poppy said.

"They'll be here soon," Stella said. "I'm sure the garden will only be more beautiful by July."

"Are you ready?" Andrew asked after he took the picture. "Gabe will have a breakdown if we aren't on time."

Poppy and Sorrel walked arm in arm. It felt good to both of them to be linked.

"I don't think I've seen Dad this excited since, oh, ever," Poppy said. "You'd think he'd planted the thing himself."

"Well, I couldn't have planted a thing without his faith," Sorrel said.

"And his cash."

"That, too." Sorrel laughed. "I've worked for a fair number of wealthy summer people back home, but I've never been given quite such free rein. It really has been heavenly."

Poppy watched Sorrel as she walked. Everything about her had been softened in her time at Kirkwood Hall. Perhaps it was the garden, perhaps Andrew and his own awakening, but Poppy suspected it was both. She hoped nothing would change, hoped that it was only the beginning.

Gabe was standing at the garden gate when the family arrived. Graham was pleased to see that the wall was restored and solid, the creaky gate cleaned and polished in the sun and the bricks softened by a froth of pale purple and white creeping phlox. Stella was thrilled to see Gabe's shy smile, and Sorrel checked his face for reassurance.

"Sorrel," Graham called, "is there anything we need to know before we fall about in paroxysms of joy and wonder and a bit of misplaced panic?"

Sorrel glanced at Gabe, who shook his head.

"Just that I am honored to have made this garden for you and grateful to Gabe for being by my side."

"Well then, let me say welcome to the Shakespeare Garden, one and all!" Graham opened the gate and ushered everyone in.

The sundial stood at the center of the garden, its shiny brass gnomon flashing light into the air and casting a thin shadow

precisely on eleven o'clock. The Kirkwoods stayed in a tight, silent unit for a moment before all bursting into talk and laughter at once.

"Oh, it is magnificent," Stella said.

"Perfect," said Poppy.

"I am speechless," Graham said and proceeded to be anything but. "I knew it!" he crowed. "Didn't I say she could do it? Didn't I tell you the Sparrow was our answer?"

"I never doubted you, darling," Stella said and rolled her eyes.

Andrew turned in a circle. Not a blossom was out of place, and every bud seemed on the verge of blooming. Those that were in bloom made the scent heady; waves of it broke over him with the clean effervescence of good champagne and the sweetness of summer itself. He looked at Sorrel and saw clearly how transformed she was by the power of this garden, just as the garden had been transformed by her. The hopefulness that had tiptoed into his heart when Sorrel came into his life blossomed into the possibility of true happiness.

Everyone spread out across the space murmuring and marveling at all the changes Sorrel had wrought. The small markers Sorrel had fashioned for each specimen charmed Poppy. Sorrel had labeled the copper tags in her careful upright hand and they stood, still bright as a new penny, telling the story of each plant and herb.

Graham hardly knew where to start as he all but ran along the gravel paths. When he reached the sundial, he stopped.

Such an appropriate centerpiece in this garden that time forgot, he thought. Now it will stand and mark the hours for generations. Gabe came up behind him, and Graham turned to shake his hand and thump his shoulder.

"It is done," he said. "It is begun as well."

Gabe looked long at his chief, and his friend, before he gave a nod and looked to the dark corner. Graham followed his gaze.

"Unfinished?" he asked, nodding at the shovel leaning against the wall.

Gabe turned back to Graham and raised an eyebrow. He felt like a fake and a liar in his silence. He felt like Graham Kirkwood in his deception.

"Perfection is an unattainable thing, you know that," Graham said. "At least put the shovel away for now." Graham blithely moved on to another parterre.

While everyone was captured by the garden, Delphine appeared at the gate. She watched in silence, listening to Poppy's laughter, Stella's dulcet murmurs, and Sorrel's clear voice describing what to expect as the garden grew. Delphine hesitated before entering. She wasn't true family, even though Graham was her old friend and he had expressly invited her to be there at the opening of the garden. In that moment Delphine felt keenly the absence of Mathilde, the loss of her own innocence, and the almost unbearable burden of knowing how very fragile everything could be, including this garden, including the very visible joy of Andrew's newfound faith in love—especially that

joy. But if she didn't embrace the changes here, and Graham's childlike belief that all would be well as long as the garden thrived, what could ever be her place in all this? Delphine took a single step and joined her true family.

Gabe hovered at the edge of the garden. If he only looked at everyone chatting in the sun, he could almost believe that all was well indeed. But behind him, the failure chilled his back as if it had actual, physical reach. He saw Delphine walk into the garden. Her steps were tentative. Stella turned and gathered her into her arms, waving and pointing around her, and Delphine smiled. Gabe caught Sorrel's eye, and they both looked to the corner. If Delphine made her way over, she would raise questions neither of the gardeners was ready or willing to answer. Gabe was afraid to leave or stay. He shuffled as if he were about to steal a base and then walked quickly toward the gate. When he was only feet away, he felt her hand on his wrist.

"Did you think I would not see you?" Delphine asked.

Gabe didn't bother to respond. He simply looked at Delphine.

"When did it start?" she asked.

Gabe pointed at the ground.

"Today?"

He nodded.

"What does Sorrel think?"

Gabe lowered his head so that he could speak to Delphine without being overheard.

"She is unsure," he said in a slurred growl.

"Will she try again?" Delphine asked.

"Tomorrow," Gabe said.

"I will join you both," Delphine said. "Don't tell Sorrel."

Now Gabe was keeping secrets from Sorrel, and the weight was enough that he felt ill. He might have been concerned that it was the garden infecting him, punishing him for having any hope at all for the benighted place, but he was a man and never had a man been affected.

He caught Sorrel's eye again and waved her over.

"What's up with Delphine?" Sorrel asked. "She didn't stay long."

Here was the moment Gabe could come clean, tell Sorrel that both he and Delphine had bad feelings building. Then at least he wouldn't be quite as false-hearted as Graham. But he only shook his head.

"Well, I'm sure she'll reappear at lunch, ideally with sweets!" Sorrel laughed and gave Gabe a pat. "We really are pretty terrific gardeners, aren't we?"

Gabe thought he might just burst out with every lie and secret, vomiting up his culpability, poisonous as anything stirring in the garden. But again he was silent and smiled before he left to clean up for lunch. If he didn't return for the meal, Sorrel would surely notice and sound the alarm, which would only bring Graham running, which would unleash Stella's concern and send Poppy off on one of her investigations. All these years with this family and it would be his absence that would reveal his secrets.

"Gabe?" Sorrel asked, touching his arm. "We *are* terrific gardeners, aren't we? I mean, we're OK, right?"

Gabe nodded and signaled that he was going to change out of his dirty work clothes, and Sorrel shooed him off with a smile.

Sorrel drifted back into the garden. If the failed plants troubled her, it didn't show. Andrew took her hand.

"You should be so pleased," he said. "This is a wonderland."

"Thank you, Andrew," Sorrel said. "I was a little worried that you'd be spooked again."

"I was startled, that's all," he said. "Your little town may be used to your magic, but it's new to me and I needed a moment to let it work."

Sorrel stroked his jaw, finding a whiskery spot Andrew had missed shaving.

"You know, of course," she said, "this isn't magic, just rich soil and hard work and the gift of good weather."

"Oh, I'm sure all that had something to do with it," Andrew said.

"I'm ready for lunch," Poppy called out.

"I'm in," said Andrew.

"Of course you are," Sorrel muttered.

When everyone arrived at the formal garden, lunch had been laid out on the terrace by unseen hands. Bowls of strawberries and frosty buckets of champagne waited beside iced platters of salmon and dill, sliced cold flank steak and a salad composed of all the kitchen garden's earth-bound magic. A

tiered cake stand held scores of *macarons*—pistachio, chocolate, raspberry and the more exotic lavender and vanilla, thyme and honey, rose and tea, each topped with the corresponding herb or flower. Delphine had set her staff to work as per Stella, and now she and Arthur stood like proud parents before the beautiful tableau.

Naturally, Graham had another toast ready.

"To all the hidden fairies in our garden and our lives. You have made us very happy today!"

Gabe didn't drink. He was still too anxious to join in the celebration. At the word "fairies," in fact, he jumped a little. Delphine saw his reaction. Poppy did, too. Graham was oblivious, and Stella was so relieved to have the garden completed without the loss of man or beast that she could hardly see beyond the lovely posies Sorrel had placed in tumblers and silver campaign cups around the table. Gabe had to settle down. He waved to everyone and went back to his cottage. Maggie lay on his bed, a place where she was not welcome, but Gabe hadn't the heart to move her. He stretched out beside her and fell asleep.

Sorrel and Andrew strolled in the formal garden. He'd brought four *macarons* wrapped in a napkin. As they approached the maze, he handed Sorrel one and said, "If we are lost, at least we will not starve."

Sorrel laughed. "As if this is enough to sustain you for even an hour!"

"With me as your guide we'll be out in ten minutes. I've been mapping this maze since Stella married into the family." Andrew held out his hand, "Come on, then, it'll be fun."

Sorrel hesitated. She'd avoided the maze itself when she talked with Gabe; she never did like enclosed spaces or being told which way to go, so this wasn't her idea of fun, but she followed Andrew in because, well, it was Andrew.

The high boxwood was fresh and fragrant with new, electric green growth on every branch, but the maze itself held the metallic hint of winter. Perhaps it was the shadows that never lifted as the path wound tight and tighter toward the center. Sorrel had kept her right hand on the hedges; somewhere she'd heard that if you just kept turning right you'd never get lost, but Andrew made what felt like entirely random turns, chatting all the while about how the weekend Stella married he'd had to go in to rescue a couple who drunkenly wandered off at the rehearsal dinner.

Sorrel had stopped listening. The constant turning was making her feel sick. The enveloping, unrelenting green had become cloying, and Sorrel wiped sweat off her upper lip.

"I hope we're almost there," she said and swallowed the saliva that filled her mouth.

"We are indeed," Andrew said and paused to open the *macarons*. "Reward," he said and held one out to Sorrel.

She turned her head and waved it away.

"Suit yourself," Andrew said as he popped it whole into his mouth.

And then there they were at the heart of the maze, a perfectly square moss lawn and a statue of Puck from Shakespeare's *Midsummer Night's Dream.* It was pitted with age, so worn that Puck's smile was nearly gone and the inscription on its base was barely readable.

"'Lord, what fools these mortals be!'" Andrew crowed. "I think it was a joke by the maze designer, you know, about how silly people were to try to find the secret."

Sorrel nodded, she didn't trust herself to speak, certain she was going to throw up. *This is so Patience,* Sorrel thought and put her hands on her knees.

Andrew peered down at her. "Good God, Sorrel," he said. "You are as white as anything. Are you all right?"

Sorrel shook her head and then stopped. "I'm going to be sick," she whispered and was, directly into the roots of the hedge behind her.

Andrew came up and pulled her hair into his hands while Sorrel heaved.

After a bit she sat back on her heels. Andrew handed her the napkin he still held and sat down beside her.

"Poor thing," he said. "If Delphine hadn't been in charge of lunch, I'd think food poisoning."

Sorrel ran her finger across her neck. "No food talk," she whispered.

"Of course not, sorry," Andrew said. "When you're ready, I'll lead you out and we'll put you to bed straightaway. There's been entirely too much excitement for one day."

"I'm not a child, Andrew, but thank you," Sorrel said and put her head down on her knees. "I could sleep right here, I swear."

"That's not going to happen," Andrew said. "Give me your hand." He stood and reached out to Sorrel. She took his hand and wobbled as she rose.

"This may be the most embarrassing thing ever," she said. "Patience is the barfer, I'm the swollen glands one."

"I hate that word 'glands,'" Andrew said. "Lean on me, darling. I'll bring us home."

A feeling of absolute peace and trust stole over Sorrel. She couldn't remember if anyone had ever made her feel safe like this. Certainly not her father in his last years, and more often than not, Sorrel found herself playing the role of rescuer. So she did as Andrew asked, leaned against him, her head on his shoulder, his arm threaded around her waist, and let him lead her back to the light. They emerged from the maze onto the wide green lawn. The terrace had cleared save for Delphine's workers, who were busy clearing away the lunch.

"I can't pass by the food," Sorrel mumbled.

"Of course you can't," Andrew said and swung wide of the terrace under the weeping willow and around the house to the Tithe Barn.

After he settled Sorrel in bed, a ridiculously overwrought process that involved much protest on Sorrel's part, Andrew sat down at the dining table to work through his consecration papers. He'd barely gotten past *"When the Bishop and the Clergy*

(of which there shall be two at least) have entered the Church or Chapel in their several habits, let them, as they walk up from the west to the east end, repeat alternately the 24th Psalm, the Bishop beginning, 'The earth is the Lord's,' with 'Gloria Patri.'" when there was a rapid tapping at his door. Andrew dashed to it before the noise woke Sorrel to find Gabe holding a blanket bundle.

"Hello," Andrew said in a whisper as he signed. "Sorrel's ill so let's be quiet."

Gabe held out the bundle to Andrew. His face was nearly as white as Sorrel's.

"Gabe?" Andrew asked as he held the bundle. The blanket fell away revealing Maggie, dead.

"Oh my God, Gabe! What happened to her?" Andrew couldn't sign with his arms full.

Gabe spoke because his hands were shaking.

"The garden, the damn garden," he said.

"That's not possible," Andrew said and wondered if it was.

Gabe shook his head. "You know nothing," he hissed.

"Now that's not on," Andrew said. "When have I ever crossed you?"

"You had best watch over Sorrel," Gabe said and, taking Maggie from Andrew, turned and left before Andrew could say anything. He tiptoed back into the bedroom to do as Gabe said. Sorrel was lying on her side, her hair spread out over her back like a wave, smelling of salt and sea. It took all he had for Andrew not to lie down beside, to keep her safe, to, in fact, believe that what Gabe said about the garden was true. But

Sorrel was asleep, quiet and calm in the big bed so Andrew left her to rest.

He sat back down at the table and began taking notes. Whatever was going on in the garden, the chapel would be consecrated on the summer solstice, and the longest day of the year would end with a new church to serve the Kirkwood family and perhaps the village as well. For Andrew the real question was whether he would be their leader.

CHAPTER 19

Foxglove

Gabe ran with Maggie in his arms. He ran until he skidded into his cottage and then stood, chest heaving while he tried to understand why his dog was killed by the garden. He scoured his memory for the stories he'd heard over the years, how the garden refused to bear, how at night no one went near it because the unearthly sounds that rose from its shattered remains were too much like a woman crying, how, when Mathilde died, the village gossip had tried to convince everyone that the garden curse was real. He remembered when Delphine walked into the post office for the first time after losing her daughter. He was collecting the estate post and was bending over the box, pulling the last of the bills out when he heard Marta, the newsagent's wife, suggesting that someone should bulldoze

the place before it struck again. It was Delphine's sharp intake of breath that made Gabe turn and stand so fast his head swam. He shoved the post into his bag and rushed over; taking Delphine's arm he guided her quickly out of the post office.

He took her shoulders and stooped to look in her eyes.

"It is not true," he rasped, the first time he had spoken aloud to Delphine. "Cruel gossip," he said and handed her his handkerchief.

Delphine covered her face with the hankie and let out her breath.

"I know," she said. "You are very kind, Gabe."

Gabe accepted his handkerchief and let Delphine walk back to her inn. It would be days before she returned for her post.

Even now, as he laid Maggie gently in her bed Gabe couldn't think of a single incidence of a dog being affected by the garden. Still, he was convinced and now he would have to convince Andrew for good and all. Later, after Gabe picked at the leftovers Delphine had packed for him, after he heard Graham and Stella and Poppy laughing as they walked by on their way to the village, after it was finally dark, long past nine, he took Maggie and walked as far into the woods as he dared. He dug a small grave for her and placed her in it, still in her bed, still wrapped in her blanket. He began to shovel dirt in when he remembered the little wren from the garden. He jogged to the shed and opened the steamer trunk. He gathered the bird and the handkerchief in his hand and locked everything up again. But Gabe was drawn to the awful gar-

den, the stillness in the air around it, the lack of birdsong, of insects, the absence of any sound at all.

When he entered through the gate, Gabe sensed the change. The poison was spreading. He strode to the back corner and even before he reached it, he could smell the rot. The darkness crawled toward him, draped with dead and dying plants. It had reached the first parterre, the low boxwood hedge had yellowed, and when he brushed it, white dust and mites flew out. Just inside, the dense little row of pinks Sorrel had planted for the intense scent had closed into brown nubs, and if there was any scent it was only of decay. There was no way to gauge how fast it would move, this ugliness, now that it had begun in earnest. But Gabe knew he had to move faster. He returned to the forest and finished burying the first victims before the Kirkwoods came home from the village. Then he lay in bed, eyes wide the whole night through. Tears stood as if unable to fall because the loss now and that of the future was simply too great.

Sorrel was worse in the morning. Andrew had trouble rousing her, and her lips were dry and cracked from fever. When she finally sat up, Andrew was shocked at how pale she was. Even the sun-kissed tops of her shoulders looked pallid. There were dark circles under her eyes, and her hair was tangled in a salty wad.

"No work for you today," Andrew said as he brought a cool, damp washcloth in from the bath.

"I'm afraid the garden won't wait for me to get over the creeping crud," Sorrel said. "In fact, it has its own creeping crud to get over." She swung her feet over the side of the bed. "Man, I feel rotten," she said and flopped backward.

"Can't Gabe do whatever needs doing?" Andrew asked. Then he remembered the night before. It had faded as he slept until it took on a dreamlike distance. But now, looking at Sorrel, who was fragile in a way Andrew had never seen, the logical part of his mind clashed with the overwhelmed-by-love part, and those ran into his clergy self, which vacillated between wonder at the power of belief and horror at the power of, well, belief.

"Shit," Andrew said. "I need to talk to Gabe."

"Why?" Sorrel asked from the bathroom.

"Because he might have an answer to your 'whatever this thing is' thing."

Andrew stuck his head around the door of the wet room.

"Don't go anywhere till I get back, yeah," he said.

Sorrel had turned on the shower. "Yeah," she said and leaned against the sink waiting for the water to warm.

Gabe was standing outside the garden walls by dawn. He'd been standing there for two hours by the time Andrew found him and tapped him gently on the shoulder so as not to startle him.

"Sorrel's really ill," Andrew said.

Gabe pointed. "So's the garden," he said.

"I don't give a fuck about the damn garden," Andrew shouted, the noise lost on Gabe, but the anger and fear apparent without a sound.

"You must," Gabe signed. "This is where it started."

"Oh God, Gabe," Andrew said, "You can't really believe that?"

Gabe took Andrew's arm and all but dragged him into the garden. He pulled him toward the back, and they both had to step over fallen stems and crushed blossoms.

When Andrew saw the ruined parts, he heard Sorrel's voice talking about creeping crud.

"All this since yesterday?" he asked Gabe.

Gabe nodded.

"Well, clearly there's something toxic in the soil, something neither of you twigged to when you started."

Gabe shook his head.

"OK then, blight, bugs, mold in the irrigation hoses."

Again Gabe shook his head.

"What is it then?" Andrew asked. "And don't tell me the Kirkwood curse."

Gabe said nothing and stepped gingerly through the mess to collect his shovel. Whatever was happening here, Gabe planned to remove as much of the filth as possible and burn it. He grabbed the shovel and turned to leave. Andrew was pointing behind him.

"What in the world?" he asked.

Gabe looked back. *Damn it,* he thought, and lunged for the fairy house in the corner.

"Gabe, is that one of Mathilde's?"

Gabe had no answer for Andrew.

"Jesus, Gabe, what did you think the fairy house was going to do here?"

Gabe signed with vigor. "I hoped that putting them back where they belonged one by one might keep everything from going wrong again," he said.

"Them? All the houses are still around?" Andrew spluttered.

"I kept them. It was too sad to burn them," Gabe signed.

"You have to tell Delphine, now, today, Gabe."

Gabe looked at Andrew pleadingly.

"No, you have to do it," Andrew said. "I'm going to ask Stella about her flu last February. Maybe there's a link between my sister's bug and Sorrel's."

Gabe watched Andrew go. He envied him his ignorance.

STELLA AND POPPY were in the kitchen, naturally, when Andrew found them.

"Listen," he said, "Sorrel's ill, fever, stomach, general mess."

"Oh, poor thing," Stella said. "I can call Dr. Hancock, have him come out."

"I'm not sure Sorrel would agree to that," Andrew said. "She seems less concerned than I am."

"Maybe you should talk to her sister, Patience," Poppy said.

"Oh, good, let's get the witch of Granite Point involved in our haunted garden," Andrew said.

"Whoa," Poppy said. "What are you on about?"

"Sorry, I'm a little worried, and Gabe's got me all bollocksed up with his superstitions and then that puppy."

"Maggie?" Stella asked. "I think it's sweet the way she's his shadow."

"Not anymore," Andrew said. "She's dead, and Gabe thinks it's the garden."

"Oh God. Did she eat something?" Poppy asked.

"Might have, but Gabe is certain it's more than that, and now he's got me spooked."

"What does Sorrel think? She's got more experience with all this stuff," Poppy said.

"What stuff?" Graham said as he came into the kitchen. "By stuff I hope you mean pancakes and grits or some such American delicacy. I'm starved." He rubbed his hands together.

Poppy rolled her eyes, Stella sighed, and Andrew made a fist under the table.

"Honestly, Graham," Stella said. "Sometimes you are such a cliché."

Andrew explained his situation, and Gabe's theories, including the fairy houses hidden away all these years. Graham's brow lowered, and his expression darkened until finally he held up his hand to stop the story.

"Enough, I've heard enough," he said with uncharacteristic force. "Stella, Poppy, you are to stay out of the garden until we've halted the newest assault on our happiness." He strode out of the room without his breakfast or even tea.

Poppy convinced Andrew to let her come back to the Tithe Barn to see Sorrel, and Stella agreed to check on Delphine. If Gabe had already gotten to her, she'd need counsel. If he hadn't, Stella might just spirit away a couple of *croque-madames* for lunch while Delphine was still in a reasonable mood.

Sorrel was sitting on the edge of the bed when Poppy and Andrew returned. She actually looked a bit better, but to Poppy, who hadn't seen her the day before, Sorrel had never looked worse.

"We are here to help," Poppy said. "Andrew has gotten us all in a swivet over the grotty garden and Gabe's dodgy theories about Maggie and the fairy houses."

"I almost wish I knew what you were talking about, but mostly I wish my head would just fall off and put me out of my misery," Sorrel said.

"She doesn't know?" Poppy asked Andrew.

"I didn't know until I hit the garden with Gabe."

Sorrel shuffled over to the chaise by the big window and lowered herself onto it.

"Start at the beginning," she said. "Don't assume I'll believe you, but do start talking."

Of all the people who should have believed in the innate evil, or good, of a garden, it was Sorrel. She knew in her blood and bone what ugliness could prevail, what history left behind in the land. But this story was exactly what she didn't need or want to hear. The fact that Andrew had gotten himself all tied up in Gabe's superstitions was almost more upsetting than the

idea that her garden was as thwarted as Sorrel once was. Never mind Graham's useless theories.

"You guys," she said, "if you could hear yourselves."

"I'm only filling you in on what's happening," Andrew said.

"And the fact that everyone's gone bloody mad," Poppy said.

"The only thing to do is go see what's gone wrong," Sorrel said. "Gabe and I were going to clear out that corner this morning anyway."

"It's not just the corner anymore," Andrew said as he helped Sorrel off the chaise.

"Well, shit," she said. "Let's leg it, then."

A ramshackle bunch, that's what they were as Sorrel slowly walked between Poppy and Andrew. When they got to the gate, Poppy hung back, a sheepish look on her face.

"Your dad?" Sorrel asked.

"Yes, but now I'm going to ignore him," Poppy said and stepped up.

"Actually," Sorrel said and put a hand on her arm, "Let's play it safe. If the garden is contaminated, I want to limit the damage to a party of one."

Andrew hadn't mentioned Maggie, party of two. He wasn't sure if it was because her death was so heartbreaking for Gabe or because it would only upset Sorrel.

Poppy lingered at the wall feeling useless. It was another beautiful day, which seemed particularly insulting given how ugly everything was. She closed her eyes and tipped her face

into the sun. Andrew's shout came only minutes later, and Poppy skinned her elbows pushing off from the brick wall. She spun to run through the gate but Andrew barreled through first with Sorrel in his arms.

"She passed out, just out!" he said. "Call 999, and Stella and, Jesus, just get someone!"

Poppy did as she was told, calling emergency services and then running for her mother while Andrew half-carried, half-walked a now conscious Sorrel to the Tithe Barn.

"I'm feeling better," Sorrel whispered.

"Excellent, Monty Python girl, I'll just call off the dead cart, then."

"Seriously, dehydration, flu, whatever. It's not an emergency."

But it was to Andrew. He'd seen the look on Sorrel's face when she saw how the garden rot had spread. He watched what little color she had drain when she rustled the boxwood, letting loose so many mites it looked like snow. When she saw the fairy house, she gasped and put her fingers to her mouth. She'd turned to Andrew in that moment, and then she went down. There was an angry scrape from the gravel on her chin, she'd bitten her tongue in the fall, and her shirt was fouled with decay.

The ambulance arrived at the drive just as they did, so Sorrel simply sat on the edge of the open back while the medics tended to her.

"I have to agree with your wife, sir," the EMT said.

Andrew and Sorrel spoke as one. "We're not married."

"In any event, while her blood pressure is a little low, and she still has a fever, this is a matter of dehydration and too much sun on top of a stomach bug," she said. "Rest, fluids, and shade."

Sorrel was so embarrassed that she agreed to everything and let Andrew lead her away. Poppy and her mother arrived shortly afterward.

"You do look wretched," Stella said.

"She's going to follow orders," Andrew said. "Perhaps for the first time ever."

They left Sorrel in bed, the long linen curtains pulled over the windows. She felt more than awful, although she'd never admit it. The enforced rest was welcome. As for the garden, it was so disturbing that all Sorrel could do was compare it to the state of the Nursery last summer. The combination of human destruction and whatever blight Patience's state of mind threw over the whole town seemed much too close to what was happening here. She drifted off, determined to contact Patience when she woke.

In the living room Stella was handing out sandwiches from Delphine. She had in fact beaten Gabe into the village, probably because he was dawdling. No one enjoyed a tongue lashing from Delphine. Considering how sensitive the subject, Stella could only imagine that Gabe was putting off the confrontation.

"I think we should still call Patience," Poppy said. "She should at least know that Sorrel's not well."

"And then she panics right along with Andrew," Stella said. "Why don't we leave it to Sorrel to contact her sister?"

GABE FINALLY CAME to Delphine after the lunch rush at the inn. He stood for a long time in the shade of the laburnum allée that led to the beer garden. There were still a few stragglers enjoying the last of their drinks. Gabe thought they looked happy and carefree, and he wanted to slap them all.

Delphine came out to clear the last of the glasses and saw Gabe.

"You are lurking," she said. "I'll take these in and we can sit."

Gabe felt even worse in the face of Delphine's hospitality. When she returned, she was carrying a tray with her *citron pressé* and glasses.

"Something is on your mind," she said. "Tell me."

Gabe let the story spill out, alternately signing and scribbling. He watched Delphine carefully, waiting for the anger to rise, the explosion that was surely coming. But when he finished, Delphine reached out her strong hand and covered his worn ones.

"You are expecting blame?" she asked. "A lecture about privacy and respect, perhaps? How the weight of grief that you cannot know and must not trifle with transforms one, maybe?"

Gabe nodded. He was as still as a hare in a hedgerow.

"Oh, Gabe," Delphine said and patted his hands again. "I did not know how much I wished for those little fairy houses until you told me they survived."

Gabe closed his eyes in relief.

"And," she continued, "now that Sorrel is ill and the garden is failing, it is essential that we put them back to work, yes?"

Gabe might have let it go at that, but given the terrible state of the garden, and her little gardener, he made a decision that he knew would probably end his time at Kirkwood Hall. He spoke slowly and carefully so that there would be no misunderstanding.

"The final tapestry is in the crypt," he said. "Richard hid it. Graham knew that much. He lied to you."

Delphine froze. Not even the bee that alighted on her shoulder stirred her.

"When was this?" she asked.

"The year you found them, when the chapel was such a ruin no one ever went in it."

"And you knew this?"

Gabe nodded. "I had to keep the secret. Kirkwood is my life," he wrote, giving up on the spoken word.

"Of course you did," Delphine said. "I can't blame you, not at all."

Gabe's eyes filled. The relief of telling the truth made all the anxiety of the last weeks fade.

"Now we will go get it and see what it has to tell us."

Gabe started to protest. "Graham will not allow," he said.

"I don't care what Graham will or will not allow," Delphine snapped. "It is time to end this charade of his before anyone else is hurt."

Delphine removed her apron, instructed her husband to stir the veal stock, and led Gabe back to Kirkwood Hall.

On the way she learned about Maggie and cooed her distress as Gabe swiped at his tears. She catalogued the symptoms of Sorrel's sudden illness with Gabe and heard how the garden seemed to be eating itself alive. When he told her that he had wanted to put the fairy houses in the garden to protect it, Delphine nodded.

"Of course this makes sense," she said. "It is what Mathilde did, why she made them."

"Too late," Gabe said.

"We'll see," Delphine said. "We'll see."

THE GARDEN GROANED as it oozed toward the sundial. Any bird that had begun to feel safe again inside the walls was long gone. A meadow vole who thought to burrow under the soil and nibble on the tasty bulbs when autumn arrived lay dead in a small indentation caused by the collapse of the lady's smock. Three holly blue butterflies grown accustomed to the revived ivy were left stranded when the vine fell away from the wall and lay curled in upon itself in the shadows. The silence was absolute. If ever there was a call for a fairy house to keep watch, it was now.

CHAPTER 20

Hemlock

Andrew finally caved the next morning and rang Patience Sparrow on his mobile. Nettie answered the Nursery phone, and when she heard Andrew's voice, she shouted for Patience before he even had a chance to tell her why he was calling.

"What's wrong?" Patience asked, her own voice sharp and demanding.

Andrew found himself babbling as he tried to present the situation both in the least worrying light and without the questionable occult bits.

"So is Sorrel sick enough for me to come over?" Patience asked. "I mean, what is it you want me to do, exactly?"

"Mostly she's been sleeping," Andrew said, "We had her

seen by a medic, but she doesn't seem to be making any improvement."

"I'm still confused," Patience said. "Put her on the phone."

"That's just it, Patience. She doesn't want to get out of bed, and she won't let me call the doctors back."

"Oh, for fuck's sake," Patience spat.

"Well, my thoughts exactly," Andrew said.

Poppy grabbed the phone from Andrew.

"Hi, I'm Poppy, and I think Skype is the way forward here," she said. "Andrew's too upset to be of any use, but I am ready to tell you what you need to know to devise a remedy for this."

Poppy and Patience organized themselves with admirable speed and before long they were sitting across a computer screen and an ocean trying to fix Sorrel. Andrew paced behind them until Patience finally told him to sit still or get out. He got out, taking Wags, on lead to avoid any garden-related danger, for a walk.

Patience asked Poppy to get Sorrel's list of herbs for the physic garden and the plan she'd drawn up for the Shakespeare Garden as well. She asked her pointed questions about Sorrel's state. Only when she asked about the state of the garden itself did Poppy stumble.

"OK, what are you hiding?" Patience asked.

So Poppy told her everything, including how her father was convinced there was a Kirkwood curse and Gabe was certain the garden, his puppy, and Sorrel had succumbed to it.

"First of all," said Patience, "I don't believe in curses, only

in ignorant people and really bad luck. Second, if something is wrong in that garden and it sounds like something is very wrong, it can be explained without witchery, I promise."

Poppy felt the lightness and sense of wellbeing that comes from finding help just when you need it, or when a fever breaks. She agreed to come back to Patience once Sorrel's sister had time to digest the materials Poppy was sending. She took Sorrel's list of herbs and the garden plan and scanned them into the computer in her mother's office and emailed it to Patience. Then she went looking for everyone. She didn't trust the quiet that had come over the house and grounds. Just then Wags came flying around the corner of the stables followed by a shouting Andrew.

Poppy knelt down and grabbed Wags while Andrew caught his breath.

"What did you learn?" he asked.

Poppy told him that she was waiting for Patience's call and he asked to see her phone.

"Stop it," she said, holding the phone behind her back. "Isn't there someone else who needs you?"

"Gabe and Delphine are at the chapel. They seem to think—"

Poppy interrupted him. "Great. Go help them, and I'll sit with Sorrel while we wait for Patience."

Andrew handed off Wags, and the two parted. Poppy could see by the slump of Andrew's shoulders that he was struggling. As for herself, she found it unsettling that Sorrel was not in

charge. Poppy had gotten used to her calm certainty, the way she tilted her head as she listened to her plants, the sound of Sorrel's ethereal humming as she moved from parterre to parterre, music that seemed to call the birds to the garden and the bees to the blossoms. Poppy was a sensible sort, so this kind of musing was so out of character that she mimed a quick slap to her own cheek before she entered the Tithe Barn.

Sorrel was still asleep. Her skin was pale, but her cheeks were red, as if Poppy had actually slapped her. Poppy straightened the sheet and coverlet over Sorrel, and Wags jumped up on the foot of the bed.

"No!" Poppy hissed. "Get down, silly." She reached to scoop Wags off the bed.

Wags growled low and long. She bared her teeth, and Poppy saw her hackles rise into a ridge. She'd never seen Wags do anything but smile and cuddle, and she stepped back with her hands up.

"Steady, steady," she said. "I'm leaving." Poppy backed out of the room.

Wags turned in a circle before settling in the crook of Sorrel's knees with a sigh.

Poppy waited in the living room, leafing through Andrew's unspeakably boring church stuff, checking his fridge for Delphine leftovers, snooping in cupboards for biscuits to have with her tea. When her phone rang, she jumped.

Patience didn't even greet Poppy, just started talking.

"Have you got a pen and paper?" she barked.

Poppy grabbed Andrew's pad and a pen and sat as if ordered, her hand poised for note taking.

"Ready?" Patience asked.

"Quite," said Poppy and bent to her task.

Twenty minutes later Poppy had two pages of instructions, lists of herbs and proportions, and a bunch of doodles along the margins that now made no sense. Thankfully, Patience had agreed to Skype with Poppy while she made the remedy.

"It won't be mine, exactly," Patience said. "But at least I'll know you won't kill her."

The last thing Patience asked was what Sorrel smelled of.

"I beg your pardon?" Poppy said. "I don't fancy sniffing for whatever it is you think I should sniff for."

"No, no, jeez, you people are so literal," Patience said. "Just tell me what the air around her says."

Poppy crept into the bedroom thinking that Patience was probably the rudest person she'd ever encountered, and the strangest. That was saying something lately.

Yet there it was, a scent that lay atop the air, a breeze of it that Poppy inhaled and tried to identify. She ran back to the phone before she forgot.

"Marigolds, she smells like marigold leaves," Poppy said. "Sharp, acrid but also kind of nice."

"OK, that's helpful," Patience said. "Come back when you have everything."

"Wait, wait," Poppy said. "I'm not supposed to go into the garden."

"Really?" Patience said. "You're going to follow the rules now?"

"Right, right, I'm off," said Poppy and put down the phone.

Poppy did tie a scarf around her nose and mouth while she worked: a Hermès silk scarf that belonged to her mother, which was very soon coated in fine grit and damp with Poppy's breath. It was alarming, the garden, so Poppy moved quickly, keeping her list held high as she stopped to cut the herbs. It seemed as if the rot was claiming plants like a wave on the shore. The physic patch was close enough to the wall that, while scraggly, it was for the most part intact. Poppy threw everything into the Pyrex bowl she'd brought and ran back to the Tithe Barn.

IF GRAHAM HAD seen his daughter even pass by the garden gate, he would have lifted her by her shirt collar and carried her away. But Lord Kirkwood was in his library surrounded by family history, desperate to stop the disaster he saw coming. Of course, had he paid any attention at all to his current family or, to be more exact, if he had told them the truth from the start, the disaster might have been averted altogether. At least that's what he thought. Instead, Graham sat at his desk, his hair standing on end from being scrubbed back and forth, a scattering of hives already climbing his neck. He blamed himself for everything, as he should have, and for the life of him, he could see no way out. It wasn't that he expected a plague to take his family one by one, it was that however this most recent failed

attempt at garden saving ended up, Graham knew his family might never forgive him for his part in it. Nor should they, he thought as he ran his hand through his hair again.

In the crypt Gabe was on his knees beside Thomas's sarcophagus. He was digging around in the space between the stone and the stone wall with Andrew's sponge pole, minus the sponge and with the addition of a hook made of baling wire. The scraping sound made Delphine cover her ears and Andrew wince. Finally there was a muffled thump and a dry dragging as Gabe snagged the tapestry roll.

"Don't tear it," Delphine shrieked, but Gabe was turned away. The thought of the sharp wire ripping through the delicate threads, the linen and silk and perhaps even gold embroidery, made her shudder. But she also knew why they were all in this suffocating place and she closed her mouth.

The roll was wrapped in a muslin drop cloth so that the sound Delphine heard was only the hook in the muslin. Gabe and Andrew carried the tapestry out between them and laid it on the widest part of the transept at the foot of the altar. They pulled the muslin off bit by bit, sending plumes of stone dust into the air.

"Before I open this," Andrew said, "have you seen it, Gabe?"

Gabe shook his head and bent down again, waving an impatient hand at Andrew.

"Fine, I'll do this with you but whatever it shows, can we

agree not to blame Graham? We can be pissed that he's been so secretive, we can be irritated that even in the face of your certainty, Delphine, he denied it was here, but we can't blame him for the subject matter, right?"

Everyone nodded.

The two men gave a shove and the tapestry unrolled, the colors so bright after the shadows in the crypt that everyone gasped. No stone dust had marred the panel, no light since the day Richard Kirkwood had found it and dragged it into a box room in the public wing, away from prying eyes. The tapestry went into the crypt immediately, but not until Richard had shown his son the awful thing. He swore Graham to secrecy and never told him specifically where it was hidden. Gabe knew though, but he kept Richard's secret as well as his own. Nevertheless, Graham's superstition and his unease knew no bounds. Still, promises had been made so, as gruesome as the subject on display was, all three standing in that chapel on this day held their tempers and their tongues.

This last panel of the so-named Hunt of the Innocent was different from the other six; it was twice the size of the others, for one thing. It was also divided into three sections, like a triptych or a grotesque altarpiece. The first section gave the impression that the woman in the sixth had leapt from that panel into this one. As Sorrel and Poppy had seen earlier, her foot was bloodied, but now everyone could see against the frayed edges of her nightdress that her leg and her arms were almost flayed. In this section her face was visible for the first

time, and even with the terror in her eyes, picked out so intricately by the weavers, Delphine swore that she could see the reflection of her pursuers in them. The woman was beautiful. Her tangled hair was long and black, her neck a fine column of white stained by blood drops. Snarling hounds snapped at her heels as she turned her face over her shoulder to watch them. In the second section the woman had been caught. She was on the ground, her hands held above her by one of the hunters. The dogs were still now, and a row of men stood behind them, a silent jury passing judgment without compunction. All around the woman plants, herbs, and broken flowers lay scattered. If Sorrel had been well and with them, she could have identified them all. Shattered glass phials were ground under the feet of the hunters, and a mortar and pestle were overturned at her feet. Behind her a tall stake stood at the center of a pyre waiting to be lit.

This section, this chapter of The Hunt of the Innocent, struck Poppy with the force of a blow. This was Anna, it had to be: Elizabeth's mentor, the village midwife, Elizabeth's own midwife, and her friend. This was what had happened to Anna; she was the innocent hunted by Thomas and his savages. In fact, Thomas was the man holding Anna's hands in a cruel grip, a black cord wrapped around her wrists. He was instantly recognizable by his height, his hair, and his unsmiling face. Poppy longed for Sorrel's insight and also for her comfort as she looked at the awful man.

Slowly, slowly in the quiet of the empty chapel all four

viewers turned to the last section of the oversized final panel. Even knowing what to expect was no preparation for the hideous completion. Lord Kirkwood and his men stood beside the flaming pyre. Thomas held his torch high and smiled at last, an ugly, ferocious grin that split his face like a wound. The hounds were cowering at the edge of the frame, clearly spooked by the fire. At the very center was Anna. Tied to the rough-hewn stake, she was half consumed by the flames. Her face was absolutely expressionless, her eyes closed. Smoke rose around her in a nimbus and her black hair was filled with sparks. In the distance was the walled garden and farther away still, the tiny chapel. None of it was to perspective or scale or even in the right arrangement. Clearly, the nuns had made some dangerous choices in the composition of the last panel and had concealed clues in the ones that came before. Each building, landmark, image, even the botanicals, held a message for those who wished to see.

"Jesus." Andrew finally spoke. "I can hardly look at this."

"That must be how Graham felt when he found it," Delphine said. "It is hard to fault him, no?"

"Christ, what a lovely family I've got," said Poppy.

Gabe signed, it was clearer and faster than speaking, and with Andrew at hand to translate, everyone would now know what he did.

"You are all missing the bigger point," he signed as Andrew spoke quickly, his eyes on Gabe's hands.

"This last panel holds the key to rescuing the garden," Gabe said.

"I don't think anyone gives a shit about the garden right now," Poppy said.

"I know I only care about Sorrel," Andrew said.

Gabe began signing again. "Exactly, the secret to the garden is the secret to saving Sorrel."

"What are you going to do about Sorrel, Gray?" Stella asked.

They were sitting in the library with untouched tea before them.

"Please, Stella," Graham said. "Can I have just a moment to think?"

"No, you may not," Stella said. "You made this mess, you gormless twit!"

"Stella!" Graham was shocked that his wife would speak to him with such a lack of affection.

"We've got no time for your games now, Gray," Stella said. She softened. "I know you've only been trying to protect us, but what you've done instead is throw Sorrel into harm's way, just as I warned, and lost the garden at the same time. How do you think Poppy's going to feel about her father when she realizes everything that's gone wrong stems from you?"

"Bugger," Graham said without much energy.

"Bugger indeed," Stella said and pulled Graham to his feet. "Let's go then."

"Where are you taking me?"

"To find the rest of this motley crew and make a plan."

Poppy propped her laptop on the table in Andrew's kitchen and let Patience walk her through the remedy. While she measured and ground, mixed and shook the ingredients in a jam jar, she told Patience about the latest discovery.

"So you guys have figured out what, exactly?" Patience asked.

"Well, it looks like, from the tapestry at least, that Anna was burned as a witch."

Patience shuddered. "Assholes," she spat.

"Exactly," Poppy said. "Now Gabe, he's our caretaker—"

"You all need one," Patience said.

"Fine, I'll acknowledge that," Poppy said. "Gabe claims that Anna's bones or ashes or something equally disturbing, are buried in the Shakespeare Garden and that's why it's cursed."

"Let's put aside for a moment the impossibility of everything you just said and accept that Anna's remains were buried centuries ago in the garden your father hired Sorrel to restore," Patience said and held up her hand. "Wait, the lovage root has to be grated and then the liquid squeezed out."

"Oh, right," Poppy said and did as Patience instructed.

"So, if Anna's whatever are in fact in the garden all these years later, in theory they could have tainted the soil."

"And that's what made Sorrel, and the others in the past, ill?"

"I don't know. I'm just thinking out loud," Patience said. "And to be honest, I don't care about the others or the damn garden. I only care about my sister."

"I'm with you on that," Poppy said. "But, to be clear, no one other than a Kirkwood has ever succumbed to the garden."

"Don't you see?" Patience snapped. "The minute Sorrel fell for Andrew, the minute she took you all into her heart, she became a Kirkwood."

"Oh dear," Poppy said.

"Yes, oh dear," Patience said. "Now, let's get back to the remedy."

Poppy strained the remedy through the finest sieve in the Tithe Barn kitchen. There were still bits floating but Patience assured her it was fine and besides, there was no more time to fiddle. She instructed Poppy on the dosage and told her that under no circumstances was anyone to go into the garden again. Poppy dreaded sharing that news with the others. Then she decided she didn't give a fig.

"Let that steep for one hour," Patience said, "before you administer it. Then after the first two doses, call me back."

"I'm on it," Poppy said.

"And, Poppy," Patience said, "Sorrel had better recover, fast."

"HERE'S A THOUGHT," Andrew said after he and Delphine left Gabe to re-roll the tapestry. "What if we reinter Anna properly in the chapel?"

"Don't you need permission for that?" Delphine asked. "Certainly you can't go burying people willy-nilly."

"No, not like, say, Thomas did to the midwife," Andrew said sourly. "But given that the bishop is joining me for the consecration at the solstice, I'm pretty sure I could convince him that Anna deserves a Christian burial."

"Even though she's a witch?"

"Well, she's not, obviously, so that's not an issue."

"How do you explain her then?" Delphine asked.

"We just spin a story about the garden restoration uncovering ancient human remains and take it from there."

"We don't even know if she's there," Delphine said.

"One way to find out," Andrew said. "I'm going to Sorrel. If she seems stable, we'll get Gabe and excavate together."

"And Graham?" Delphine asked.

"He'll be right there with us."

CHAPTER 21

Morning Glory

Andrew sat by Sorrel's bedside waiting for a sign. Poppy had given her the first dose and was anxious to give the second. Sorrel was awake but utterly wiped out.

"I wish you wouldn't stare at me like that," she whispered.

"I wish you weren't so ill," Andrew said. "I wish you'd never undertaken that garden."

"If I hadn't, I wouldn't be here with you."

"Precisely," Andrew said. "I mean; you wouldn't be laid out like a flounder."

"Lovely," Sorrel said. "Fish."

"Henry thinks it's a mold thing," Andrew said.

"You talked to Henry?"

"No, Patience did. I guess she's covering all the bases."

Sorrel nodded and put her arm over her eyes.

"Of course, Gabe has his own idea," Andrew said. "Do you want to hear it?"

"I guess." Sorrel sighed.

Andrew told Sorrel the story of the last tapestry. He watched as her eyes widened and her mouth opened in surprise or shock or disbelief or all three, he couldn't tell which without words. Poppy sat by the window holding the remedy as if it were the grail and checked her watch repeatedly.

"This is beyond spooky," Sorrel said.

"Or," said Andrew, "it makes complete sense."

"Either way, the revival was false, the garden is a failure and so am I," Sorrel said. "I'd cry if I had the energy."

Poppy stepped in with Patience's remedy. Unlike her sister's beautifully clear and clean concoctions distilled and decanted in the peace and comfort of the Sparrow Sisters Nursery, this jam jar was full of a murky liquid, and Poppy had to shake it to redistribute the sediment.

Sorrel was smart enough to take it without protest, but she gagged all the same.

"You needn't be so dramatic. I've been taking my Heart's Ease for a month now without a single blech," Andrew said.

"*Your* Heart's Ease?" Sorrel asked. "And, *how long?*"

Poppy attempted to slip out but Sorrel stopped her with a puny clap.

"Don't blame it all on Poppy, Sorrel," Andrew said. "She may have started it, but I'm the one who kept it up."

"I can't trust either of you," Sorrel said. Then she looked at Andrew. "Can I trust your feelings for me or is this just another story I'm being told?"

Poppy turned away and eased out of the room.

Andrew climbed onto the bed with Sorrel and put his arms around her, pulling her into his chest.

"I have never felt anything like the love I have for you," Andrew said. "It was not engendered by potions or nurtured by anything more enchanted than your love for me. You must know that, Sorrel, here," he thumped his heart.

Sorrel nestled into Andrew's arms, and he felt her nod against his chin. In minutes they were both asleep.

SORREL DREAMT OF the garden, or rather she dreamt of a Shakespeare Garden that was resplendently in bloom. She dreamt that her sisters were with her and that they were as happy as she. Patience carried a basket and plucked herbs and flowers with her tiny, sharp scissors. Nettie had a canvas bag slung across her chest. She began to pick vegetables and slip them into the bag, all the while telling her sisters what she planned for dinner. Sorrel had already gathered a bouquet of sweet peas so fragrant the bees were drunk on the nectar and were compelled to alight in the branches of a dogwood to sleep it off. She planned to put them at her bedside. Nettie already had a bushel basket of pears and passion fruit, and out of nowhere Patience had lined up her blue bottles around the sundial.

There was a wood just beyond the garden walls. Sunlight

played through the leaves, and birdsong floated in to the girls. Strangely, a rill ran right through the garden, bending around the sundial and disappearing into a small opening in the brick wall. The sisters had left the gate open as they worked so that Wags and Maggie wandered along with them, drinking from the rill, nibbling at the grasses that grew amidst the gravel. Sorrel bent to pat Maggie as Nettie tsked over her malformed leg. Maggie was not the least bothered, and Wags nudged her along as they snuffled.

"Everything is just right," Sorrel said. "All the hard work has paid off handsomely."

"If only Anna were here to see it," Patience said. "She promised to come, but it's too late for her now."

Sorrel looked up to see that it had darkened in the garden. Shadows climbed the brick walls and crawled across the gravel paths. She checked her watch, but the numbers were blurry. She couldn't use the sundial, crowded as it was with Patience's bottles. And Anna, how could she be coming? She was long dead and buried. Patience must be confused. Nettie toed her basket of fruit down the path toward the gate.

"We'd better move along if we don't want the fruit to go over," she said. "It'll be no use in my pie."

Sorrel looked in the basket to see that already the pears were softening and the passion fruit had split open, spilling seeds and flesh in a sticky mass.

"I don't understand," Sorrel said. "What's going on?"

"Oh," Patience said, "you know you can't make a garden without us, you shouldn't have even tried."

"But it's beautiful," Sorrel said, waving at the garden. "It's perfect."

"Is it?" Nettie asked, and Sorrel saw that everything was spoiled, every plant and flower and fruit was furred with rot. She thought for a moment that she was back home at the Nursery during the trial when everything went so wrong for the Sisters. She wondered if, in fact, she was in Granite Point and that everything that had happened to her from the invitation to Wiltshire, to meeting Andrew, to the secrets revealed by the garden was just dreams. Perhaps, standing in the center of her own ruined garden, she'd imagined another one entirely.

"This can't be," Sorrel said. "You can't be here, this is mine. The garden is mine, Andrew is mine, my life here belongs to me."

Patience and Nettie looked at Sorrel with pity.

"Sorrel," Patience said, "you'll forget all this once you're home where you belong."

"I don't want to go home," Sorrel said and began to cry.

Andrew woke her gently. Her mumbling and restless shifting beneath the sheets made him afraid her fever was back, but Sorrel's brow was cool and dry and other than her confusion as she swam up from her dream, she looked far better than she had only hours before.

"Darling," he whispered, "come back now."

While the lovers slept and Sorrel dreamt her way into a nightmare, Gabe gathered his tools. He knew that digging around in the garden would be nasty, unhealthy stuff, so he took a stack of facemasks and a pile of Tyvek bunny suits from the restorer's offices in the public part of the house. Next he chose his sturdiest shovels and a tarp to hold whatever he unearthed. They would all have to move quickly if they wanted to avoid village gossip.

He drove his materials over in the truck and unloaded everything into a large barrow. The light was good enough until nearly ten these days, so Gabe decided to make his move. Stella brought Graham over, and Andrew left Poppy and Delphine with Sorrel so he could help. None of them had any desire to be witness to what Gabe was certain would be an exhumation.

No matter what the plan, Graham did not take part in the digging. Instead, Gabe cleared away the last of the rotted vegetation, and he and Andrew began together. Stella turned away and gazed in horror at how far the decay or blight or curse had spread. Only the two parterres just beside the gate remained completely untouched. If Sorrel thought she could repair the ravages before she left in little more than a week's time, Stella could not imagine how.

The first few shovels full of dirt raised a smell as pungent as fox piss. Everyone had their facemasks on, and Gabe and Andrew were in the bunny suits, giving the entire operation an unsuitably comic aspect. In minutes they'd dug beyond the

three feet of new soil that had been put in and had begun to reach the rocky pale gray layer beneath. It was harder to make progress here, as the dirt was so fine it kept drifting from the shovels or blowing back into the hole. Gabe sprayed the area with the hose to make the dust lie, and they went back to digging. No one spoke, no bird sang, and not a single bug fizzed through the dusky air.

Andrew and Gabe stopped once to lean on their shovels and drink bottled water under their masks. Stella and Graham stood next to the sundial feeling pointless. It was close to eight when Andrew's shovel struck something. Everyone jolted at the sound, and Gabe grabbed Andrew's arm to stop him.

"By hand now," he signed.

The men went to their knees around the hole. It was not a terribly big hole in a little corner of a garden that might have been anywhere, but Gabe was certain that it was Anna's grave. They leaned in together, their hands tangling with each other as they scooped. They found a box, wood with leather straps, or at least that's what the tattered bits around the buckles seemed to be. The box itself was rotted through, stove in on one side perhaps by other shovels or other gardeners. Gabe and Andrew lay down, letting their chests down into the hole and together they brought the box out. It was no bigger than a shoebox, and Stella let out a sob before she gathered herself and stepped forward to the tarp.

"I'll take that," she said and removed her mask.

"No, Stella, leave it on," Graham said.

"I will not approach this victim of your ancestors as if she is the tainted one."

"You've no idea what's in there," Graham said.

"It's not a jack-in-the-box, so you can come closer, dear," Stella said.

It hardly seemed possible, but as Stella gingerly picked the lid apart, the smell of soot and char drifted out. The bone fragments were clearly visible amidst the gravelly ash and filtered dirt.

"How do we know it's Anna?" Graham asked.

Stella shook the box gently. "Because of this," she said and lifted a blackened medallion from the box.

It was hanging from a tangled chain, a flat metal disc with a carved plant or branch in the center. "It's a rose of Jericho," she said, "also called Maryam leaf, and traditionally used by midwives during labor." Stella rubbed it on her sleeve. "This is our Anna."

CHAPTER 22
Nigella

Andrew spent the night in the chaise by the windows. He wasn't afraid of falling ill. He was afraid of jinxing Sorrel's slow but steady recovery. By nightfall she was sipping bone broth brought by Delphine and by ten she was in the kitchen, wobbly but determined to find the éclair Delphine had left for her.

Poppy had left before sunset, buoyed by Sorrel's improving health and feeling more than a little heroic as she gave the remedy a final shake and left it in the fridge with instructions from Patience for the final dose. She thought that perhaps, after she had her degree, she might spend some time in the colonies, New England to be precise, studying art, and a bit of magic with the Sisters if they were willing.

When she reached the big house, she found her parents and Andrew in the kitchen scrubbing their hands and arms up to the elbow, a puddle of Tyvek coveralls and facemasks by the larder door.

"Result," her father said when he caught sight of Poppy.

"Oh, Poppy, we found Anna, just where Gabe said she would be!" Stella said. She grabbed a towel off the stove and rubbed as if she'd just been given a poor tour of the Hartlepool nuclear plant.

Stella reached for the medallion. "Look, this was hers and now we can bury Anna where she belongs, beside Elizabeth in St. Mary's crypt."

Poppy wanted to be pleased, she wanted to board the happy trolley, but she could still see Sorrel as pale as death itself, and anger rose unbidden.

"Oh fab, brill, no, really, this is great news," she sneered. "Sorrel Sparrow, your handy dandy miracle worker, nearly succumbed to whatever shit has been brewing in that garden for generations, but by all means, let's make sure the dead woman gets a decent burial. Well done to us!"

"Now listen here, madam," Graham began.

"Oh shut up, you great clod," Stella said. "Sorry, darling but you really have no standing here."

Poppy had to stifle a laugh.

"Poppy, you are right, and wrong," Stella said as she steered her to a seat. "Sorrel has suffered under our watch, but Anna did as well, and I believe, if you give it a little think, you will

see that the circle has at last been rejoined. Anna will find her rest. Sorrel, thanks to you, and Patience, of course, has found her health again and, if all goes well, the garden will recover, the chapel will be consecrated, and you will forgive your father for his blinding drive to keep his family safe."

"When you put it that way," Poppy said. "Yeah, but no. Dad, you really have cocked it up this time."

"And don't I know it," Graham said. "I am no better than Thomas, no more enlightened than the idiot Kirkwoods who trampled the original monastery to ruins and then thought to distract God and man by building a great estate and an even greater fortune."

Poppy had no response.

"There is nothing I can do or say to undo what has come before, but I promise you, on my honor—not the honor of my forbearers, clearly—that I will never break trust with my family and the land we steward." Graham crossed the kitchen and held out his hand as his bond. Poppy, naturally, shook it. What else could she do? And, honestly, what a relief it was to be a united front against whatever challenge came next, instead of a rabble of village idiots chasing shadows.

Andrew looked a bit shambolic the following morning as he tiptoed around the kitchen making coffee, spooning out yogurt and fruit into bowls and measuring out Sorrel's next dose of remedy. She'd slept quietly through the night, no nightmares or restless movements. Andrew, on the other hand, had

felt like bad origami as he folded his long frame in half just to keep from falling out of the chaise. It was a relief to rise with the light. If he'd learned anything about Sorrel these last weeks it was that she too would rise with the light, even if she felt like death on toast.

And he was right. Sorrel appeared in the kitchen, Andrew's dressing gown even looser now. She was still pale and thin, but she was Sorrel again. Andrew gathered her gently into his arms. She smelled of summer air again, of green things, of living and growing, and Andrew felt tears threaten.

"I was awfully worried about you, my love," Andrew said.

"I was awfully worried about me, too," Sorrel said and nuzzled into Andrew's chest. "But I think it's past, whatever it was, and if I don't get into that garden, there'll be nothing for your altar come next Sunday."

"Listen, there's been a development," Andrew said.

Sorrel tilted her head back to look at him. Her chin was sharp against his breastbone.

"It's good, I think," Andrew said. "At least it's a resolution of sorts."

He explained all that had transpired while Sorrel lay insensate. She listened, drawing away from him with each new revelation until she sat slumped in a chair with both elbows up on the table. Andrew brought her the remedy and a glass of water. Sorrel took it without noticing and then drank the entire glass down. Finally, Andrew came to the part about Anna and the chapel, and he saw a slight smile come to Sorrel's lips.

"Coffee," she said and reached out a hand.

"That's it? Coffee?" Andrew said as he poured a mug. "No clever boy, no hallelujah?"

"I need to reorganize my brain before I can respond," Sorrel said. "You know I had the oddest dream the other night, or maybe it was day. I can't remember how long I've been sick. Anyway, my sisters and I were in this garden, here, and it was beautiful and unsullied, but then Patience mentioned Anna, and this filth began creeping through until everything was ruined."

"That sounds dreadful, and all too real," Andrew said.

"I know, except that my sisters were cruel to me, and that is never real or true. They told me I wasn't any good on my own, that this garden couldn't possibly thrive, and that I needed to go back to Granite Point with them."

Andrew felt his heart clutch, the beat off, just a flutter as he took in Sorrel's words. In the midst of her illness, the surreal garden horror, all the intrigue and revelations about the tapestries, Andrew had been able to put away the reality that Sorrel would leave him, and soon.

"That doesn't seem very Sparrow-like," he managed.

"No, it's not," Sorrel said and ate some yogurt. Yellow and red raspberries mixed with sliced peaches mounded her spoon. She ate silently for a minute or two until the yogurt was gone.

Andrew couldn't have taken a single mouthful without gagging, and he wondered at Sorrel's equanimity. He waited

for her to add something for as long as he could and was about to dive in when she finally spoke into the quiet. He startled.

"I told them, my sisters, that I didn't want to go home," Sorrel said. "Not yet, at least." She didn't look up from her bowl.

"Oh, thank God," Andrew said and pulled a chair over in front of her. He put his hands on her knees and pressed a flurry of kisses to her hands in her lap.

"I'm not sure I can swing it," Sorrel said. "The Nursery needs me as much as my sisters do, but perhaps I could stay just a while longer to make sure the Shakespeare Garden recovers?"

Andrew just nodded. He didn't trust his voice and he thought a whooping cheer was inappropriate, given the gravity of Sorrel's choice.

"I'm going to dress," Sorrel said. "Then can you take me to the garden?"

THE CORNER AT the back of the garden, Anna's corner as Andrew thought of it, was still raw. The hole had been filled in, and Gabe had raked fresh, healthy soil over everything but there was no ignoring the lack of anything growing. Sorrel stepped carefully through the gate, holding Andrew's elbow to steady her. The damage had stopped in its tracks, leaving the front parterres untouched. Beyond that almost everything would have to be replanted. And, depending on how receptive one was to fairy stories, those plants would either flourish in celebration of a wrong righted, or do no better than the last.

Either way, Sorrel was eager to get started. She was too experienced to expect a Shakespeare Garden of full and florid bloom by the solstice, but she was determined that whatever she could do would be done.

"Is the garden center at Codswallop open today?" she asked.

"Middle Wallop." Andrew laughed. "Yes, I'm sure it is but not for an hour at least."

"Where's Gabe?" she asked.

Gabe rounded the corner just then, and a great grin spread across his face at the sight of Sorrel. He approached, and Sorrel reached out with both arms. Gabe rocked her in a hug as Andrew stood by beaming.

"We'll have to get back at it," Sorrel said to Gabe.

He nodded and led her over to the greenhouse. Just inside it were flats and flats of plants. Not just seedlings this time but some strong, nearly full-grown specimens as well. There were trellised pots of sweet peas, already out of season but somehow bursting, seven peony bushes lined up like frivolous soldiers, their blossoms heavy and round, golf-ball-sized buds bobbing in the breeze, and a cluster of rose bushes, sparkling in the sun, the soil in their containers deep and dark and damp from Gabe's hose. A pallet of herbs and low-growing ground cover sat beside a small lilac tree, and a long row of boxwood marched tidily along in blue-green splendor.

"How, when, where . . .?" Sorrel darted between the plants, brushing her hand across each one, cooing and laughing, the damp flicking sand and soil up her calves.

"I kept some plants back," Gabe signed. "I had the nursery open early for us."

"You wonderful elf, you!" Sorrel sang. "Come on, then. Let's get started. It's going to be a hot one."

Gabe and Sorrel began loading the barrow, happily up to their elbows in dirt and leaves. Today, reckless in their joy, neither wore gloves. Sorrel, adrenaline high, would not notice her fatigue until she paused at the end of the day.

Andrew left them to their work and drifted off to the chapel. He hadn't even glanced at the plans for the solstice service, and now he'd have to buckle down if he wanted to serve Anna as well. It was cool in the chapel as Andrew went to find the sponge pole. He remembered that he'd left it with Gabe. He'd have to jury-rig something to check the water level. Andrew walked to the altar and stood looking out over the small nave. He pictured the pews full of family and friends and wished that there were an organ for service instead of the piano borrowed from the primary school. The altar cloth Delphine had made was beautiful, Andrew could see that now. It seemed like yesterday and a hundred years ago that Stella had tried to catch his interest by pointing out the intricate embroidery, the flowers and herbs scattered across it as if an unseen gardener had left a drift of nature's finery to honor the chapel. He bent closer, almost certain he could smell the scents of the garden in the cloth itself. He ran his finger over the stitches and found, at the hem, a tiny fairy house sewn into the ribbon trim. Andrew smiled

and understood that Delphine, too, had found a resolution in the garden and in this soon-to-be-sacred house.

As he stood, Andrew began to settle into the idea of making this church his own. He felt, for the first time in months, the swell of love and gratitude that formed the base of his faith, the bedrock of his confidence. His certainty grew, like the garden, until there was no room for doubt. Andrew would make this little chapel a place of comfort and joy. He would shape the primary school in the village after his beloved Chelsea school, and he would ensure that the old and young in this village always knew they could come to him in sorrow and in celebration. With Sorrel by his side, at least for some weeks to come, Andrew would answer God's call to minister with a resounding yes.

Andrew spent the rest of the day at the Tithe Barn working on the consecration service while Sorrel and Gabe dug and planted with single-minded devotion to the garden. It seemed that every able-bodied soul was engaged in the work of life at last. Sorrel was shaky but determined. Her shorts were soon splattered with mud, and she'd tossed her straw hat away because it threw shade over her work. Her sunburn returned, but the heat felt fine as she worked. Gabe mopped his face, handed her bottles of water, and followed behind her tamping down the soil with his hands, spreading mulch and manure around each fresh plant. They missed lunch without missing food so

that by three o'clock when clouds rolled in and a hint of rain nudged at their bent backs, Gabe and Sorrel were ready to stop for the day.

THIS IS HOW it went for them all: hard work followed by rest followed by more hard work. Andrew found a wellspring of hope and purpose as he readied the chapel and himself. Each afternoon he came home to Sorrel in the Tithe Barn. They made love and laughed and scattered soil and scented herbs around them as they tumbled across the sheets. Wags was easily distracted with a chewy treat while her master wove his love around Sorrel until she couldn't think, only feel.

In the evenings the family gathered at Kirkwood Hall. Sometimes Andrew cooked, sometimes Delphine. There was a bounty of vegetables from the kitchen garden: tiny patty-pan squash, radishes both peppery and sweet, beets striped deep magenta and white, golden and green, butter lettuce and spinach and peas, zucchini blossoms stuffed with Graham's mozzarella and salty anchovies. Delphine whipped eggs from the chickens into soufflés. Chicken—from the chickens, sadly—were roasted in a Dutch oven or grilled under a brick. Plump strawberries from the fields and minuscule wild ones from the forest were served with a drizzle of balsamic syrup or a billow of whipped cream. Delphine's baking provided custardy tarts, flaky pastries, and deep, dark chocolate cake. She'd recently begun experimenting with ice cream, to Poppy's huge satisfaction, and Stella, a benevolent smile wreathing her face,

sat regally, drinking in the happiness. Those days were an idyll that they all deserved but still could not entirely trust. Perhaps that is what made it so very sweet.

Sorrel's decision to stay on had been greeted with joy in Wiltshire and a mixture of glee and disappointment in Granite Point. Patience wasn't surprised and Nettie was delighted, but there were three brides and a new mother who felt utterly robbed of Sorrel's floral gifts. Patience and Charlotte Mayo teamed up to fill in in Sorrel's absence, and Charlotte found that she rather liked getting her hands dirty now and then. The baby sat on a blanket in the shade and gnawed at Nettie's homemade zwieback. Henry mooned around the Nursery while the sisters worked. He'd forgotten how little he saw of Patience during the high season. He, Ben Avellar, and Simon met for beers at the end of each day in the Nursery shed while the Sisters tidied up for the next one. Henry and Ben had lugged a dorm fridge over at the start of the season and filled it with local ale and Nettie's watermelon juice. Sometimes she made them snacks, and sometimes Patience made them take some remedy or other, and the men found that they'd never felt better. All in all, it appeared that Granite Point would weather Sorrel's time away.

THE NIGHT BEFORE the solstice, after Andrew had collected his pressed vestments from the cleaners, set out his sermon in a leather folder embossed with the Kirkwood heraldry, and made his final notes on a couple of index cards, Sorrel drew him into

the garden while the sky was still pale blue and the sun above the horizon.

"I wanted to spend a little time in here alone with you," she said as she opened the gate. "Close your eyes. I will lead you." She took his hand and guided him in.

"Will there be bumbling?" Andrew asked.

"I believe we are all bumbled out, Reverend Darling," Sorrel said.

"Never!" said Andrew and slipped his hands down Sorrel's shorts, cupping her bottom and pulling her close.

Sorrel extricated herself and turned to face Andrew.

"OK, open," she said.

Andrew didn't need to see to know that enchantment had returned to the Shakespeare Garden. The scent was overwhelming in its beauty, but not overpowering. He could not untangle the threads of scent, so he let the whole curl around him. When he did open his eyes, he was stunned.

Gabe and Sorrel had in fact wrought a miracle within the walls. It was almost impossible to believe that anything had ever been so terribly wrong there. Anna's corner was perhaps a little fragile still, but everything else seemed to have not just recovered but thrived. It was nothing less than a transformation from ruin to rebirth.

Sorrel looked to Andrew. "So, what do you think?" she asked.

"I am in awe, Sorrel," Andrew said. "I am a man whose faith has been renewed by nature. Will you share that faith with me?"

"I will," Sorrel said and found that she meant it.

"Come to me, little gardener, let me show you how much I love you."

THERE WAS MUSIC in the garden all through the night. It came from the mouths of snapdragons, through the twining vines of the wild sweet peas Sorrel had brought from Granite Point, threading its way along the tops of the shiny boxwood hedges. The notes hung in the air above the garden as a murmuration of starlings made their final flight in the last of the light. The rampant morning glories that Sorrel had wrestled into good behavior along the outside of the walls opened long before dawn, and the roses and peonies nodded their blossoms toward one another in tribute to beauty beyond words. There was no darkness left in this garden, no sadness lingered where Anna had been so cruelly thrown away. She was gone from here and with her the sorrow that manifested as death. On this night and into the days to come, only delight would find a home here in the Shakespeare Garden of Sorrel Sparrow.

ACKNOWLEDGMENTS

My thanks are genuine and full of heart, as are the people who helped me plant this particular garden. Faye Bender of The Book Group is an uncommon woman who brings out the brave one in me. Lucia Macro is an editor with a gardener's touch, planting seeds that allow my words to flower. Laura Hartman Maestro is the artist who draws my gardens to life. My writing cohorts, Anson and Yun Soo never let a weed make its way into the story. My children are my finest blossoms and they keep me walking forward on this winding writing path. My husband David makes our garden green, whether in the pages of this book or in all the years of our partnership. I am enormously grateful to him.

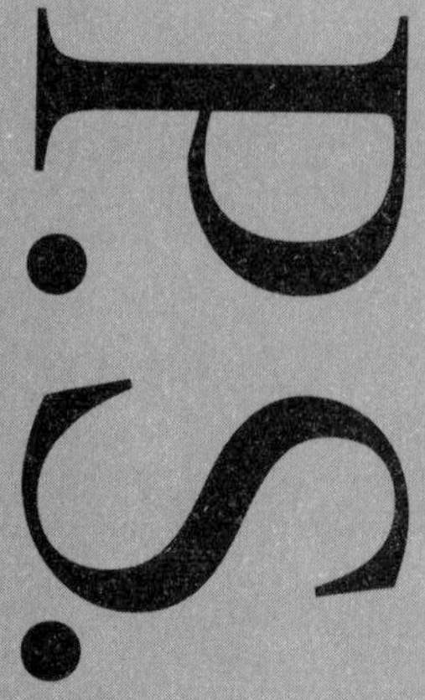

About the author

2 Meet Ellen Herrick

About the book

3 Reading Group Discussion Questions

Read on

5 Excerpt from *The Sparrow Sisters*

Insights,
Interviews
& More . . .

About the author

Meet Ellen Herrick

Susan Lapides

Ellen Herrick was a publishing professional in New York City until she and her husband moved to London for a brief stint; they returned nearly twenty years later with three children (her own, it must be said). She now divides her time between Cambridge, Massachusetts, and a small town on Cape Cod very much like Granite Point.

Reading Group Discussion Questions

1. Discuss the role that family secrets and family legends play in *The Forbidden Garden*. Is it possible that the secrets of the past—real or imagined—can still affect families generations later?
2. From the outset Graham Kirkwood says that the Shakespeare Garden is cursed. Do you think it's actually possible for a place or thing to be "cursed" or somehow tainted?
3. From the outside, the Kirkwood family appears perfect but the reality is somewhat different. How does the novel make use of the concept of appearance being different from the truth where it pertains to the Kirkwood and Sparrow families?
4. Graham Kirkwood originally approaches Sorrel by writing a letter. What does it tell you about Lord Kirkwood that he would use such an old-fashioned method of communication in this day of emails, texts, and even phone calls?
5. The Kirkwood family seems to have their own private language. How much of this do you think is used to keep strangers at a distance? How much of this is mere whimsy, or simple age-old English tradition on their part?
6. Andrew is a minister who appears to do some very unreligious things. Is ▸

Reading Group Discussion Questions
(continued)

this what a modern cleric looks like today? Does this startle or upset you? Why or why not?

7. Graham sometimes acts in ways that are protective of his family but detrimental to others. Do you feel he is justified in his actions? Are there ever times when protecting one's family at the expense of others is acceptable?
8. The Sparrow Sisters have deep ties and ways of communicating that seem, at times, almost paranormal. Have you ever seen members of a family who are able to communicate in these ways?
9. How do you think Andrew and Sorrel are going to live out their futures?
10. Is it possible for one's faith to be restored by nature? By extension, can one be a person of religious faith who is also a person of pure science?

Although there is no evidence that Shakespeare ever planted a garden, there are Shakespeare Gardens all over the United States, and naturally in the United Kingdom. They are, for the most part, open to the public—from the Brooklyn Botanic Garden in New York to Golden Gate Park in San Francisco.

If you want to plant your own Shakespeare Garden, the New York Botanical Garden has a handy how-to web page!

www.nybg.org/gardens/home-gardening/tips/shakespeare-garden.php

Excerpt from *The Sparrow Sisters*

Prologue

"ALL STORIES ARE TRUE. Some of them actually happened."

Three sisters in the third pew nodded sharply in unison as John Hathaway looked out over his congregation; this made him stutter in an otherwise seamless sermon.

Patience Sparrow rocked in the pew until she made her sister Sorrel look away from the altar. Nettie Sparrow leaned in so that she could see both her sisters and smiled when she noticed they were already bent toward each other. Someone's stomach growled. It was Easter Sunday and the women were ready to bolt. It wasn't that the sermon was dull, or that they already knew how right the Episcopal minister was. Some stories, told enough, became as true as their words. Any of these sisters could tell you that. It's just that they were *hungry.* The three swayed back and resumed their attentive poses.

In the last pew but two, Henry Carlyle sat on the aisle. He was not a regular at the First Episcopal church on the green. He was too new in town to be a regular anywhere, although he thought the ▸

Excerpt from *The Sparrow Sisters* *(continued)*

little bakery down the street from his house was so good he might start showing up there every day. The phone in his pocket vibrated against his thigh, and he put his hand over it before the woman next to him got the wrong idea. She'd already shot him several curious glances, and he'd let his heavy, dark forelock fall over his eye to block her out. Henry needed a haircut. The phone buzzed again. He knew it was work; Henry didn't have a friend in Granite Point, not yet anyway. Sampling the churches in town was his sorry attempt at meeting people. He watched the three heads a few pews up from his. He'd seen them laughing, acting up really, their shoulders shaking like naughty kids. A soft snort floated up from the redhead when the blonde in the middle nudged the others. Their behavior seemed so unlikely; one of the women (they were women, he had to acknowledge) had graying hair. Henry knew he'd have to slip out to answer the call, but before he did, he told himself a story about the women: how they couldn't convince their husbands or kids to come to church with them, how they were best friends or neighbors who would pick up their Easter desserts at the bakery after the service. But his story wasn't true because how could he know anything at all about the Sparrow Sisters? The true story would come later.

Chapter One

LUPIN CREATES a fresh color in the cheek and a cheerful countenance

Once there were four Sparrow Sisters. Everyone called them the Sisters, capitalized, and referred to them as a group, even when just one had come to the post office to collect the mail. "The Sisters are here for their package," the postmistress would say, calling her clerk to the desk. Or, "What do you know, the Sisters are taking the train into the city." All four had left Granite Point over the years on school trips to Boston for the symphony or the museum, but they always came back; it was home. The only Sparrow sister who did leave town forever, did so in the hardest way. The oldest Sparrow, if only by seven minutes, was Marigold, Sorrel's twin. She was the real homebody, the one people still shook their heads over, and she actually left Granite Point just twice; the first to accompany her father to a meeting with lawyers upon the death of her mother and the last upon her own death, in a smallish wooden box nestled inside an Adams's Hardware bag on the arm of her twin. Sorrell took Marigold to the Outer Beach, past the break north of the seal colony, to scatter her ashes in the Atlantic.

Now there were only three Sparrows left in the house at the top of the hill ▸

overlooking the far harbor. Long ago this house that their great-great (and more) grandmother Clarrissa Sparrow built had rung with the shouts and laughter of her four sons and the many Sparrow sons that followed. It was made of the timber used to craft the whaling fleet that sailed out from the harbor and into the dark waves. Her husband was a sea captain so fond of his trade that Clarissa chose wood from her father's shipyard with the idea that if George Sparrow loved his boat so much, surely he would be called home to a house made of the very same wood. She'd even built a widow's walk high above the street so that she could watch for him to sail back to her. Eventually, the widow's walk would earn its name several times over.

By the time the Sparrow Sisters lived in the house on Ivy Street, lanes and hedges and other houses had grown up, blocking all but a narrow sliver of the deep blue water of Big Point Bay. Ivy House, as everyone called it, stood tall and white as it had for all those years, home to the last of the Sparrows altogether. The house was beautiful and spare with high ceilings and windows of wavy glass. It was most often filled with the flowers and herbs, vegetables and fruits of the Sparrow Sisters Nursery. Like their mother, Honor Sparrow, dead now for twenty-some years—gone on the very day her youngest daughter Impatiens, arrived—the sisters all had green thumbs. It was ordained, really. They had each been named after a

botanical, mostly flowers, and as their mother kept producing girls, the names became slightly ridiculous. But Honor was a keen gardener and in darkest winter, calling her daughter's names reminded her that spring would come again. For months after her death the older girls hated their names and all they recalled for them. By the time they founded the Sparrow Sisters Nursery, though, each thoroughly embraced their names as the sign they were.

Sorrel, Nettie, and Patience, might well have gone on as they were accustomed, planting and reaping, selling the abundance of their labors, cooking for each other and listening to the opera every Saturday afternoon as Sorrel did the ironing, fulfilling the roles of town eccentrics. Although to be fair, Sorrel was not yet forty, hardly biddy material. But then the old town doctor, Eliakim Higgins, retired and set in motion everything that came after. He'd delivered all but one of the girls and cared for each of them on the rare occasions that they fell ill. He had diagnosed Marigold, and overseen her chemotherapy, as pointless at it turned out to be, in the seven months it took her to die. Dr. Higgins was very attached to the sisters; even more so after he'd been unable to save their mother and then Marigold. But at seventy-six his hands were not as steady nor his eyes so clear. He decided to leave his practice for the creosote-scented air of Arizona. Although there was a group medical ▸

practice in Hayward seventeen miles west, Dr. Higgins had always been the town's first choice. Well, he and then Patience Sparrow, whose reputation for curing everyday maladies like cradle cap and insomnia had turned her gift into an unexpected sideline. She was more often paid in eggs and striped bass, hand-knitted sweaters and fresh quahogs, than cash, but still. Her ability was cultivated along with the plants at the Sparrow Sisters Nursery and it wasn't long after college that Patience decided she would stay in Granite Point and go to work with her sisters. Her degree in botany wasn't the reason the Nursery called to her. It was the Nursery that called her to study. In fact, if the older girls hadn't invested their inheritance, and even more, their hearts into the land, Patience might well have wandered away and had a very different story indeed.

The Sisters remained close to the doctor (he was, after all, as alone as they were), but after Marigold they were never his patients again. The spring after Dr. Higgins left town, a young doctor straight out of Massachusetts General by way of the Army bought the small, shingled house and practice on Baker's Way where Dr. Higgins had lived and worked for over forty years. The arrangements were made quietly through a Boston firm, leaving little time for speculation in town and even less for real digging. The young man remained a mystery.

Henry moved in quickly, alone, on a cold Wednesday in April. He'd collected few things over the years in medical school and then the service. The neighbors watched Dr. Carlyle, muffled in a dark blue sweater, sleeves pushed up over his elbows as he unloaded the rented van. Movers had already brought all the big stuff, so what Henry now carried into the house was expected: boxes, lamps, two suitcases, and a large duffel. The oddest item was a long single shell and oars. Henry slid it out effortlessly, shouldering the impossibly thin boat before he went back for the oars. His little audience behind their twitching curtains might have wondered where he meant to row—the glacial lake, Frost Fish perhaps, or the still pond down Arey's Lane? But the snoopers were more curious that the tall, broad-shouldered doctor limped, and as the van began to empty, the hitch became more pronounced. By the time Henry Carlyle climbed into the van to return it to the U-Haul in Hayward, he'd begun to wince with every step. His first patients would try to divine how he'd been hurt but, although he was attentive and gentle in his examinations, Dr. Carlyle revealed nothing personal beyond the fact that he was a product of Yale medical school (class of 1999, the diploma was on his wall).

Henry Carlyle was just a year or so younger than Nettie Sparrow, and on the day she came to see him, she couldn't help but notice the way his dark hair ▸

curled behind his ear. There were strands of gray in it that led Nettie to think that while it might be youthful in its length, perhaps it showed he hadn't had things so very easy. She sat on the crinkly paper covering the old leather examination table, the first and likely the only sister to consult Dr. Carlyle. She was a bit of a hypochondriac, but really, who could blame her after Marigold and her parents? Nettie had been fighting a chest cold for weeks, it seemed, so she made an appointment, convinced it was pneumonia. The nurse who doubled as receptionist at the practice had gone to high school with Nettie. Sally Tabor waggled her eyebrows as she beckoned Nettie closer to the counter. She leaned in to whisper, which wasn't easy given that Sally was heavily pregnant.

"Look out," she said, glancing behind her to be sure her boss wasn't in earshot. "He's as handsome as anything and as chilly as Big Point Bay in January."

Nettie was in mid-giggle when Dr. Carlyle came to the doorway and called her name. She followed him down the hall, her fingers at her lips as she saw his limp. Now, as she sat watching him glance through her chart (a thin file that was proof of both the Sparrow Sisters' hearty constitutions and their mistrust of doctors), she hoped that Sally was wrong about him.

Dr. Carlyle looked straight into Nettie's eyes as he put the file on the table beside her, which made her heart flutter just enough to worry her.

"Nettie, is that short for Annette?" Dr. Carlyle asked.

"It's short for Nettle," Nettie hated the way her voice quavered as she shivered in the office gown. "Stinging nettle tea was the only thing that soothed my mother's hives when she was carrying me."

Henry laughed and then apologized. "That's unusual."

"Yes, well," Nettie said, "all our names are unusual."

Henry took her pulse and temperature, laying a gentle hand against her forehead for a moment. He breathed onto his stethoscope to warm it before he slipped it under her gown. Nettie noted the small courtesy and decided there and then that this Dr. Carlyle was a suitable replacement for Dr. Higgins—not that she would be seeing him again. Just being in his office made her feel traitorous, and she regretted her moment of panic. Or was it rebellion? Patience could smell a doctor a mile off.

After listening to her lungs, Dr. Carlyle determined that she did not have pneumonia but rather a stubborn case of bronchitis, and prescribed antibiotics and rest. Nettie left his office in an unreasonably grateful state, prescription in hand, feeling better already. There was only a moment of hesitation when she considered the reaction of the pharmacist. Since Marigold's death none of the Sisters had needed Mr. Howe's services. It had not gone unnoticed. As she waited for her medicine Nettie knew that his clerk had her ears pricked as ▸

she unnecessarily straightened the magazines on the rack next to Nettie.

When Dr. Carlyle brought her chart to Sally, he saw that Nettie had left her jacket on the chair nearest the counter. It actually belonged to her sister Patience but Nettie was feverish and distracted; she'd grabbed the first thing she saw as she snuck out of Ivy House that morning. He picked it up to give it to his nurse but the smell of tarragon and thyme and something almost *cool*, made him pause and hold it a little closer. Sally eyed him as she took the coat from his hands and signaled the next patient. Henry was already planning what would be the first of many house calls since arriving in a town that seemed absolutely determined to stay trapped in the amber of a time long past. The last patient was dispatched by 5:30 so Henry had just enough time to listen to a filing lecture from Sally before he washed the disinfectant off his hands and face. As Henry picked up the jacket Nettie had left behind, he remembered how his father had always told him that he should start as he meant to continue, so Henry decided that he'd make Nettie Sparrow his first house call. He buttoned his vest and stepped out into the slanting light.

BACK AT THE HOUSE Sorrel and Patience settled their sister in her room. Patience brought her white pepper, ginger and honey mixed into hot water and tied a length of eucalyptus-scented flannel around Nettie's neck. Then she went back to the Nursery. Patience had a talent for healing but she wasn't much for nursing and certainly not for a sister who chose to bypass her in favor of a stranger.

This is how Dr. Carlyle found Nettie that early evening when he stopped by to check on his patient and return the jacket. Propped up in her bed, a thick eiderdown pulled up to her shoulders, even in the warmth of the house, Nettie was shocked when the tall doctor walked into her room followed by a clearly discombobulated Sorrel.

"Well," he said. "I see someone has their own ideas about medicine." Dr. Carlyle leaned down, his hand on the iron bedpost for balance, and took a deep sniff of Nettie's flannel. "Eucalyptus?" he asked, cocking his head as he inhaled, his long

lashes casting his gray eyes in darker shadow. Poor Nettie felt a shiver leap up her neck.

"My sister made this," she stuttered. "And the tea."

Henry picked up the cup and sniffed again. It was an odd smell, sharp from the pepper, soft from the honey.

"Patience has the gift," Sorrel added from the end of the bed. "She's quite popular here in town."

"Popular as in all the boys like her?" The doctor laughed.

"Oh, no," Nettie said. "Patience isn't interested in boys anymore."

Henry laughed again. "All grown up or already taken?"

Sorrel gave a laugh. "Patience is the baby, Dr. Carlyle, and none of us are taken." She blushed and desperately wanted to unsay the last bit. "She has a gift with herbs and plants," she continued. "Everyone comes for her remedies."

Now Henry turned to look at Sorrel. "Remedies?" he said with a frown.

"Oh, yes." Nettie sat up straighter; she had heard the disapproval in the doctor's voice and was already on the defensive. "Patience has inherited an ancestral ability and the recipe book. She has the touch; ask anyone."

Henry Carlyle didn't know whether to be alarmed or just amused that this unseen Sparrow sister had managed to hoodwink an entire town. He was pretty sure that he didn't like it. He might have left with nothing more than a vague feeling of disappointment about how gullible people could be had Patience not come home just then, the back screen door slamming behind her with a loud clap. Nettie started and Sorrel escorted the doctor from the room, down the front stairs, away from the kitchen, hoping to get him out of the house before he had a chance to meet their sister. She nearly made it, too. Henry had his hand on the front door when Patience wandered in from the kitchen, her arms full of chamomile. The little flowers brushed her chin with yellow pollen and her hair had sprung loose from its messy twist.

The Sisters had lived in an isolated state for so long that Patience was shocked to see a strange man in her front room. Almost as soon as she felt that shock, Patience was embarrassed, and then she was irked. ▶

"Who is that?" she asked her sister, completely ignoring the man himself. Sorrel spluttered out Henry's name and purpose. She saw the face-off that was setting up and clapped her hands at Patience, an unspoken request for civility from her prickling sister. The entire scene was so unexpected it brought out the worst in all three players. Henry didn't want to lecture this very pretty girl he'd barely met. He realized she was the snorter in church on Easter, the redhead, and as he stared at her he became fascinated by the precarious nature of her hairdo. In the last of the sun it appeared like a halo around her head. But, perhaps because he was new to Granite Point and eager to establish his authority, Henry spoke, his voice harder than he meant it to be.

"What's all this I hear about your remedies?" The dismissal was clear and Patience, for the first time in days (a record), turned snappish.

"I beg your pardon?" Patience asked with a bit of a bark. Out of the corner of her eye she saw Sorrel flinch.

The doctor looked at Patience with a mixture of surprise and anger. It was not a pretty look. His brow lowered, and his jaw stood out sharply as he clenched it. As for the object of his irritation, two hectic spots of red bloomed on her cheeks and, to her horror, tears sprang to her eyes, threatening to spill over her burning face.

Sorrel ushered Henry out as she excused her sister's outburst in calming tones. As soon as the door clicked into place, she rounded on Patience.

"How could you be so rude!" she snapped. "Honestly, I think you put all your care, every bit of it, into your remedies."

She stomped out into the back garden leaving Patience staring at the black-and-white checked floor. A hot tear dropped at her feet. It smelled of chamomile, as did her skin and clothes, but there was nothing soothing in it for Patience. Sorrel lost her temper with her sisters so infrequently that Patience wasn't sure if she was (damn it) crying because of Sorrel's angry words or over the very odd reaction she'd had to Henry Carlyle. Simmering under her anger with Dr. Carlyle was a wholly unexpected tug. If Henry had been captured in that moment, Patience had been caught, too. She would never tell her sisters but Patience had

already noticed Henry, twice. One evening as she walked home from Baker's Way Bakers Patience looked up to see him standing at his window. He hadn't seen her in the darkness, but she was able to pick out the slump of his shoulders, his fingertips pressed against the glass. She'd wondered what his story was. Patience had sidled closer to the building across the street so she could look at him for another minute. When she saw him coming out of the post office a week later, she ducked her head and fiddled with her phone.

Patience swiped at her cheeks and pulled her heavy hair back up into a ponytail. "Really," she muttered, "get a grip," and walked down the hall to the kitchen.

The air around her had taken on a sharp, astringent smell, the soft chamomile burned away in a matter of moments. Sorrel smelled it as she gathered laundry from the line; it was so strong even the sheets were imbued. She knew that sometimes Patience's rich interior life, a thing of bright colors, strong scents, and a good deal of swearing, burst forth. The smells that followed her were the most noticeable, and even the town had learned to interpret at least some of the scents that wrapped around the youngest sister. Her graceful surface was often at odds with the force of her emotions. When that happened, everything and everyone around her knew it. Her sisters had gotten used to it: her internal struggles externalized. In fact, they could read Patience as easily as Patience read the people she helped. The three sisters were as tightly entwined as the bittersweet they battled each fall, and as stubborn. If the town ever wondered why they didn't break away—and it did—no one dared to ask them.

All the Sparrow sisters were naturally beautiful, each in very different ways—except for the twins, of course, who were eerily identical. So even the three who were left in the house had the certain confidence that came with knowing you needn't worry about your looks. They were never self-conscious around the men in town, which made Patience's reaction to Dr. Carlyle all the odder. In fact, as the years passed and neither Sorrel nor Nettie married, everyone stopped bothering about them. A natural New England reserve meant people didn't give in to curiosity often, and really, it was easier to assign them the status of the slightly ▸

sad single Sisters than to keep wondering. The girls seemed unconcerned and went about their days, each as lovely in their own way as the flowers they tended. Sorrel's black hair became streaked with premature white, which gave her an exotic air, although the elegance was somewhat ruined by the muddy jeans and shorts she practically lived in. Nettie, on the other hand, had a head of baby-fine blond hair that she wore short, thinking, wrongly, that it would look less childlike. Nettie wouldn't dream of being caught in dirty jeans and was always crisply turned out in khaki capris or a skirt and a white shirt. She considered her legs to be her finest feature. She was not wrong.

Patience was the sole Sparrow redhead, although her hair had deepened from its childhood ginger and was now closer to the color of a chestnut. It was as heavy and glossy as a horse's mane, and she paid absolutely no attention to it or to much else about her appearance, nor did she have to. In the summer her wide-legged linen trousers and cut-off shorts were speckled with dirt and greenery, her camisoles tatty and damp. The broad-brimmed hat she wore to pick was most often dangling from a cord down her back. As a result, the freckles that feathered across her shoulders and chest were the color of caramel and resistant to her own buttermilk lotion (Nettie smoothed it on Patience whenever she could make her stand still). When it was terribly hot Patience wore the sundresses she'd found packed away in the attic. She knew they were her mother's, and she liked to imagine how happy Honor had been in them.

On the surprisingly warm June day on which Dr. Carlyle threw the Sparrow Sisters into a swivet, Patience was wearing a pair of Sorrel's too-loose shorts rolled down at the waist until her hip bones showed below her tee shirt. She hadn't expected a visitor, and certainly not a stranger, so it wasn't until she went back into the kitchen and caught sight of herself in the French doors to the dining room that Patience realized how undressed she really was. She stared for a minute and then she laughed. *Ha!* she thought, *No wonder he was so unbalanced.*

Patience wasn't vain, but she knew what the sight of her bare midriff could do to a man. It made her laugh again as she pulled the chamomile flowers from their stems. But when she thought

about how silly her sisters were, how completely "girly" their behavior had been in front of the doctor, her smile faded. And when she recalled how Henry Carlyle's jaw had hardened as he looked at her, Patience dropped the chamomile into the sink and slapped the cold porcelain, her tears completely dried, as teed off at him as Sorrel had been at her.

Outside Ivy House, the doctor stood for a full minute before he turned to walk back to his practice. The scent of herbs and grass and damp soil trailed in the air behind him. He turned in a circle trying to focus on the scent, and for the second time that day he sniffed like a rabbit and tried to pinpoint what it was.

When Henry got back to his shingled house on Baker's Way, he wavered in front of the door to the apartment he lived in over the "shop." It was after six, and there was no real reason to go back into the office, but he did so anyway. It was too quiet in his apartment, which struck him as funny, really. The one thing he'd craved in the hospital was quiet. The one thing he didn't have when he was deployed was solitude. Now that he had both, it made him restless. So he unlocked the door and turned on the lights in the office. There were always notes to dictate, charts to catch up on; paperwork was not Henry's strong suit, and he usually left anything to do with organization to the last minute, or to Sally, who he'd inherited from Dr. Higgins. He found a pile of patient files with a yellow sticky on his desk and growled as he toed his chair out.

"Dr. Carlyle, please try to keep up," Sally had written in purple ink. He huffed and deliberately moved them aside so he could put his bag on the desk. Henry opened the old satchel, meaning to restock it with saline, Tylenol, a suture kit. The scent of chamomile slipped out, or at least that's what Henry thought. He snapped the bag shut and crossed to lie down on the exam table. The paper rattled under him as it did under his patients. Not for the first time he wondered what he thought he was doing in this town of fishermen and spinsters, shopkeepers and faith healers.

The smell of cookies replaced the chamomile, and Henry figured that the little store down the street, Baker's Way Bakers, was probably just closing, the last of the stock set aside for ▸

discount sale in the morning. Henry coughed, certain he could feel the flour on the back of his throat. He gave in to fatigue, a very different kind than that of his residency in Boston. There he'd felt hollowed out by exhaustion, a dark place inside waiting to be filled by the desperation and panic of a city hospital. Remembering that, Henry understood, again, why he'd left and why he'd come to Granite Point. He dozed off, slightly hungry for cake, the ache in his leg a nervy hum.

When Henry woke it, was full dark, and a small circle of lamplight puddled on his desk. Sitting up, he had a renewed sense of purpose; maybe it was the half hour of oblivion. Henry had trained himself to sleep quickly and deeply. He grabbed the charts and made his way upstairs, opened a beer, swallowed three aspirin, considered a Vicodin, and sat at the kitchen counter to work. There weren't too many patients yet: Dr. Higgins's practice had begun to wind down before he did, but Henry had high hopes. Already word of his kind manner and good looks had filtered down to the young mothers, their babies swaddled tight even into June, their toddlers already in bathing suits. News traveled fast, no doubt about it; rumors even faster. The women speculated that he'd left heartbreak behind in Boston, and their husbands figured he'd seen too much death in Iraq, too many sick people, accidents, and car wrecks at the hospital. Both were right, although his heart had broken far from Boston.

Hunger drove Henry back outside. He set aside his papers and slipped on the blue sweater. He was more susceptible to the cold since his return. The tree peepers seemed to echo the insistent buzz of pain in his leg. He walked slowly, trying to make his gait as even as possible. He was used to the way people's eyes flicked to his leg when he walked through the hospital or into his own waiting room. But, he realized now, Patience hadn't lowered her gaze, not even for an instant, as she stood with her arms full of damp flowers. Henry stuck his hands in his pockets as he rounded Main Street, glad that the lights of Doyle's were bright.

He took a seat at the bar. Frank Redmond approached, drying his hands on a stained white cloth.

"What'll you have, Doc?" he asked, and Henry snorted.

Frank looked at him, eyebrows raised.

"It's just that you're so welcoming and I just had a run in with . . . I have no idea what." Henry laughed. "Pretty tight, this town."

"Well, now," Frank said, already pulling a pint for Henry. "There's some who might take offense at that, coming from an inlander."

"Oh, I'm sorry"—Henry raised his hand—"I only meant that nearly everyone I've met is . . ." He stopped. "Just, I'm sorry."

Frank was chuckling as he watched Henry fumble. "Shit, Henry, I'm just messing with you. Inlander, like that's even a word." He handed Henry a menu and moved off, still smiling.

Henry looked at the menu, not really seeing any of it. He'd have a grilled cheese and leave it at that. What Henry was seeing was Patience: the way her hair stuck to the dampness at her neck, the smudge of dirt over her eyebrow, the spark of anger he'd drawn from her even as he suspected that the last thing he wanted to make her was angry. Henry thought that making her smile would be wonderful and he felt his own lips twitch.

"So?" Frank was back. "See something you like?"

"Oh yes," said Henry and shook his head to clear it of the springy green scent that seemed to cling to Patience, even in memory.

When his sandwich came, he ate it in silence, listening to the chatter of the locals who were Frank's bread and butter until the summer season got underway. He wiped his mouth and reached for his wallet, shifting on the stool until he had to slide off to keep his balance. He landed harder than he meant to on his bad leg and grimaced, dropping the wallet.

"A quart of the chowder, Frank." Patience stood at the end of the bar, an old hoodie over her tee shirt. The stretched hem came to the middle of her thighs; she looked naked beneath it, but her dirty boots and slouchy socks dismissed that image with an oddly childish look.

Henry paused, his head just below the bar, his wallet halfway to his hip pocket. *Damn it,* he thought. It felt as if his little reverie had called Patience to Doyle's long before he was ready to see her again.

"How's Nettie?" Frank asked. ▸

"She's better," Patience said shortly.

Frank lowered his voice, and Henry had to strain to hear him.

"She went to the new guy, didn't she?"

"Yeah," Patience said. "She gets nervous, you know." She shuffled through some bills as Frank brought the soup.

"No charge, P," Frank said. "I still owe you for Claire's migraines."

"Thanks." Patience shoved all but a couple dollars back into her pocket. "See ya."

"Yup." Frank turned back and Henry stood up slowly, careful not to look toward the front door, as it swung shut behind Patience.

"Where'd you go, there?" Frank asked.

"I dropped my wallet," Henry answered and opened it to pay for his dinner. Frank took the money, and Henry asked, "Not on the house for me?"

"When you cure my wife's headaches in the time it takes to make a martini, I'll tear up your bill too."

Henry felt the heat rise up his throat. He put a hand on the bar to stop Frank. "You seriously think her stuff works?"

"I seriously think it does, and so do most of the people in this town." Frank looked at Henry. "What do you know about the Sparrow Sisters?"

"There are three of them," Henry said. He took a last swallow of his beer. "That's all."

"That's true," Frank said and let the name Marigold flit through his head. "And you were hiding from Patience because, what? She doesn't like you?"

That was a question; she sure didn't seem to like him. "I wasn't hiding," Henry said. "How long am I going to be the new guy?" he asked.

"A while," Frank said.

Henry stepped back, preparing to leave, but Frank stopped him.

"You should know that the Sparrow Sisters are something of a legend in Granite Point. Their family history, hell their own story, it's as much a part of this place as the harbor." Frank closed the register. "I'm surprised you've seen one in your office. They aren't

much for doctors after Marigold. Dr. Higgins was one thing, but the rest of the medical world, let's just say the Sisters aren't exactly fans." Henry faked a shudder. "I wouldn't want any of them pissed off at me."

"I'll remember that," Henry said. *Too late,* he thought as he walked out and right into Simon Mayo.

"Whoa, there," Simon said as both men grabbed each other's elbows.

As Henry apologized, he gave a slight hop to take the weight off his leg. He watched Simon's eyes travel down.

"So, the city doctor meets the country lawyer," Simon said as he stuck out his hand. "I'm Simon Mayo."

"Henry Carlyle," Henry said as he shook. "The new guy. How do you know me?"

Simon gestured to Henry's face and leg and smiled. "I'm afraid you're already famous."

"Oh" was all Henry could come up with.

"Can I buy you a beer?" Simon asked.

"I've got work to do," Henry replied.

"Another house call to the Sisters?" Simon's voice thinned and Henry heard the shift.

"No, I'm finished there." Henry shook his head. "How does everybody know everything?"

Simon nodded and smiled again. "Very small town," he said. "I'll let you go, then."

Henry watched him walk into Doyle's. The light spilling around Simon's ▸

shoulders and the familiar greetings he got from people in the bar reminded Henry of the extent to which he was under scrutiny in Granite Point. Somehow Henry had ended up in a town with three odd sisters digging around at their nursery, making "remedies" in a cauldron, no doubt, and *he* was the curiosity.

Frank had slipped out from behind the bar to watch Simon and Henry through the big window. He reckoned that the new doctor had a lot to learn about the Sisters if he wanted to belong in Granite Point. Frank understood, or at least his wife had taught him, that each sister had a life that held in its smallness all the detail of a much larger tragedy. He'd listened to the story of the Sparrows because Claire had told it to him. If Henry seemed a bit undone by Patience, maybe it was because her story was still unwritten.